Politics and Government in Britain

KU-486-387

Politics and
Government in Britain
An Introductory Survey

T. Brennan

Cambridge at the University Press 1972

Published by the Syndics of the Cambridge University Press
Bentley House, 200 Euston Road, London NW1 2DB
American Branch: 32 East 57th Street, New York, N.Y.10022

© Cambridge University Press 1972

Library of Congress Catalogue Card Number: 78-171673

ISBN: 0 521 08366 4

Printed in Great Britain by Jarrold & Sons Ltd, Norwich

ACKNOWLEDGEMENTS Thanks are due to Her Majesty's Stationery
Office for permission to include the material in figure 8, appendix III
and appendix IV. Figure 4, which is redrawn from the diagram in
A Guide for visitors to the House of Commons, is also reproduced by
their permission.

Contents

Tables

Figures

Preface

This book is designed to provide an introduction to the study of the political system in Britain. The aim throughout has been to include material which will assist in an understanding of the political process in British society today. It is intended primarily for students in the upper forms of secondary schools and in technical colleges who are embarking upon a systematic examination of the structure and functioning of government in Britain. Every effort has been made to keep in mind the needs of those who are preparing for examinations. I hope also that it will be of use to non-specialist teachers undertaking some work in this field and interested students in departments and colleges of education.

The treatment takes account of recent developments in political studies and includes a consideration of pressure groups, mass media, political socialisation, voting behaviour and the pattern of participation in politics. The institutions through which government operates are, for the most part, examined both descriptively and analytically. Parties and policies are dealt with in considerable detail.

The political system operates within a wider social system and attention is drawn to the way in which society influences and is influenced by the political system. The fundamental consensus on political institutions and procedures is emphasised but conflict is also a basic element in political activity and no attempt has been made to disguise this fact. I have attempted to define the nature and scope of activities which we refer to as politics and have incorporated some discussion of the notion of democracy. It is hoped that the case studies and illustrative examples provided will assist in developing an understanding of the interplay between institutions and ideas and give some insight into the political behaviour of individuals and groups. My assumption is that the book will supplement and support the teacher's approach rather than dictate it.

Having in mind the need to concentrate on those aspects of the political process necessary to a proper understanding of the system as a whole, some topics have been treated at greater length than is customary in an introductory book and others are correspondingly dealt with in a more summary fashion. My hope is that this will result in a more realistic appraisal than might otherwise have been the case. In this respect I am encouraged by those examiners, especially at G.C.E. Advanced Level, who are now setting the kind of questions which demand thoughtful and well-argued answers rather than mere statements of received opinion.

Although I have generally tried hard to present a balanced treatment of the more controversial issues, I have, here and there, given rein to my personal preferences and prejudices; the sections on local government, the House of Lords, delegated legislation and administrative tribunals, suffer or gain most from this indulgence. There will doubtless be some teachers who will feel that I have gone too far in jettisoning ideas which are often more conservatively expressed, but I know there are others who believe that I have not gone far enough.

An introductory volume can only hope to scratch the surface of this vast field and there is a real danger that important arguments and findings will lose overmuch by undue compression. My hope is that students will be encouraged to explore at first hand at least some of the works which are referred to; the brief quotations used are intended to give the flavour of some important books which are fairly readily accessible. Above all, the present volume is intended to provide a framework of reference against which political ideas and events can be examined and evaluated.

My indebtedness to a number of authors and their publishers will be clear from the text; for the privilege of drawing so extensively upon the concepts and knowledge to which they have addressed themselves, I am deeply grateful. Prominent among these is Professor Bernard Crick of Birkbeck College, University of London, who, along with Mr Derek Heater of Brighton College of Education, played a leading part in helping to found the Politics Association, which is the professional organisation of teachers of politics in schools and colleges. My general orientation and the treatment of certain topics has been considerably influenced by his ideas and beliefs. I can only hope that he will not be too disappointed at the result. Should any acknowledgements due to writers and official publications have been inadvertently omitted I should be grateful to know of them so that formal acknowledgement can be made in future editions.

I should like to take this opportunity of expressing my gratitude to the editorial staff of the Cambridge University Press, with whom the outline of the book was first discussed and whose professional guidance throughout the period of writing has been both kind and helpful. My thanks are also due to a number of friends and colleagues at Bingley College of Education. Mr Peter Squibb read the drafts of one or two of the early chapters from the point of view of a former sixth-form teacher and an 'A' level examiner; Miss Hilda Watkinson typed nearly the whole of the first draft of the book from a sometimes very untidy manuscript; Mr Denis Yeadon prepared most of the diagrams and Mrs Shirley White drew one of the maps; Mr Adrian Shaw and a small group of my own students subjected some sections to critical examination. My former teaching colleague, Mr Peter Hardy, M.P., received me at the House of Commons and offered helpful comments on the chapters on Parliament and Local Government; Mr Alfred Morris, M.P., went to considerable trouble in meeting me at the House and providing the background information for the case study of the Chronically Sick and Disabled Persons Act, 1970; Mr Richard

Kelley, M.P., kindly helped me with some queries on recent changes in parliamentary procedure.

Some parts of the text have been used in a study of some aspects of politics and government made with a group of sixth-form girls at Lawnswood High School, Leeds. I am grateful to the Headteacher and staff of the school for affording me the opportunity of this partial trial run and to the girls concerned for a series of enjoyable and interesting discussions.

T. Brennan
10 October 1971

Part 1 Political Democracy

---

1 The Basis of Politics

Politics arises only because neither accidental self-interest, nor some arbitrary idea of the common good, provides a sufficient warrant to govern a free community.

Bernard Crick *In Defence of Politics*

Politics and people

In Britain, 'politics' and 'politicians' are words which are frequently used as terms of abuse. 'Politics is a dirty business', and 'They're only in it for what they can get', are comments that are heard over and over again. Similarly, the 'government' is more often abused than praised. 'I'm not interested in politics', is a recurring refrain and real knowledge of political matters is, for the majority, very restricted indeed. To those who are actively interested in politics this may seem to present an unduly pessimistic picture and certainly it is one which needs to be qualified in some important respects. Few, however, would seriously challenge the view that both the Government and politicians are generally unpopular. What then is the essential basis of politics and how far is the popular impression justified?

Politics is connected with government and the activity of politicians is concerned with agreements and, more frequently, disagreements about what Governments should, or should not, do. The basis of the British system rests on the existence of a Parliament which is elected by all those over the age of 18 who take the trouble to vote. The party which gains the most seats forms the Government which thereafter for a limited period takes the decisions which, for good or ill, affect the nation's destiny. Almost every action a government takes is the subject of criticism and controversy, and few decisions command universal approval; when there is general agreement the decision is nearly always one connected with national emergency, such as defence against an aggressor, or the meeting of manifestly humanitarian needs, as in the case of relief for the victims of flood, earthquake or other natural disasters. In normal times, political activity in a system like this is ceaseless; political parties publicise their policies, pressure groups make their demands, newspaper and television commentators churn out their views and individuals and groups approve

1

or disapprove of the decisions which finally result.

These activities are the hallmarks of political rule, under which the law-making body is created with the consent of the electors and not established by coercion, and in which criticism is a major activity. Political rule is, for the most part, characterised by free debate and open argument; opposition is allowed and even institutionally encouraged. Not all acts of government, however, are open to public scrutiny; some matters connected with internal security are kept secret, but even here there is fairly widespread agreement on the basic rules, and a high degree of co-operation between Government and Opposition.

The British are accustomed to political rule and perhaps too readily take it for granted, for it is only one of the methods which can be employed to ensure stability and order in society.

Provided that a Government has the power to enforce its wishes, it does not need to allow criticism or argument. A powerful Government could, if it was so minded, put everyone who disagreed with it behind bars. Past and present alike abound with examples of very successful tyrannies, oligarchies and dictatorships, where the only voice that matters is the voice of the group holding power. Clearly, these Governments are not political in the sense that we have used the term. In totalitarian regimes political activity in the sense described here is minimal; overt criticism of the Government is regarded as a threat to its survival and opposition is, therefore, either stifled or rigorously controlled.

The allocation of resources

The decisions of government on relationships with other states and on the use to which resources are put is the stuff of which politics is made. Politics, as the late Professor H. V. Wiseman often remarked, is about 'who gets what, when and how'.[1] Resources in any society are always in short supply. The shortage may be relative but it is nevertheless real, for no society can hope to meet all the wishes and needs of its inhabitants. Resources in this context must be taken to mean not only material goods but facilities, space, availability of skills, etc. Even then the term is not wide enough. Human needs include not only material requirements, but status, freedom of movement and all those less tangible factors, the presence or absence of which makes life pleasant or painful according to individual tastes. No one person or group can have everything it wants and criteria for the sharing of resources must somehow be arrived at. In many important respects the government is faced with the impossible task of reconciling the irreconcilable. Under political rule the distribution of goods and resources at any particular time is affected by the actions of the Government itself and by the kind of pressure which individuals and groups are able to bring on the Government. What the Government does is to ensure that, however disappointed some groups may be, the decisions

[1] H. V. Wiseman, *Politics in Everyday Life* (Blackwell, 1966), p. 8.

2

and settlements are as far as possible implemented in a peaceful and orderly way. As Professor Crick puts it: 'Politics is, as it were, the market place and price mechanism of all social demands – though there is no guarantee that a just price will be struck; and there is nothing spontaneous about politics – it depends on deliberate and continuous individual activity.'[1]

Professor Raphael observes that: 'The whole process of political behaviour turns on the fact that there is a set of institutions called government for regulating the affairs of society',[2] and politics can be defined as the expression of demands and wants and the process through which resources are allocated among the various groups on whose behalf these demands are made. This system has its weaknesses but it also has its strengths. Decisions which are the outcome of an electoral process, which is preceded and followed by discussion and debate are time-consuming and in any event are likely to fall short of what any particular person or group would ideally like. There may well be a case for allowing a much wider basis of participation than exists at the moment and for introducing more efficient methods of arriving at decisions but this involves a refinement of political rule and not its replacement; the main alternatives to political rule are tyranny or anarchy and only a minority would welcome the prospect of either of these. The continuation of the British system therefore, whatever adaptations are eventually made, involves a pattern of government in which political activity has an important and integral part to play.

The necessity of politics
Many individuals may profess to dislike politics but they cannot, under a system of political rule, be avoided. The management of the economy, the level of wages, the scope of the social services, which foreign sports teams should visit Britain, the organisation of education, the pattern of television and radio broadcasting, and a thousand and one other aspects of our everyday lives are affected by the kind of political decisions which are made. This is to say nothing of the far reaching questions of relationships with other countries and international organisations. Whether or not the Government takes active steps to prevent continuing pollution of the environment or to spend more money on education may have important consequences for the future of Britain. Still more crucial are the kind of decisions which have had to be made twice in this century as to whether or not war should be declared. Decisions on whether or not to have this or that level of armaments, to maintain armed forces East of Suez, or to support the American intervention in Vietnam have both moral and economic implications. All of these, in the British system, are political matters, but the same kind of questions would still arise even if arbitrary non-political decisions were made.

[1] B. Crick, *In Defence of Politics* (Penguin, 1964), p. 23.
[2] R. R. Raphael, *Problems of Political Philosophy* (Macmillan, 1970), p. 28.

3

From time to time we hear the cry that this or that question should be 'taken out of politics'. Education is a frequent runner in this race. Almost invariably it turns out that what the individual or groups making this plea mean is that the particular question should be moved from the political arena only if everyone agrees with their own highly political point of view. Thus, the claim that 'Grammar schools should not be the plaything of politicians', is a political attitude because it means, to those who support the introduction of comprehensive schools, that what they see as the existing pattern of privilege should remain. No question therefore is necessarily political but almost any matter can become political. When disagreement arises upon which a governmental decision must at some stage be made the issue is a political issue.

Politics, although it stems from individual and group preferences, prejudices and passions, is the activity which brings order and coherence to the diverse needs and demands of men and women in a complex society. It is concerned with ends and their attainment, with policies and their fulfilment. The machinery of government is complicated and its tentacles far reaching because the apparatus of politics and government has to provide for all kinds of rational and irrational acts on the part of members of society. A few are politically active but the majority are not. Some profess to be promoting the general welfare, others are consciously pre-occupied with their own concerns. There are general ideologies expressed through political parties and particular viewpoints expressed through interest groups of all kinds. All of these attitudes, aims and activities are reflected in the ongoing activity of politics.

Professor Crick has made the simple but important observation that people are disillusioned with actual Governments and hence with politics because of what Governments do; because of the limitations under which Governments operate; and because they expect too much.[1] It may well be true that in this situation politicians are more to blame than the public because the former make claims which are extraordinarily difficult to realise, but the harsh fact is that the limitations on any Government are there and are most difficult to overcome. A Government in Britain is, for example, at the mercy of the international money market and it has to retain confidence in sterling; to fail in this is to court economic disaster. Because of this certain external demands must be met by internal regulation. The desire to effect a change in the climate of industrial relations is one thing, the difficulty of bringing it about is another. Increased expenditure must be linked to increased revenue and most people, sadly, are more eager to receive than to give. Factors of this kind are part of the reality of politics and cannot be ignored, for politics can never really provide panaceas; politics is essentially the art of the possible, and the possible, almost invariably, involves some degree of compromise.

[1] B. Crick, 'The Introducing of Politics' in D. B. Heater (ed.), *The Teaching of Politics* (Methuen, 1969), p. 8.

4

Politics and society

The political system reflects the society of which it forms part and the system itself influences changes within the society. The two systems are intimately connected and the relationship between them functions on a reciprocal basis. A change in one of the components of the political system affects not only the political system but the wider social structure as well. Similarly, a basic change in the social structure is likely to have political consequences. Within the political system, there is general consensus about the form of political machinery but much less about the details of the ends it is designed to serve. But even the means, the institutions through which government works, are constantly brought into question by those who have a committed interest in politics. Some of the questions which are raised in this connection are examined in more detail in subsequent chapters of this book. What, for example, should be the role of the House of Lords? Is the British system of representation grossly unfair to smaller parties such as the Liberals? Are the procedures of the House of Commons hopelessly out of date? Does the Prime Minister really have more power than the President of the U.S.A.? Is power too heavily concentrated in the hands of a few? Is the existence of a complex structure of local government really worthwhile?

Many related questions on the changing pattern of society will also need to be considered. Does the lowering of the age at which people can vote make any appreciable difference to the outcome of general elections? Are working-class electors becoming less deferential? What is the effect of television and newspaper reporting? Is there a 'ruling circle' and, if so, is admittance to it more easy than it was? Why do only a minority of people take an active part in politics? Would there be any dangers in a much wider degree of participation?

The British system of government is described as a political democracy, but democracy is a notoriously elusive term and, having given some indication of the nature and scope of politics, it will be helpful to look much more closely at the notion of 'democracy' which is so often bandied about in political arguments. To do this is much more than an academic exercise because, as the late Professor J. L. Austin has pointed out: 'in searching for and finding such definitions we are looking not merely at words...but also at the realities we use words to talk about. We are using a sharpened awareness of words to sharpen our perception of the phenomena.'[1] Democracy and politics are closely linked and it can be forcibly argued that each is inseparable from the other.

[1] J. L. Austin, quoted in W. J. M. Mackenzie, *Politics and Social Science* (Penguin, 1967), p. 13.

5

2   The Nature of Democracy

Democracy is not a particular kind of civilisation; it is rather a civilised way of taking political action.

R. Bassett *Essentials of Parliamentary Democracy*

What is democracy?

'Democracy', writes Professor Crick, 'is perhaps the most promiscuous word in the world of public affairs. She is everybody's mistress and yet somehow retains her magic even when a lover sees her favours being... illicitly shared by another.'[1] Countries as far apart, both geographically and politically, as the U.S.S.R. and the U.S.A. call themselves democracies as do Britain, West Germany, the Scandinavian countries and many new African states; the 'People's Democracies' of Eastern Europe swell the numbers of candidates for possession of this political label. In Britain, use of the term is now applied in aspects of life not directly connected with the State; thus the government of schools, colleges and universities is described as being 'democratic' or 'undemocratic'; the administration of factories and commercial undertakings is also discussed in these terms. The adjective 'democratic' is sometimes applied to style of speech, dress, manners and other forms of social and personal behaviour.

The common factor in all of these is the acceptance of the notion of democracy as being desirable, commendable and progressive. Nowadays, in spite of varying interpretations, widespread ambiguity and vagueness, the notion of democracy meets with almost universal acclaim. This is one of the most significant developments of the last 100 years. A hundred years ago the idea of democracy could still be treated with scorn but since the turn of the century only the Nazis and Fascists have openly used it as a term of abuse.

Although applied from differing bases and in widely different contexts, the idea seems to have an important influence on the attitudes and assumptions of those who accept it. Literally, the word democracy means 'rule of the people'. This immediately makes it clear that in origin it is concerned with the government of states and that only by extension is it

[1] Crick, *In Defence of Politics*, p. 56.

6

applied in smaller groupings such as universities and factories. But the original definition does not take us very far because some important questions are left unanswered: Who are the people? What is the machinery of rule-making? Towards what end are the rules made? It seems that two sets of considerations are involved: firstly, the word democracy is connected with particular kinds of political institutions and secondly, it relates to certain social ideals. It may, then, be associated with the *form* of government, the *purpose* of government, or both.

Although they are both self-styled democracies, it is unlikely that the political leaders of the U.S.A. and the U.S.S.R. would wish to have their social ideals and systems of government too closely identified. The U.S.A. has a President directly elected by the people, and a legislature elected from candidates representing the major political parties. In the U.S.S.R., elections are held but only candidates approved by the Communist Party are allowed to present themselves. There is little doubt that most Americans would regard the system of government in the U.S.S.R. as undemocratic and that Communists everywhere would condemn American society, where racial integration has proceeded slowly and private enterprise is so strong, as being undemocratic.

Political democracy and social democracy

If we apply the two sets of considerations mentioned above to the U.S.A. and the U.S.S.R. it might at first sight seem reasonable to suggest that the U.S.A. claims to be democratic because it attaches prime importance to the *form* of its government and regards itself as a *political democracy*, whereas the U.S.S.R. has the *purpose* in mind and attaches importance to the idea of *social democracy*. This distinction is important but it must be remembered that in both countries, ideals and institutions are very closely connected and it is necessary to examine closely the different political realities which lie behind the descriptive labels.

This much at least is clear: the concept of democracy held by Britain, the U.S.A., several European countries and Commonwealth countries like Canada and Australia is vastly different to the view held by Communist countries. To say this is not to imply that one is 'better' than the other but to underline that they are different from assumption, purpose, and machinery of government. Our main concern in this book is with the Western conception of democracy, in which is implied the existence of a popularly elected legislature and an emphasis on liberty and equality. It will therefore be helpful to look first at the political method in this conception and then to examine more closely the associated ideals.

In discussions of democracy, phrases like the 'sovereignty of the people' and 'majority-rule' are frequently used. To what extent are these meaningful descriptions of what actually takes place? J. A. Schumpeter defines the democratic method as 'that institutional arrangement for arriving at political decisions in which individuals acquire the power to decide by means of a competitive struggle for the people's vote'.[1] In a democracy, he suggests, the primary function of the elector's vote is to produce a Government. In advanced industrialised states, sheer numbers obviate the possibility of *direct* democracy; the process has necessarily become *indirect*. All qualified individuals have the opportunity of choosing between organised political parties who are making a bid for power and, having chosen between the alternatives, it is the few and not the many who make all major decisions in affairs of State until the time for a renewal of the selection procedure arrives. Competing parties, popular election and a Government accountable to the electorate form the essential basis of representative and responsible government in Western democracies but they do not, of themselves, guarantee that a Government, once elected, will relinquish its power. How then can the continuation of the system be ensured?

Essential features

The late E. F. M. Durbin suggested that political democracy exists when three fundamentally important features are accepted both by governors and governed.[2] Firstly there must be the right to choose a Government; this implies both the power of the electors not only to choose but also to dismiss a Government and this condition can only be fulfilled if a real choice of Government exists. The second requirement, therefore, is that there must always be more than one party able to place its views before the electorate, and that parties are free to offer themselves as alternative Governments. It necessarily follows from this that opposition parties must always be free to criticise and compete with the Government of the day; whether or not opposition parties can function freely and openly is the acid test of democracy as it is understood in the West.

These two features, responsible Government and legal opposition, provide the characteristic institutions of democracy but they are not its guarantor. The doctrine of parliamentary supremacy (see chapter 10) admits the possibility that a Government could, if it so desired, extend its own life indefinitely but in Britain this never happens. This is because all concerned in the process of government subscribe to the values which make the continuance of democratic procedures possible: there is widespread agreement that Governments shall allow opposition and submit themselves for re-election at constitutionally agreed intervals. It is evident that the third factor which does provide the guarantee of the democratic method is 'an implicit undertaking between the parties contending for power in the state not to persecute each other'. In the British Parliament, the existence of this agreement is symbolised by the payment of a substantial salary to the Leader of the Opposition.

[1] J. A. Schumpeter, *Capitalism, Socialism and Democracy* (Allen and Unwin, 1963), p. 269.
[2] E. F. M. Durbin, *The Politics of Democratic Socialism* (Routledge, 1948), pp. 235–43.

Institutions and ideals

It would seem, then, that the attitudes, expectations and values of the electorate and especially of those who are politically active, are vitally important in the existence and continuance of the structure and form of government which we refer to as political democracy. It seems reasonable to argue from this that the more deep-rooted these values are in the population at large, the more likely it is that the institutions and procedures will give expression to them. Democracy, as S. I. Benn and R. S. Peters suggest, 'is not merely a set of political institutions like universal suffrage, parliamentary government, and decisions by majority procedure, but also a set of principles which such institutions tend to realise'.[1]

These writers also draw attention to the fact that, although the notion of 'majority-rule' plays such a prominent part in discussion about the nature of democracy, the majority is not a single interest, but 'a shifting aggregate of interests'. Large numbers of people rarely agree about a whole range of issues. Some will agree with some proposals but not with others. The individuals who comprise the majority on one issue will not all be the same people who form the majority on a quite separate question. Neither, indeed, does democracy imply majority approval of every decision that it takes. As is often said the 'business of government is to govern' and any Government must expect that at least some of its measures will, for one reason or another, be distasteful to the electorate. What any Government does is to proceed in the hope that, in the long run, a majority of the electors will, on balance, be reasonably satisfied with the overall pattern of their administration or that they are at least less dissatisfied with them than with their opponents. In this situation Government must be acutely sensitive to all sections of opinion; because it will in due course be seeking a renewal of the licence to govern, the Government must take the reactions of the whole of the electorate into account.

In a political democracy, discussion, argument, the representation of interests and their conciliation, criticism and the advocacy of alternative policies are characteristic and necessary processes. Democracy does not dispense with the need for authority, nor can it guarantee that Governments will be particularly competent. Its institutions are designed not only to administer a complex society but to highlight deficiencies and prevent the abuse of political power. The part of the electorate in the process may be in one sense small, but in another, it is all important. In Britain, the 'sovereignty of the people' comes actively into play only at election times, but because it can confirm or reject the Government in office when the time comes, its reactions cannot be ignored.

The democratic ideal

We have already observed that in a democracy, ideals and institutions are

[1] S. I. Benn and R. S. Peters, *Social Principles and the Democratic State* (Allen and Unwin, 1959), p. 355.

closely connected and it is now necessary to consider further the main components of the democratic ideal and to make an assessment of the extent to which it influences the actions of government. The democratic ideal is characterised by the importance attached to the rights of individuals. A society which claims to be democratic places considerable emphasis upon the notion of equality, particularly the idea of equality of opportunity. It stresses the necessity of the greatest possible measure of freedom of expression and association. The American philosopher, John Dewey, was one of the leading exponents of the democratical ideal in education, but his views are relevant to a consideration of the nature and purpose of the political system as a whole. For Dewey democracy was a moral idea, implying a political system superior in form and purpose to other systems. He saw democracy as an attempt to embody in society the principle that each individual possesses intrinsic worth and dignity. Democracy, in his view, implied a society in which the welfare of individuals was of the highest importance and institutions were to be designed and developed with this end in view.

Democracy, if it is to be no more than an empty shell, necessitates actions on the part of Governments embodying genuine attempts to realise these ideals. Among different groups at different times, expectations will be different. Democracy, liberty and equality are closely connected but they do not necessarily go hand-in-hand. Before democratic ideals can be realised, strong and effective government must be established and both Government and governed must care deeply about the condition of the society of which they form part. Inevitably the demands made will be conflicting and contradictory. It is the function of Government to reconcile them as best it can. Pressure groups, political parties, factions within parties, the press and other agencies, will each have their preferences and priorities. The views expressed by the groups competing for attention are themselves likely to be the outcome of discussion and compromise.

It can be argued that, in modern times, the fairly widespread acceptance of the democratic ideal, however nebulous this may be, serves to provide a moral basis for politics. Actions by Governments may fall short of stated intentions but the existence of the ideal provides the basic framework of reference within which they must operate. S. I. Benn and R. S. Peters express this viewpoint in the following terms: 'It encourages rulers to behave *as if* they were virtuous, because it lays their decisions open to the scrutiny of rivals as competent as themselves, who have their own interests in drawing the voters' intention to partiality or corruption.' They add: 'the whole process presumes the give and take of criticism and justification, conducted within the framework of moral criteria'.[1]

Government in a democracy
The government of a modern, industrialised society is an extraordinarily

[1] Benn and Peters, *Social Principles and the Democratic State*, pp. 351–2.

difficult and complex task. Democracy may not be the most efficient method of government but, in Britain, it is generally believed to be the most desirable. The gap between peoples' wishes and their realisation is likely to remain considerable and it is this which provides the continuing impetus of political activity. The successful functioning of a political democracy demands that certain central questions must be asked over and over again. Does it provide strong and stable government? Does it prevent undue abuses of power? Does it safeguard freedom of speech and association? Does it provide the basis of social justice? Does it adapt itself to changing circumstances and conditions? Does it allow the opportunity for further realisation of the ideals which it embodies? It is, therefore, important that the principles and practice must as far as possible be in harmony and that the machinery of government will be designed towards this end.

Government in a political democracy, such as Britain or the U.S.A., requires the existence of institutions which can regulate the clashes of interest that arise from within society. There must be a *legislature* for the making of laws, an *executive* which is responsible for carrying them out, and a *judiciary* which adjudicates on disputes between individuals and between the citizen and the State. In Britain these requirements are met respectively by Parliament, which is the supreme law-making body; Ministers, Government Departments and the Civil Service, who are responsible for the administration of Government policy; and the Courts which interpret and adjudicate when the law is contravened or brought into question.

The relationship between the various branches of government involves a consideration of the doctrine of the 'separation of powers' and the relevance of the 'rule of law' in the British system. (See chapter 20.) It also raises the question of the powers of the various institutions, the rights of individual citizens and the way in which these are determined in a constitution which is said to be unwritten. It seems preferable, however, to look at these matters at a later stage after the actual working of the system has been more extensively examined.

3 The Electoral System

I think the idea that we should make this House an exact replica of opinions held in the country is, first of all, quite impossible, and, if it were possible, that it would be undesirable.

Clement Attlee – From a speech in the House of Commons, 6 December 1933

Introduction
In the British pattern of political democracy it is the general election which gives one or other of the parties the necessary authority to govern. The party forming the Government at the time of the election may be confirmed in office for a further period or it may be dismissed and replaced by its opponents. The result of a general election is determined by the nature of the electoral system, the qualifications for voting, whether or not the vote is actually used and the way in which the vote is cast when the franchise is exercised. Because of the fundamental importance of the electoral system in British politics these matters will be examined in some detail.

Who can vote
The franchise in Britain is based on the principle of adult suffrage. The qualifications for registration and the subsequent right to vote are that the person concerned must be a British citizen (or a citizen of the Commonwealth or the Republic of Ireland resident in Britain) who is over the age of 18 years and who does not fall into one of the categories excluded from the franchise. Those excluded are peers and peeresses, persons who have committed serious criminal offences and individuals who have been convicted of electoral offences during the five years prior to the compilation of the register. Registration is compulsory but there is no penalty for the failure to vote in an election.

The register is renewed each autumn and provides a record of those entitled to vote on the 'qualifying date' which is 10 October. The list, however, does not come into operation until 16 February of the following year. This means that the register upon which a particular general election is held would be relatively 'new' if held in March but 'old' if held in January. Provision is made in the electoral legislation for individuals who will reach the age of 18 within the period during which the register is operative. They are placed on the register as 'Y' voters and these can vote if they have reached the minimum age at the time of the election. Provision is also made for postal voting in certain approved categories such as serious illness or infirmity.

History of the franchise
The development of the electoral system in Britain has been slow and spans a period of nearly a century and a half from 1832 to the present time. Before 1832 only about 3 per cent of adults were entitled to vote and the so-called 'Great Reform Act' of this year extended the franchise to the extent that now 5 per cent of the total adult population were able to vote, but did little to curb the extensive electoral malpractice that then existed; it did, however, provide the beginnings of a climate of opinion in which further reform was possible. The Representation of the People Act, 1867, extended the franchise further but still only about 13 per cent of the adult population were entitled to vote. The Ballot Act of 1872 made provision for secret voting and this had the effect of ending the intimidation of voters which had continued unchecked after the legislation of 1832 and 1867. A further spate of legislation followed in the early 1880s. The statutes enacted during this period included the Corrupt and Illegal Practices Act, 1883, which was designed to curb bribery and corruption; the Franchise Act, 1884, which gave the vote to working men in country areas, especially agricultural workers, and increased the proportion of adults able to vote to about 25 per cent, and the Registration Act, 1885, which brought about a radical distribution of seats based on population figures. David Butler suggests that 1885 can be regarded as the climax of the evolution of the development which had begun in 1832.[1]

The nineteenth-century legislation, however, concerned only men; women had to wait much longer before they were enfranchised. The first step in this direction came with the passing of the Representation of the People Act of 1918. A woman of over 30 years of age was entitled to vote provided that she or her husband was qualified to vote at local government elections, and the percentage of the adult population now having the vote rose to 75 per cent. This legislation also contained some other important provisions. The qualification for entitlement to vote was now that of residence, or the occupation of land or business premises in a constituency; the disqualification of persons in receipt of poor relief was removed; elections in all constituencies were to be held on the same day and no individual could vote in more than two constituencies (e.g. a person could qualify in a constituency on the residence qualification and in another on the basis of business premises, but if he had business premises in two constituencies he

[1] D. E. Butler, *The Electoral System in Britain Since 1918* (Oxford University Press, 1963), p. 2.

could only vote in one of these). The Act also introduced the requirement that candidates must deposit £150 which was forfeited unless he received one-eighth of the total votes cast. University graduates retained the right to an additional vote and university seats were included in the House of Commons up to the general election held in 1945. In 1928 the age qualification for women was reduced to 21 and this brought the proportion of the adult population entitled to vote to nearly 100 per cent.

Further changes were introduced by the Labour Government after the general election of 1945. Under the terms of the Representation of the People Act of that year the qualification of a spouse to be registered as a business premises voter was abolished and a person qualified for the parliamentary franchise received an automatic right to vote at local government elections. The Representation of the People Act, 1948, finally gave effect to the principle of 'one man – one vote' in parliamentary elections when, in the face of fierce Conservative opposition, the qualifications based on the occupation of business premises and the possession of a university degree were abolished. In April 1969 the age qualification was reduced to 18 and people of this age voted for the first time in the general election of 1970. (The qualifications of local government electors and membership of local authorities are discussed in chapter 16.)

Criteria for evaluation
Professor A. H. Birch observes that: 'The way in which an electoral system works will depend partly upon the methods adopted of dealing with certain practical problems of electoral organisation which arise in every country.'[1] He lists five main features:
  (i) the compilation of the electoral register;
  (ii) the division of the country into constituencies in a way which will be accepted as fair and impartial;
  (iii) the decision on how votes are to be counted and the result arrived at;
  (iv) agreement upon rules for the nomination of candidates;
  (v) the control of expenditure on elections.
Professor Laski postulated four conditions which a democratic electoral system must fulfil. These were:
  (a) the electoral system should enable the legislature to embody the opinions of the majority and the minority on the great issues of public interest;
  (b) constituencies should be small enough for candidates to be known and to cultivate personal relations with their constituents;
  (c) there should be some means of checking the drift of opinion between elections (he quotes by-elections as a useful means of achieving this);
  (d) the voters should be as directly related as possible to the government in power, which should be seen to be their choice.[2]

[1] A. H. Birch, *The British System of Government* (Allen and Unwin, 1967), pp. 75–7.
[2] H. Laski, *A Grammar of Politics* (Allen and Unwin, 1938), p. 315.

These two statements, taken together, provide us with a useful framework of reference in considering the main features of our electoral system.

The register
As we have already seen, the responsibility for the electoral register rests with officials duly appointed to do this task. In practice the duties of returning officers are undertaken by personnel who are already working as full-time local government officers in County Boroughs and County Councils. In normal circumstances about 96 per cent of persons qualified to vote are registered, the remaining 4 per cent being missed in the canvass. The register on which the 1970 election was fought had numerous omissions, however, arising from the lowering of the voting age to 18; a spokesman for the Home Office explained that many householders did not appreciate that the names of those reaching the age of 18 during the twelve-month life of the register should have been included in the form supplied by registration officers. In all, about a quarter of those qualifying for the vote were not registered. It is expected, however, that when this new situation is properly established the position will revert to the normal very full registration. The register nowadays presents few difficulties and cases of falsification or impersonation are very rare.

First past the post
The United Kingdom is at present divided into 630 [635] single-member constituencies, and each constituency returns one member. Each elector votes for only one of the candidates who submit themselves for election. The winner is chosen on the simple plurality of the votes cast. In this 'first past the post' system the candidate obtaining the most votes becomes the M.P. There are no qualifications like obtaining at least 50 per cent of the votes cast and large numbers of M.P.s have in fact been elected on 'minority' votes. This means that over the country as a whole a government can be elected on a minority of votes cast; thus in 1929 and 1951 the party with the largest number of votes did not win a majority of seats. (See appendix I.) It is, in fact, mathematically possible for one party to obtain the highest aggregate vote over the country as a whole and yet not to win a single parliamentary seat. It is evident that under this system there is no attempt to ensure that representation in the legislature reflects with mathematical accuracy the votes cast by the electorate. The position of the Liberal Party illustrates this point. Between 1951 and 1959 the Liberal Party more than doubled its share of the vote but the number of seats gained remained the same; the 1966 election, however, saw a drop of 25 per cent in the Liberal vote but the number of seats *increased* by more than 33 per cent. In 1970 they obtained 7.4 per cent of the votes cast and the number of seats held dropped from 12 to 6.

Closely related to these facets of the electoral system is the existence of the so-called 'wasted' vote. As we have seen, in order to be successful in a

15

British election the candidate need only obtain one more vote than his nearest opponent. All the rest of the votes are in a sense 'surplus'. In some constituencies one party, for reasons that will be discussed later, nearly always wins by a large majority, sometimes amounting to 30 000 votes or more; all of these votes are surplus to requirements and are given no credit in terms of parliamentary seats. Constituencies vary tremendously in voting population. In 1970, the largest constituency was Billericay with 124 125 voters and the smallest the Ladywood division of Birmingham with only 18 884. The system allows 'one man – one vote' but does not provide 'one vote – one value'.

It is for reasons such as these that it has from time to time been suggested that some other system of voting should be introduced which will give parliamentary representation more directly proportionate to the votes received by a particular party. There are various forms of proportional representation but the one most favoured by British critics is the single transferable vote.[1]

The single transferable vote

Under the single transferable vote system the country would be divided into multi-member constituencies each returning, say, five members. To be elected each candidate has to obtain a 'quota' of votes. The quota is determined by the following formula:

$$\frac{\text{total votes cast}}{\text{number of seats} + 1} + 1$$

Candidates receiving the quota are automatically elected and the 'surplus' votes are transferred to other candidates in accordance with the voters expressed second preferences. Candidates reaching the quota after the distribution of surplus votes are also declared as elected. If no candidate reaches the quota on the first count, the candidate receiving the least votes is eliminated and his votes are redistributed in accordance with the stated second choices. The procedure is slow but it can be seen that by the application of these procedures the required number of candidates will emerge when the necessary counting and redistribution have been finally completed. The best way of understanding the procedures is to make assumptions about the total number of votes in a constituency, the number of candidates, the number to be elected, the number of votes cast for each candidate and the allocation of second-preference votes. This can then be systematically worked through and the final result on this basis determined. Thus, let it be supposed that in a given constituency 240 000 votes are cast and five members are to be elected from fourteen candidates. The process of deciding who are the elected candidates will begin with the formula:

$$\frac{240\ 000}{5 + 1} + 1 = 40\ 001$$

[1] See W. J. M. Mackenzie, *Free Elections* (Allen and Unwin, 1958), and P. G. J. Pulzer, *Political Representation and Elections in Britain* (Allen and Unwin, 1968).

16

Candidate A receives 40 501 votes, is elected and has 500 surplus votes to be redistributed on the basis of second preferences; which of the remaining candidates are elected will be decided by the number of votes obtained and the distribution of second preferences.

Clearly, under this system, as compared with our existing 'first past the post' pattern, the counting of votes changes from a quite simple matter to a very complicated one and, additionally, special arrangements would have to be made for by-elections. It is also difficult to see how, on the single transferable method, elected members could be so closely identified with electors as they are in the present single-member constituencies. Against this it must be said that the introduction of multi-member con- stituencies would allow the individual voter a wider choice of candidates which might well have important effects on the procedures for selecting candidates. Contrary to the claims expressed by small parties, there is no evidence to support the contention that a system of proportional representa- tion would seriously alter the present monopoly position of the two major parties.

Stability in government
In the British electoral system great importance is attached to the need for stability in government, the belief being that a general election should desirably result in one party having a majority large enough to enable it to govern for a full term of office, and to provide electors going to the polls at the time of a general election with a clear choice between well organised and disciplined parties. The anomalies which arise from the 'simple plurality' system in single-member constituencies are, in the view of many observers, greatly outweighed by the advantages which accrue from decisive majorities, remembering that, in modern conditions, Govern- ments can function with majorities which are quite small and which as recently as 1950 would have been thought to be impossible. Countries which have adopted systems of proportional representation have fre- quently found that this results in short-term coalition Governments which makes the continuity and planning much more difficult than it would otherwise be.

In reciting the pros and cons of this argument, however, it is important to avoid the temptation to place overmuch reliance on assumptions which are only partially valid, for a particular type of electoral system does not, of itself, ensure stability of government. Fundamentally, political stability involves respect for established institutions and procedures on the part of the majority of the people. Attitudes favourable to stability derive from the overall pattern of the political culture as discussed in chapter 2 and chapter 6 and it is perhaps best to view the electoral system in Britain partly as a reflection of such attitudes and partly as one of the factors in maintaining them.

Proposals for the adoption of the principle of the single transferable vote were examined by the Speaker's Conference on Electoral Reform in 1944 but the ideas were decisively rejected. After the 1950 election, Winston Churchill, referring to the Liberal vote, pointed to the 'constitutional injustice' which had been done to the 2 600 000 voters who had been able to return only nine members. He proposed the setting up of a Select Committee to inquire into the whole question of electoral reform. However, four years later, when the Conservatives were in office and Churchill himself was Prime Minister, a request in Parliament for a Royal Commission on voting systems was rejected. There are at present no signs that either of the major parties would seriously entertain any basic change in the existing pattern, except perhaps in that they might be willing to support the introduction of some kind of system of proportional representation in Northern Ireland in an effort to contribute to the solution of the special political problems which exist in the province.

Finally, it is worth asking the question, what would have been the difference in the results of post-war elections if the single transferable vote system had been in operation? There are too many imponderables in the situation to do much more than make intelligent guesses, but it has been estimated that it would have made no difference in 1945, and that in 1950, 1951 and 1964 no single party would have had an overall majority in the House of Commons. If this is in fact the case, it underlines the choice which has to be made between a system which in modern conditions results in majorities large enough to remove doubts about the composition of a government, and one which allows a level of representation to smaller groups which is commensurate with their electoral strength.

If the present system is to be retained it is important that it should be as fair and impartial as it can possibly be made, and this involves a consideration of the size of constituencies, the nomination of candidates, the regulation of expenditure and other related questions.

Boundary commissions

The drawing of the boundaries for constituency areas presents a most difficult problem to those who have the responsibility for doing this because their recommendations are always open to criticism of all kinds. The main problems in achieving a satisfactory pattern are:
    (i) the number of constituencies should not be much in excess of 600;
   (ii) constituency boundaries should, as far as possible, match local government boundaries;
  (iii) the number of electors in each constituency should not be excessively different;
  (iv) the geographical size of any one constituency should not be impossibly extensive;
   (v) account must be taken of the movement of population.
It will be seen that if one of these criteria is met it makes it all the more difficult to meet the others effectively. Perhaps the best that can be hoped

for is that the recommendations will be made by people who have no vested interest in the result and that their recommendations will strike a balance between the needs and demands which are often mutually exclusive. Additionally it must be recognised that it is much more difficult to effect a satisfactory situation in single-member constituencies than it is in multi-member constituencies.

The abuses and inequities of parliamentary representation in the eighteenth and nineteenth centuries are well known. Before 1832 large and growing towns like Manchester, Leeds, Sheffield and Birmingham were without separate representation while Old Sarum, where no shelter could be found for the returning officer, and Gatton, which had only half a dozen electors, both returned members to Parliament. The Redistribution Act of 1885 brought about a radical distribution of seats and introduced a much fairer system that was based on the numbers of electors in each area. At the end of the First World War an attempt was made to introduce a pattern of constituencies which were equal in numbers of electors but this proved to be impossible in practice; indeed after the 1918 redistribution some of the largest constituencies had three times as many electors as the smallest. By the beginning of the Second World War the scale of disproportion in terms of numbers of electors had become even greater. Up to 1944 boundaries were revised from time to time by Acts of Parliament and each change was accompanied by bargaining between the parties and much resentment on the part of those who were, from their point of view, adversely affected.

In 1944, following the recommendations of the Speakers' Conference, four permanent Boundary Commissions were created for England, Scotland, Wales and Northern Ireland, each of which had a separate body with power to consider necessary changes and to make recommendations to Parliament. The task of the Boundary Commissions is to ensure that discrepancies between constituencies, especially in terms of numbers of electors, do not become too big and to make recommendations which take into account problems of administrative convenience, local government boundaries and geographical and natural regions.

Clearly too frequent changes are undesirable because of the upset caused to electors, M.P.s and candidates, party organisations and the administrative readjustment necessary. The Redistribution of Seats Act, 1944, provided for revisions to be made every three to seven years, but this came to be regarded as impractical and in 1948 the period was extended to each ten to fifteen years. The first major revision resulting from the new Commission was introduced in 1948 when the boundaries of over 80 per cent of the constituencies were changed. At this time the number of seats was reduced from 640 to 625. Further alterations in 1954 adjusted the number to 630 and the number of constituencies has remained constant since that time. At the time of the general election, 1970, England had 511 seats, Scotland 71, Wales 36 and Northern Ireland 12.

19

Further changes in the pattern of constituencies resulting from the recommendations of the Boundary Commissions which were approved by Parliament in 1970 will become operative at the next general election. Under the new pattern 325 of the constituencies result from major boundary changes and in a further ninety constituencies there have been minor boundary alterations. The number of constituencies in Scotland, Wales and Northern Ireland remains the same but the number of English constituencies is increased by five, making the total number of constituencies 635.

Nominations

Persons ineligible for membership of the House of Commons include: those under 21; aliens (excluding citizens of the Republic of Ireland), the Clergy of the Established and Roman Catholic Churches, Peers and Peeresses (excluding Irish Peers), bankrupts, those convicted of election offences and other serious crimes, civil servants, members of the armed forces, police and judges.[1] These disqualifications, however, do not apply to actual candidatures in an election; thus, legally there is nothing to stop a serving soldier or a peer standing for election and the decision as to whether or not a person elected is disqualified is decided by an Electoral Court after the election has taken place. One of the classic cases in this field is that of Anthony Wedgwood Benn, who, before the passage of the Peerage Renunciation Act, 1963, became ineligible to be a member of the House of Commons on inheriting his father's peerage in 1960. He did, however, contest and win the by-election caused by his own disqualification. After the election he was declared to be ineligible and the seat was awarded to the candidate receiving the second highest number of votes. This procedure applies when the ineligibility of the candidate for membership is known. When the ineligibility is for some reason not widely known until after the contest, a further election is held.

Each candidate forfeits the deposit of £150 if he fails to obtain one-eighth of the votes cast. The intention here is to deter frivolous candidates. The smallness of the amount and the relatively few candidates who contest elections, however, is a reflection of the electoral strength of the major parties. Independent or minority party candidates are few and far between and the vast bulk of candidates are representatives of the party organisations. A characteristic feature of the British system is that there is no residential qualification for parliamentary candidature, indeed a high proportion of candidates seeking election for the first time come from outside of the constituency.

In the elections held in the inter-war period, there were relatively large numbers of uncontested seats; only three, however, were unopposed in 1945 and since 1951, virtually every seat at general elections and by-

[1] Disqualifications on grounds of age is not altered by the lowering of the voting age to 18. The House of Commons Disqualifications Act, 1957, clarifies the position relating to the categories of persons formerly described as holding an 'office or place or profit under the Crown'.

elections has been contested. Independents and representatives of smaller parties and organisations are much more likely to lose their deposits. Of the 400 candidates who lost their deposits in the general election of 1970 only a handful were Conservative and Labour candidates. Each nomination at a parliamentary election must be supported by ten duly registered electors; an individual elector can support only one nomination. It is important that this procedure is correctly executed in every detail as an error would result in an invalid nomination. Each candidate is allowed a short description on the ballot paper and this usually includes his occupation and, since 1969, the name of the party he represents.

Expenses

It was not until the passing of the Corrupt and Illegal Practices Act of 1883 that expenses in British elections were first controlled. Before this time bribery and corruption were almost universally rife; public houses dispensed beer to the electors for which the candidates paid!

Although there is no limit on the amount of money which a party can spend on propaganda up to nomination day the expenses from this date are strictly regulated by law. Each candidate is required to appoint an agent who is generally responsible for his campaign and it is the agent's responsibility to ensure that a proper statement of expenses is submitted to the returning officer at the end of the campaign. The Representation of the People Act, 1969, lays down the current limits. Candidates in a county constituency can spend a maximum of £750 plus 5 pence for every six registered electors. Candidates in borough constituencies are allowed £750 plus 5 pence for every eight electors. Thus a candidate in a county constituency of 60 000 would be legally entitled to incur expenses of up to £1250. If a candidate and his agent were so inclined, however, it would not be difficult to circumvent the law by spending more than this. But, as far as can be determined, substantial infringements of the legal limits are few and far between, and in many cases the amount spent is considerably less than the maximum legal amount involved. An additional safeguard is that the accounts are made available for public inspection, when agents have the opportunity of inspecting the accounts of their opponents.

In the 1970 general election, by far the smallest expenditure was that of £1 only, incurred by Mr H. Button, an independent candidate at Folkestone and Hythe, who received 129 votes. The biggest expenditure was that of Mr R. McCrindle (Conservative), who was elected as M.P. for Billericay. He incurred total expenses of £1767 which fell only £18 short of his legal limit. The exception which proves the rule is Mr S. O. Davies, the 84-year-old former Labour M.P. for Merthyr Tydfil who stood as an independent candidate after being rejected as the official Labour candidate on the basis that he was too old. He gained 16 701 votes, against the official Labour candidate's 9234 and the Conservative's 3169, and won the seat with an expenditure of only £212 for printing and stationery.

The 1837 candidates in the election spent a total of £1 329 796, mainly on printing and publicity, together with £73 184 on personal expenses. Generally Labour candidates spent less than Conservative candidates. Both parties spent considerable sums on publicity and advertising in between elections.[1]

Conclusion

For better or worse, the practical effect of a general election in Britain is to elect a Government from one of the major parties contending for power; with a few possible exceptions, the party to which a candidate belongs looms much larger than his individual personality. The electorate, in effect, uses the polls to reward or penalise the party which has held office in the preceding period. By-elections and local government elections, to some extent, give an indication of the electorate's mood but, as was the case in the election of 1970, their probable reactions can sometimes be severely misjudged by politicians, pollsters and experts. (See chapter 8.)

The British system, whatever its defects and anomalies, is free of corruption and it does result in Governments which are remarkably stable. The electorate is free to elect the Government of its choice and as David Butler and Donald Stokes have pointed out, and as the result of the 1970 election confirms: 'the public is not the creature of the parties, and the ebbs and flows of popular favour affect, often in unexpected ways, the whole conduct of British Government'.[2]

---

[1] See *Election Expenses*, H.C. 305 (H.M.S.O., 1971).
[2] D. Butler and D. Stokes, *Political Change in Britain* (Macmillan, 1969), p. 3.

22

4 Political Parties

Parties are part and parcel of the real life of elections and of Parliament.
Professor Jean Blondel *Voters, Parties and Leaders*

The party system
Nowadays in Britain most people take for granted a number of practices which are politically of fundamental importance and among these is a virtually unquestioned acceptance of the party system. They are used to the idea that at the time of a general election the vast majority of electors will vote for a political party, whether Conservative, Labour or Liberal, rather than for an individual candidate. It is assumed that the major parties will put before the electorate, in greater or lesser detail, statements of the policy which we expect to see pursued if they are successful in the election. As David Butler and Donald Stokes observe: 'The role played by the parties in giving shape and direction to the behaviour of voters is so taken for granted that its importance is easily missed. Without it, however, the mass of the people could scarcely participate in regular transfers of power. The individual elector accepts the parties as leading actors on the political stage and sees in partisan terms the meaning of the choices which the universal franchise puts before him. British Government would be fundamentally changed if the parties were absent from the voter's mind.'[1]

It is by means of the party system that the electorate is linked to the Government. Votes are cast for candidates representing the parties and the leader of the party gaining the most seats at a general election becomes the Prime Minister and forms his Government. These elements are essential if the party system is to function efficiently and the business of government is to be carried on.

The existence of political parties and the way in which they function is, then, of central importance in our system of government. Parties focus attention on the outstanding political issues of the day and competing policies are hammered out between which the electorate is invited to choose. Parties form the pivot of political action at all levels and provide the impetus of organised political activity at the national level, whether

[1] Butler and Stokes, *Political Change in Britain*, p. 23.

23

this be policy-making, campaigning, governing or criticising the actions of government.

Writing at the end of the eighteenth century, the famous parliamentarian, Edmund Burke, described a political party as 'a body of men united for promoting by their joint endeavours the national interest upon some particular principle upon which they are all agreed'. This definition may be contrasted with that put forward by the eminent sociologist, Max Weber, who refers to a party as 'a voluntary society for propaganda and agitation seeking to acquire power in order to provide channels for its active militant adherents to realise objective aims, or personal advantage, or both'. Both of these statements give clues as to the essential nature and purpose of the parties in our political system. The major parties select and put into the field opposing teams of potential parliamentarians. They also provide the organisation and means for publicising their cause in attempts either to stay in office or to oust their opponents.

Historical development

Political parties have been in existence for much longer than the modern party system. Kenneth Mackenzie suggests that: 'Party, in the bare sense of a group of men of similar views and who act together in parliament for common purposes, appears at least as early as the reign of Elizabeth.'[1] In the later parliaments of this reign the Puritans persistently acted together to oppose the Queen's prerogative on issues affecting both Church and State.

The origins of the Conservative and Liberal parties can be found in the period after the Restoration. The Earl of Danby, who became the King's principal adviser in 1673, attempted, by the use of royal patronage, to maintain a group of loyal supporters in the House of Commons, which we can refer to as the 'Court' party. At the same time the Earl of Shaftesbury assumed the leadership of a 'Country' party which opposed the 'Court' party. These two groups came to be known respectively as 'Tories' and 'Whigs', both of these descriptions being originally used as terms of abuse: the former term referred to Irish brigands and the latter to Scottish rebels. A broad distinction between the two groups was that the Tories supported the Royal prerogative and the Whigs opposed it. A less clear-cut distinction was the Tories' acceptance of the High Church and the Whigs' inclination towards Protestant dissent. The Tories were the forerunners of the Conservative Party and the Liberal Party was the successor to the Whigs.

Kenneth Mackenzie also notes that 'though the names served to indicate these broad distinctions, they did not by any means indicate two clear-cut parties. The high-handed action of James II served to unite the parties in a common resistance to royal pretensions, and the Revolution was the work of a coalition.'[2] We would do well, therefore, to bear in mind

[1] K. Mackenzie, *The English Parliament* (Penguin, 1969), p. 108.
[2] Mackenzie, *English Parliament*, p. 109.

the caution issued by Sir Ivor Jennings who reminds us that 'the two words, Whig and Tory, were less used by contemporaries than by historians of a later generation, who read the divisions of 1688–1714 in terms of the party history of the nineteenth century'.[1]

At this early stage, and for a long time to come, the activities of the parties were far removed from anything like the modern pattern. There were no generally agreed policies and no sustained organisation; family cliques were prominent and personal allegiances often cut across the two groups. The parties existed only in Parliament and there was no supporting organisation in the country at large. Their aim was to obtain office but no policy statements were issued and no binding promises were made at election times. Professor Robert McKenzie states: 'At the end of the third decade of the nineteenth century it was still impossible to identify within Parliament or outside it anything that resembles the modern party system.' He adds that after the general election of 1830 the situation was so confused that it was impossible to get agreement between the Government and the Opposition as to which side had won. This, he points out, is in striking contrast to the situation today when 'party is the overwhelmingly dominant factor in British politics' and where, within Parliament, 'party lines are drawn with rigid strictness'.[2]

The development of national networks of political party organisations went hand in hand with the widening of the electorate following the successive Reform Acts. The Tories established the Carlton Club in 1832 and two years later the Whigs set up their Reform Club. Until party headquarters were formally established these clubs served as the centres of political organisation which reflected deepening political divisions and increasingly partisan alignments. The organisational development of the parties was facilitated by the tendency towards more forceful leadership, the establishment of better communication between different parts of the country, and the growth of the popular press.

The 1832 Reform Act made it necessary for candidates to canvass for the support of electors systematically because each voter's name had to be recorded on the electoral register and many had to be persuaded to do this. Through their clubs, therefore, both Whigs and Tories organised local Registration Societies and these gradually developed into local party organisations.

These local bodies concerned themselves with all the work necessary for the fighting of elections and were subsequently welded into national organisations. In 1867 the National Union of Conservative Central Constitutional Associations was set up and the Conservative Central Office was established in 1868. In 1861 the Liberal Registration Association was established and this became in effect a central office for the Liberal Party. The National Liberal Federation was founded in 1877.

[1] I. Jennings, *The British Constitution*, 5th edn (Cambridge University Press, 1966), p. 37.
[2] R. T. McKenzie, *British Political Parties* (Heinemann, 1963), pp. 1–3.

The mandate

From the time of the first Reform Bill to the end of the nineteenth century other important changes were taking place in the political scene. In particular, the notion of the 'mandate' was gaining ground. The mandate implies the acceptance of the principle that political parties at the time of a general election will put forward specific proposals which will form the basis of the Government's programme if the party is successful in the election. This mode of seeking electoral authority for intended legislation can first be seen in the election of 1831 when Lord Grey placed before the country a detailed scheme for franchise reform and pledged himself to pursue this if elected. The importance of this development was not immediately recognised but the principle was adopted three years later by Sir Robert Peel. In 1834 Peel unexpectedly became Prime Minister at a time when Parliament was not in session and he could not, therefore, explain his policy to the House. He issued a declaration of policy to his constituents in Tamworth, and this became the platform of the Conservative Party. The Tamworth Manifesto was regarded at the time as an important change in political practice. It is important to notice, however, that the programme put forward in the Tamworth Manifesto was far from being comprehensive in scope.

By the end of the nineteenth century new types of party leaders like Gladstone and Disraeli emerged whose following depended to a much greater extent on principles and policies rather than personal loyalties. These leaders went around the country speaking at public meetings in an effort to gain support for their policies on specific issues. Gladstone's efforts on the Irish question had the effect of strengthening the idea of the need for a mandate to consolidate support in Parliament for major changes in Government policy. Gladstone had been elected as Prime Minister in 1885 and a year later he introduced the Irish Home Rule Bill which had not been mentioned at the election. The Bill was defeated in the Commons and he advised the Queen to dissolve Parliament. In the election which followed he sought a clear mandate on this issue and stumped the country in support of his programme. Since this time it has been the practice for the political parties to issue policy statements in the form of manifestoes at the time of a general election. In the earlier phases of this development, however, comprehensive statements were used only by the Liberal and Labour Parties and the Conservatives did not completely adopt the practice of its rivals in specifying policies covering the whole field of government until as late as 1950.

Nowadays these election statements are likely to cover all aspects of home and foreign affairs, as is shown in the list of main headings of the Conservative and Labour Parties, manifestoes for the general election, 1970, which are presented in table 1. Only a few issues, however, are likely to figure centrally in a given election and those so selected are publicised and expounded with all the apparatus of present day elections, including

26

TABLE I *Conservative and Labour Manifestoes, General Election, 1970*

Conservative	Labour
Theme: 'A Better Tomorrow'	*Theme:* 'Now Britain's Strong let's make it great to live in.'
Main Headings:	*Main Headings:*
Labour's Failures	The Britain We Want
The Conservative Way:	The Main Tasks:
Lower Taxes	A Strong Economy:
More Savings	Investment in Industry
Controlling Government Spending	People and Jobs
Steadier Prices	Industrial Reorganisation
Fair Deal at Work	Fighting Inflation
Training for Better Jobs	Food and Farming
Industrial Progress	Prosperity in the Regions
Prospersity for All Areas	
Food and Farming	Better Communications:
Homes for All	Roads, Railways, Air Services
Social Service Advance	Education and Social Equality
Better Education	A Great Place to Live in:
Caring for those in Need	Housing, Urban Priority Areas,
Race Relations and Immigration	New Towns
Government and Citizen	
Freedom under the Law	Caring for People
A Better Environment	A More Active Democracy:
The Arts, Broadcasting and Sport	Central Government and Parliament
	Devolution
	Industrial Democracy
	Law and Justice
	Race Relations
A Stronger Britain in the World	Britain in the World Community

public meetings, radio and television broadcasts and press conferences. This was particularly so in the 1970 election when both Mr Wilson and Mr Heath concentrated their attention on the economic situation and the alleged impact of their policies on wages and social conditions.

The relationship between party policy statements and the electorate, however, is not quite so straightforward as the doctrine of the mandate seems to suggest, because studies of voting behaviour have shown convincingly that the majority of voters support the party of their choice without giving much, if any, consideration to specific items of policy. Indeed, even party members are unlikely to support every item in a party programme. It can also be argued that the task of a Government is to make decisions in the light of the circumstances of the day and not every possible contingency can be seen in advance. This is not to suggest that Governments should not and do not have long term plans and that efforts are not made to fulfil pledges made at election times; it is merely to recognise that, in practice, detailed plans are not always capable of being completely realised and that unforeseen issues may arise which have not been referred to in party manifestoes.

The relevance of the mandate in contemporary politics has been the subject of considerable discussion, but it seems reasonable to suggest that two separate but related interpretations can be placed upon it. The first of these implies that a party intending to introduce a major change on a specific but controversial issue should have the support of the electorate at a general election before doing this. Historically, several instances of this situation can be given. Thus the 1831 election was fought on the issue of the franchise; the elections of 1906 and 1923 were fought on the free trade issue; the elections of 1910 centred on restricting the power of the House of Lords.

More recently, however, a number of important decisions have been taken by Governments without being mentioned previously in policy statements. Professor A. H. Birch notes that the Government had no mandate for the decision to return to the Gold Standard in 1925 and there was no mandate for enacting the Trades Dispute Act, 1927. He also reminds us that in 1962 'the Government did not think it necessary to go to the country before applying for British membership of the Common Market, though some Labour spokesmen suggested that this would have been appropriate'.[1] This brings us to the second interpretation; namely, that if a party wins a general election it has a general mandate to govern, the tacit assumption on all sides being that it will not lightly ignore the general lines of policy indicated in its election manifesto.

An interesting illustration of the confusion which arises between the two interpretations is provided in the account of a parliamentary debate dealing with the Labour Government's proposals to reduce further the delaying power of the House of Lords in the 1945–50 Parliament, which is dealt with in detail by Professor Bernard Crick.[2]

When this Bill was first introduced in 1947 it was rejected by the Lords and one of the reasons given was that it was a measure 'for which the nation had expressed no desire' and for which the Government had not sought a specific mandate at the election. Lord Addison, the Government spokesman in the Lords, in replying to the debate, said: 'To claim to decide whether a subject is or is not in accordance with the mandate of the people contains the implication that, if this House is of the opinion that it is not in the mandate, this House is at liberty to reject (the Bill); that is the deliberate and obvious implication. We challenge that implication from the very start. We claim that it is for the elected representatives of the people to decide whether an issue is or is not to be the subject of Parliamentary activity.' The Bill under consideration was eventually passed and became the Parliament Act of 1949. In introducing this legislation, the Labour Party could claim it was in fact ensuring that the mandate given by

[1] Birch, *The British System of Government*, p. 94.
[2] B. Crick, *The Reform of Parliament* (Weidenfeld and Nicholson, 1968), pp. 124–8.

the electorate in approving that policy statement at the 1945 election could be fulfilled and that they were making sure that this intention was not frustrated by the House of Lords.

Generally, it is suggested, the strict interpretation of the doctrine of the mandate is no longer applicable, if indeed it ever was, but it can be claimed that the notion has a strong persuasive effect on parties which requires them as far as possible to fulfil specific election pledges without preventing them from governing in the light of the circumstances prevailing when they are actually in office.

Similarities and differences

The Conservative, Labour and Liberal Parties provide most of candidates at present day general elections, and in the period since 1945 it is the Conservative and Labour Parties which have won the vast bulk of the seats. (See appendix 1.) There is a substantial Liberal vote but the number of seats gained is relatively small. The British electorate seems to favour a two-party system and the fact that the Labour Party supplanted the Liberals as the second major party in 1922 (thus avoiding a situation in which there were three major parties with substantial electoral support) is frequently taken as evidence of this. Seats are, of course, contested by independents and representatives of smaller parties but these are rarely successful. In the months before the dissolution of Parliament in 1970 a number of by-elections were won by candidates of the Welsh and Scottish Nationalist Parties. In the general election, however, the Nationalist parties fared very badly, only one Scottish Nationalist candidate being elected.

We will now examine the way in which the main political parties are organised, highlighting, as far as possible, points of similarity and difference in the modes of working of the Conservative and Labour Parties. Historically the Conservative Party grew up within Parliament, and, as we have seen, gradually extended its activities throughout the country at large. The Labour Party on the other hand, to use Ernest Bevin's phrase, 'grew out of the bowels of the trade union movement'. It was originally a pressure group to obtain parliamentary representation for the organised labour movement and it was not until 1906 that the Labour Representation Committee, which had been set up in 1900, was formally renamed as the Labour Party. (See chapter 5.)

The objectives of both Conservative and Labour Parties are identical in that they both seek to obtain office and form a Government in order to put their policies into effect. To do this they need the best possible organisation at national, regional, constituency and local levels in attempting to create a climate of public opinion favourable to their respective political aims. To do this successfully they need money to maintain their organisation and to pay for propaganda and election campaigns. They both have the job of formulating and amending programmes and policies

29

in the light of changing economic and social circumstances.

In the national network of organisation there are some striking similarities, at least on the surface. They are, however, some important differences between the Conservative and Labour Parties in the way they operate, which include:

   (i) the powers of the leader, at least in so far as these are constitutionally established;

 (ii) the machinery for policy-making;

(iii) the financing of the organisation;

(iv) the degree of professionalism.

These differences reflect the different historical background and ideological development of the two parties.

The Labour Party

The Labour Party is a federal body. It links together constituency and local organisations, trade unions which are affiliated to the Trades Union Congress, Co-operatives, and Socialist societies such as the Fabian Society. Individuals may be members of one or more of these societies. The trade unions have a considerable influence in the Labour Party and play a vital role in financing it. The general nature of the organisation and functioning of the party can best be illustrated by reference to figure 1. It will be seen that the trade unions and Socialist societies are separately represented at each level. The Constituency Party can be regarded as a kind of pivotal organisation in that it has direct links with local parties, the regional councils, and the Annual Conference. The respective functions of the various levels can be shown by starting at the local level and working upward.

The Local Labour Party is composed of individual members; representatives of trade unions and other bodies must also be individual members, and this requirement applies similarly at other levels of representation. A chairman, vice-chairman, secretary and treasurer are elected annually and they are responsible to the combined body of members which comprises the local party. The local party encourages the specialised activities of the Young Socialists and Women's Section, and ideally receives help and support from them. It selects and finances candidates for local councils and assumes responsibility for canvassing and other activities at both parliamentary and local elections.

The Constituency Labour Party General Management Committee is made up of delegates from local parties, trade union branches and Socialist societies in the constituency. It elects a chairman, vice-chairman, secretary and treasurer, each delegate having one vote in the election of these officers. The smaller Executive Committee, which is responsible for the conduct of business in between meetings of the General Management Committee, is elected by sections: the delegates from the Local Labour Party elect from their members the required number for their section and

30

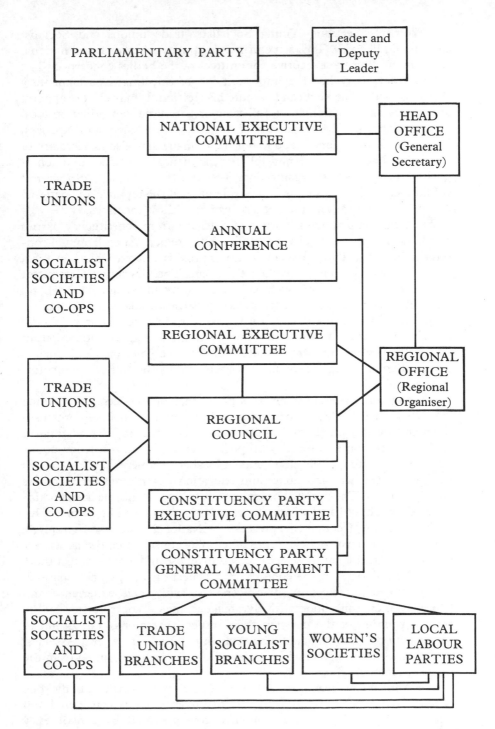

Figure 1. Structure of the Labour Party

the Women's Sections, Young Socialists, trade unions and Socialist societies do likewise. This same principle applies at regional and national levels in electing the executive committees of the bodies concerned. The constituency party has the important job of selecting a parliamentary candidate and doing all it can to secure his election. It may elect *or* appoint an election agent who may be full-time or part-time depending on local circumstances and the availability of funds to pay his salary and expenses. When a full-time agent is appointed he normally acts also as secretary of the party. The agent is responsible for the management and direction of parliamentary election organisation. The constituency party can submit resolutions and amendments for consideration at the regional and national Annual Conferences, and it elects delegates to these meetings.

The Regional Council is formed of delegates from constituency parties and trade unions and Socialist societies in the region. At each annual conference of this body an Executive Committee is elected which, in turn, elects its own chairman and vice-chairman. The Executive Committee reports to an Annual Conference on its year's work and arranges for debates on resolutions received from constituency parties, trade unions and other bodies who are represented. Until the constitution was changed in 1971 resolutions were restricted to regional matters and consideration of national policy matters was not allowed. The Secretary of the Council is also the Regional Organiser and he is appointed by the National Executive Committee.

Although unimportant in terms of policy making, the Regional Council plays a significant role in providing links between its constituent organisations and deals with many important political matters. For example it gives detailed consideration to proposed changes in constituency boundaries and encourages developments in local government; it also arranges regional conferences and rallies and educational gatherings for members and supporters. The regional organiser has an important role in maintaining an oversight of party affairs generally in the region and he, or one of his senior assistants, frequently represents the National Executive Committee at meetings of constituency parties when they are selecting parliamentary candidates. His job on these occasions is to advise and to ensure that there are no irregularities in the conduct of the meetings. Regional organisers are usually experienced party officers and with their experience and expertise they can, unobtrusively, make a major contribution to the smooth running of the party in their respective regions. The group of senior national party officials who include the National Agent, Assistant Agent, and National Women's Organiser are normally recruited from the ranks of regional officers.

The Annual Conference is the Labour Party's policy-making body. The Annual Report of the National Executive Committee is considered and debated. Delegates to the Conference are appointed by constituency parties and trade unions, the number from each organisation being dependent upon the size of membership. Delegates from Co-operative organisations and Socialist societies also attend. M.P.s, prospective parliamentary candidates, party agents and regional organisers may attend as observers. If an M.P. wishes to stand for election to the various offices, or participate actively in the debate, he must be a fully accredited delegate of one of the constituent organisations and, particularly for the more active and best known M.P.s, this is frequently the case. Resolutions and amendments are submitted by the constituent organisations and, if these are approved, become the official policy of the Party.

The Conference elects the National Executive Committee which is responsible for the organisation and development of the party throughout the country. The National Executive Committee is made up of 28 members, 12 are elected by and from trade unions, 7 by and from constituency parties, 1 by or from Socialist societies and Co-operative organisations, and 5 women members and the Treasurer are elected by the whole of the Conference. The person elected as Treasurer is normally an M.P. who ranks high in the party leadership. The leader and deputy leader of the Parliamentary Labour Party are ex-officio members. The person who is to occupy the important position of General Secretary of the Party is appointed by the National Executive Committee subject to the approval of the Conference. A high proportion of the delegates elected to the National Executive in the constituency party and women's sections are prominent members of the Parliamentary Labour Party.

The fact that the Annual Conference is officially the policy-making body creates difficulties when the Labour Party is in office for it is now clearly established that a Labour Government is not bound by the decisions of the Party Conference. It must rule in accordance with its own judgement of political, social and economic circumstances. This was made clear by Mr Attlee when he was Prime Minister at the beginning of the 1945–50 Parliament, following the alleged efforts of Professor Harold Laski, who was Chairman of the party at the time, to interfere with the actions of the Government. This also applies even when the party is in opposition; thus in 1960 the leader, Hugh Gaitskell, made it clear at the Conference that the Parliamentary Labour Party would not be bound by a Conference decision in favour of unilateral nuclear disarmament. This decision was in fact reversed at the annual conference in the following year.

At the 1970 Annual Conference a resolution deploring the Parliamentary Party's refusal to act on Conference decisions was passed by a narrow majority. In replying to the debate Mr Wilson explained that, in accordance with the party constitution, the Parliamentary Party's function was 'to give effect, as may be practicable, to the principles from time to time approved by the Party conference'. Mr Wilson insisted that the timing and priorities of items in a Labour parliamentary programme were matters for the Prime Minister to decide when the Party was in power.

The Labour Party Head Office works under the direction of the

National Executive Committee. It has various departments (e.g. Finance, Research, Organisation, Publicity) which are managed by paid employees. In recent years a number of senior members of the Head Office staff have gained seats in Parliament and some have later achieved high Government office.

The Leader of the Party is elected by the Parliamentary Party. The procedure used is that of the 'exhaustive' ballot which can be outlined by reference to the occasion when Mr Gaitskell died and Harold Wilson was elected as Leader in 1963. If a candidate receives an overall majority of votes cast in the first ballot he is declared as the winner; if there is not an absolute majority the candidate with the least number of votes is deemed to have withdrawn and a second ballot is held. A further ballot is held and the same criteria again apply. If necessary the process is continued until only two candidates remain. In 1963 there were three candidates. In the first ballot Mr Wilson obtained 115 votes, George Brown 88 and James Callaghan 41. There was no absolute majority and a second ballot was held, with Mr Callaghan being eliminated in accordance with the rules. In the second ballot Mr Wilson received 144 and Mr Brown 103.

No election is held when the party is in office but when in opposition provision is made for the annual election of a Leader. In practice the election in these circumstances is normally not contested. Mr Attlee remained unopposed for twenty years. Atypically, Mr Gaitskell was unsuccessfully opposed on two occasions.

The Labour Party publishes its accounts annually in the report of the National Executive Committee and it is clear from this that a large proportion of its income is derived from the trade unions by way of affiliation fees and grants; in 1969 the trade unions contributed £272 000 in affiliation fees. From time to time special fund-raising campaigns are held; thus in 1969 members and supporters were invited to contribute 'Fighting Fivers' to the election fund. In 1969 the party claimed 680 656 individual members and nearly 5½ million affiliated trade union members. The individual membership subscription is still only 60p per annum. This seems an extraordinarily small amount by modern standards.[1]

The Labour Party has a smaller number of paid officials than the Conservative Party. Only in a minority of constituencies is there a full-time agent and even where one exists he is likely to spend a good proportion of his time in fund-raising activities, part of the proceeds of which at least is required to pay his salary. At election time there is a widespread reliance on voluntary efforts by members and supporters and those who work at the 'grass-roots' rarely, if ever, receive any recompense for their sometimes strenuous activities. Although great efforts have been made in recent years towards 'streamlining' the organisation it seems virtually certain that some seats are lost in general elections through an absence of professionalism in the organisation at the local level. Thus, agents may be inexperienced and

[1] The individual membership subscription has now been increased to £1.20 per annum.

34

have insufficient time to devote to the job. Although posters may be ordered in large numbers the distribution may be so badly handled that only a few of them are actually displayed. On the day of the election, cars may be plentiful but uneconomically deployed; liaison between the 'committee-room', the polling station, and those 'knocking up' reluctant voters may be inadequately organised with the result that a great deal of effort is wasted.

The Conservative Party
The structure and functioning of the Conservative Party, although very similar on the surface to that of the Labour Party, differs in a number of important respects. (See figure 2.) We will first look briefly at the national level to make clear an important distinction and then move upwards from the local to the national level. It is easier to understand the structure if initially we think of the whole organisation as being divided into two inter-connected halves. The first of these is the National Union of Conservative and Unionist Associations, representing the constituency and area organisa-tions, and the second is the Conservative Party proper which controls the Central Office and the main party officials. The Chairman of the Party Organisation and other officials are appointed by the Leader. The complete division between the two halves is more apparent than real because there are in practice a number of important points of contact. Thus some seats are reserved on the two governing bodies of the National Union (i.e. the Executive Committee and the General Purposes Sub-Committee) for the parliamentary party and the party organisation.

The Conservative Party aims to have branches in each ward or polling district and their main function is to keep in touch with the electors and publicise the activities of the M.P. or candidate. The basis of membership in a branch is the same as that of a constituency association and membership of a branch automatically entitles the subscriber to membership of the association. The officers of the branch normally include a chairman, one or more vice-chairmen, a treasurer and a secretary. These are elected at an annual meeting of the branch and, together with such other members as the meeting may decide, they constitute a committee which manages the affairs of the branch. A number of local branch members are normally appointed as representatives from the branch to the Executive Council of the Constituency Association. In marked contrast to the Labour Party most members of the Conservative constituency and local associations rarely discuss questions of policy or pass resolutions intended to influence the parliamentary party. Generally their function is regarded as that of rendering voluntary assistance in supporting the Conservative cause.

As in the case of the Labour Party, the Conservative constituency asso-ciation is the basic unit in the structure of the Conservative Party outside of Parliament. The whole organisation of the National Union is built on the foundations of the Constituency Associations. Committees with special responsibility in Local Government, Trade Unions, Women's activities,

35

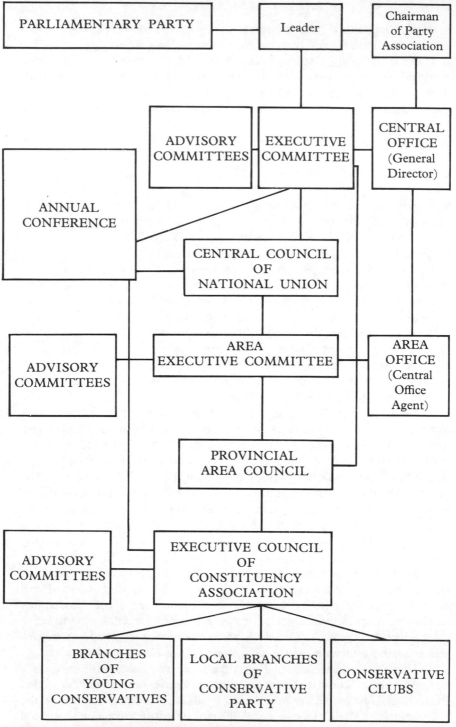

Figure 2. Structure of the Conservative Party

36

Young Conservatives,[1] Education, etc. are paralleled at constituency, area and national levels. Representatives from the Associations constitute the largest element in the provincial Area Councils, the Central Council and the Annual Conference.

The Associations elect their own officers, and select and appoint their own agents, although these are recruited and trained by the Central Office. They raise their own funds, adopt their own candidates for parliamentary and local government elections, and promote their own publicity and election campaigns on behalf of the party. The constituency association works through an Executive Council made up of the officials of the association, representatives of the ward and polling district branches, Young Conservatives, subscribing Conservative Clubs, and certain co-opted members.

The provincial Area Councils are voluntary federations of constituency associations. Their function is to co-ordinate and administer the affairs of the party within the area to provide a source of information and advice for the party leaders. The Council includes in its membership representatives from every unit of the party organisation within the Area. It debates and forwards to the National Union resolutions on policy originating either in the constituencies or in the Council itself. It allocates funds to assist constituency associations in the areas where there is special need. The principal organs of the council are the Area Executive Committees and a range of advisory committees similar in scope to those at national and constituency level. The Chairman of the Area plays an important and responsible role and is required to devote a great deal of time and energy to his duties.

The Central Office is represented in each area by an Area Office, which is under its direct control. The senior official of the Area Office, the Central Office Agent, acts as secretary to the Area Council. This pattern again applies at the national level where the General Director of the Central Office acts as honorary secretary to the National Union.

The Area Council has substantial representation on the Executive Committee of the National Union. Each area sends its Chairman, Treasurer, Chairman of the Women's Advisory Committee, Young Conservative, trade unionist and additional representatives. This strong link between the area and national levels, plus the fact that in the Conservative Party policy matters can be dealt with at area levels, provides a striking contrast to the pattern in the Labour Party. Professor R. T. McKenzie has observed: 'Limited though the influence of the Conservative provincial areas may be, it is probable that the work of the Conservative Party at this level has greater meaning for members of the party than is the case with Labour.'[2] Whether the recent changes in the Labour Party constitution affecting the regional organisation will invalidate this comparison remains to be seen.

It has a President but this is largely an honorary post. The really

---

[1] The maximum age for Young Conservatives is 30; for Young Socialists it is 25.
[2] McKenzie, *British Political Parties*, p. 432.

exacting work is undertaken by the Chairman who is assisted by three vice-chairmen. All of these are elected by the Central Council. The secretaries to this body are the General Director of the Central Office and an additional secretary, both of these being appointed by the Executive Committee of the National Union. The offices of the National Union are within the premises occupied by the Central Office and this provides a further link between the two 'halves' of the party.

The Annual Conference is made up of all members of the Central Council and three additional representatives from each constituency along with the honorary treasurer and the agent of each Association. The Conference receives and debates briefly reports from the Central Council and the Executive Committee and debates resolutions on policy. The decisions on policy, however, are not binding on the Leader, and it is generally agreed that the Conference serves primarily as a demonstration of party solidarity. Before Mr Heath's election as Leader it was customary for the Leader merely to address the closing rally.

The governing body of the National Union is the Central Council which normally meets once a year. Its membership includes the Leader of the Party and other leading officials, including the Chairman of the Party Organisation, the General Director and other senior officials of the Central Office; all Conservative M.P.s and peers, prospective candidates; members of the Executive Committee of the National Union; representatives of the National Union advisory committees, and four representatives from each constituency association, together with representatives of Area Councils.

This body is so large that its day to day work is carried out by a General Purposes sub-committee which meets monthly. In view of the nature of its task, this is again a relatively large body. It has about fifty members who include the principal officers of the National Union, the Chairman of the Party Organisation, the General Director of the Conservative Office, the Chief Whip in both Houses of Parliament, the chairman of each Area Council, and twelve representatives of the Executive Committee. The Executive Committee has a number of Advisory Committees, each consisting of about fifty members made up mainly of representatives appointed at area level.

Until recently the Leader of the Conservative Party was said to 'evolve' naturally from within the party by a process which was not made clear publicly but seemed to involve consultations with the Parliamentary Party, constituency associations, the National Union, prospective M.P.s etc., organised by senior statesmen within the party. The detailed process followed seems to have varied from time to time. An outline of the course of events which occured in the changes of leadership in 1957 and 1963 is given in chapter 9. On both of these occasions there was considerable criticism of the methods used from both inside and outside the Conservative Party and eventually a more straightforward system was adopted.

In October 1963, Mr Macmillan, who was then in hospital, announced that he intended to resign and this event coincided with the Conservative Party Conference which was being held at Blackpool. Those who were thought to be in the running to succeed Mr Macmillan included R. A. Butler, Lord Hailsham, Edward Heath, Lord Home, Reginald Maudling and Iain Macleod. According to press reports there was an unprecedented amount of open lobbying for support and the fact that Lord Hailsham took steps to renounce his peerage was taken as evidence of his desire to be selected as Leader. Unexpectedly, Lord Home was announced as Leader and the Queen was duly notified. This was followed by allegations that the Monarch had been involved in the appointment of a Prime Minister who had been put forward following a dubious process of selection.

In February, 1965, a new procedure for the election of a Conservative Leader was agreed and this was first used later in the year when Lord Home resigned. The revised procedure provides for a first ballot in which all Conservative M.P.s take part. In order to be elected at the first ballot a candidate must obtain an overall majority of the votes cast and he must also have 15 per cent more votes than the 'runner-up'. If the result is closer than this a further ballot is held within four days in which candidates from the first ballot must be re-nominated and new nominations may be made. In the second ballot a candidate may be elected merely by having an overall majority of the votes cast. If this does not happen a third ballot is held which is restricted to the three candidates who received the greatest number of votes in the second ballot. On this occasion votes are given with first and second preferences made clear. If necessary the third candidate is eliminated and the result is decided by the redistribution of the second votes to the two remaining candidates.

In 1965 there were three candidates in the first ballot. Mr Heath received 150 votes, Mr Maudling 133 and Mr Powell 15. Mr Heath had not received the required 15 per cent lead but, before a second ballot was held, Mr Maudling and Mr Powell withdrew leaving Mr Heath as the unopposed candidate.

The Leader so chosen is confirmed in office by a meeting of Conservatives made up of M.P.s, peers, prospective candidates and members of the Executive Committee of the National Union. The Leader continues in office as long as he retains the confidence of Conservative M.P.s and has general support from the wider party organisation.

It is the Leader's prerogative to pronounce on policy and although he inevitably takes account of the views of the Conference he is not bound by its decisions. He appoints his own nominee to the powerful post of Chairman of the Party Organisation. Professor J. Blondel notes that 'although the leader is officially all-powerful in matters of policy, he has come to be advised by an Advisory Committee on policy of about twenty members. This committee technically falls under the party half, not under the National Union half of the Conservative structure. It is none the less comprised of representatives of the National Union, the parliamentary party, and the party organization. The real power of this committee is not well known.'[1] R. T. McKenzie concludes: 'The party does make every effort to protect the Leader and his colleagues from any attempt by the National Union to exert over them any form of arbitrary control. In practice, however, the Leader's powers are in no sense those of an autocrat; it can be further shown that he ignores the moods and opinions of the National Union at his peril.'[2] It may be deduced from these observations that, in practical terms, the power of a Conservative Leader is not distinguishably greater than that of a Labour Leader.

The Conservative Party does not publish detailed accounts of its finances and until recently little firm information was available on the sources of funds other than those received from constituencies under a quota scheme. The Companies Act of 1967 (passed by a Labour Government) now requires companies to disclose details of donations made to political parties. In 1969 the Labour Party produced a list of the donations made to the Conservative Party. These add to something like £900 000 received from various companies. Banking, insurance and hire-purchase companies account for £228 000 of the total and the breweries contributed £71 000.

The Conservative Party employs a higher proportion of paid officials than does the Labour Party and they draw higher salaries. The Conservatives tend to be much more professional in organisational matters at constituency and local level than the Labour Party. This is reflected in procedures such as making arrangements for postal voters. David Butler states: 'There is no doubt that the great majority of these votes went to Conservative candidates.'[3] He notes that calculations have been made which suggest that between nine and twelve seats in post-war general elections may have been gained by the Conservatives because of the postal vote.

The total membership of the Conservative Party is estimated to be between two and three millions.

The Liberal Party
The Leader of the Liberal Party is elected by M.P.s receiving the Party Whip. As in the case of the Conservative Party, the Liberal Leader is formally accorded a dominant role in the organisational structure. (See figure 3.)

The Liberal Party Organisation includes the whole of the party network outside of Parliament. The President and other officers are elected by the annual conference of the party which is known as the Assembly.

Those entitled to attend the Assembly include representatives of the constituency associations together with various *ex officio* members such as M.P.s, parliamentary candidates, agents and organisers, and representatives of the Women Liberals and the Young Liberals. The Assembly

[1] J. Blondel, *Voters, Parties and Leaders* (Penguin, 1965), p. 116.
[2] McKenzie, *British Political Parties*, p. 221.
[3] Butler, *The Electoral System in Britain*, pp. 210–11.

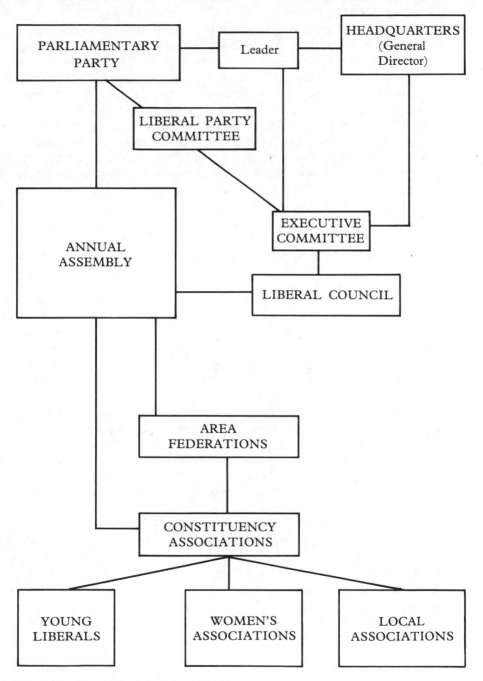

Figure 3.   Structure of the Liberal Party

41

receives a report from the Council and debates resolutions on policy matters which have been submitted by constituency associations and other authorised bodies within the party.

The Liberal Council is made up of thirty representatives elected by the Assembly, representatives of the Parliamentary Party, representatives elected by the Area Federations, the Women's Association and the Young Liberals and all members of the Executive Committee. This body meets at least every three months and is responsible for stimulating and maintaining support for Liberalism throughout the country. It issues pronouncements on behalf of the party on current issues. The Council officially has the task of maintaining the Party Headquarters, raising funds, the adoption of candidates, and initiating various forms of publicity and propaganda. A smaller Executive Committee which meets more frequently is elected by and from the Council. This smaller body supervises the day to day activities of the organisation.

The Party Headquarters is responsible to the Executive and the Council. It provides administrative and secretarial assistance for all the national bodies of the party and their associated committees. It undertakes work in the fields of publicity, propaganda and research. The senior official is the General Director.

The Liberal Constituency Associations are grouped together in Area Federations which are responsible for the co-ordination of the party activities within their respective areas. They are responsible for their own organisation, working arrangements and finance. They undertake the same sort of propaganda and educational work as in the Conservative and Labour Parties and sponsor Liberal candidates for parliamentary elections, and encourage local government candidatures.

A most important body in the Organisation is the Liberal Party Committee which is responsible for the co-ordination of the party's activities both inside and outside of Parliament. The elected leader automatically becomes President of this Committee.

The Liberal Party has considerable difficulty in raising funds because, unlike the Conservative and Labour Parties, it cannot rely upon the continued financial support of bodies which are sympathetic to its policies. In 1951 its income was as low as £11 000. During 1965–6 its income was £66 000 and its expenditure £92 000. The Report and Accounts for 1969 presented to the 1970 Conference, however, record a very encouraging response to appeals which had been launched to raise funds. The Report states: 'In consequence of these appeals, the Party's accounts for 1969 show a surplus for the first time in many years. The income of the Party, too, is the highest for a considerable period.' During 1969 no less than £113 000 was received by way of appeals, subscriptions and donations from individuals and Associations.

In spite of the fact that its members and supporters are numerically fewer than those of the major parties, it can be seen that in its organisa-

42

tional structure the Liberal Party is very similar to that of the Conservative and Labour Parties.

Selection of parliamentary candidates

Among the principal factors which determine the public reputation of all political parties is the calibre of M.P.s and parliamentary candidates. It is important, therefore, to consider the way in which the selection process operates. In any general election the probability is that eight out of every ten candidates will be representatives of the Conservative and Labour Parties and nearly all of those elected will be members of the major parties. Furthermore, something like two-thirds of all constituencies in the country are more or less 'safe' seats in that they are won by the same party in successive general elections; in these cases, therefore, 'selection is tantamount to election'.[1] Electorally, the Liberal Party has a thin time, with only a handful of the many candidates having any real prospect of success.

One striking feature of the British system, which applies to all parties, is the absence, except in a minority of cases, of any previous personal tie between the individual seeking a candidature and the constituency where the selection is taking place. It is quite common for a candidate not to have set foot in the locality concerned before the day of the selection meeting. In many cases the continuing association with a constituency begins after one of the candidates is elected as M.P. There is a marked tendency, however, for constituencies in Scotland, Wales and Northern Ireland to be represented by their countrymen, and a small number of constituencies in all three parties seem to prefer local candidates.

While there are differences between the parties in the detailed procedures followed, the choice of a candidate is characterised in all cases by a mixture of the principles of selection and election; the difference is mainly in the extent to which the procedure is regulated by the national organs of the respective parties. In the case of the Labour Party the selection process is carefully regulated by the party's Constitution, which provides that 'The National Executive Committee shall co-operate with the Constituency Labour Party for each constituency in selecting a Labour Candidate for any Parliament Election.' The detailed rules lay down that the National Executive has the power to:

    (i) decide in association with the constituency party if the constituency is to be contested;

    (ii) decide the timing of the programme for the selection procedure;

    (iii) approve the nominations submitted before the selection meeting;

    (iv) be represented at the selection meeting to ensure that it is properly conducted;

    (v) endorse or reject the candidate chosen after the selection meeting;

    (vi) to order if necessary, a further selection meeting.

[1] M. Rush, *The Selection of Parliamentary Candidates* (Nelson, 1969). (This book contains detailed case-studies of selection meetings in a number of constituencies.)

These powers are extensive but while there are cases of each one of them being used, the need to apply the more restrictive provisions is rare in practice. The Head Office of the party maintains two lists of potential candidates. List *A* includes those who are 'sponsored' by trade unions; this in effect, means that if a person from this list is selected as a candidate the trade union concerned will pay a substantial part of the election expenses. List *B* includes all other persons who wish to be considered as potential candidates. Inclusion in the list is not a condition of nomination.

Constituency Labour Parties, however, are jealous of their right to select their own candidates and normally resent any suggestion, real or imagined, that the National Executive wish to foist a particular person on them. In fact it is probably true that in the vast majority of constituencies, for a nominee to have, or to appear to have, the support of the Head Office is in most cases a virtual guarantee of non-selection. Thus when the candidature in North-East Derbyshire became vacant in 1959, the then General Secretary, Mr Morgan Phillips, personally made known his willingness to be considered. This was apparently interpreted locally as Head Office interference and Mr Phillips was not included among those finally considered. Nevertheless, some constituencies do co-operate with the National Executive in finding seats for ex-Ministers or individuals whom a Government might wish to bring into Parliament, as for example in the cases of Frank Cousins and Patrick Gordon Walker during the early months of the 1964–6 Government.

The first practical step in the process of selection is that all local parties, trade union branches, etc in the constituency are invited to submit nominations. Sometimes, Lists *A* and *B* are referred to locally, probably more often they are not. Individuals on List *A* can almost always arrange to be nominated in a given constituency. The number of nominations varies in accordance with the 'winnability' of the constituency. In safe and marginal seats there are adequate numbers forthcoming and frequently unofficial canvassing takes place, but in 'hopeless' seats it is often difficult to find suitable candidates. In seats where there is a good or reasonable prospect of success between twenty and thirty nominations may be received. The Executive Committee then considers all nominations received and proposes a short list of five or six persons to the larger General Committee for approval. The selection process is conducted at a specially convened meeting of the General Committee. Each candidate is allowed 10 or 15 minutes to address the gathering after details of his qualifications have been read out or circulated. A similar period is allowed for questions from delegates. When all nominees have been heard the delegates complete the ballot forms, each person having one vote. If a candidate has an overall majority of votes in the first ballot he is deemed to be elected, if not the person with the least number of votes is eliminated and a further ballot is held. This process is continued until one person has a clear majority. After endorsement by the National Executive Committee

44

he is formally adopted as the prospective parliamentary candidate.

A Conservative Constituency Association is not subject to detailed supervision by the national body as is the case with the Labour Party; neither is any standard pattern for the selection process laid down. The Conservative Central Office publishes a pamphlet which is used as a guide to selection procedure. This states: 'Subject to certain simple Party rules each association has complete freedom to select the man or woman of its choice.' The purpose of this pamphlet is to assist associations in discharging their responsibility in the interest both of the country and of the constituency.

The National Union has a Standing Advisory Committee on Candidates (S.A.C.C.) which functions under the general direction of the Vice-Chairman of the Party. The S.A.C.C. maintains a list of potential candidates but inclusion in the list is not a condition of selection. Selection meetings are attended by the Central Office Area Agent and the S.A.C.C. has the right to approve or disapprove the person selected before he or she is formally approved as the prospective candidate by the constituency association concerned. Only on two occasions since 1945 has approval been withheld. The first of these was at Chorley in 1949 when the local association adopted Andrew Fontaine who held markedly right-wing views and who had made these known at the Party Conference in 1948. This did not deter the local association and he fought the 1950 election as the unofficial Conservative candidate. After the election Lord Woolton, the Chairman of the Conservative Organisation, threatened to withdraw recognition of the local association if Mr Fontaine was again adopted as candidate and finally an alternative choice was made. Mr Fontaine became President of the British National Party in 1962. The second case occurred at Newcastle North in 1951 when there was disagreement between two factions within the Conservative Association which led to official and unofficial candidates being adopted. The S.A.C.C. supported Major G. Lloyd George, the former M.P. for Pembroke, and ruled against the other candidate.

The selection procedure begins by inviting applications to be considered and about 100 names may be considered which arise either from personal application or names supplied by the Vice-Chairman from the S.A.C.C. list. These are then considered by a selection committee on behalf of the Executive Council and a dozen or more of the applicants are interviewed, possibly accompanied by their wives, by the selection committee. After this a short list, probably of four or five, is drawn up and these then appear before the full Executive Council. Half an hour or so is allowed for speeches and questions, following a pattern similar to that outlined for the Labour Party, and a vote is then taken. Some significant variations from this general pattern have occurred in a number of constituencies; perhaps the most dramatic of these was the Reigate Conservative Association's selection in 1968 when, after 267 applications had been reduced to two, the final choice was made by 600 members of the local association in a meeting which was open to television and the press. This represented the nearest ever approach in Britain to the American system of 'primaries'.

Liberal constituency organisations have much more freedom than either of their Conservative and Labour counterparts in the selection of parliamentary candidates. They find it more difficult to find suitable candidates and are given virtually unlimited freedom in their choice. A list of candidates is drawn up by a sub-committee of the national organisation but the National Executive Committee of the Liberal Party Organisation has no power either to prevent the local organisation from contesting a seat or to veto the candidate chosen.

Principles and policies

In recent years the view that the lines of demarcation between the major parties have appreciably narrowed has received support from a number of political commentators and academics. Samuel H. Beer, for instance, writes: 'If one asks whether during the sixties there has been a further lessening of the ideological distance between (the) two parties, the answer is clearly yes.'[1] But, in assessing the attitudes and actions of political parties, it is necessary to look at both basic principles and detailed programmes. Differences which are regarded by some as marginal may well be regarded as central by others. The important question to be asked is whether or not the confrontation between parties is a sham battle and if the respective policies are significantly different and politically relevant.

The Labour Party describes itself as a party dedicated to the ideal of democratic socialism. Clause IV of its constitution sets out the objective of the party as being 'to secure for producers by hand or brain the full fruits of their industry, and the most equitable distribution thereof that may be possible, upon the basis of the common ownership of the means of production and the best obtainable system of popular administration and control of each industry and service'.

The Labour Party still sees itself as accepting and being motivated by the principles of the brotherhood of man, equality of opportunity and the just society. It believes that a large percentage of public ownership and control of industry and government planning is necessary to achieve these ends. It eschews the principle of free enterprise and protests against human discrimination in all its forms. The late Arthur Greenwood summed up the party's basic attitude in the following terms: 'Socialism is a philosophy of life which, when translated into policies and programmes, offers this country and the world the means of establishing human society as a real community based upon co-operation.'

The philosophy of the Conservative Party is in marked contrast to that of the Labour Party. 'Conservatives', says Lord Hailsham, 'are sometimes impatient when they are asked to explain in simple terms "what their party stands for"'. Conservatives do not accept that the political needs of

[1] S. H. Beer, *Modern British Politics* (Faber, 1969), p. 409.

46

society can be summed up in a few phrases and they consider that 'a living society can only change healthily when it changes naturally – that is, in accordance with its acquired and inherited character and at a given rate'.[1]

In the view of Conservatives, politics is not the best or the only way of changing society. Human beings, they suggest, are capable of considerable development without the aid of government. They believe that as large an area as possible of life should be free from government interference; and that regulation and control of men and resources should be minimal. Personal initiative is important and rewards should be matched with efforts made. Freedom of choice is, in their view, vital and people must not be pressed into a universal mould. Social services should be for those really in need. Conservatives place high store on patriotism and contend that loyalty to country 'stands over and above party affiliation'. They dislike abstractions and prefer to concern themselves with concrete situations.

Both parties have to a large extent accommodated themselves to changing social and economic conditions and neither has been able, when in office, completely to translate their principles into a practical reality. There has been considerable bi-partisanship, especially in foreign affairs and neither party has attempted drastically to undo the changes made by its predecessor in government. Thus, when the Conservatives took office in 1951 after six years of Labour legislation they did not attempt to return the basic industries of coal, gas and electricity to private ownership, nor did they significantly alter the framework of the social services which had been developed since 1945. Similarly, successive Labour Governments have left virtually untouched whole areas of private industry. This is not to suggest that there is complete accord in these and other areas of policy because the contrary is the case as the respective approaches to the control of steel, road haulage and civil aviation show. Since 1950 both parties have tended to concentrate their energies on the central problem of the economy and its relationship to living standards in terms of the level of employment, wages, taxation, and welfare services. But fairly clear cut divisions between Conservative and Labour approaches which reflect their differing premises and assumptions are still apparent. In the months following the general election of 1970 this centred on the issue of supplying arms to South Africa; charges for school meals; prescriptions and dental treatment; assistance to industry; and trade union legislation. All of these debates made it clear that, in the view of the parties themselves, Conservative and Labour are still a long way from unanimity in the approach to political and social problems. The Conservative view of the aim of government remains markedly different to that of Labour and, as Professor Beer observes, 'the old party dualism would seem likely to have a long, vigorous and useful future'.[2] Certainly, the Parliamentary Session

---

[1] Q. Hogg, *The Conservative Case* (Penguin, 1959), pp. 28–9.
[2] Beer, *Modern British Politics*, p. 432.

1970–1 proved to be the most politically divisive year since the end of the Second World War.

Pros and cons of the party system

A number of claims are frequently cited as to the merits and demerits of the party system as it operates in Britain. The points made referring to the advantages of the system include the following. Firstly, it contributes to the need for stability in the process of government. (The same claim could, of course, be made for the government of the U.S.S.R., which has a *one party* system.) Secondly it ensures that governments must be concerned with the issues which really matter and that they are clearly responsible for the policies which are pursued. The existence of an official Opposition ensures that these policies are the subject of continual scrutiny and criticism. Thirdly, the existence of the parties brings about a situation in which the electorate is presented with a clear choice. The result is that party politics represent a crystallisation of many points of view, indeed the parties themselves are coalitions of opinion and belief. The formulation of policy and the arguments within and between parties, it is claimed, play a vitally important role of informing and educating the wider public. Additionally, in framing and implementing their policies, the parties must take into account the fact that they will in due course have to submit themselves for re-election.

The nature of these advantages gives rise to corresponding disadvantages. Thus the major parties have a strong interest in maintaining the existing pattern and the very nature of our electoral system makes it extremely difficult for new parties to gain a foothold. New parties seem to flourish only in exceptional situations. Sir Richard Acland's Commonwealth Party grew up during the Second World War when there was a coalition government and 'normal' political activity was severely restricted; its decline after the end of the war was rapid. Under the two party system, the electorate is presented with a kind of 'package' deal. The individual elector has to accept the whole of the package or none. He cannot register the fact that he is in general sympathy with the Labour Party, but is opposed to the further extension of government control of industry. The Conservative elector cannot indicate that, while generally approving the party's programme, he is unhappy about the proposals for education. The two party system has meant the virtual exclusion of the independent M.P. Apart from the difficulty of financing a parliamentary candidature an Independent, if elected, finds his opportunity for influencing policy strictly limited. The legislative programme is dominated by the Government and a Private Member's Bill has little hope of success unless it receives support from the Government or both major parties. It is sometimes suggested that the present pattern precludes the possibility of a number of important issues being considered. The validity of this particular claim depends on a definition of what constitutes 'importance' in the political context, but marriage-law reform and local-government reform have been quoted in recent years as examples of topics which may be in danger of being rejected. In the event, both these matters have received the attention of recent Governments.

It is further argued that strong party discipline in the House of Commons means that the individuality of M.P.s receiving the Party Whip is suppressed. Part of the answer to this is that discipline is the price to be paid for the coherence and stability of the system but it must be borne in mind that the individual M.P. has a voice both within party meetings and in the House of Commons. M.P.s sometimes defy the Party Whip and, as a last resort, resign their membership. Finally, the spectre of the danger of rule by an outside party caucus is sometimes raised. The evidence, however, suggests that in the case of both the Conservative and Labour Parties this fear is unfounded.

Conclusion
In Britain political parties clearly hold the centre of the political arena but they are not all powerful. The composition of the parties themselves provides strong regulating mechanisms and they are subject to numerous pressures from interest groups of all kinds. It was the parties themselves who gave the vote to an ever increasing number of the population and they are dependent upon the support of the public which they have enfranchised. There is nothing automatic about this and the electorate from time to time acts in a way that defies the forecast of opinion polls and 'expert' commentators. In 1945 the Labour Party won an overwhelming victory; a quarter of a century later a Conservative Government was elected, in spite of the fact that every public opinion poll except one had forecast the return of a Labour Government.

5 Pressure Groups

Pressure Groups are necessary to the government of our complex society. The coherent expression of opinion they render possible is vital.

J. D. Stewart *British Pressure Groups*

Organised groups and the political process

Throughout Britain today there are literally thousands of organised groups based on interests which their members have in common. The direct contact of many of these with government bodies is limited or non-existent. Local dramatic societies, gardening associations, chess clubs and netball teams flourish and fade without having any effect whatsoever on the development of the political system. A group, whether national or local, becomes a pressure group when it becomes formally organised and sets out deliberately to influence the decisions made by governmental bodies.

Pressure groups include trade unions, employers' associations, motoring organisations, welfare societies, and groups promoting a variety of causes ranging from facilities for the chronically sick and disabled to world peace. A realistic view of the political process must take account of the activities of these groups because both the process of legislation and the pattern of administration may be affected by them.

Among organisations as diverse in aim, interest and outlook as the Transport and General Workers Union, the Abortion Law Reform Association, the Royal Automobile Club, the Fish Friers' Association, and the Child Poverty Action Group, there are, of course, important differences in the composition and size of membership of the groups, the way in which objectives are pursued and the extent to which they are likely to influence political decisions.

Pressure groups and political parties

Firstly, it is important to recognise that the role of pressure groups is different to that of political parties. J. Blondel suggests that they 'differ from political parties by their aim, which is not to take power but only to exert pressure. They differ from parties in their objects, which are usually limited in scope. They differ from parties in their membership, which is often limited to one section of society.'[1] But even here the line is not always easy to draw; pressure groups have occasionally put up candidates in parliamentary elections, especially in by-elections, in order to draw attention to the issue which is of concern to them. The picture is also blurred by the existence of nationalist parties and regional parties whose nature is rather different to that of the major parties. Until a few years ago there was a Lancastrian party seeking home rule for Lancashire, whose founder, Tom Emmot, stood for election in the Nelson and Colne constituency, and today there is Mebyon Kernow which aims to establish home rule for Cornwall. Quite frequently Welsh and Scottish Nationalist Parties put up candidates at by-elections and general elections and a few of these have from time to time been elected.

There are also close links between the major parties and pressure groups which share common interests. There are formal organisational links between the trade unions and the Labour Party and many individuals are active in both groups. The Conservative Party has close connections with business organisations and again some of the people involved have influence in both fields. Pressure groups such as the Aims of Industry and the Economic League seek to promote the interests of private enterprise and have much in common with the general objectives of the Conservative Party.

Protective groups and promotional groups

Classification of these organisations presents some difficulties, but a broad distinction can be made between *sectional* or *protective* groups, and *cause* or *promotional* groups. Protective groups include trade unions, motoring organisations, and associations devoted to the defence of particular individuals or institutions. Membership of these groups is normally limited to those sections of the community who directly benefit from the services offered. Promotional groups are those which seek to gain widespread support for given objectives ranging from private enterprise to nuclear disarmament. They are open to all who share their view and who are prepared to give time, energy or cash to seeking its realisation. These divisions are not hard and fast because many groups seek both to protect the interest of their members and to promote ideas and practices which will facilitate this task. The degree of overlap is considerable and the category into which any one group is placed depends largely on the aspect of its organisation under consideration. This fact should be taken into account when looking at table 2, which attempts to give some indication of the variety of groups with which we are concerned.

The general nature of a group, or the particular objectives being emphasised at a given time, tends to determine the channels used in an attempt to exert pressure and the extent of its influence. By and large, promotional groups have a harder task in gaining official recognition and

[1] Blondel, *Voters, Parties and Leaders*, p. 160.

TABLE 2 *Types of Pressure Groups*

Protective (sectional)

Business	Institute of Directors
	Confederation of British Industries
Labour	Trades Union Congress
	National Union of Mineworkers
Professional	British Medical Association
	Society of Civil Servants
Ethnic	Society of Jewish Refugees
	Indian Workers Association
Religious	Free Church Federal Council
	Student Christian Movement
Property	National Federation of Property Owners
Welfare	National Federation of Old Age Pensioners
	British Limbless Ex-Servicemen's Association
Local government	County Councils Association
	National Association of Parish Councils
Recreational	Ramblers Association
	Lawn Tennis Association
Transport	Road Hauliers Association

Promotional (causes)

Educational and cultural	Council for Advancement of State Education
	Third Programme Defence Society
Environmental	Council for the Preservation of Rural England
	National Society for Clean Air
Economic/political	Aims of Industry
	Economic League
Human welfare	N.S.P.C.C.
	SHELTER
Animal welfare	R.S.P.C.A.
	League Against Cruel Sports
Religious and anti-religious	Catholic Truth Society
	British Humanist Association
Socio-medical	Family Planning Association
	Abortion Law Reform Committee
Penal	Howard League for Penal Reform
	National Campaign for Abolition of Hanging
International (cultural/social)	Rotary International
	English Speaking Union
International (policy)	United Nations Association
	Parliamentary Group for World Government

are less likely to be consulted by government bodies than are protective groups who can frequently give assistance to government departments as well as making demands upon them.

The study of pressure groups

The importance of the part played by pressure groups in the political process was recognised by the American writer, F. A. Bentley, at the beginning of this century. His book, entitled *The Process of Government : A Study of Social Pressures* was first published in 1908 and this was almost entirely concerned with the political influence of pressure groups. It was not, however, until the period after the Second World War that these groups came to be studied extensively in Britain. More recently, they have attracted the attention of prominent politicians. Mr Anthony Wedgwood Benn, for example, suggested that these groups 'have now become an integral part of a new style of parliamentary democracy'.[1] It is now argued that we have in this country a system of representation which rests on two main bases. We have firstly, *political* representation organised territorially in that M.P.s are elected for the constituencies into which the country is at present divided. Secondly, the holders of this view suggest, there is additionally a form of *functional* representation which results from the vast variety of organised groups which are constantly pressing the Government in pursuit of their members' interests.

Historical development

A number of political and economic reforms have been greatly influenced by the activities of organised groups which were established to pursue specific aims. The Committee for the Abolition of the Slave Trade, the Anti-Corn Law League and the Suffragette movement provide well known examples of this type of activity. S. H. Beer has shown how, in the period covering roughly the last quarter of the nineteenth century up to the beginning of the First World War, a new pattern of politics emerged. He writes, 'the key element in it was the organised interest group based on an occupational stratum of what had become a highly industrialised economy'.[2] Thus, in the late nineteenth century railway politics were dominated by the activities of nationwide associations of manufacturers and traders, and the Employers Parliamentary Council was formed in 1918. Farming and landed interests also established representative groups, the Central Chamber of Agriculture being founded in 1865 and the National Farmer's Union in 1918. This pattern also applied to other occupational groups as in the case of the National Union of Teachers which from its beginnings in 1870 adopted pressure group tactics.

During the nineteenth century there developed a close identification between political parties and pressure groups with similar aims. The Liberal Party had links with the Temperance movement and at the same time the Conservative Party formed connections with brewing interests. The trade unions, through the Parliamentary Committee of the Trades Union Congress, sought parliamentary representation initially in association with the Liberal Party but later through the Labour Party, which was formed by bringing together trade unions and other socialist groups. A characteristic of this phase was the way in which connections were formed

[1] Reported in *The Guardian*, 6 November 1968.
[2] Beer, *Modern British Politics*, p. 109.

between the pressure groups and Members of Parliament. This took a variety of forms ranging from individual M.P.s who were willing to act as spokesmen for particular interests, to groups of M.P.s who were sponsored by groups outside Parliament. This kind of relationship still prevails and is in many cases very systematically organised.

Pressure groups and public opinion

The extent to which any particular group is likely to influence political decisions at a given time is dependent upon a number of factors. One of these factors, it is suggested, is the extent to which the objectives being pursued coincide favourably with the attitudes of the general public, or important sections of it. Richard Rose refers to this as the relationship between pressure group aims and 'cultural norms'. His argument implies that the receptivity of those making decisions is to a greater or lesser extent affected by the general attitudes, beliefs and expectations of the community. Changes in attitude normally take place over a period of time but, in exceptional circumstances, they may be quite sudden. Professor Rose suggests no less than six forms of this relationship.[1]

Firstly, there may be harmony between cultural norms and pressure group aims, e.g. the welfare of animals is generally accepted as a desirable aim in our society. This means that a group such as the R.S.P.C.A. does not have to embark upon campaigns to convince the public of the desirability of its objectives but it can, instead, concentrate upon bringing about legislative and administrative improvements which will facilitate its work. Secondly, there may be a gradual increase in the acceptance of norms associated with certain demands, such as the granting of independence to colonial territories or the abolition of hanging. Thirdly, groups may have to bargain in situations of fluctuating support for their demands; trade union or employers' groups, for example, may have to adjust their tactics accordingly. Fourthly, groups may have to pursue their aims in the face of general indifference; groups in this situation having perhaps the hardest task of all. Fifthly, they may have to carry on their activities in opposition to long term changes; a group such as the Lord's Day Observance Society, once strong enough to influence legislation, now has to fight a holding operation in an attempt to prevent further changes which are contrary to its aims. Finally, there may be outright conflict between values generally held and the goals of some pressure groups. Thus a group seeking to abolish the institution of private property would find it exceedingly difficult fully to realise its aims.

Pattern of activity

Various methods are employed by pressure groups in their efforts to influence the decisions of government. They range from informal consultations to public demonstrations. The general position has been

[1] R. Rose, *Politics in England* (Faber, 1965), pp. 130–2.

summarised by Richard Rose in the following terms: 'the elements of the political system provide a multiplicity of access points for pressure groups – government departments, political parties, Parliament and the peripheral public. But these access points are not all of equal significance, and at some points governmental resistance to pressure is great.'[1] The fact that in Britain power is concentrated in the hands of the central government means that pressure groups concentrate their activities on Ministers, M.P.s and senior civil servants in government departments. Efforts to persuade the public to support a particular point of view are merely an indirect method of seeking to influence the Government.

The close interconnection and interpenetration between the major political parties and some pressure groups has already been noted. Of the 287 Labour M.P.s elected in 1970 132 were sponsored by trade unions and many others who were not formally sponsored have close associations with individual unions in which they have been members or officials. Similarly a substantial proportion of Conservative M.P.s have active connections with industry, commerce and farming interests. The National Union of Teachers currently sponsors candidates from all three political parties and many other organisations have M.P.s among their officers, members and supporters. Some M.P.s voluntarily promote the aims and interests of the groups to which they are attached in Parliament. Others are retained by groups as advisers and consultants, who are paid for their services and similarly attempt to promote and safeguard the interests which they represent.

The House of Commons offers a number of opportunities for these activities. Question Time, Adjournment Debates, Private Members' Bills, major debates on Government Bills, can all in one way or another be used for this purpose. Some good examples of the connection between M.P.s and groups outside of Parliament are provided by a study of the use of the time allotted by Parliament for the consideration of Private Members' Bills. Thus the Protection of Animals Anaesthetics Bill, 1954, was promoted by the British Veterinary Association. On other occasions Bills not likely to be approved are promoted by M.P.s in order to gain publicity for particular issues they are seeking to promote. Some groups which have powerful financial support actually employ professional lobbyists known as Parliamentary Agents. Even small organisations which have substantial backing by M.P.s and peers can make considerable headway. Thus, the Parliamentary Group for World Government, which is virtually unknown to the general public, has some distinguished politicians from both the House of Commons and House of Lords amongst its senior office holders. This group has been successful in arranging debates in the House of Lords and for influencing the Government in issuing a circular on education, which, to some extent, reflects the views which it seeks to propagate.

[1] Rose, *Politics in England*, pp. 135–6.

There has now been established a strong tradition of consultation between government and groups representing major interests. The groups consulted in this way are those which can be said to represent fully a defined section of the community. Thus the British Medical Association, which can claim to represent the majority of doctors, is more likely to be consulted than the Socialist Medical Association, which represents only a proportion of them. The Government is not likely to consult groups which represent interests that are completely at variance with its own policy. Bodies such as the C.N.D. and various pacifist groups are compelled to direct their efforts towards the general public.

Sometimes legislation makes specific provision for consultation. Under the provisions of the Agriculture Act, 1947, the Minister is required to consult 'with such persons or bodies as appear to him to represent the interests of producers in the agricultural industry'. When Royal Commissions and Committees of Inquiry are set up, groups representing interests which are likely to be affected are formally consulted and requested to submit their views. Thus, all Local Government Associations were consulted by the Maud Commission on Local Government. Frequently alterations can be made to legislation when it goes through Parliament to accommodate views expressed when a Bill has been published. Amendments made in this way are likely to be matters of detail rather than substance, but occasionally substantial changes in policy are made, as was the case, for example, in the passage of the Race Relations Bill (see below).

There are many public bodies and advisory committees which, as a matter of common practice, receive the views of organised groups affected by their respective spheres of responsibility. These range from bodies such as the National Economic Development Council, with wide terms of reference, to the National Advisory Council for the Motor Manufacturing Industry, which has more specific objectives. In all of these the government receives technical advice from the groups which are represented. (See also chapter 13.)

Sometimes there is direct personal contact between the officials of groups and civil servants. Where the proposals on detailed matters made by group spokesmen are not contrary to Government policy and the intention of the relevant legislation, minor amendments may be made in regulations in order to meet their wishes. The legal and constitutional position is safeguarded in that the resulting delegated legislation is subject to parliamentary sanction.

In view of what has been said earlier about the relationship between the major parties and powerful pressure groups, it might be thought that this widespread pattern of consultation would be affected by a change in the party dominant in government following a general election. This is not the case. The Trades Union Congress faced this question when the Labour Government was defeated in 1951. The T.U.C., after careful considera-

tion, issued a statement which declared: 'Since the Conservative administrations of pre-war days the range of consultation between both sides of
industry has considerably increased, and the machinery of joint consultation has enormously improved. On our part we shall continue to examine
every question in the light of its industrial and economic implications.'
Similarly, the Federation of British Industries said: 'Whatever the
government in power, [the Federation] seeks to create conditions in which
each firm has the maximum opportunity to turn its own ideas and recources
to the best account in its own and the national interest.'[1]

In discussing the convention of consultation Professor B. Crick has
stated: 'It is now a long-established practice for civil servants to consult
at the very earliest stages of the new policy or legislation with all organized
interests who might be affected. This is done regularly and thoroughly.
In some respects, the political results are excellent. Governments are
seldom caught by surprise at unexpected opposition from industrial and
union leaders; and very often essentially political compromises can be
made before ever the Bill becomes public and is debated in Parliament
and in the Press.' Professor Crick, however, criticises the practice on the
grounds that the compromises reached in this way may be excessive and
that the spokesmen may not be representative of the membership. He
believes that Ministers have become unduly pessimistic about their own
room for manoeuvre and suggests the possibility that 'they could reach out
above the heads of the leaders of pressure groups to the members of the
groups, and also to those who are not represented in this way'.[2]

In some instances, pressure groups are even more directly involved in
administration. The Law Society, for example, administers the Legal Aid
scheme and the Marriage Guidance Council receives a subsidy to support
the work which it undertakes. This practice, however, does not prevent the
organisations from actively pursuing their objectives and from bringing
pressure to bear in much the same way as other established groups.

Some groups co-operate with each other; others are diametrically
opposed. As J. D. Stewart puts it: 'The group cannot ignore the attitude
of other groups. Other groups are making decisions on matters that
concern it. Some may be hostile to it, others may be friendly to it. The
group must adapt its tactics to these circumstances.'[3] Thus, the Lord's
Day Observance Society is opposed by the Sunday Freedom Association;
the Popular T.V. Council, which sought the introduction of commercial
television, was in direct conflict with the National T.V. Council which
opposed it; currently the group which is advocating the establishment of
commercial radio is challenged by another which prefers the extension of
B.B.C. local radio stations. There are allied as well as opposing groups. The

[1] The Federation of British Industries joined with the British Employers Federation and the
National Association of British Manufacturers to become the Confederation of British
Industries.
[2] 'Put politics back into Parliament', *The Observer*, 23 October 1966.
[3] J. D. Stewart, *British Pressure Groups* (Oxford University Press, 1958), p. 43.

Politics Association, an organisation of teachers of politics, works closely with the Hansard Society, which seeks to strengthen and extend the institution of parliamentary government, and uses its London offices; the variety of groups opposing blood sports work together on some issues but not on others. One of the most interesting examples of co-operation in recent years is the arrangement arrived at in the autumn of 1970, under which the Child Poverty Action Group and fifteen trade unions agreed to work together to help the poor and to press the claims of lower income groups.

Efforts on the part of organised groups to influence public opinion are conducted in a variety of ways. In the contemporary situation we have at one extreme, large well-organised demonstrations, such as those undertaken by nurses and teachers in the pay disputes and by anti-racialist groups against the South African Rugby team's tour; at the other there is the method whereby groups arrange for a large number of individuals to write to M.P.s and other influential people on a specific matter in the hope of gaining their support. Bodies such as the Aims of Industry and the Economic League conduct long term campaigns to persuade the general public of the desirability of free enterprise. They produce literature and films, provide speakers which are made available to all kinds of groups. Sometimes much shorter campaigns are mounted, a good example of this type of operation being provided by the Road Haulage Association's attempt to prevent the nationalisation of the road haulage industry during 1945–7. Hundreds of telegrams were signed and in all, the campaign cost about £100 000. The campaign, however, failed to affect the Government as the legislation went through without any concessions being made. Long term anti-nationalisation campaigns have been conducted by both steel firms and sugar firms.[1] An excellent recent example of successful activity by a pressure group formed for a particular purpose was the Cublington residents' campaign to defeat the Roskill Commission's recommendations to site the third London airport in the area.

It has been suggested that discreet negotiations are more likely to be successful than public campaigns and mass protests, and until recently this was probably true. The practice of holding public demonstrations and 'taking a tough line' appears to have become much more widespread and in some cases at least appears to have produced the desired result. The method has recently been used by farmers, nurses, council workers and electricity workers as well as students. It is difficult to lay down any hard and fast rules and it seems likely that the outcome of a public campaign depends on a number of factors such as the nature of the group concerned, the extent to which it is representative of the opinion of its membership, the attitude of the general public and the way in which the issue under consideration relates to government policy.

[1] For some interesting detailed examples see: R. Rose, *Influencing Voters* (Faber, 1967); and S. E. Finer, *Anonymous Empire* (Pall Mall, 1966).

58

The Government is subjected to continual pressure from a variety of sources, each group using the means most readily available to it and joining with other individuals and groups which have the same or similar objective in view. Sometimes the effect is swift and dramatic as when the leaders of the Campaign Against Racial Discrimination working with a group of M.P.s, manoeuvred to effect major alterations in the Race Relations Bill when it was before Parliament in 1965.[1] On other occasions the build-up towards the cumulative effect of pressure is relatively slow as in the case of draft legislation considered by the County Councils Associations in 1970, which was designed to give powers to local authorities to control the organisation of large open-air gatherings such as the 'pop' festivals held in the Isle of Wight in the two previous summers.

Pressure groups and government

It is difficult to come to a firm conclusion about the contribution of pressure groups in the successful working of political democracy in Britain. Professor W. J. M. Mackenzie writes: 'The structure of British Government includes besides the hierarchical world of public servants and the parliamentary world of party politics, a very complex world of organised groups: and public decisions are the result of interplay between these three worlds. Does the public get left out in this process? Perhaps, but then no public or publics exist politically except in so far as they express themselves through this process: access to it is open to all and the entry fee can be paid in brains and energy as well as in cash.' He recognises, however, that this statement may appear to be complacent and states his personal view in the following terms: 'We are gradually shifting back into a situation in which a man is socially important only as a holder of standard qualifications and as a member of authorised groups.' This situation he characterises as the 'new medievalism'.[2]

The validity of the representations which are made by a number of groups have been brought into question on two main scores. Firstly, it seems certain that the views submitted by the leaders of some organisations do not represent the views of the mass membership. If this criticism has any validity, it applies to bodies as diverse in character as the Transport and General Workers Union, the National Farmers Union and the Royal Automobile Club. Secondly, there is the problem of finding satisfactory ways of adequately representing consumers in all manner of undertakings. Governments frequently consult producers and planners, but there is little machinery for obtaining the views of consumers of goods and resources. This problem has become all the more serious following the Government's decision, made in 1970, to wind up the Consumer Council.

[1] See K. Hindell, 'The Genesis of the Race Relations Bill' in R. Rose (ed.), *Policy Making in Britain* (Macmillan, 1969).
[2] 'Pressure Groups in British Government' in R. Rose (ed.), *Studies in British Politics* (Macmillan, 1967), p. 218.

Other writers have expressed fears and reservations about the nature of pressure groups and their effect on the political system. Some take the view that the present practice has resulted in an abdication of responsibility on the part of the Government. Paul Johnson for example, suggests that: 'Acts of policy are now decided by the interplay of thousands of conflicting interest groups, and cabinet ministers are little more than chairmen of arbitration committees.'[1] It can be argued, however, that the Government is far from being the mere clearing house of pressure group demands. The Government has the power to say 'no' and has on occasions come out strongly against giving concessions to sectional interests. The power of the electorate is real and the Government must eventually submit itself to its judgement. Pressure groups submitting demands frequently press their claims as being in the 'national interest', the same argument being used by farmers, teachers, industrial leaders and others. By the same token their claims can sometimes be rejected!

R. T. McKenzie, although recognising that many interests are un-organised and that some groups are much more effectively represented than others, concludes that pressure groups are an inevitable concomitant of the party system. They provide, he suggests, 'an invaluable set of multiple channels through which the mass of the citizenry can influence the decision-making process at the highest levels'.[2]

[1] P. Johnson, 'The Amiable Monster', New Statesman, 12 October 1967.
[2] R. T. McKenzie, 'Parties, Pressure Groups and the British Political Process' in R. Rose (ed.), Studies in British Politics, p. 262.

Part 2 Society and the Political System

6 The Social Structure

If we are to comprehend the politics of a country, we cannot confine our studies exclusively and narrowly to the formal institutions of government, for governments do not exist independently of the men who work them and the society around them.

Richard Rose *Studies in British Politics*

Introduction

The nature of a political system can only be properly understood by reference to the wider social system of which it forms part and with which it is inextricably interwoven. The relationship between the two is complex but reciprocal; each influences and is influenced by the other; the political system is in part both the product and the perpetrator of the social system; changes in the social system inevitably have their impact upon the political system. All or most of the forces which impinge upon society, whether historical, geographical, social, economic, demographic or cultural, impinge upon and influence the political system; the political system in turn affects the character and composition of the social system.

The characteristics of the British political system which strike most informed and experienced foreign observers are its continuity, stability and homogeneity. These three aspects are clearly closely inter-related, each reacting positively upon the other. Consensus of outlook and attitude is conducive to stability, and stability makes for continuity. Britain is politically homogeneous in the sense that there is a widespread acceptance of existing institutions and a willingness to work within the norms of behaviour which have existed over a long period of time. Although there are significant differences between various groups in other respects including those based on region, social class, style of life, political beliefs and attitudes, and other attributes, this does not significantly alter the basic consensus on the political way of life.

In this chapter we will examine some aspects of the social structure and consider the way in which they have contributed to or detracted from the tendency towards continuity, stability and homogeneity.

Historical development of the United Kingdom

Britain has a long and relatively untroubled history of independent nationhood. Its political institutions have developed slowly over a long period of time through a process of cautious adaptation rather than radical or violent change. The peoples of England, Wales, Scotland and Northern Ireland make up the United Kingdom and are joined together in a unitary pattern of government.

Wales was conquered by the English and has for all practical purposes been governed as part of England since the Act of Union, 1535. Scotland was never finally vanquished by the English and it remained as an independent Kingdom until the Act of Union, 1707; it has retained and developed certain institutions and patterns of life significantly different to those in the rest of the United Kingdom. In 1922 Ireland was divided into the Irish Free State, which became fully independent, and Northern Ireland, which comprised the six counties remaining under the jurisdiction of the British Government.

Wales has a tradition and culture different from that of England. The Welsh language is spoken by about a quarter of the population, although all but a few speak English as well. The Welsh Language Act, 1967, affirmed the equal validity of the Welsh language with English in the administration of justice and the conduct of government and business throughout Wales. Scotland has retained its own legal system based on Roman Law, its own local government and educational systems and its established Church is the Scottish Presbyterian Church. Only about 80 000 people, mainly in the northern counties, speak the Scottish form of Gaelic. For both countries provision is made for an appreciable degree of administrative devolution, which does, however, fall a long way short of the complete domestic self-government demanded by some nationalist groups. Northern Ireland does have its own government for domestic affairs but the province is much less politically stable than the rest of the United Kingdom.[1] Life in Northern Ireland is characterised by rifts between Catholic and Protestant populations and between Republicans and Loyalists, which have persisted over a long period of time and which are liable to erupt in outbreaks of public disorder. In the United Kingdom as a whole, the overriding authority of the Westminster Parliament is virtually unchallenged and only a few clamour for national or regional secession.

Active participation in politics is very much a minority activity and criticism of the Government by the mass of the electorate, as opposed to the relatively small proportion of political activists, turns largely on matters which affect the material standards of individuals and groups rather than on deep-seated ideological divisions. In spite of the diversity of cultural background, socio-economic status, attitude and aspirations, there is a high measure of acceptance of the framework of government based on parliamentary institutions and representative democracy.

A non-isolationist island

The fact that Britain is an island has had important consequences –

[1] Northern Ireland Parliament suspended in March 1972. See footnote page 202.

historical, economic and social. The surrounding sea has not only made invasion more difficult but speeded up and strengthened the development of a common language and national identity.

The mainland of Europe in terms of time and distance is very close but until relatively recent times Britain has been reluctant to commit itself firmly to a close involvement with the Continent and even today there is considerable disagreement about the wisdom, both economically and politically, of 'going into Europe' by joining the Common Market. Britain's island position has, however, not resulted in a markedly isolationist outlook. By the nature of its size and geographical position Britain has had to depend on international trade and, as a consequence of colonial expansion, it has developed close ties with a world-wide Commonwealth of Nations whose opinions and interests cannot lightly be offended or ignored. Britain also maintains a close liaison with the United States which, as well as having a bond of a common language and linked historical development, has common interests in the North Atlantic Treaty Organization and other spheres of commitment.

Britain is no longer a world power in economic and military terms but it still has considerable influence in the comity of nations. Its Parliament has provided a model for numerous legislatures overseas and the English language is the main means of communication in some parts of all continents.

The basis of Britain's foreign and economic policy alike is affected by its island position. The balance of payments, the need to import food and raw materials, the corresponding necessity to produce for export, all have their consequences for internal industrial organisation; decisions on external commitments have to be made, at least in part, against a background of historical interests and responsibilities and the demands for national economic and social development.

Demographic background

Britain is densely populated and heavily urbanised; the expectation of life is higher than at any time in the past and as the aggregate size of the population goes on increasing its age-composition is significantly changing.

The estimated total population of Britain in 1968 was nearly 55.3 millions compared with 52.7 millions in 1961, 38.2 millions in 1901 and 6.5 millions in 1700. The continued growth in total numbers results mainly from a gradual reduction in death rates and the persistence of high birth rates for substantial periods in this century. Britain's density of population, with 587 persons to the square mile, is one of the highest in the world. This overall figure is deceptive because it conceals significant local and regional variations; thus the density for England and Wales is 833 and Greater London has 12 600 persons per square mile. On the basis of present population trends, taking into account birth rates, death rates and the balance of migration, the total population is expected to reach 59 259 000 in 1980, 63 165 000 in 1990 and 68 190 000 in the year 2000.

TABLE 3   *Population of Great Britain, 1901–68*

		1901	1931	1961	1968
England	Persons	30 514 967	37 359 045	43 460 525	45 873 000
(excluding Monmouthshire)	Males	14 717 155	17 839 205	21 012 069	22 305 000
	Females	15 797 812	19 519 840	22 448 456	23 568 000
Wales and Monmouthshire	Persons	2 012 876	2 593 332	2 644 023	2 720 000
	Males	1 011 458	1 293 805	1 291 764	1 325 000
	Females	1 001 418	1 299 527	1 352 259	1 395 000
Scotland	Persons	4 472 103	4 842 980	5 179 344	5 188 000
	Males	2 173 755	2 325 523	2 482 734	2 490 000
	Females	2 298 348	2 517 457	2 696 610	2 698 000
Great Britain	Persons	36 999 946	44 795 357	51 283 892	53 781 000
	Males	17 902 368	21 458 533	24 786 567	26 120 000
	Females	19 097 578	23 336 824	26 497 325	27 661 000
Northern Ireland	Persons	1 236 952	1 243 000	1 425 042	1 502 000
	Males	589 955	601 000	694 224	733 000
	Females	646 997	642 000	730 818	769 000
Totals (Great Britain and	Persons	38 236 898	46 038 357	52 708 934	55 283 000
Northern Ireland)	Males	18 492 323	22 059 533	25 480 791	26 853 000
	Females	19 744 575	23 978 824	27 228 143	27 430 000

Source: Census Reports and Estimates by Population Authorities.

(Changes in the population of Great Britain between 1901 and 1968 are given in table 3.)

The death rate has remained almost stationary since 1920 at about 12 per thousand and the expectation of life has increased to nearly 69 years for males born between 1965 and 1967 and to 75 for females born during the same period. This compares with an expectation of 48 for males and 52 for females born 1900–10. Comparing the nineteenth century with the twentieth century, the steady fall in the birth rate in this century ceased in 1933 and during the Second World War it rose again and reached a peak of 20.7 per thousand of population in 1947. There was a further reduction as against the pre-war level in the early 1950s but it rose again from 1953, reaching a peak of 18.7 in 1964. The present level is about 17 per thousand. This has resulted in the presence of a high proportion of young people and old people in the present population compared with those in the 15–64 age groups which are normally regarded as the working population. While the pattern of the working population is not as straightforward as this the changing age composition of the population is a fact of considerable economic and social importance. (See table 4.)

The distribution of the population is extremely uneven, with a particularly heavy concentration in southern England. Since 1920, nearly 40 per cent of the total population has concentrated in the seven conurbations of Greater London, South-East Lancashire, the West Midlands, Central Clydeside, West Yorkshire, Merseyside and Tyneside. Associated

TABLE 4 *Age groups as percentage of total population of England 1901–61 and projections to 1981 and 2001*

Age group of population	Census populations			Registrar-General's Projections	
	1901	1931	1961	1981	2001
Persons 0–14	32.32	23.64	22.93	25.39	26.79
Males 15–64 and females 15–60	61.53	66.68	62.20	58.42	59.77
Males 65+ and females 60+	6.15	9.68	14.87	16.19	13.44
All ages	100.00	100.00	100.00	100.00	100.00

Source: General Register Office. (Census reports and projections; Welsh Office.)

with this development is the increasing tendency for people to live in the suburbs rather than in the centre of the city, and where necessary to travel in to work. (See table 5.) Whole areas from the centres of major cities have been rehoused on the outskirts many miles from their previous homes, causing massive upheavals in established social patterns. Where residential property remains standing near the city centres there is, with the notable exception of London, a marked tendency for it to be occupied by the poorest sections of the community and immigrant groups.

In the period from 1950 to 1962 there was a relatively high rate of immigration from Commonwealth countries, particularly the West Indies, India and Pakistan. In the three years 1960–2 the total net immigration amounted to some 38 000 persons, about 75 per cent of whom were from the Commonwealth. This rate of inflow was arrested by the Commonwealth Immigrants Act, 1962, and further restrictions were introduced in 1968. The coloured immigrants are concentrated in the larger cities, notably

TABLE 5 *Increases in Commuting 1921–66 by Standard Regions in England*

Standard region	Percentage of population working outside own area of residence at 1921 census	Percentage of population working outside own area of residence at 1966 census
Northern	24.0	37.5
Yorkshire and Humberside	16.4	28.3
North-Western	21.7	40.3
East Midlands	18.3	35.1
West Midlands	19.5	28.9
East Anglia	11.6	29.0
South-East (excluding Greater London)	28.0	40.2
South-West	11.9	29.3
England (excluding Greater London)	20.7	34.9

Source: 1921 and 1966 censuses.

London, Birmingham, Liverpool, Manchester, Bristol, Leeds, Coventry, Sheffield, Bradford and Nottingham. Other towns which have sizeable immigrant populations include Bedford, Dudley, High Wycombe, Newcastle upon Tyne, Slough, Smethwick and West Bromwich.

Each facet of the demographic background of society has political effects and implications. The consequences arising from the fact of coloured immigration on a scale to which the indigenous population is unaccustomed are perhaps the most obvious. There were ugly racially based disturbances in several parts of the country before the end of the 1950s of which the Notting Hill riots in 1958 are among the best known. Experienced observers in the general election of 1964 spoke of racist overtones in a number of constituencies, and in the Smethwick constituency, Patrick Gordon Walker, ex-Cabinet Minister and 'Shadow' Foreign Secretary, lost to a Conservative who was alleged to be something less than liberal in relation to immigration questions. In the 1970 election Mr Enoch Powell, who urged the massive but voluntary repatriation of immigrants, was returned for Wolverhampton with a large majority. We have also seen the unusual spectacle in recent years of a substantial number of London dockers marching behind racist banners.

In February 1971, the Government introduced a Bill designed to regulate further the procedure for immigration. The Bill differentiates between Commonwealth citizens with British ancestors, who are referred to as *patrials*, and for those without, who are called non-patrials. It makes provision for putting non-British immigrants on a common basis; creates a new offence of assisting illegal entry, with up to seven years' imprisonment for offenders; widens the Government's power to assist repatriation; extends the time-limit for the prosecution of illegal immigrants; abolishes appeals against political deportation; and extends the repatriation regulations which apply to immigrants; new immigrants are to be admitted only on a temporary basis and will be required to report to the authorities at regular intervals. It remains to be seen whether this Bill will pass into law in its present form. What does seem certain is that the whole field of coloured immigration is one which continues to exercise the minds of statesmen, politicians and pressure groups and which for the foreseeable future is likely to carry in its wake important social and political consequences.

Occupations

Britain is a predominantly industrial country. Of a total working population of approximately 25 million only about 2 per cent are engaged in agriculture, forestry and fishing. (See table 6.) About 40 per cent of all employees are employed in mining and manufacturing and over 55 per cent of those involved in manufacturing are in the metal, engineering, vehicles and chemical industries. The numbers employed in agriculture, forestry and fishing have decreased steadily over the last few years. In

66

TABLE 6   *Principal Civil Occupations in Great Britain**

Industry or service	Number in thousands		
	Males	Females	Total
Agriculture, forestry, fisheries	336	77	413
Mining and quarrying	465	21	486
Manufacturing industries:			
Chemicals, and allied industries	361	136	497
Metals, engineering and vehicles	3 421	996	4 417
Textiles	343	347	690
Clothing and footwear	127	365	492
Food, drink and tobacco	462	345	807
Other manufacturers	1 200	510	1 710
Total : manufacturing industries	5 914	2 700	8 613
Construction	1 417	89	1 506
Gas, electricity, water	353	57	413
Transport and communications	1 315	269	1 584
Distributive trades	1 236	1 538	2 774
Professional, financial and miscellaneous services	2 145	3 310	5 455
National government service	373	211	584
Local government service	595	224	818
Total employees	14 151	8 494	24 645
Employers and self-employed persons			
(all industries and services)	1 320	361	1 681
Total in civil employment	15 471	8 855	25 326

* Figures are for 1968.
Source: Department of Employment and Productivity.

1954 the total was 1 013 000; by 1961 this had dropped to 890 000; by 1968 it had decreased dramatically to 413 000.

The numbers in the armed forces have also fallen steadily in the last decade. In 1959, some 569 000 were so engaged, but by 1968 this figure had dropped to 400 000.

There is always a proportion of the total adult population which is unemployed. Comparing the post-war with the pre-war period this proportion is relatively small, although for those concerned it is, of course, an extremely serious matter. The numbers of those registered as totally unemployed has, however, increased over the last few years. Thus, in 1969 the total was 533 816; in 1970 it was 578 751. By February 1971, the number had risen to 721 143; these, apart from the bad winters of 1947 and 1963, were the highest figures for thirty-one years. By August 1971 the number of unemployed had reached a total of 904 000. There are marked regional variations in the incidence of employment with northern England, Wales and Scotland usually having the highest percentage.

It can be seen that the occupational pattern of Great Britain is characterised by relatively full employment with the vast majority in the working age groups being employed in industrial concerns. Women form over half of the total working population.

The age of affluence

Comparing the period since 1945 with that of the inter-war years there is considerable accuracy in describing Britain as an affluent society. There has been a significant increase in real incomes, especially for manual workers, the basic working week is shorter, nearly half of the 18 million dwellings existing in 1968 were owner-occupied, the possession of cars and televisions is spread widely throughout the population, more and more people take holidays abroad, vast sums are spent on home improvement, the standard of nutrition is relatively high and there is a greater degree of geographical and social mobility than ever before. It must be remembered, however, that there is still a small but significant proportion of society which exists in poverty.

The notion that rising material standards necessarily induces inclination towards Conservatism, is a dubious one and this is discussed further in chapter 8, but geographical and social mobility, which frequently involves drastic changes from a previous pattern of life, may in some cases affect political loyalties and attitudes.

The extension of home ownership, together with a concentration on home improvement and the facilities for family outings which arise from the possession of a car, may have considerable political consequences, especially if one takes into account the overall changes likely to occur over a period of time. Mr Mark Abrams, for instance, speaks of a 'Home-Centred Society' which may have the result of decreasing the sense of political solidarity which was formerly experienced by substantial sections of the population in less affluent circumstances.[1] As we shall see, the locality in which the individual lives and the kind of place in which he works seem to influence voting behaviour.

Social class

There is substantial evidence that social class is the most important single factor which can be positively related to political attitudes and behaviour. Additionally, a number of studies have shown that the way in which an individual subjectively perceives his status is even more relevant than his position objectively determined by an outside investigator.

Britain no longer has absolutely clear-cut class divisions such as existed between the medieval nobles and peasants or the Marxian bourgeois and proletariat. Although, nowadays, class divisions are not so sharply defined they nevertheless exist and most individuals are consciously or sub-consciously aware of belonging to one group and being excluded from another.

In societies such as Britain, where the edges of class divisions have

[1] M. Abrams, 'The Home-Centred Society', *The Listener*, 26 November 1959.

become increasingly blurred and in which there is much more movement between different social groups than was previously the case, the concept of class is complex, and precise definition is difficult. The factors most closely associated with class are occupation, education and income which in the vast majority of cases are inseparably linked. Other criteria which have been applied in this type of analysis include speech, clothing, possessions, manners, customs, physical movement and, more generally, style of life. The description of a person or group as upper-class, middle-class or working-class may be rather vague but to most people it is nevertheless meaningful, whether they are referring to themselves or to others. T. H. Marshall states: 'The essence of social class is the way a man is treated by his fellows (and, reciprocally, he treats them), not the qualities or the possessions which cause the treatment.' Social class, he says, 'unites into groups people who differ from one another by overriding the differences between them'.[1]

Since the early part of this century the Registrar-General, in presenting census data, has included a special category described as social class. Under this classification individuals are assigned to one of five social class groups, the main occupation of the 'head of the household' being used as the basic criteria. Class I consists of high status professional and business occupations; class II includes a variety of non-manual occupations, e.g. teaching; class III is made up of a large number of individuals in various skilled manual occupations and clerical and routine non-manual workers. Class IV caters for semi-skilled workers and class V for unskilled. The overall picture which emerges from this type of classification in the 1961 census is presented in table 7.

TABLE 7   *Population of Great Britain classified by Social Class (Census 1961)*

Social class	Occupation of head of household	Percentage of total population (approx.)
I	Higher professional and managerial	4
II	Intermediate non-manual	15
III	Skilled manual and routine non-manual	51
IV	Semi-skilled	21
V	Unskilled	9
	Total	100.0

This type of classification has been criticised on a number of grounds and especially because the wide variety of jobs included in class III accounts for about half of the population. Nevertheless, it has been widely used by investigators and some of the surveys reported elsewhere in the present volume are couched in these terms. For making general comparisons between the economically 'better-off' and 'worse-off' sections of the com-

[1] T. H. Marshall, *Citizenship and Social Class* (Cambridge University Press, 1950), pp. 92 and 104.

munity the device of grouping together social classes I, II and III and matching them against social classes IV and V is sometimes used. (See e.g. chapter 17.) An alternative type of classification used by the Registrar-General provides a much more detailed breakdown into occupational categories. This is based on sixteen separate socio-economic groups and table 8 gives details of the population of England and Wales analysed by this means in the 1961 census.

TABLE 8   *Population of England and Wales classified by Socio-Economic Groups (Census 1961)*

Socio-economic group	Occupation of head of household	Percentage of population
1	Employers and managers – large establishments	3.6
2	Employers and managers – small establishments	5.9
3	Professional workers – self-employed	0.8
4	Professional workers – employees	2.8
5	Intermediate non-manual workers	3.8
6	Junior non-manual workers	12.5
7	Personal service	0.9
8	Foremen and supervisors – manual	3.3
9	Skilled manual workers	30.4
10	Semi-skilled manual workers	14.7
11	Unskilled manual workers	8.6
12	Own account workers – non-professional	3.6
13	Farmers – employers and managers	1.0
14	Farmers – own account	1.0
15	Agricultural workers	2.3
16	Members of armed forces	1.9
17	Unclassified	2.9
		Total 100.0

The various categories listed above can be grouped together for purposes of analysis and research. Thus, if groups 1, 2, 3, 4, 13 and 14 are joined they provide the category of employers, managerial and professional workers which constitutes some 15 per cent of the population; this can for some purposes be usefully measured against groups 10 and 11 which brings together semi-skilled and unskilled workers who, at the time of the 1961 census, made up about 23 per cent of the population.

Early in the 1950s a socio-economic scale was evolved by C. A. Moser and J. R. Hall in connection with a study of social mobility undertaken by D. V. Glass and his associates, which has been much used in social research.[1] This ranked thirty occupations on the basis of their social prestige and there was a high measure of acceptance of this ranking, especially at the two extremes, by those interviewed in the investigation. This resulted in a seven-fold socio-economic scale which is outlined in table 9. Examples of the occupations included in the respective categories are included to

[1] See J. R. Hall and C. A. Moser, 'The Social Grading of Occupations' in D. V. Glass (ed.), *Social Mobility in Britain* (Routledge and Kegan Paul, 1953).

TABLE 9 *The Hall-Jones Scale of Socio-Economic Categories*

Group	Description and examples of occupations included	Percentage of males 1949
1	Professional and high administrative (colliery manager, chartered accountant)	2.9
2	Managerial and executive (works manager, civil servant – executive branch, headmaster of secondary school)	4.5
3	Inspectorial, supervisory and other non-manual, higher grade (teacher, police inspector)	9.8
4	Inspectorial, supervisory and other non-manual, lower grade (costing clerk, insurance agent)	12.7
5	Skilled manual and routine grades of non-manual (boilermaker, bricklayer, routine clerk, storekeeper)	41.2
6	Semi-skilled manual (boot machinist, boilerman)	16.5
7	Unskilled manual (bath attendant, porter)	12.4
		Total 100.0

give an indication of the general nature of their composition. It will readily be appreciated that the existence of these groupings and others which have been devised can make comparison between different sets of data very difficult. Thus the only exact correspondence between the Registrar-General's five social classes and the sixteen socio-economic groups is between class I and group 3. The Registrar-General's classes IV and V can, however, be readily compared with groups 6 and 7 on the Hall–Jones scale.

The consideration of class categories is further complicated by the fact that their own social status is differently perceived by different individuals and there is a marked reluctance on the part of a significant number of people to see themselves as being part of the class category which is, on an objective basis, associated with their occupational grouping. Thus, a bank clerk may see the middle-class as being made up of people who have had a secondary education, speak reasonably good English, go to work in a formal suit and draw a monthly salary cheque; a foreman electrician may see it as a group consisting of 'steady' workers in regular employment who are buying their home on a mortgage and who earn above a given amount per annum. A lecturer with high academic qualifications who has a working-class background may still prefer to have tea when most of his colleagues have coffee and may feel that he would be in danger of being thought a snob if he overtly referred to himself as middle-class. The type of hypo-thetical example just given does occur in practice but the tendency for many individuals is to place themselves in a class higher than that to which

71

they would be allocated by objective criteria. The investigation conducted by D. V. Glass and his associates referred to above showed that about a quarter of those in groups 5, 6 and 7 on the Hall–Jones scale placed themselves in the middle-class. The same survey revealed that women are more prone than men to 'upgrade' themselves in this way while a significant number of men who are the sons of manual workers see themselves as working-class regardless of occupation and qualifications.

The connection between class categories, whether objectively or subjectively determined, and political attitudes is an important one especially in relation to voting behaviour. The nature of this relationship is discussed further in chapter 8.

Education

There is a marked correlation between objectively measured social class and educational achievement. As shown in chapter 7, the products of the public schools occupy a percentage of the elective and non-elective positions in the upper echelons of government which is altogether out of proportion with their overall numbers in society. These individuals have been socialised into expectations of a high level of social success and political participation. The children of semi-skilled and unskilled workers, on the other hand, the majority of whom spend their schooldays in secondary modern schools or the lower streams of comprehensive schools, tend generally to become socialised into expectations of low social achievement and minimal political participation. Richard Rose goes so far as to suggest that: 'The English educational system implicitly emphasises cultural norms concerning inequality.'[1]

A number of studies have indicated that the school system exercises a selective function which has a close connection with social class criteria. Jean Floud's study of Middlesbrough and South-West Hertfordshire, for example, showed that sons of professional workers had six or seven times the chance of unskilled workers' sons of entering grammar schools in these areas.[2] The *Report on Early Leaving* revealed that whereas 46.8 per cent of boys and 41.1 per cent of girls from professional and managerial backgrounds entered sixth forms of secondary schools, the corresponding figures of children from the homes of unskilled workers was 7.2 per cent and 6.1 per cent.[3] Professor William Taylor has presented a helpful analysis showing the position in higher and further education.[4] This shows that only 7 per cent of all university undergraduates in universities in the academic year 1961–2 were offspring of parents employed in semi-skilled and unskilled occupations. (See table 10.) An inquiry conducted by the present writer and his colleague indicates that this trend applies even in

[1] Rose, *Politics in England*, p. 64.
[2] J. Floud, *Social Class and Educational Opportunity* (Heinemann, 1956).
[3] Ministry of Education, *Report on Early Leaving* (H.M.S.O., 1956).
[4] W. Taylor, *Society and the Education of Teachers* (Faber, 1969).

TABLE 10   *Occupations of Students' Parents, 1961–2*

	Non-manual			Manual				
	Higher profes-sional	Other profes-sional and mana-gerial	Clerical	Skilled	Semi-skilled	Un-skilled	Not known	All
University undergraduates								
Men	17	40	12	19	6	I	5	100
Women	20	43	II	16	6	I	5	100
Postgraduates	10	37	14	25	7	2	6	100
Training college students								
Men	5	27	16	32	13	2	5	100
Women	8	36	14	27	7	2	5	100
Full-time further education students	12	32	14	28	8	2	4	100
Part-time further education	6	20	16	39	12	4	3	100

Source: Derived from *Students and Their Education* (Report of the Committee on Higher Education, Appendix Two (B), 1964). Tables, 5, 65, 81, 102, 135, as presented by W. Taylor in *Society and the Education of Teachers* (Faber, 1969), p. 186.

attendance at non-vocational classes. In the evening institute investigated, professional groups formed a high percentage of the students attending classes against less than 3 per cent of students in unskilled jobs.[1]

There is further evidence that the explanation for this is not simply that children of parents in managerial and professional groups have a monopoly of inborn scholastic potential, although they clearly derive considerable benefit from being brought up in a social climate which is conducive to academic and social success. Surveys suggest that, for one reason or another, there is in fact a considerable wastage of talent. The *Crowther Report* showed that 44 per cent of the highest ability groups among 5940 National Service recruits had left school by the age of 15.[2]

Religion

Historically religion has made a considerable impact upon political affairs in Britain from the time of the early Whigs and Tories respectively opposing and supporting the Established Church, to various inter-denominational wrangles especially on educational issues which were hotly debated at the start of the century. The settlement of the Irish question in

[1] T. Brennan and D. McDowell, 'Non-Vocational classes: is there a social barrier?', *Adult Education*, vol. 4, no. 5, 1969.
[2] Ministry of Education, *15–18 Report of the Central Advisory Council for Education-England* (H.M.S.O., 1959), p. 9.

1922, however, marked the end of the deep-seated religious controversy and since that time religious allegiance has played only a minor role in British politics and where it does have an effect this tends to be regional or local. In England and Scotland, the constituencies where the impact of religious adherence is most marked are Liverpool and Glasgow, both of which have a relatively high percentage of Roman Catholics in their populations; there are also a number of constituencies in Wales, and possibly elsewhere, where Nonconformist candidates have a better chance of success than others.

The major denominations are nowadays less prone than was once the case to take stands on political issues, at least in the case of most internal affairs. T. Brennan and his colleagues have shown that in south-west Wales the leaders of the chapels have concerned themselves with matters such as Sunday Observance, temperance, pacifism, gambling and the preservation of Welsh culture, to the exclusion of more politically contentious issues. These authors conclude that 'the social integration attributable to religion has markedly declined during the last two generations. The long term decline in religion is associated, here as elsewhere, with the growth of secular education and the interpretation of life in materialistic, rather than spiritual terms.'[1]

TABLE II   *Strength of Main Denominations in Great Britain, 1947–57*

Denomination	Members (%)	Members attending weekly (%)	Claiming affiliation (%)
Church of England	6.5	4.9	53.0
Roman Catholic	7.3	3.75	10.0
Nonconformist	3.0 }	4.5	15.0
Church of Scotland	3.1 }		7.5
Small Protestant Sects	0.8 }	1.75	4.0
Jews	0.8 }		1.0
	21.6	14.9	90.5

Source: M. Argyle: *Religious Behaviour* (Routledge and Kegan Paul, 1958), p. 37.

The precise numerical strength of the various denominations at the present time is not easy to ascertain and various sets of figures published are at variance with one another. Table 11, compiled by Michael Argyle will help to indicate the general nature of the situation. It will be clear from this that there is a vast discrepancy between claimed affiliation to a given religious group and the actual degree of religious involvement.

Nevertheless, socially and politically, the churches probably still have an appreciable influence, especially where moral questions are concerned: many religious pressure groups are well-organised and active and the

[1] T. Brennan *et al.* (This author is not the present writer.) *Social Change in South-West Wales* (Watts, 1954), p. 137.

74

Government and individual M.P.s appear to be susceptible to pressure from these sources.

The mass media

The term 'mass media' includes radio, television and the press. These media, and especially newspapers and television, are examined in some detail because of the important role they play in publicising political events. Adults in Britain today purchase more newspapers per head than any other country in the world, and at least one newspaper is read by nine out of every ten persons. Practically all households possess a radio and something like 90 per cent now have television sets.

TABLE 12   *Circulation of National Daily and Sunday Newspapers*

Paper	Daily circulation	(Millions)
Dailies		
The Times	437 278	0.4
Daily Telegraph	1 380 367	1.4
The Guardian	292 602	0.3
Daily Express	3 731 673	3.7
Daily Mail	1 992 591	2.0
Sun	951 132	0.9
Morning Star	52 097	0.05
Daily Mirror	4 924 157	4.9
Daily Sketch★	871 041	0.9
Sundays		
Observer	879 024	0.9
Sunday Times	1 454 079	1.4
Sunday Telegraph	753 441	0.7
News of the World	6 227 684	6.2
People	5 455 372	5.4
Sunday Express	4 235 326	4.2
Sunday Mirror	5 008 731	5.0

★ *Daily Sketch* has now ceased publication.
Source: *The Newspaper Press Directory*, 1969.

NEWSPAPERS

The distinctive features of the press in Britain are the dominant position of national daily and Sunday newspapers and the fact that ownership is concentrated mainly in the hands of a comparatively small number of large press groups. Table 12 gives details of the circulation of the main daily and Sunday newspapers. The *News of the World* has the largest circulation of any newspaper in the world. The total circulation of provincial and evening papers is estimated at about eight million. Of the morning papers the *Journal* (Newcastle), the *Yorkshire Post* (Leeds), the *Northern Echo* (Darlington) and the *Western Mail* (Cardiff) have circulations of over 100 000 and two provincial Sunday papers, the *Sunday Sun* (Newcastle upon Tyne) and the *Sunday Mercury* (Birmingham), have circulations of over 200 000. Scotland has six morning, seven evening and two Sunday newspapers, in addition to Scottish editions of the *Daily Express* and *Sunday Express*. The leading morning papers are the *Glasgow Herald* and the *Scotsman*. Northern Ireland has two morning papers, one evening paper and one Sunday paper, all of which are published in Belfast. The foremost London evening papers are the *Evening News*, with a circulation of over a million, and the *Evening Standard*, with half a million.

Although the political leanings of most newspapers are characteristically Conservative, they are financially independent and do not necessarily follow strict party lines. The papers which are more or less inclined to Conservative support include the *Daily Telegraph*, the *Daily Mail*, the *Sunday Times*, the *Sunday Express* and the *Sunday Telegraph*. The *Sun* and the *Daily Mirror* are inclined to be much more left-wing; the *Sun* replaced the former *Daily Herald* which, until 1969, was partly owned by the Labour Party and the T.U.C. and was for a long time regarded as 'Labour's own newspaper'; the *Sun*, however, has no official connection with either the Labour Party or the trade unions. *The Guardian* and the *Observer* are generally liberal in outlook. Only one newspaper has direct links with a political party; this is the *Morning Star*, the successor of the *Daily Worker*, which is owned by a co-operative society and gives consistent support to the Communist Party.

Labour politicians are prone to be highly critical of what they consider to be the Conservative dominated press; but against this it is sometimes argued that the *Daily Mirror* and the *Sun* are sympathetic to the Labour viewpoint and these have a combined circulation of nearly six million which approaches the total circulation figures of the 'Conservative' papers; but overall the Conservative emphasis is dominant because Sunday papers and the more popular regional dailies and evening papers to some extent reflect this outlook. In any event all the evidence points to the fact that the majority of individuals do not buy newspapers because of their political complexion and what they read confirms existing views rather than moulding opinion. Furthermore, newspapers are primarily a business undertaking and the concern of proprietors is to publish what sells.

The standards of the coverage of political news varies considerably. The 'quality' papers, *The Times*, *The Guardian*, *Daily Telegraph*, *Sunday Telegraph*, *Observer* and *Sunday Times*, give news and articles in some depth but in the rest, issues and events are more briefly and dramatically treated.

A General Council of the Press with certain 'watch-dog' functions was established in 1953. Ten years later this was reconstituted as the Press Council, which now has a lay chairman and twenty-five members. The objects of the Council now include: preserving the freedom of the press; maintaining the highest professional and commercial standards; keeping under review any developments likely to restrict the supply of information of public interest and importance; dealing with complaints about the conduct of persons and organisations towards the press; reporting publicly on developments tending towards greater concentrations or monopoly in the press and publishers of relevant statistical material.

Generally speaking there are in this country no laws specifically relating to the press but a number of statutes include clauses which apply to the press particularly; some of these, for example, relate to limitations on newspaper ownership in independent television companies, restrictions on the reporting of the preliminary hearing of indictable offences, and the right of the press to be admitted to meetings of local authorities. The press is also subjected to certain restrictions under the Official Secrets Act.

Although the question is difficult to judge it would appear that the political effect of newspapers is not so widespread as some people suppose and almost certainly whatever influence it had has been reduced by the advent of television. The probability is that newspapers may confirm and canalise deep-seated public reactions to the attitudes and actions of politicians but they do not create them. It also seems likely that the effect of newspaper comment is more telling when a traditionally Conservative newspaper such as the *Daily Telegraph* strongly criticises Conservative leaders, or a pro-Labour newspaper, e.g. the *Mirror*, mounts an attack on Labour policies.

TELEVISION AND RADIO

The British Broadcasting Corporation, which was established under Royal Charter in 1926, at present retains a monopoly on sound broadcasting (although commercial radio is to be introduced shortly) and until 1954 it had sole rights in television broadcasts. The B.B.C. was launched as a public corporation 'acting in the national interest' to be financed by licence fees paid by owners of receivers. B.B.C. Television at present operates two television broadcasting channels, B.B.C. 1 and B.B.C. 2. The Independent Television Authority was set up in 1954 and its function is to license programme contracts companies and to regulate their output. The financing of independent television is dependent on advertising revenue and the Television Act, 1954, forbids the 'sponsoring' of programmes on the American pattern. In 1967 new contracts were issued to companies which will operate between 1968 and 1974. These include Anglia Television, A.T.V. Network, Border Television, Granada Television, Harlech Television, London Weekend Television, Scottish Television, Southern Independent Television, Thames Television, Tyne-Tees Television, Ulster Television, Westward Television and Yorkshire Television. A common news service is provided by Independent Television News Limited.

Both the B.B.C. and the I.T.A. are independent authorities in the day-to-day operation of broadcasting, including the nature and content of programmes. The Minister of Posts and Telecommunications is, however, answerable to Parliament on broad questions of policy and may issue appropriate directions to both bodies. Both organisations are expected to show balance and impartiality in the presentation of programmes, especially in matters of public policy and controversial matters. In the last resort the Minister has power to prohibit the broadcasting of particular programmes in any general class of matter and to revoke the licenses of either the B.B.C. or I.T.A. at any time.

Broadcasts on political matters include daily accounts of proceedings in Parliament transmitted on B.B.C. Radio 4 and weekly parliamentary reports on B.B.C. 2 and I.T.N. Regular current affairs programmes with a high level of political content are transmitted by both B.B.C. and I.T.V. Ministerial and party political broadcasts are regulated by rules agreed between the major political parties and the broadcasting authorities. In 1968 experimental closed-circuit sound broadcasts of the proceedings in both Houses of Parliament, and a three-day close circuit experiment of televising the proceedings of the House of Lords were carried out.

The impact of television upon the elections of 1959 and 1966 has been studied and it is evident from the reports of the surveys made that, of all the media, television contributes most to increasing awareness in the electorate of political personalities and issues.[1] These studies suggest that the mass media does not significantly affect political attitudes and, like newspapers, television tends to confirm existing predilections rather than alter them. (See also chapter 8.)

From a number of quarters there has been criticism of the handling of television programmes dealing with political events. The form, content and impartiality of programmes have all been questioned. Some important criticisms were raised by Mr Richard Crossman, then a Minister in the Labour Government, in his Granada lecture on 'The Politics of Television' delivered in 1968.[2] In this lecture, Mr Crossman drew attention to what he conceived to be two main dangers which he referred to as the 'gladiatorial' approach and the 'trivialisation' effect. He argued that 'the coverage of politics, outside the news bulletins, consists chiefly of interviews, arguments and confrontations between the spokesmen of the two parties which play up the gladiatorial aspects of politics and gives the impression that it consists in a mere conflict of personalities rather than a conflict of ideas carried by the personalities'. Mr Crossman also expressed the view that in the search for mass audiences important social and economic issues will be treated 'as an inferior form of entertainment which has to be gimmicked up in order to be made more palatable to an indifferent audience'.

There seems little doubt that both the form and content of political

---

[1] See J. Trenaman and D. McQuail, *Television and the Political Image* (Methuen, 1961), and J. G. Blumler and D. McQuail, *Television in Politics: its Uses and Influence* (Faber, 1968).

[2] Reported in *The Guardian*, 22 October 1968.

programmes could be improved, and claims have been made that more issues should be treated in depth and more time should be given to serious political programmes. In this connection Mr Crossman observed: 'Whereas television authorities are not afraid to risk losing the mass audience for two hours to stage a grand opera or a ballet or a horse show, this privilege is never accorded to any political event in between elections.'

In order to deal with allegations of unfairness and other matters for dispute it has been suggested that a Television Council should be established which would work on a basis similar to that of the Press Council. In 1971, following a dispute between Mr Harold Wilson and the B.B.C. about being questioned on the earnings from his book giving a personal account of the Labour Government 1964–70 and between the Labour Party and the B.B.C. over the screening of a programme called 'Yesterday's Men', in which a number of ex-Labour Ministers took part, the Labour Party decided to press for the establishment of a Television Council. A body such as this would not solve all the problems which arise but some informed observers believe that it would at least go some way to providing an avenue through which criticisms could be submitted and properly evaluated.

Convincing arguments have been adduced both for and against proposals to televise Parliament, but Parliament has decided that, for the time being at least, television coverage will be restricted to reported news and its day-to-day proceedings will not be televised.

Politics and society
The aspects of the social structure which have been briefly examined in this chapter will perhaps serve to underline the emphasis which has been placed upon the inter-connectedness of society and its political system. Parties, pressure groups and the machinery of government do not exist in a vacuum but are part and parcel of the ongoing life of the community. What happens in any one element or part of the overall structure affects the rest of the structure. Political beliefs, attitudes and assumptions do not mysteriously appear and are far from being completely rational; they spring, in large measure, from the social context in which individuals are born and develop and they can be seen as the outcome of the individual's inborn potential as it is affected by his life experience and the wider cultural context in which this development takes place.

7 The Pattern of Participation

Most Englishmen gradually fit into social roles involving little expectation of political activity; a small minority are socialized for active participation in national politics. The political division of labour is largely completed by the time an Englishman is old enough to vote.

Richard Rose *Politics in England*

Introduction

In this chapter we consider questions such as: What proportion of people play an active part in politics? What is the level of political knowledge and interest? Are political leaders representative of the electorate at large? What influences determine whether a given individual will be active or not? Are we governed by an elite? This will involve an examination of the process known as political socialisation and an analysis of the social and educational background of those who occupy influential positions in the political hierarchy.

Extent of participation

Although precise information is lacking we can obtain some indication of the size of the body of people who contribute actively in political affairs by reckoning together, as far as this is possible, the numbers of those individuals who are members of political parties, hold party offices at various levels, are local councillors or candidates, M.P.s or parliamentary candidates and so on. Table 13 makes an attempt to do this. This is, at most, a very crude estimate of the numbers involved but it can be seen that, on this reckoning, out of the total population over the age of 18 less than 4 per cent take any real responsibility in the work of political parties. In the whole area of political activity the role of the parties is, of course, supplemented by thousands of other individuals including the leaders of pressure groups, members of advisory bodies, civil servants, and others who occupy a variety of technical and advisory posts.

Compared with other European countries the proportion of voters who are party members is high. As J. Blondel points out, the figures for British parties 'are particularly impressive on the Conservative side, because right-wing parties usually have much smaller membership totals than

TABLE 13 *Extent of Political Participation*

	Number (in round figures)	Percentage of electorate (approximate)
Size of electorate	39 000 000[a]	100
Number voting	28 000 000[a]	72
Membership of political parties	3 530 000[b]	9
Conservative 2 500 000[b]		
Labour 680 000[c]		
Liberal 350 000[d]		
Active Members (e.g. holding office at local or constituency level, attending meetings fairly regularly and assisting with activities, member of or candidate for local council, parliamentary candidate, etc.)	1 143 000[e]	3
Full time officials at national level	60[f]	
Full time officials below national level	800[g]	
Regions 100		
Constituencies 700		
Members of Parliament	630	
Peers regularly attending the House of Lords	200	

[a] Figures are for 1970 election.
[b] Estimated figures.
[c] Report of National Executive Committee, 1970. This does not include trade union affiliated members.
[d] Based on 1964 census of membership.
[e] Based on assumption that about 30 per cent of *overall* party membership is active in accordance with criteria given. The percentages for *Labour* and *Liberal* parties are almost certainly significantly higher than this.
[f] See W. Guttsman's *The British Political Elite*, p. 196, Table 1. Only those with primarily *political* responsibility are included.
[g] Based on figures published in *New Society*, 8 August 1963.

left-wing parties'. He adds that because of its favourable financial position, the Conservative Party has been able to afford paid canvassers on a bigger scale than the Labour Party.[1]

Level of political knowledge

Whatever the reason, knowledge of and interest in political matters is generally very low. It is estimated that only about half of the electorate can, in between election times, name their M.P. A survey of one constituency, conducted by Richard Rose in the 1964 general election, showed that only 41 per cent of the sample interviewed could do so even though the M.P. had represented the constituency over a long period of time.

A most revealing survey is reported by Mark Abrams. In 1960, a fully representative sample of 1500 persons was interviewed and in answer to the question: 'How would you describe your interest in politics?' answers were given at four levels: 15 per cent described themselves as 'very interested'; 37 per cent as 'interested'; 33 per cent as 'not really interested'

[1] Blondel, *Voters, Parties and Leaders*, pp. 90–5.

and 15 per cent as 'not at all interested'. The percentage claiming to be very interested was much bigger among people aged 45 or more, among those who had followed courses of higher education and among middle-class adults.

A further survey conducted just before the 1959 election which is reported in the same article shows that 'it is not false modesty which leads so many people to disclaim lively interest in politics'. Here each respondent was asked to name three leaders of the Conservative and Labour Parties and one leader of the Liberal Party. The definition of 'leader' used for this purpose was very generous indeed and names of any of nineteen Conservative Ministers, eighteen Labour front-benchers and three Liberal M.P.s was accepted as being correct. Even so only 30 per cent of all respondents could give five correct names and 20 per cent were unable to provide even one correct name.[1]

Constituency and local leaders

E. G. Janosik has made a study of the social background of fifty-four 'leaders' in thirty-six constituency Labour Parties. The sample is too small to enable firm conclusions to be drawn but the findings are of considerable interest as indications of a definite trend. In this study, the 'leaders' included ten M.P.s, twenty-five prospective parliamentary candidates, thirty-five chairmen, thirty-five secretary-agents, thirty-one conference delegates and eighteen others. No less than 49 per cent of these were categorised as having professional, business or white-collar occupations, 12 per cent were skilled workers, 14 per cent semi-skilled, 16 per cent trade union or party officials and 9 per cent were housewives. Not a single unskilled worker was included.[2]

The study also revealed significant differences in the educational background of M.P.s and prospective parliamentary candidates as compared with those holding office in the constituency party. The overall situation in this respect is shown in table 14.

Professor Birch's study of the Borough of Glossop outlines the social background of the local political leaders, and a sample of party members and voters in the locality and this information is summarised in table 15. It will be observed that although all the leaders are included the numbers in the other two categories are relatively small. It is important also to recognise that this study deals with a local party and not a constituency party.

While the studies of both Janosik and Birch are probably indicative of the general situation it is likely that there will be considerable variations in different constituencies. Thus in areas where the proportion of working-class residents is particularly high we would expect to find that this group

---

[1] M. Abrams, 'Social Trends and Electoral Behaviour' in Rose (ed.), *Studies in British Politics*, pp. 133–6.
[2] E. G. Janosik, *Constituency Labour Parties in Britain* (Pall Mall, 1968), pp. 16–17.

TABLE 14   *School-leaving age of Constituency Labour Party leaders expressed as percentage of leadership category*

| | Age of leaving school | | | |
	12–14 (%)	15–18 (%)	Over 19 (%)	All groups (%)
M.P.s	30	0	70	100
Parliamentary candidates	16	40	44	100
Chairmen	66	28	6	100
Secretary-agents	63	24	13	100
Delegates	61	26	13	100

Source: E. G. Janosik, *Constituency Labour Parties in Britain* (Pall Mall Press, 1968), p. 24.

is more heavily represented at the leadership level. The studies which have been quoted suggest that, at both constituency and local levels, the leadership of all political parties tends to have a higher proportion of middle-class members than in the wider membership and in the population in the locality as a whole. It has yet to be proved that this is universally true, but the findings are probably indicative of a general trend. This survey is supported by the results of studies in which the social backgrounds of councillors and candidates at local elections have been investigated (see chapter 17).

TABLE 15   *Types of Occupations of Party Leaders, Members, and Voters*

| | | Type of occupation | | | | | |
Party	Position of informants	Business proprietors (%)	Professional or managerial workers (%)	White-collar workers (%)	Industrial workers (%)	Total (%)	Total No.
Conservative	Leaders	62	15	15	8	100	13
	Members	19	28	14	39	100	36
	Voters	10	17	22	50	100	272
Liberal	Leaders	33	22	39	6	100	18
	Members	9	27	30	34	100	33
	Voters	6	22	8	64	100	50
Labour	Leaders	6	28	33	33	100	18
	Members	7	—	17	76	100	30
	Voters	1	4	18	77	100	227
Whole sample	Electors	6	11	20	63	100	697

Notes: (1) The figures regarding voters relate to voters in the general election of 1951. (2) The figures regarding members do not include office-holders.
Source: A. H. Birch, *Small Town Politics* (Oxford University Press, 1959), p. 81.

Other studies show that men are much more numerous than women in political activity and that the middle-aged are numerically more preponderant. This applies to voluntary societies generally as well as to political parties, as is shown in T. B. Bottomore's study of 'Squirebridge' and Margaret Stacey's survey of Banbury.[1] The common characteristic of all voluntary groups is that they are predominantly male, middle-aged and middle-class.

Members of Parliament

It we turn from the constituency and local leaders to M.P.s we find that in terms of social background a similar picture emerges, but the discrepancy between the social composition of the House of Commons and that of the population in the country as a whole is even more marked. Table 16 shows that white-collar, semi-skilled and unskilled workers are virtually non-existent among Conservative M.P.s. The proportions of businessmen, farmers, and former military personnel among Conservative M.P.s are relatively high.

In both Conservative and Labour Parties, lawyers provide a substantial source of recruitment; this is probably because they have an occupation which can conveniently be combined with membership of the House of Commons. The same consideration applies to journalists, publicity experts and similar occupations.

Labour M.P.s are much more representative of society as a whole in that about a quarter come from industrial occupations; miners being still the most numerous group in this category. A very high proportion are lecturers and teachers; this to some extent arises because teaching is one of the most common routes through which people from working-class families reach middle-class status.

The educational background of M.P.s must also be noted. No less than 170 out of 330 Conservative M.P.s and 72 out of 287 Labour M.P.s in the Parliament elected in 1970 had been to Oxford and Cambridge. Only 35 Conservative members as against 104 Labour members had finished their education at the end of the elementary or secondary school stage.

Top decision makers

T. Lupton and C. Shirley Wilson give a summary of the educational background of a number of individuals whom they refer to as 'top decision makers'. This group includes six categories: (i) Cabinet Ministers and other Ministers of the Crown; (ii) senior civil servants; (iii) directors of the Bank of England; (iv) directors of the 'Big Five' banks; (v) directors of 'City' firms; (vi) directors of insurance companies. They show that 50 per cent of the Ministers included in the investigation, 19 per cent of

---

[1] See T. B. Bottomore, 'Social stratification in voluntary organisations' in D. V. Glass (ed.), *Social Mobility in Britain*, and M. Stacey, *Tradition and Change: a Study of Banbury* (Oxford University Press, 1960).

TABLE 16   *Occupational Background of M.P.s, 1970*

		Conservative	Labour	Liberal
Professions				
Barrister		60	34	3
Solicitor		14	13	1
Doctor/dentist		6	7	—
Architect/surveyor		3	2	—
Civil engineer		1	2	—
Chartered secretary/accountant		6	6	—
Civil servant/local government		12	3	—
Armed services		24	—	—
Teaching:				
university		1	⎱13	—
adult		2	10	—
school		6	33	1
Other consultants		14	9	—
Scientific research		—	5	—
	Total	149	137	5
Business				
Company director		80	4	—
Company executive		14	10	—
Commerce/insurance		3	5	—
Management/clerical		1	7	—
Small business		3	2	—
	Total	101	28	—
Miscellaneous white collar		1	3	—
Private means		4	—	—
Politicians/organisers		10	11	—
Publisher/journalist		30	27	1
Farmer		31	1	—
Housewife		1	1	—
Local administration		1	3	—
	Total	78	46	1
Clerk		—	4	—
Miner		—	22	—
Skilled worker		2	33	—
Semi-skilled/unskilled		—	17	—
	Total	2	76	—
	Grand total	330	287	6

Source: Abstracted from table in *The British General Election of 1970*, D. Butler and M. Pinto-Duschinsky (Macmillan, 1971), p. 302.

the senior civil servants and 66 per cent of the Bank of England directors had been educated at the major public schools. Seventy-one per cent of the Ministers and 68 per cent of the civil servants had studied at Oxford or Cambridge.

The study also examines an actual situation in which a number of top decision makers were involved and charts the family connections of some of the people concerned. In 1957 a group of Labour M.P.s alleged that the decision to raise the bank rate had been improperly disclosed and the Parker Tribunal was set up to investigate. The tribunal rejected the

TABLE 17 *Labour Cabinet Ministers, 1916–35 and 1935–55*

	1916–35	1935–55
Class background		
Aristocracy	3	1
Middle-class	12	14
Working-class	19	19
University education		
None	20	17
Oxford	5	6
Cambridge	2	5
Other universities	7	6

Source: Adapted from W. L. Guttsman, *The British Political Elite* (MacGibbon and Kee, 1968), p. 244.

allegations but the sections of its reports quoted by Lupton and Wilson illustrate the kind of personal relationships which existed between some of the major participants. Thus, when Lord Kindersley (a director of the Bank of England) was questioned by the Attorney-General as to why he (Lord Kindersley) and not Mr C. F. Cobbold (the Governor of the Bank of England) had gone to see Lord Bicester (a senior director of Morgan Grenfell and Company, an important 'City' firm, and also a Governor of the Bank of England) about the effect the rise in the Bank Rate would have on a particular issue of stock, Lord Kindersley said: 'I consider it perfectly natural that I should be allowed to go and talk to a colleague in the Bank of England...I do not think that Lord Bicester would find it in the least surprising that I should come to him and say to him: "Look here, Rufie, is it too late to stop this business or not?"' and: 'I have discussed this with Jim – with the Governor and I am coming to see you.'

In order to show the family connections of these and other central figures who gave evidence at the Tribunal, Wilson and Lupton constructed a series of 'family trees' which were presented in twenty-three separate diagrams. The first of these, for example, shows that 'Mr C. F. Cobbold is related on his father's side to the late Lt. Col. John Cobbold who married a daughter of the 9th Duke of Devonshire.' Another 'traces some of the connections of the Prime Minister's nephew by marriage, the 11th Duke of Devonshire, a brother-in-law of the writer Nancy Mitford; she married a son of Lord Rennell. Lord Rennell's wife is a sister of Lord Bicester...'. A further diagram shows that Lord Kindersley's brother 'married a niece of the 2nd Earl of Iveagh, father in law of the Rt. Hon. Lennox Boyd, M.P., Minister of State for Colonial Affairs'. The study shows the way in which, of these groups and others, including the Hambro family, Mr R. A. (now Lord) Butler, the Astor family, several Conservative M.P.s and Ministers, and several other titled families are interconnected.[1]

[1] T. Lupton and C. Shirley Wilson, 'The Social Background and Connections of "Top Decision Makers"' in Rose (ed.), *Policy Making in Britain*, pp. 5–25.

Labour Cabinet Ministers

The previous section shows the educational background of Conservative Ministers only and the question arises as to whether the composition of Labour Cabinets is dramatically different. W. L. Guttsman provides information which enables us to contrast the social and educational background of the members of Labour Cabinets in the periods 1916–35 and 1935–55.[1] This is presented in table 17.

Richard Rose observes that in the 1945–51 Labour Government, four of the six men who held the offices of Prime Minister, Foreign Secretary or Chancellor of the Exchequer had been at major public schools. He adds that the 1964 Labour Cabinet 'was unusual in having six members who had been manual workers'.[2]

Political socialisation

Socialisation, in its broadest sense, refers to the process through which individuals develop a view of the society to which they belong and their particular place within it. Socialisation creates in the individual a tendency to see things in a certain way and to have certain beliefs, values and assumptions about his own role and that of others. It is a process which begins in infancy and continues throughout life, but the earliest phase of development seems generally to be of greatest importance. The family is the most important single influence, but friends, neighbours, education, workplace and other factors may make important contributions, each tending usually to reinforce the other. Political socialisation is part of this process and the outcome determines the individual's attitude towards the political system and the kind of part which he expects to play within it.

Only a few people are socialised in a way which leads them to play an active part in politics and, as we have seen, the vast majority are inactive, the activity of this latter group being limited to voting and casual discussions on the way in which government actions affect their personal welfare. In some cases, it is clear, a lively political interest passes from father to sons and daughters. Thus Winston Churchill and Harold Macmillan belong to well-known 'political' families. Similar traditions seem to be developing on the Labour side: Anthony (now Lord) Greenwood, Roy Jenkins, Anthony Wedgwood Benn, Lord Caradon, Sir Dingle Foot and the 'rebel' Michael Foot, all had fathers who had been M.P.s. Both the daughter of Morgan Phillips (who was Secretary of the Labour Party) and her husband, Dr Dunwoody, were M.P.s and junior Ministers in the 1966–70 Parliament. Family influences are also evident in political activities at a much less elevated level. In one family well known to the author a tradition of political interest extending over four generations can be traced: the great grandfather (born 1865), an Irish immigrant, was active in the Sinn

[1] W. L. Guttsman, *The British Political Elite* (MacGibbon and Kee, 1968), ch. IX.
[2] Rose, *Politics in England*, p. 96.

87

Fein and kindred organisations; the grandfather (born 1891) was a member of the Independent Labour Party and later the Labour Party; the father (born 1925) was a Labour parliamentary candidate and the son (born 1953), has been a local official of the Liberal Party. Each of these had begun their political activity at very early ages. It seems reasonable to suppose that negative attitudes are similarly transmitted. In a much broader context, Gabriel Almond and Sidney Verba, in their survey of political attitudes in five nations, show that there is a tendency for people who have had the opportunity for discussion of decision-making in the family, at school and at work to be more inclined to believe that their actions can influence political decisions.[1] These authors point out that the effect of these experiences is cumulative: thus, British subjects investigated whose family participation was followed by opportunities to take part in decision making at work scored much higher on a 'subjective competence' scale than those whose family experience in this respect was not reinforced at work.

The operation of the socialising influence is, of course, diverse and complex but a brief indication of the main factors can be given. 'Within the home', as Richard Rose points out, 'children early become aware that sex differences are related to differences in adult political roles.'[2] In many families women are not expected to do certain things and active participation in politics is one of these. The fact that there are so few women M.P.s in Britain is a result of the pattern of socialisation; the common practice of women voting 'the same way as their husbands' is also a reflection of this.

Education also has a marked influence. We have already seen that those who are educated at the major public schools and the older universities dominate the upper echelons of political life. We have also noted that the majority of adolescents and especially those who are not in the top rank of educational achievements are only rarely encouraged to believe that their views and actions will make a vital difference to the nature of the body politic. Home environment and the place of work are also relevant. Thus, communities which are relatively stable and where there is a predominant industry such as mining result in a greater cohesiveness of political attitudes than areas where the population is transitory and the work pattern varied.

The earliest influences shape the probable direction of the individual's political outlook; later experience may confirm, amend or in a few cases drastically alter it. Changing social conditions and experiences of life in abnormal circumstances such as war, are also likely to have some effect. Affluence may not eradicate discontent but it alters its nature.

Except within the limits previously mentioned religion appears to have little effect on political attitudes generally. There are, however, indications that in the earlier part of this century it had a considerable formative

---

[1] G. A. Almond and S. Verba, *The Civic Culture* (Princeton University Press, 1963), ch. 12.
[2] Rose, *Politics in England*, p. 61.

88

influence in the attitudes of a number of individuals who later became Labour M.P.s. An article quoted by Richard Rose shows that in the first large group of Labour M.P.s returned to Parliament in 1906, *Pilgrim's Progress* was mentioned more frequently than any other book as having influenced their thinking.[1] In individual cases this connection between religion and political attitudes may still be applicable and in this connection one thinks of the way in which the religious and political convictions of men like Sir Stafford Cripps and Sir Richard Acland were very closely intertwined.

Are we ruled by an elite?

In recent years it has frequently been suggested that Britain and certain other countries are governed by an 'establishment' or an 'elite'. These terms are used loosely and are suggestive rather than precise, the general notion being, in the case of Britain, that Ministers, higher civil servants, industrial and business leaders share a common background and outlook which results in them sharing common values and assumptions. The elitist view seems to suggest that these groups are very closely linked and that they make decisions which are conducive primarily to their own well-being and are not really concerned with the welfare of other groups in society even though in their public statements they may be at pains to avoid giving this impression.

Professor Blondel has examined this thesis in some detail. He points to the difficulty of defining words like 'power' and 'domination' and concludes that before the argument can be confirmed it must be shown that the people 'at the top' form a united group who are in a position which cannot seriously be challenged. Their basic values must be identical and their rule must be permanent. If another group, e.g. the Labour Party, are seen to be radically different in social composition and personal values and the gaining of office means the gaining of real power, then the argument, by definition, falls to the ground. If the Labour Party is seen as similar in some respects but different in others, (e.g. it seeks to acquire power but is not anxious to perpetuate a relationship between government and powerful economic groups) then there are two ruling groups and not one. If, however, the 'establishment' keeps its influence when Labour is in office then the Labour Party is really irrelevant because government, in all important particulars, will be carried on as before.[2] T. B. Bottomore suggests that there is no conclusive evidence for the existence of a single dominating establishment group. He observed that the groups concerned 'are not a single establishment but a ring of establishments with slender connections'.[3] It seems clear, however, from the Lupton and Wilson investigation quoted above and from other studies, that a common social

[1] Rose, *Politics in England*, p. 79.
[2] Blondel, *Voters, Parties and Leaders*, ch. 9.
[3] T. B. Bottomore, *Elites and Society* (Watts, 1964).

and educational background produces intellectual and attitudinal cohesiveness but that this does not extend to the sharing of common political opinions and policies.

Should there be greater political participation?

Practising politicians and others with strong social commitments are often keen to increase the numbers of those who take an active part in political affairs. They bemoan the low level of political interest and what they see as widespread political apathy. They urge improvement in the level of political education and an increase in the degree of 'participation' and 'involvement'. Views such as these usually meet with acclaim from audiences which are likely to be composed of individuals who are themselves politically active.

Perhaps less frequently an opposing view is expressed. The level of participation, it is suggested, is low because the majority of people are basically satisfied with the political system as it is and do not feel impelled to exert themselves unduly because they are suffering no real hardship and the outcome of an election only marginally affects their welfare. Furthermore, as Seymour Lipset argues, it may in fact be dangerous to increase the level of participation because increased activity may indicate that the fundamental cohesion which is characteristic of political democracy is breaking down as it did in Germany in the 1930s.[1]

Both of these arguments are interesting and important and they merit the attention of all those who attach importance to the nature of government in contemporary society. Political behaviour is dynamic, not static, and changes in attitude and perception which have been taking place slowly and are not immediately evident are liable to make an impact quite suddenly. This kind of change can be observed in student attitudes and behaviour, both in Britain and overseas in recent years; it must be assumed the wider electorate is similarly affected by social changes and the ongoing process of government as it is seen by them. Some insight into the phenomena of constancy or change in political attitudes (and the difficulty of making firm pronouncements on these) can be derived from a study of voting behaviour which is examined next.

[1] See S. Lipset, 'Political Sociology' in R. K. Merton, *et al.*, *Sociology Today* (Harper and Row, New York, 1965), p. 95.

8 Voting Behaviour

This is a realm in which the understanding of human nature is so incomplete that it would be grotesque to portray the electorate as playing out any fully determined role.
David Butler and Donald Stokes *Political Change in Britain*

Introduction

In the last twenty years or so electoral support for the major parties has been fairly evenly divided and one outstanding characteristic of voting behaviour in Britain is the consistency with which the vast majority of electors support one party or the other. In all general elections since 1950 the 'swing' between the parties has been small, ranging as it has between 0.9 and 4.7 and averaging out at approximately 2.5. (See table 18.) The fact that most Governments during this period have had sizeable majorities stems from the variations in the numbers of electors in different con-stituencies which have resulted in a substantial disproportion between the total votes cast for each party and the number of seats gained.

What then are the factors which influence electors in their voting decisions? One thing at least is certain: the way in which votes are cast is not wholly determined by judgements of a Government's performance or responses to campaign propaganda. Politicians and commentators grossly over-simplify the situation when they attribute a direct cause and effect relationship between party policy and the voters' response. While a good deal of research in this field has been done, we are far from having a comprehensive explanation of voting behaviour. As D. Butler and D. Stokes in a recent detailed study confirm: 'Any catalogue of the factors involved in these processes must include some that are found in the voter's mind, in the circumstances that govern his chances of being born and of surviving in any given age, some in the interaction with his family and with his neighbours and workmates, some in the structure and operations of the communications media, some in the behaviour of political leaders and party organisations and some in the trend of the economy or in world events – and even this list is far from exhaustive.'[1]

[1] Butler and Stokes, *Political Change in Britain*, p. 441.

TABLE 18   *Extent of 'Swing' in General Elections, 1945–70*

Year of election	Swing to Conservative	Swing to Labour
1945		11.3
1950	2.8	
1951	0.8	
1955	2.1	
1959	1.1	
1964		3.1
1966		2.6
1970	4.7	

Note: The Swing is arrived at by calculating the averages of the differences in the Labour and Conservative share of the total votes cast, comparing the current with the previous election. This can be done for an individual constituency, groups of constituencies or the country as a whole. This measurement enables the change in a given constituency or region, or in the country as a whole, to be expressed in single figures, which facilitates comparisons. The example for a hypothetical constituency given below makes clear the method of calculation.

	Percentage of vote, 1970	Percentage of vote, 1966
Conservative	49.4	44.5
Labour	41.2	43.1
Liberal	9.4	12.4
Conservative majority	8.2	1.4
Swing to Conservative	8.2 − 1.4 = 6.8	
	= 3.4	

We will examine the influence of at least some of these factors and look at some of the associated aspects such as the phenomena of the so-called 'floating voter', and 'non-voter' or abstainer. This will be done by reporting the results of a number of studies in order to illustrate the range and character of the investigations which have been undertaken. The place of opinion polls in forecasting the results of British general elections and the part which they might possibly play in influencing the result will also be discussed. It must constantly be borne in mind, however, that society is not static and the influence of the various social forces which impinge on electoral behaviour are liable to change. The result of this, in course of time, might conceivably be to alter the present pattern of voting.

In one study or another, social class, sex, age, work situation, trade union membership, neighbourhood connections, parents' voting preferences and religion of samples of electors have been examined in order to see whether or not they are significantly related to voting behaviour.

Before summarising some of these studies it should be noted that the demonstration of a positive statistical correlation between two factors does not necessarily imply a causal relationship. All that can be said in these cases is that there is a connection between the two factors. Occasionally we shall speak more loosely of the influence of this factor or that. Where this is done there are reasonable grounds for assuming a causal relationship but this is an assumption and not a proven fact.

TABLE 19   *Class Differences in Voting Behaviour* (shown as percentages)

Party	1945	1950	1959	1964
Upper middle-class				
Conservative	76	79	87	77
Labour	14	9	6	9
Liberal	10	12	7	14
Middle-class				
Conservative	61	69	76	65
Labour	24	17	16	22
Liberal	15	14	8	13
Working-class				
Conservative	32	24	25	32
Labour	57	64	68	59
Liberal	11	12	7	9

Source: Adapted from H. Durant, 'Voting behaviour in Britain, 1945–64', in R. Rose, *Studies in British Politics* (Macmillan, 1967), p. 123.

Social class and voting

The relationship between social class, sex, age and voting behaviour are examined by Mr Henry Durant, the director of Gallup Poll, in an article included in a valuable compendium of studies edited by Professor Richard Rose.[1] This study shows that while there is a definite and persistent relationship between social class, as objectively determined, and voting behaviour, this is not equally strong between all classes. The figures given in table 19 show that the upper middle-class is by far the most homogeneous

TABLE 20   *Sex Differences in Voting Behaviour* (shown as percentages)

Party	1945	1950	1955	1964
Men				
Conservative	35	41	47	40
Labour	54	46	51	49
Liberal	11	13	2	11
Women				
Conservative	43	45	55	45
Labour	45	43	42	39
Liberal	12	12	3	16

Source: Adapted from H. Durant, 'Voting behaviour in Britain, 1945–64', in R. Rose, *Studies in British Politics* (Macmillan, 1967), p. 125.

[1] H. Durant, 'Voting behaviour in Britain, 1945–64' in Rose, *Studies in British Politics*, pp. 122–8.

in its voting behaviour and gives massive support to the Conservatives. The remainder of the middle-class also heavily favours the Conservatives. Working-class voters favour the Labour Party but by much smaller margins than the middle-class as a whole favours the Conservative Party. The phenomena of working-class voters who support the Conservative Party and middle-class members who support Labour are interesting ones and they will be examined in detail later in this chapter. R. Alford, also using Gallup data, made an extensive comparative study of voting behaviour in Britain, America, Australia and Canada, in which he concluded that Britain has a higher and more stable level of class voting than any of the other countries surveyed.[1]

Sex differences
Henry Durant shows that when voting preferences are analysed in terms of sex differences (see table 20), men show a consistent bias in favour of the Labour Party and women similarly favour the Conservative Party. As Seymour Lipset has shown, these differences are also found in a number of Western countries. Durant, however, points out that the differences are so small proportionately that sex has very little accuracy as a predictor of any individual's vote.[2]

Age
In looking at the differences in voting patterns between various age groups it is important to remember that the membership of any one group will have changed completely in the course of a decade. It is necessary, therefore, that a study of this aspect of voting behaviour should extend over a reasonably long period of time. Henry Durant's report shows that while Gallup polls have made clear the preference of the 21–9 age group for the Labour Party at each election between 1945 and 1964, the margins have varied between 1 per cent and 28 per cent (see table 21).

TABLE 21   *Voting Behaviour of 21–9 Age Group, 1945–64*

Party	1945 (%)	1950 (%)	1951 (%)	1955 (%)	1959 (%)	1964 (%)
Conservative	29	36	44	43	46	39
Labour	57	52	53	54	47	47
Liberal	14	12	3	3	7	14
Labour lead	28	16	9	11	1	8

Other data show that, over the same period, those aged between 30 and 49 divided fairly evenly and the age group 50–64 consistently favoured the Conservatives. The preference of the 65+ group shifted

[1] R. Alford, *Party and Society* (Murray, 1964).
[2] S. Lipset, *Political Man* (Heinemann, 1960).

TABLE 22   *Party preference; by self-rated class within occupational stratum*

Party	Non-manual		Manual	
	Self-rated middle (%)	Self-rated working (%)	Self-rated middle (%)	Self-rated working (%)
Conservative	52	23	36	16
Liberal	25	23	19	16
Labour	11	37	31	55
Other	1	0	0	1
Don't know or refuse	11	17	14	12
Total	100	100	100	100
Number	363	124	303	610

Source: W. G. Runciman, *Relative Deprivation and Social Justice* (Routledge and Kegan Paul, 1966), p. 171.

back and forth between the parties and moved counter to the national swings at the same election. It is clear from this that age alone is not a very helpful indicator of voting behaviour.

It is convenient to add here that the lowering of the voting age to 18 appears to have made little if any difference to the overall results in the General Election of 1970. Whether or not the fuller registration of this age group and the passage of time will have a more marked effect in future elections remains to be seen.

This analysis of the relationship between class, sex, age and voting, Henry Durant states, 'makes clear how misleading are attempts to explain voting behaviour in terms of a single social characteristic', because even the significant relationship shown between class and voting 'leaves un-explained the voting behaviour of that third of the British electorate which does not vote in agreement with its objective social class'.

Self-assigned social class
The consideration of social class and voting given above indicates the picture which emerges on the basis of *objective* social class, i.e. the categories into which individuals are placed in accordance with some objectively determined criterion such as income or occupation. A different and almost certainly more accurate representation is arrived at when the relationship between the way in which an individual votes and the social class to which he *sees himself* as belonging is investigated; this phenomena is variously referred to as 'self-assigned', 'self-rated' or 'subjective' social class. A survey made by W. G. Runciman in 1960 and 1961 (see table 22) suggests that the relationship between self-assigned class and party preference is strong in the case of Conservative and Labour voters but

that it makes little or no difference to support for Liberal candidates.[1]
A survey made in Greenwich by M. Benney, A. P. Grey and R. H. Pear
also suggests that subjective class membership shows a much
stronger relationship with voting behaviour than does objective class
position.[2]

Workplace, neighbourhood and trade union

A number of environmental factors and their relationship to voting
behaviour have been discussed by Professor Blondel.[3] The workplace of
the elector seems to be related to his voting behaviour. He suggests, for
example, that workers in large plants are more likely to vote Labour than
workers in small plants. This is supported by Mrs Stacey's study of
Banbury which showed that manual workers employed in 'traditional'
firms (e.g. small family businesses) are more likely to vote Conservative
than those in non-traditional firms, such as large factories.[4] Professor
Blondel also gives details of the voting behaviour of trade unionists who
formed 41 per cent of the sample in a survey conducted by the British
Institute of Public Opinion in 1964. Of these, 53 per cent were regular
Labour voters and 22 per cent were Conservative supporters. He points
out, however, that trade unionism is stronger in some industries than
others and, even among trade union members, there is a sizeable minority
of Conservative supporters which is considerably larger than the minority
of Labour voters among professional and managerial employees.

In the same book reference is made to the influence of the home sur-
roundings. The writer suggests that individuals have a strong tendency to
conform to the area in which they live and he reports that studies in
Sweden, the U.S.A. and France have shown that 'the more an area is
inhabited by manual workers, the greater is the proportion of manual
workers who vote for a left wing party'. Professor Blondel also found from
his participation in the study of Newcastle under Lyme that in middle-
class districts, manual workers are less likely to vote Labour than those
in working-class districts.[5] This phenomenon is confirmed in a study by
M. Young and P. Willmot who write: 'The rule seems to be that the more
the middle class predominates in a district, the more working class people
identify themselves with it.'[6]

The inclusive effect of this group of influences is characterised by
Blondel in his reference to miners, in whose ranks are included a higher
proportion of Labour voters than in any other group. He writes: 'Miners
are at the intersection of a number of pressures which all seem to work in

[1] W. G. Runciman, *Relative Deprivation and Social Justice* (Routledge and Kegan Paul, 1966).
[2] M. Benney, A. P. Gray and R. H. Pear, *How People Vote* (Routledge and Kegan Paul, 1956).
[3] Blondel, *Voters, Parties and Leaders*, ch. 3.
[4] Stacey, *Tradition and Change in Banbury*.
[5] F. Bealey, *et al.*, *Constituency Politics* (Faber, 1965).
[6] M. Young and P. Willmot, *Family and Class in a London Suburb* (Routledge and Kegan Paul, 1960).

Respondents' own first preference	Parents' partisanship		
	Both parents Conservative (%)	Parents divided Con./Lab. (%)	Both parents Labour (%)
Conservative	89	48	6
Labour	9	52	92
Liberal	2	—	2
	100	100	100

Source: D. Butler and D. Stokes, *Political Change in Britain* (Macmillan, 1969), p. 47.

TABLE 24   *Present Party Preferences by Parents' Conservative or Labour Preferences*

Respondents' own present preference	Parents partisanship		
	Both parents Conservative (%)	Parents divided (%)	Both parents Labour (%)
Conservative	75	37	10
Labour	14	49	81
Liberal	8	10	6
None	3	4	3
	100	100	100

Source: D. Butler and D. Stokes, *Political Change in Britain* (Macmillan, 1969), p. 48.

the direction of a Labour vote. They are engaged in one of the more traditional industrial occupations, they usually live in self-contained housing estates, they are often the sons of miners. Finally, they are heavily unionised....' Although the influence of workplace, unionisation and neighbourhood are important they do not stand alone. Voting behaviour is the outcome of a diverse and complex set of forces, and closely linked to factors just examined are the influences of the individual's family, his education and, perhaps, religion.

Family influences

A most interesting statement on the relationship between an individual's voting preference and the party supported by his parents is provided by David Butler and Donald Stokes. They write: 'A child is very likely indeed to share his parents' party preference. Partisanship over the individual's lifetime has some of the qualities of a photographic reproduction that deteriorates with time: it is a fairly sharp copy of the parents' original at the beginning of political awareness, but over the years it becomes somewhat blurred, although remaining easily recognisable.'[1] Table 23 examines the

[1] Butler and Stokes, *Political Change in Britain*, p. 47.

remembered early preferences of the individuals included in the survey; table 24 gives the preferences of the same group as indicated at the time of the investigation in the mid-1960s.

Religion

In some countries religion has a marked influence on political attitudes but, in general, the association between religion and voting behaviour in Britain, with one or two regional exceptions, does not seem to be particularly strong. As we have seen in chapter 6, in Northern Ireland the Protestant–Catholic antipathy spills over into the political scene and in Wales there is the widespread influence of the Nonconformist tradition. Elsewhere it is difficult to disentangle the influence of religion from the influence of occupation and social class. Surveys show considerable local variations but overall there appears to be a tendency for Catholics and Nonconformists to support Labour rather than Conservative and for members of the Church of England to be more Conservative than Labour. This association, however, could be explained in terms of social class because, for example, the Church of England has a relatively high proportion of middle-class supporters, and a high proportion of Catholics are working class. As Professor Blondel observes: 'the precise impact of religion on voting is thus difficult to determine'.

It can be seen from the aspects of voting behaviour already discussed that a variety of forces impinge on the individual who is to a large extent 'socialised' into a particular attitude in electoral terms. In many cases the attitude will persist throughout life, in others it will be altered in response to experiences and circumstances encountered. This is not to suggest that the individual's behaviour is wholly determined by external factors but it is important to recognise their considerable impact. Voting behaviour may also be affected by the individual's response to the performance of particular Governments, his impression of the party leaders, his 'image' of the political parties and the impact of press, television and the election campaign. Whether or not an individual votes, and the party he supports when he does vote can be viewed as the resultant of all these forces upon his own personality.

Party images

It is clear from a number of surveys that the majority of voters possess only a highly generalised view of what the parties stand for. Thus, Mark Abrams points out, the Labour Party is viewed, by Conservative and Labour supporters alike, as 'standing mainly for the working class'. The Conservative party is seen as 'standing mainly for the middle class', and one likely to 'give more chances to a person who wants to better himself'.[1] Furthermore, the fact that an individual votes for a party does not necessarily imply support for its policies. The survey conducted by M. Benney

[1] Abrams, 'Social trends and electoral behaviour' in R. Rose, *Studies in British Politics*.

and his colleagues in the 1950 general election referred to earlier showed that the proportion of Labour voters agreeing with a particular item of Labour policy ranged from 79 per cent (on full employment) to 49 per cent (on nationalisation). The point is further emphasised by the fact that the same survey showed that an average of 41 per cent of Labour voters approved of some plans in the Conservative platform and an average of 31 per cent of Conservative voters approved of some Labour policies. It is clear that the support given to parties is frequently based upon continuing loyalty rather than rational consideration of specific policy issues. As early as 1908, long before the time of the sophisticated surveys to which we can now refer, Graham Wallas pointed out that the parties can draw upon emotional loyalty. He wrote: 'Something is required simpler and more permanent...which can be recognised at successive elections as being the same thing that was loved and trusted before; and a party is such a thing.'[1] The reference to 'love and trust' may raise a sceptical eyebrow in the contemporary setting but the point he is making is clear. Professor Cotgrove submits that 'the fact that voters support a party for its image rather than for any specific item of policy facilitates the task of the party in aggregating a variety of issues into a coherent policy, and ensures continued support in the face of disagreements on specific issues'.[2]

Leaders and candidates

It is part of the folk-lore of politics that 'no candidate is worth more than 500 votes'. This kind of statement is simply a way of expressing the fact that in Britain, parliamentary elections are primarily contests between parties and not between personalities. The investigations of the Bristol North-East constituency by R. Milne and H. C. McKenzie in 1951 and 1955 show that only 1 per cent of the electorate felt that the local candidate influenced their decision.[3] In a national sample interviewed in 1966 by National Opinion Polls, only 3 per cent mentioned the qualities of candidates. It seems, however, that there are exceptions to this rule, and it is possible that one or two outstanding candidates have a substantial personal following. On this, however, no firm evidence can be presented. Additionally, it should be borne in mind that some candidates have gained benefit from the existence of a strong local organisation; it is very easy to confuse organisational success with personal success. On this question, D. Butler and D. Stokes state: 'The results of every election since the war have been sifted for traces of "personal" votes and the findings are impressively negative.'

The same authors draw attention to the fact that until recently little has been known about how a leader's personality intertwines with his party's

[1] G. Wallas, *Human Nature in Politics*, 4th edn (Constable, 1948).
[2] S. Cotgrove, *The Science of Society* (Allen and Unwin, 1967), p. 166.
[3] See R. Milne and H. C. McKenzie, *Straight Fight* (Hansard Society, 1954) and *Marginal Seat* (Hansard Society, 1958).

image or with other issues of politics in the voter's mind. They observe that the mass media focus a sharper spotlight on leaders than ever before but suggest that the leader phenomenon is not new. 'The qualities of Gladstone and Disraeli – and even Baldwin – were projected as central issues in election campaigns.' They take the view that the leaders do enter into the voter's calculations to varying extents. 'Some who voted in 1966', they suggest, 'identified Mr Wilson with the defence of the pound, Britain's presence East of Suez, firm handling of strikes and other actions which were by no means simple extensions of Labour's traditional policies.' From their own investigations they provide evidence which indicates that some voters' attitudes toward the party leaders do in fact involve shifts in votes between the parties.[1]

Election campaign and the mass media

The parliamentary election campaign makes little impact upon the majority of voters. Only a small percentage attend public meetings (probably not more than 7 per cent) and a high proportion of these are party members and activists. Voters are subjected to a bombardment of literature, posters, as well as extensive coverage in the newspapers and on radio and television. The great bulk of the British electorate appears to be virtually immune to blandishments of this kind as far as changing of attitudes is concerned and the greatest attention is focused on the activities of the party of their own, and usually prior, choice.

In 1959 an extensive study of the impact of television on political attitudes was made by J. Trenaman and D. McQuail.[2] This showed that although viewing election programmes on television enlarged the electors' knowledge of activities and issues it had no effect on their political attitudes. The same study confirmed the negative effect of radio on local election campaigns. Indeed, as far as the press is concerned, it is pointed out that as the campaign progresses readers become more sceptical of the treatment of issues which is presented to them. The authors of this survey conclude that there is 'a definite and consistent barrier between sources of communication and movements of attitude in the political field at the general election'.

The value of electioneering?

As we have seen, the amounts of money spent by political parties at parliamentary elections and in the intervals between them is considerable and it is clear that the direct result of this in terms of change of allegiance is minimal. It should not be concluded from this, however, that there are no results and that the money is entirely wasted. In contradiction of the view frequently expressed that propaganda activities, particularly at

[1] Butler and Stokes, *Political Change in Britain*, ch. 17.
[2] J. Trenaman and D. McQuail, *Television and the Political Image* (Methuen, 1961).

100

election time, make no difference to the result it can be argued that such activity does occupy an important role in British politics. Thus:

(i) The excessive amount of energy put into the campaign by candidates and party workers which is extensively reported does at least make voters aware that an election is impending and probably contributes to the high turn-out which is characteristic of British elections. Whether or not there is a large scale turn-out of supporters for a particular party may make all the difference in 'marginal' constituencies.

(ii) It is of importance both in the short-term and the long-term, for the parties to keep up the morale of their members and most active supporters. An energetically fought campaign is an excellent way of doing this.

(iii) Although the proportion of the electorate which is not constant in its voting habits is small it is there and must be courted. In some seats only a small 'turn-over' in votes can make the vital difference between success and defeat.

(iv) Elections undoubtedly contribute to the diffusion of political knowledge.

Although, therefore, techniques alter with changing social conditions it seems unlikely that the degree of effort and proportion of money expended by political parties is likely to diminish.

Characteristics of British voters

It has sometimes been observed that the chief characteristics of the British electorate are a remarkable consistency in individual voting behaviour and a high turnout at general elections. The extent to which this is valid depends on the criteria applied. Firstly, as far as the question of turnout is concerned, the proportion of the electorate voting in general elections in the post-war period has ranged between 75 per cent and 85 per cent; in the nineteen elections since 1900 an 80 per cent poll has been exceeded five times but three of these occasions occurred before 1914. When it is remembered, however, that only 90 per cent of those registered (at least in the more recent period) are likely to be able to vote, because of deaths, removals, illness, absence from the constituency on polling day, etc., and that mobility has greatly increased since the end of the Second World War, it is submitted that compared with other Western countries where there is no compulsory voting this is remarkably high. A comparison with the U.S.A. is interesting. In the presidential election of 1968 only 61.7 of the electorate voted and since 1916 the turnout for a presidential election has never exceeded 65 per cent of those able to vote; on two occasions (1920 and 1924) it was below 50 per cent. In mid-term elections for Congress and many state offices, the turnout in the last fifty years has never exceeded half of the electorate and on three occasions (1922, 1926, and 1942) it was smaller than one third.

It should be noted that the reference to relatively high turnout in elections in Britain applies only to general elections and that the proportion of the electorate voting in by-elections and local government elections is, by comparison, low. (See chapter 17.) The same kind of situation applies in the U.S.A. where voting in local elections and 'primaries' is at a much lower level than for presidential and congressional elections.

Taking into account that in Britain the level of political interest is generally low and that there is a marked tendency to resist the blandishments of campaign propaganda, the high turnout at general elections may appear paradoxical. This is probably explained by the fact that the general election is a popular talking point and that polling day takes on something of the expectancy that surrounds a major sporting event. To vote is to have participated in a national event and the cultural pressure to exercise the franchise is, in this respect, strong. It may also be that the majority of people recognise that their lives are affected by the decisions of government and feel impelled to do what they can to influence the general direction of these events.

To what extent are individuals consistent in the support given to a particular party from one level to another? Mark Abrams conducted a survey immediately before the general election of 1959 to elicit information on this point which is reported in 'Social trends and electoral behaviour' referred to earlier. This showed that 87 per cent of those interviewed who intended to vote Conservative in 1959 stated that they had voted Conservative in 1955. The corresponding figure for Labour supporters was 86 per cent. A further study made in 1960 indicated that 86 per cent of the Labour supporters interviewed had voted Labour in the 1951, 1955 and 1959 elections. Sixty-nine per cent of Conservatives were constant in this respect. The more recent survey made by D. Butler and D. Stokes, however, observes that: 'The most notable feature of the shifts in individual preference is their sheer volume.' These writers report that in the 'three intervals of change' which they examined in the 1960s, 'there were never more than seven-tenths of the public positively supporting the same party at two successive points of time; the fraction remaining steadfast through several successive intervals was even smaller'.[1] It appears, therefore, that in recent years the degree of volatility in voting behaviour has increased. It remains to be seen whether or not this is a transient phase and there is evidence to suggest that the allegiance of many groups to a particular party is strong (see e.g. Goldthorpe and Lockwood's study of affluent workers below); if this trend continues, however, it will bring into question many of the assumptions which have been made about the behaviour of the British electorate especially as it has hitherto been expected that, because there are thought to be relatively large reservoirs of consistent support, swings between the parties will continue to be small.

[1] Butler and Stokes, *Political Change in Britain*, p. 293.

102

'Floating' voters and non-voters

There is now evidence that in each general election a proportion of the voters change their party allegiance, some abstain from voting and some are voting (or abstaining) for the first time. As we have seen, the popular conception of a constant and identifiable group of voters who change their allegiance from one election to the next is erroneous, because the composition of this group will vary from election to election. It needs to be borne in mind that the nature of the contest in some constituencies varies from one election to another, thus on one occasion there may be a Liberal as well as Conservative and Labour candidate, but on a subsequent occasion there may only be Conservative and Labour candidates. The possibilities open to a convinced Liberal in the latter circumstances are: (*a*) to vote Conservative, (*b*) to vote Labour, (*c*) to abstain. Discussions on the 'floating' vote are, therefore, bedevilled by problems of definition. If the term is restricted to those who switch between two successive elections the number is comparatively small. R. S. Milne and H. C. McKenzie, referring to the 1955 election, state: 'On this definition, only 4 per cent of the electors in the Bristol sample were floaters; just over 3 per cent changed from Labour to Conservative and fewer than 1 per cent changed in the other direction.'[1] This group is not made up of cool, calculating, discriminating voters who provide the stereotype of ideal electors. The reasons for change are frequently quite trivial and their basis for it quite irrational.

Surveys conducted by the British Institute of Public Opinion in 1959 and 1964 show that, of those who abstain from voting, the working-class and the poor are likely to be much more numerous than the middle-class and well-to-do; and there are unlikely to be more young and old persons than middle-aged. (See table 25.)

Some recent surveys

It has been repeatedly emphasised that social change and political change are closely inter-related. What signs are there that the present pattern of electoral behaviour is likely to alter? Some interesting studies have been made in recent years which throw some light on this prospect and give insight into the present situation and one or two of these will now be examined.

AFFLUENT WORKERS

Let us take, for example, what has been referred to as 'the embourgeoisement thesis'. This suggests that as workers become more affluent they will increasingly adopt the style of life of the middle-class and eventually become Conservative rather than Labour in their support.

This view was extensively investigated by J. H. Goldthorpe, D.

[1] R. S. Milne and H. C. McKenzie, 'The Floating Vote' in R. Rose, *Studies in British Politics*, p. 145.

TABLE 25   *Social Characteristics of Abstainers*

		Non-voters 1964 (%)	Whole sample 1964 (%)
Sex	Male	50	48
	Female	50	52
Age	21–4	16	8
	25–34	24	19
	35–44	16	20
	45–64	28	37
	65 and over	16	16
Class	Well-to-do	4	6
	Middle	18	22
	Lower-middle and working	63	61
	Poor	15	11

Source: J. Blondel, *Voters, Parties and Leaders* (Penguin, 1963), p. 55.

Lockwood and their colleagues.[1] The group studied were well-paid workers in Luton, a town which was extremely favourable for testing the validity of the embourgeoisement thesis. The main sample consisted of 229 manual workers aged between 21 and 46, who were married and living with their wives, and earning relatively high wages. For comparison, 54 'white-collar' employees were also studied.

These investigators found no support, however, for the view that this group, because of their affluence, were in the process of becoming Conservative supporters. Indeed a striking feature of their findings was that support for the Labour Party was unusually strong and stable. In the general elections of 1955 and 1959 no less than eight out of every ten votes were cast for Labour and the proportion was the same for voting intentions

TABLE 26   *Voting for three main parties in General Elections of 1955 and 1959, and voting intentions 1963–4 : manual and white-collar samples*

	Labour (%)	Conservative (%)	Liberal (%)	Totals (%)	Number
Manual					
General election 1955	83	15	2	100	157
General election 1959	80	16	4	100	188
Voting intention 1963–4	79	14	7	100	199
White-collar					
General election 1955	32	55	13	100	40
General election 1959	30	55	15	100	47
Voting intention 1963–4	32	58	10	100	50

Source: J. H. Goldthorpe and D. Lockwood *et al.*, *The Affluent Worker : Political Attitudes and Behaviour* (Cambridge University Press, 1968), p. 13.

[1] J. H. Goldthorpe and D. Lockwood *et al.*, *The Affluent Worker : Political Attitudes and Behaviour* (Cambridge University Press, 1968).

in the 1964 election. There is, however, a marked difference between the voting pattern of the manual workers and those employed in 'white-collar' jobs. (See table 26.) A high proportion of the Labour voters are also consistent supporters of the party, 62 per cent of them having supported Labour on every occasion since they have been eligible to vote.

For a majority of the manual workers identification with Labour as the 'working-class' party was strong. Some stated that the Labour Party, as against other parties, commands their adherence because it can 'do most for the working man' by increasing living standards and improving the social services. From other evidence collected the authors suggested that 'the affluent workers, support for Labour is probably less *solidaristic* and more *instrumental* than that of the many traditional workers from whom the Labour Party has in the past received almost unconditional allegiance'. By this they mean that this group tend to make decisions on the basis of what the parties have to offer rather than on the basis of the kind of allegiance which stems from unquestioning loyalty. This interpretation is supported by another finding that nearly half of the intending Labour voters were not in favour of trade unions financially supporting the Labour Party and a quarter of this group had actually contracted out of paying the union political levy. Both trade unions and political parties are judged on their merits.

Goldthorpe and Lockwood remark that 'poll-type' surveys of election behaviour do not take into account the wider environment in which individuals are located including, for example, those of the work organisation and the local community. They themselves had assumed that these were important in understanding changes in working-class life and their research was designed to provide for this possibility. They state that: 'Becoming affluent does not mean that the worker becomes a member of middle-class society or even aspires to such membership', and conclude: 'the understanding of contemporary working-class politics is to be found, first and foremost, in the structure of the worker's group attachments and not, as many have suggested, in the extent of his income and possessions'.

Working-class Conservatives

It has already been seen that a substantial section of the working-class support the Conservative Party. This fact is of immense political importance because without this support the Conservatives would have no hope of obtaining office. The topic has aroused great interest among political scientists and at least two books and a number of articles have dealt with various aspects of it. (See section on Further Reading.) The most recent of the major publications on this topic is that of Robert McKenzie and Alan Silver.[1] These authors show how the actual course of events (in terms of voting behaviour) over the last hundred years or so has upset the predic-

[1] R. McKenzie and A. Silver, *Angels in Marble: Working-class Conservatives in Urban England* (Heinemann, 1968).

tions of major figures both on the left and right of the political spectrum. Thus Karl Marx, referring to the carrying of universal suffrage in England, wrote in 1852: 'Its inevitable result, here, is the political supremacy of the working class.' Lord Cranborne, who resigned from the Derby Government in protest against the 1867 Reform Bill said in the House of Commons Debate on the Bill: 'The Conservatives have dealt themselves a fatal blow by the course they have adopted.' The account is rich in historical detail and puts forward a convincing argument to show how the Tory Party since Disraeli has monopolised the sense of nationalism in British political life.

In the detailed investigation of the characteristics of working-class Conservatives in urban England in the contemporary setting, the authors make use of enquiries undertaken over a six-year period. The principal findings of this part of the study are that working-class Conservatives form a representative cross-section of the social class to which they belong. They are not the richest or the poorest, and they are if anything better informed on politics than the majority of the working-class.

McKenzie and Silver make a broad distinction between two groups; 'deferentials' and 'seculars'. Twenty-six per cent of the sample of 600 are labelled as 'deferentials', and 38 per cent are 'seculars'. The 'deferentials' tend to invest Conservative leaders with an innate superiority over their rivals and see the Conservative Party as a national institution rather different in kind from the Labour Party. They see policies which benefit the working class as stemming from the benevolence or personal wealth of elitist leaders. The 'seculars', on the other hand, base their support for the Conservatives on a pragmatic assessment of their policies and performance in office. They see policies which benefit the working class as the result of sound policies or the successful management of the economy. They judge leaders on their merits or prefer those who have reached high office by their own merits. The authors conclude that the ideological basis of working-class Conservative voting is moving away from deference towards secularism in that:
  (i) the age group under 44 includes only one in ten of the 'deferentials' but one in two of the 'seculars';
 (ii) more women than men are 'deferentials' but it is generally agreed that women react more slowly than men to changes in political and social perspectives;
(iii) there is a strong and consistent association of higher incomes with secularism.

The third finding coincides closely with that of Goldthorpe and Lockwood discussed above and may be indicative of a more general trend towards 'secularism' or 'instrumentality' in voting decisions. One wonders if this trend is likely to be accelerated with the break up of traditional working-class neighbourhoods.

Middle-class radicals
Earlier in this chapter it was noted that whereas the majority of the middle-

class support the Conservative Party a significant proportion of them do vote Labour. Mark Abrams, reporting a survey of the 1964 election conducted by Research Services, found that

   (i) the younger a member of the middle-class is, the more likely he is to vote Labour;
  (ii) only one in eight of the managerial group as against one in three of the lower middle group support Labour;
 (iii) there is a marked tendency for middle-class Labour voters to describe themselves as working-class;
  (iv) those middle-class members who assigned themselves to the working-class tended to have left school at an early age;
   (v) over half of the Labour supporters who were middle-class both by occupation and self-assignment had received formal education beyond the age of 16.

Mark Abrams summarises this position by saying that 'middle-class people who voted Labour were concentrated in two socially extreme groups – those with considerable experience of higher education and those with low work-status within the middle-class group'.[1] It is convenient to mention here, as is noted by Richard Rose, that a number of surveys have shown that university graduates are less likely to vote Conservative than those whose education terminated at the end of the grammar school, 'notwithstanding the fact that university graduates are in a social class which is very heavily pro-Conservative in its party preferences'.[2]

Evidence which shows that a high proportion of middle-class left-wing supporters are to be found in 'welfare' and 'creative' professions rather than banking, insurance, commerce, accounting, advertising, etc., is provided by Frank Parkin.[3] The former are a highly educated group holding degrees and diplomas which entrance to the professions concerned demand. Parkin suggests that the explanation for this lies in the fact that this group have formed left-wing political attitudes before they start work and enter professions which are compatible with their political and social values.

Opinion polls
Finally, mention must be made of opinion polls. The British Gallup Poll pioneered political opinion surveys in England in 1938 and, as Henry Durant observed in the article quoted above in the six elections between 1945 and 1964 it forecast the distance between the two parties with an average error of 1.9 per cent; in its final pre-election survey for each of these elections, it forecast the winning party correctly. The result for 1966 was correctly forecast but in 1970, along with most other polls, it failed in this respect. In recent years the number of polling organisations has grown

[1] M. Abrams, 'Social Class and Politics' in R. Mabey, *Class* (Blond, 1967).
[2] Rose, *Politics in England*, p. 69.
[3] F. Parkin, *Middle Class Radicalism* (Manchester University Press, 1968).

considerably and many national newspapers now commission polls and publish their results. With one exception all of the forecasts published immediately before the 1970 general election, however, were wrong and the extent of this miscalculation is comparable with the U.S.A. presidential election polling disaster of 1948 when all the polls erroneously put Dewey ahead of Truman. With considerable foresight David Butler and Anthony King in their survey of the 1966 general election wrote: 'Politicians, and everyone else, can easily be misled by the apparent findings of polls. The intelligent statesman will neither ignore them nor be intimidated by them.'[1]

The forecasts of the major polls for the 1970 election are shown in Table 27.

TABLE. 27   *Forecasts of result of General Election of 18 June 1970 as published by major public opinion polls, 1970*

Poll	Fieldwork period	Forecast result
Marplan	June 11–13	9.6 Labour
Gallup	June 14–15	7.0 Labour
N.O.P.	June 11–16	4.1 Labour
Harris	June 9–14*	2.0 Labour
Opinion Research Centre	June 11–14*	1.0 Conservative

* Plus substantial re-interviewing in election week.
Source: *The Guardian*, 20 June 1970.

The actual result was, of course, a decisive victory for the Conservatives who obtained 46.4 per cent of the votes cast as against Labour's 42.9 per cent. Martin Woollacot, in a newspaper article, reported that the organisers of the Opinion Research Centre Poll which gave the best forecast arrived at their figure in the following way. A poll taken on the weekend before the election had shown a Labour lead of 4.5 per cent on the straightforward basis of expressed party preferences. This was 'trimmed' to 3 per cent to allow for the estimated actual turnout of voters which was likely to be low, a situation which normally affects adversely the size of the narrow vote. After re-interviewing a sub-sample in election week they cut back the Labour lead to zero because of switches among Labour and Liberal supporters. Finally they pushed the result over into a 1.0 per cent Conservative lead 'because Conservative voters appeared marginally more determined to support their party'.[2]

The forecast of any poll is affected by the size and nature of the sample, the nearness of the poll to the election, the weightings given for factors such as estimated turnout, etc. The whole exercise is fraught with difficulty because it is virtually impossible to anticipate some factors, for

[1] D. Butler and A. King, *The British General Election of 1966* (Macmillan, 1966).
[2] M. Woollacot, 'Turning the Tables', *The Guardian*, 20 June 1970.

example, 'turnout' of supporters for the Labour party may be high in one election but low in another.

In Germany and some other countries the publication of polls is banned because of the effect which it might have on the outcome of elections. It has also been suggested that they should be banned in Britain. It is argued, for example, that when the forecast is that one party will win by a substantial majority it lulls the supporters of that party into a false sense of security and they don't bother to vote, or alternatively, the supporters of the opposing party won't vote because the outcome is certain. The attitude of the party leaders is against the introduction of any legislation to make polls illegal. In an interview after the 1966 election Mr Heath said: 'Ban polls? Of course not. You can't do that in a free society', and in the House of Commons on 26 April of the same year, Mr Wilson refused to consider any restrictions.[1] There is no evidence that the polls affect election results and as David Butler and Anthony King observe in their 1966 election study, 'it has been normal for elections to be decided by margins in which the polls cannot forecast the winner with certainty and in which their findings therefore can only add to the excitement'.

Public opinion polls, of course, are concerned not only with forecasting the results of general elections but with testing public attitudes on a vast range of issues as and when they arise and the question arises as to what extent governments should be influenced by these.

After the general election of 1970, Mr Wilson dwelt at some length on the place of public opinion polls in British politics in an article specially written for the *Encyclopaedia Britannica Book of the Year 1971*.[2] In this he laid down two important principles, viz: (i) 'A Government cannot govern, and should not seek to govern, by relating its policies to public opinion poll results, whatever its judgement of their accuracy.' (ii) 'If a Government has embarked on a policy it believes to be right, it should stick to it despite hostile, short-term reactions.' Mr Wilson also observed that it is a 'poor democratic leader...who needs public opinion polls to tell him what is likely to be the popular reaction to particular policies', and concluded with the following advice to guide the conduct of statesmen in relation to the polls: 'Treat them with respect as you would give to any honest and expert professional assessment of facts that you have to take into account. And then recognise that you were elected, as legislator, as an executive, to exercise a judgement – not on what is expedient or electorally rewarding but on a judgement of what is right.' If all statesmen were to do this we would have little to fear in relation to the possible harmful effects of opinion polls.

---

[1] Quoted in Butler and King, *General Election of 1966*, p. 174.
[2] Published in *The Observer*, 14 March 1971 and 21 March 1971.

Part 3
Government and Administration

9 Prime Minister, Government and Monarchy

The office of the Prime Minister is what its holder chooses and is able to make of it.
H. H. Asquith *Fifty Years of Parliament*

No Government can be successfully formed or survive unless it is sustained by the House of Commons.
Lord Morrison of Lambeth *Government and Parliament*

In its blend of showmanship, religion, diplomacy and occasional public hysteria, the monarchy remains an important part of the national character.
Anthony Sampson *Anatomy of Britain Today*

Definition of terms
'Government' and 'Parliament' are both loosely used terms. Parliament, in the strict sense, means 'The Queen in Parliament' which comprises the House of Commons, the House of Lords, and the Sovereign; it is these bodies acting together which make up the legislature. In formal terms the Government is the group of Ministers and other office-holders who together comprise the political element in the executive. Also, 'Government' and 'Cabinet' are sometimes used as if these are interchangeable terms when this is not, in fact, the case. The Cabinet is an important, but distinctive part of the Government.

The Government
The Government is made up of the Prime Minister, Ministers, Ministers of State, Junior Ministers and Ministers' Private Parliamentary Secretaries. The total size of Government has increased in proportion to the growing size and complexity of governmental administration. Before 1914 Governments had less than fifty members in all but today they are likely to have about a hundred. Following the Government reshuffle in October 1970, 92 Conservative M.P.s out of 329 held offices as Ministers, Junior Ministers or Whips.

For reasons that are largely historical, Ministers have a variety of titles. The majority are either Secretaries of State, who usually head large and important departments, like the Foreign Office, and Ministers who head other departments or Ministries. Others retain the historical title connected

110

with their department, as in the case of the Chancellor of the Exchequer and the Chancellor of the Duchy of Lancaster. The law officers, including the Attorney-General and the Solicitor-General are also Ministers. Some Ministers hold offices which no longer carry departmental responsibilities but they may have specific tasks allotted to them. This group includes: the Lord President of the Council, the Lord Privy Seal, the Paymaster-General and the Chancellor of the Duchy of Lancaster. The duties virtually undertaken by the person holding office as Chancellor of the Duchy of Lancaster, for example have varied tremendously from time to time. From 1945–8 the holders were concerned with the administration of the British Zone in Western Germany; in 1951 when Lord Swinton held the office he acted as Deputy Leader of the House of Lords and was in charge of the supply of raw materials. Mr Iain Macleod became Chancellor of the Duchy in 1961; he was Leader of the House of Commons and Chairman of the Conservative Party Organisation. In Mr Heath's Government the Chancellor of the Duchy of Lancaster has responsibility for the Common Market negotiations. The Prime Minister himself nominally holds office as First Lord of the Treasury. In some Governments, Ministers without Portfolio are included; these again may have special responsibilities allocated to them by the Prime Minister.

Next in the Government hierarchy are the Ministers of State. These are appointed to assist ministers in large departments such as the Foreign Office and the Department of Education and Science. They are subordinate to the departmental Minister but are senior in status to junior Ministers. Each departmental Minister is assisted by one or more junior Ministers who have the title of Parliamentary Secretary or Parliamentary Under Secretary depending on the nomenclature of the Minister concerned. Each Minister appoints his own Parliamentary Private Secretary who renders him assistance in a personal capacity by helping with the Minister's constituency work and undertaking informal parliamentary liaison duties. There has been some controversy as to whether or not parliamentary private secretaries should be classed as members of the Government but recent evidence points to the fact that they should be included. They are closely associated with Government and are expected to resign if they cannot accept its policies. Mr Frank Allaun, M.P., who was Parliamentary Private Secretary to the Colonial Secretary, voluntarily resigned in 1965 in protest against the Labour Government's support for the American intervention in Vietnam. In 1967 Mr Wilson forced the resignations of a whole group of parliamentary private secretaries after they had declined to support the Government's economic policy.

Although the 'Whips' of the party holding office are not formally part of the Government, their *raison d'être* is to serve it and they must be included in the numbers who are *ex officio* committed to the Government. The Chief Whip and Assistant Whips receive salaries as the nominal holders of various Government offices. The total number of Ministers is about forty and roughly half of these serve in the Cabinet.

There is no statutory provision that Ministers must be M.P.s or members of the House of Lords but there is a firmly established convention which requires that the vast majority be M.P.s and the remainder must be in the Lords. In Mr Heath's Government, announced in October 1970, only one person, Mr David Brand, Q.C., the Solicitor-General for Scotland, is not either an M.P. or a peer. It is now well established that the Prime Minister must be in the Commons. Exceptions to these do occur but they normally last only for short periods in exceptional circumstances. Thus, at the time of his appointment as Prime Minister in 1963, Sir Alec Douglas-Home was a peer but he quickly took advantage of the Peerage Renunciation Act passed in that year in order to make himself eligible for membership of the Commons. When Mr Patrick Gordon Walker lost his seat in the general election of 1964 he was appointed as Foreign Secretary in the Wilson Government on the assumption that he would quickly find a seat at a by-election. Mr Reg Sorensen vacated his seat at Leyton and took a peerage and Mr Gordon Walker was adopted as the Labour candidate. He unexpectedly lost the ensuing by-election, however, and immediately resigned as Foreign Secretary.

The maximum number of Ministers which can be appointed from M.P.s is laid down by statute. Ministers in excess of this number must, in accordance with the convention outlined above, be members of the House of Lords. The Ministers of the Crown Act, 1947, provided that no more than eighteen out of twenty-one senior Ministers would serve in the Commons at any one time. These numbers were exceeded under the Emergency Powers Act during the Second World War and a number of ministerial posts created after this time were excluded from the terms of the 1937 legislature. The House of Commons Disqualification Act, 1957, laid down that not more than twenty-nine of the senior Ministers specified and not more than seventy Ministers and junior Ministers in all could serve in the Commons at any one time. When the Labour Government was elected in 1964 new legislation was needed because the new Ministers and ministerial appointments planned by Mr Wilson exceeded the number permissible under the existing law. Accordingly the Ministers of the Crown Act, 1964, was passed. This altered the total number of Ministers allowed to serve in the Commons to ninety-one and abolished restrictions on the number of senior Ministers who were M.P.s.

It is the Prime Minister and his Cabinet who determine the emphasis and direction of Government policy. The functions of the Cabinet and its place in the structure of government will now be examined.

The Cabinet

The Cabinet consists of the Prime Minister and a group of senior ministers from his party chosen by him. The Cabinet has been described by Bagehot as 'a combining committee, a hyphen which joins, a buckle which fastens the legislative part of the state to the executive part'.[1] As Sir Ivor Jennings puts it: 'The Cabinet is the core of the British constitutional system. It is the supreme directing authority. It integrates what would otherwise be a heterogeneous collection of authorities exercising a vast variety of functions. It provides unity to the British system of Government.'[2] It must be noted that the validity of these classic statements in present-day circumstances has been challenged and the controversy which has arisen on this is discussed later in this chapter.

The main functions of the Cabinet were listed in the Report of the Machinery of Government Committee, 1918, as being:

(i) the final determination of policy to be submitted to Parliament;
(ii) the supreme control of the executive in accordance with the policy presented by Parliament;
(iii) the continuous co-ordination and delimitation of the activities of the several Departments of State.

This committee, popularly known as the Haldane Committee, also stated that for the efficient performance of these tasks the following conditions were essential, or at least desirable:

(a) the Cabinet should be small in number – preferably 10 or at most 12;
(b) it should meet frequently;
(c) it should be supplied in the most convenient form with all the information and material necessary to enable it to arrive at decisions quickly;
(d) it should consult personally all ministers whose work is likely to be affected by its decisions;
(e) it should have a systematic method of ensuring that its decisions are carried out by the departments concerned.[3]

Which persons should be appointed as ministers and included in the Cabinet is at the personal discretion of the Prime Minister. There are, however, a number of factors which he must take into account. It is customary for the heads of certain departments to be members. The Lord Chancellor, the Lord President of the Council, the Chancellor of the Exchequer, the Secretaries of State for the Foreign Office, the Home Office and the large new departments such as those for Economic Affairs under Mr Wilson and for Trade and Industry under Mr Heath are virtually certain to be included.

It is important, therefore, in making these appointments, for the Prime Minister to choose individuals who will not only be capable ministers but who will also be able to work successfully together as members of a team. There will also be an understandable tendency for him to include prominent members of the party or important sections of it, even if the Prime Minister has personal doubts about their probable performance as

[1] W. Bagehot, *The English Constitution*, Fontana edn (Collins, 1963), p. 68.
[2] I. Jennings, *Cabinet Government*, 3rd edn (Cambridge University Press, 1959), p. 1.
[3] Cmd. 9230, *Report of the Machinery of Government Committee* (H.M.S.O., 1918).

Ministers. On this reasoning to be an outstanding 'rebel' might put a person high in the running for selection. Thus it seems possible that Aneurin Bevan was chosen by Mr Attlee not merely for his undoubted ability but because he also represented a strong critical element within the Labour Party who wanted a more drastic Socialist policy. Similar considerations conceivably apply to Mr Wilson's selection of Mr Frank Cousins. Some commentators suggest that in appointments such as these where the persons involved are regarded as leaders of powerful minority viewpoints, there is an element of 'buying time' because in both cases the individuals concerned eventually resigned from the Government in which they served. The same kind of analysis can be applied to the decisions of a Conservative Prime Minister. Thus, for Mr Macmillan in 1957, Mr R. A. Butler might have been regarded as representing the more radically inclined Conservatives, and Lord Salisbury as the exponent of traditional Conservatism. Again it is important to notice that Lord Salisbury later resigned from the Government and Mr Butler was twice rejected as Prime Minister.

The majority of Cabinet Ministers have had many years of experience in Parliament but occasionally there are meteoric rises to political prominence. The special circumstances of the Second World War provide the classic cases of Mr Ernest Bevin, the leader of the Transport and General Workers Union, who was brought into Mr Churchill's Government as Minister of Labour, and Lord Woolton, a prominent city businessman who became Minister of Food. More recent examples include Mr Frank Cousins, also from the Transport and General Workers Union, who was appointed Minister of Technology in Mr Wilson's Government in 1964 and Mr John Davies, the former Director-General of the Confederation of British Industries who in 1970 was placed in charge of Mr Heath's newly created Department of Trade and Industry only a few weeks after entering Parliament.

The Prime Minister must also be mindful of the size of his Cabinet. One that is too small might smack of government by a highly privileged group and thereby give too many prominent ministers the feeling that they are being excluded from the inner councils of government; it would also present major problems of parliamentary liaison. One that is too big would be too unwieldy for efficient decision taking and make more difficult the problem of confidentiality. In the inter-war years, when nearly all ministers were included, the Cabinet had between twenty and thirty members; since the Second World War the number has ranged between sixteen and twenty-three. Before becoming Prime Minister in 1964, Mr Wilson had spoken of the desirability of a Cabinet of fifteen to twenty members but on taking office created one with twenty-three members. Mr Heath's Cabinet appointed in June 1970 had eighteen members but this was reduced to seventeen in the Government reorganisation of that year.

114

During the Second World War, Mr Churchill appointed a War Cabinet of five members, which was later increased to eight. There has been much talk of 'Inner Cabinets' and their allegedly sinister implications, but the practice of most modern Prime Ministers of having an intimate working relationship with close colleagues seems merely to reflect the understandable desire of the leader of the Government to consult his senior colleagues informally. In one form or another there have been examples of this practice in most post-war Cabinets. Mr Wilson, in 1969, formed a Parliamentary Committee of six senior Ministers with himself as Chairman and this was alleged by his critics to be an Inner Cabinet, the idea of which Mr Wilson had previously rejected. This body, however, appears merely to have given a more formal structure to a well established mode of informal consultation.

Cabinet meetings

The Cabinet normally meets twice weekly for about two hours. The Prime Minister decides the agenda and matters may not normally be raised without prior notice. The Prime Minister can vary the order of business and introduce new items if he considers this necessary. As far as possible all relevant consultations take place before the meeting and papers are circulated in advance. Verbal contributions to the meeting are expected to be relevant, concise and realistic. Much business is formal in that only an indication of approval is required. When there is disagreement, no vote is taken but the Prime Minister may 'collect voices' and declare the 'sense of the meeting'. The minutes do not mention personalities and they accord with the constitutional fiction that the Cabinet is an unofficial body, the Privy Council being, legally, the executive body (see below). The Cabinet does not issue orders but 'takes note', 'approves' or 'invites'. Its decisions are recorded as 'conclusions'.

On what criteria are items included in the agenda? Matters which the Prime Minister wishes to raise are automatically included; in other cases the responsibility of asking for an issue to be considered is placed on individual ministers. Lord Morrison has suggested the following as criteria to be applied in deciding whether or not a particular issue should be raised:

(a) Does it raise new issues of government policy?

(b) Will it involve substantial parliamentary or public controversy?

(c) Is it likely to cause embarrassment to the Government at home or abroad?

(d) Will it cause difficulty among supporters in the House of Commons?

(e) Is dispute with another department involved?

(f) Is the proposal likely to be objected to by a number of ministerial colleagues?[1]

[1] Lord Morrison, *Government and Parliament*, 3rd edn (Oxford University Press, 1964), pp.27–8.

The proceedings of the Cabinet are secret and the provisions of the Official Secrets Act reinforce the oath taken by members of the Cabinet as Privy Councillors. Occasionally an agreed statement is issued to the press and now and again 'leaks' occur. Such information as we have about the actual work and decisions of the Cabinet is derived from the biographies of former Cabinet Ministers, but these are individual and subjective accounts which are always open to challenge. Cabinet minutes and other related documents can now be published after a lapse of fifty years after the time that they were compiled.

J. P. Mackintosh provides us with an interesting account of Mr Attlee's handling of the Cabinet from 1945 to 1951, and contrasts this with the methods used by Mr Churchill.[1] He records that Mr Attlee's aim at the meetings of the Cabinet was to stop unnecessary talk. His method of doing this was to put questions in the negative, saying in effect to the minister concerned, 'You don't have anything to add to this memorandum, do you?' He would then ask, 'Does any member of the Cabinet oppose this?', cutting off any attempted amplification by repeating the question. The matter was then regarded as settled. When discussion did take place Mr Attlee called for contributions judiciously and was skilful at expressing the collective view of the meeting. Each Prime Minister has his individual method of approach and what suited Mr Attlee would not suit others. Mr Churchill was, in contrast, sometimes very talkative himself and occasionally allowed quite long discussions on some items; usually he obtained compliance with his own view, 'while leaving his colleagues with the feeling that the processes had been reasonable'. Each successive Prime Minister, while following the general pattern of procedure, has placed his own stamp upon the tenor of Cabinet meetings and the conduct of government as a whole.

The Cabinet Office

Important adjuncts to the Cabinet, which are designed to assist in the efficient working of government, are the Cabinet Office and Cabinet Committees.

The Cabinet Secretariat, which formed the basis of the present Cabinet Office, dates from 1916 when the war resulted in a heavy increase in the volume of Cabinet business. The then Prime Minister, Mr Lloyd George, took over the secretariat of the Committee of Imperial Defence and gave it responsibility for servicing the Cabinet. The Cabinet Office now provides a link between Cabinet Members and Government Departments. It keeps minutes of the meetings of the Cabinet and Cabinet Committees and circulates the agenda and other relevant papers. It conveys Cabinet decisions to the Departments concerned and reports on their implementation. The Cabinet Office includes the Historical Section and Central Statistical Office.

[1] J. P. Mackintosh, *The British Cabinet* (Stevens, 1962), pp. 425–35.

Cabinet committees

Cabinet committees are subordinate to the Cabinet and exist to facilitate its work. There are two kinds: standing committees and *ad hoc* committees. Classic examples of the former are Mr Churchill's Defence Committees, one for Operations and one for Supply; and Mr Attlee's Committees on Housing and Fuel provide instances of the latter. All of these were presided over by the Prime Minister but in other committees a senior Minister takes the chair. Ministers not in the Cabinet may serve on committees and frequently do so, especially if the work of their Department is closely related to the subject under consideration.

As Lord Morrison has observed: 'Too many Committees can be the enemies of decision', but a well planned structure of committees 'can facilitate the process of government and save a good deal of inter-departmental friction'. It is for this reason that the pattern of committees is kept under constant review.

The 'new style' of Government

The Prime Minister's announcement of major changes in the organisation of Government Departments in 1970 was accompanied by a proposal to achieve the more basic aim of improving the Government's internal decision-making process.[1] It is, therefore, intended to attach to the Cabinet Office 'a small interdisciplinary review staff' which will be staffed by people drawn from both inside and outside of the government service. It will include economists, management experts, businessmen and scientists. Cabinet Committees, instead of working out their proposals for Cabinet consideration as they have done hitherto, will call in the 'review' staff to look at the particular policy being discussed in relation to the strategy of the Government as a whole.

It is also intended that the agency will provide the Cabinet with a detailed and systematic analysis of the departmental proposals that come before it. This analysis will, it is hoped, include assessments of the objectives of the Department, an evaluation of the alternative methods of achieving them, an estimate of their impact on overall Government policy and detailed costings of alternatives. This, it is believed, will be much more efficient than the present practice of taking Cabinet decisions on papers submitted by interested Departments. It is emphasised that the function of the agency is to assist and not to supplant ministers and that it will not delve into the activities of individual Departments.

Although these proposals have been criticised by Mr Wilson and others they represent the first published official thinking about the problems of government administration since the Haldane report of 1918.

Ministerial responsibility and collective responsibility

The notion of ministerial responsibility occupies a central role in the

[1] See: Cmd. 4506, *The Reorganisation of Government* (H.M.S.O., 1970).

117

British system of government. The essential features of this are expressed in the doctrines of the 'collective responsibility' of the Government as a whole and the individual responsibility of Ministers.

The basis of collective responsibility rests in the fact that the Government is the creature of Parliament and is responsible to it; it can survive only so long as it has the support of a majority of M.P.s in the House of Commons. The Government must, therefore, present a united front to the Commons and, collectively, shoulder responsibility for its actions and policies. Any member of the Government who feels that he can no longer accept this restraint must resign.

The doctrine of collective responsibility affects the whole of the Government, but it applies with particular force to members of the Cabinet. Whatever differences are expressed in the Cabinet or in personal consultations between Ministers, a veil must be drawn over them in facing the Parliament, the party and the electorate. Lord Salisbury said in 1878: 'It is only on the principle that absolute responsibility is undertaken by every member of the Cabinet, who, after a decision is arrived at, remains a member of it, that the joint responsibility of ministers to Parliament can be upheld and one of the most essential principles of parliamentary responsibility established.'

The doctrine of collective responsibility applies even when no active part is taken in making the decision or even when the person concerned has not been consulted. Severe disagreements do occur and from time to time an individual Minister will resign from the Government. Mr George Brown (now Lord George-Brown), who was Deputy Prime Minister in Mr Wilson's Government, resigned in 1968 because he objected to what he alleged was Mr Wilson's practice of taking decisions without proper consultation. Mr Anthony Nutting and Sir Edward Boyle resigned from the Conservative Government in 1956 because of their dissatisfaction with the decision taken on the Suez issue. When resignations occur there is a formal exchange of letters between the individual concerned and the Prime Minister and these letters are published. They are normally couched in polite terms but they often give a strong clue to the actual nature of the disagreement. Fuller accounts become available from what is now the well-established practice of leading politicians in publishing their memoirs.

The individual responsibility of Ministers has two separate but related meanings. Firstly, there is a legal responsibility which means that he has a *legal* responsibility for acts done by his Department. This responsibility, subject to the limitations outlined in the Crown Proceedings Act, 1947, can be forced in the ordinary courts. Beyond this lies a *political* responsibility.

Ministers in charge of departments pilot Government Bills through the House of Commons, answer parliamentary questions and are generally accountable to the Prime Minister and to Parliament for the work of their Departments and for their personal conduct insofar as this impinges on

118

their official duties. The more extreme view of ministerial responsibility as expressed by Sir Ivor Jennings is that Ministers are responsible for every single act of their Department, whether or not they had prior cognisance of it. Clearly, no Minister can familiarise himself with every detail and the question arises as to the kind of error which is serious enough to warrant resignation. The best way of testing this is to examine what has actually happened in specific cases of error, default or bad judgement on the part of Ministers, or when serious errors have been committed by his Department without his prior knowledge.

In the period since 1945 only a handful of Ministers have resigned for reasons other than policy differences with the Government. Mr Hugh Dalton resigned in 1947 after disclosing Budget proposals before they were presented to the House of Commons; he returned to the Government, however, at a later date. Mr J. Belcher, Parliamentary Secretary to the Board of Trade, resigned and left the Commons following the Lynskey Tribunal's findings in 1949, which investigated allegations of bribery in connection with the grant of licences by the Department in which he was a Junior Minister. Sir Thomas Dugdale, the then Minister of Agriculture, resigned following the Crichel Down Case in 1954, when it was established that there had been maladministration concerning an area of land requisitioned during the Second World War. (See chapter 19.) In 1962 it was thought that Mr T. Galbraith, a Junior Minister at the Admiralty, might be concerned in a security leak and he resigned; he was subsequently exonerated by a committee of inquiry and was given a new office in the Government six months later. In 1963 Mr J. Profumo, the Minister responsible for the War Office, resigned from the Government and left the House of Commons following disclosures that he had lied to the House of Commons on matters which might have had a bearing upon the security of the State.

With the exception of the Crichel Down Case, all the above resignations arose from circumstances in which the personal reputation of the Minister was at stake. The milder view of the extent of ministerial responsibility was expressed in the House of Commons in 1954 by Sir David Maxwell-Fyfe, a leading member of the Conservative Government and former Law Officer, when he suggested that a Minister should not be held responsible for the actions of civil servants which he did not know of in advance and would not have approved of. It is clear that this view is now generally accepted and there are several cases where Ministers have been more personally involved in errors of judgement or policies which have failed without resigning. Thus, Mr John Strachey did not resign after the disastrous failure of the 'groundnuts' scheme in 1949, when large sums of money were expended in experiments in tropical agriculture; and no Ministers resigned after the 'Ferranti' affair in 1967, when enormous profits were made by a firm holding major defence contracts.

When things go badly with a Department from causes that are judged to be unconnected with the Minister's personal competence, there is a strong tendency for the Prime Minister and other leading figures in the Government to support the Minister so that he can ride the storm in the House of Commons. This practice reflects and reinforces the idea of collective responsibility. Sometimes it is deemed appropriate to move Ministers from one Department to another after things have gone wrong or when decisions have been taken that have been very unpopular. Thus Mr Callaghan left the Exchequer and became Home Secretary after the decision to devalue the pound in 1967. In the latter post he made a considerable reputation for his handling of the disturbances in Northern Ireland.

'Reshuffling' and dismissal of Ministers

The tenure of office of any Minister is limited not only by the life of Parliament and the vicissitudes of the electoral system but also by the well-established practice of moving Ministers from one Department to another for reasons of promotion, demotion, resignation or the assumed need of Governments to present a new image from time to time. In the lifetime of a single Government the scope and rate of change is considerable. Of the 38 Ministers and 36 Junior Ministers in the Conservative Government who were appointed in 1951 only 10 Ministers and 6 Junior Ministers held office ten years later. Brian Lapping has analysed the membership of the Labour Cabinet covering the period from 1964 to 1970 and he shows that, apart from the Prime Minister himself, only three Ministers held the same office throughout these six years. These were Lord Gardiner, the Lord Chancellor, Mr T. Ross, the Minister of State for Scotland and Mr Denis Healey, the Minister of Defence.[1]

Ministers are removed from office because they have proved to be unsuitable for office or because, for some other reason, they must be 'sacrificed' in the interests of the Government. Some Prime Ministers are more drastic than others in the dismissing of members of the Government. Mr Macmillan dismissed no less than seven Ministers on a single occasion in 1962. Mr Wilson was sometimes accused of being too timid in not removing Ministers who were alleged to be manifestly unsuitable for office.

Strong and weak Ministers

A recent article by Bruce Headey provides an interesting analysis of what constitutes a strong Minister.[2] His findings are based on interviews with fifty Ministers or ex-Ministers supplemented by discussions with a number of senior civil servants and principal private secretaries. Mr Headey suggests that many Ministers who fail to leave their mark do so because they try to tackle all aspects of their job with equal assiduity. The

[1] B. Lapping, *The Labour Government, 1964–70* (Penguin, 1970), pp. 208–9.
[2] B. Headey, 'What Makes For a Strong Minister?', *New Society*, 8 October 1970.

strong Minister, on the other hand, concentrates on specific types of activity. He proposes three main types of strong Minister:

(i) the 'key-issues' Minister, who devotes his time and energy to formulating policy on basic issues;

(ii) the 'executive' Minister, who is good at getting decisions which have been agreed by his Department executed as government policy;

(iii) the 'ambassador' Minister, who is good at 'selling' his Department to outsiders.

A strong Minister, however, must be able to perform several roles fairly well because his effectiveness depends upon his overall reputation and credibility. Above all, it is suggested, he must be able to take decisions quickly, to win a fair share of the interdepartmental struggles and to stand up well to the rigours of the dispatch box in the House of Commons.

A Minister who allows himself to be swamped by the ceaseless flow of paper which reaches his office or who becomes merely the 'mouth-piece' of his senior civil servants is not likely to last long. The capacity to delegate successfully is an important one and Ministers who concentrate on central issues must leave to Ministers of State and Junior Ministers the more routine tasks of complaints, delegations, minor consultations and much routine committee work.

Most Ministers work long hours, and there is little doubt that political acumen, professional expertise and a clear conception of what needs to be done is greatly helped by the capacity for physical and mental endurance. It is virtually certain that more than one Minister has shortened his life by continued devotion to the exhausting tasks which are the lot of those who take major responsibility in contemporary government.

The Prime Minister

The Prime Minister is the central figure in British government. However measured, his personal prestige and political influence is great. It is he, more than any other individual, who shapes the direction of political change during the period that he holds office. His position as leader of the majority parliamentary party provides both the basis for his appointment as Prime Minister and reinforces his political power. The office which he holds carries with it the right of appointing and dismissing Ministers and gives him control of a whole series of patronage appointments. His right to arrange the Cabinet agenda and announce its decisions, together with his power in arranging the business of the House of Commons enable him to decide the priorities of government. The party 'Whips' are responsible to him; he controls the Civil Service and the Cabinet Office; and he may have a personal office which enables him to draw upon information and advice not available to other members of the Government. He has the responsibility of maintaining personal contact with the Sovereign and he meets Commonwealth Prime Ministers and Heads of foreign States face to face.

121

It is he who decides the timing of a general election, and through the mass media he is constantly in the public eye and he can make his views known to the country at large.

This is an impressive list of powers and responsibilities and it is this concentration of power which has given rise to views such as those of Mr Richard Crossman who, in an introduction to Bagehot's *The English Constitution*, has alleged that: 'The post war epoch has seen the final transformation of Cabinet Government into Prime Ministerial Government', and Mr Humphrey Berkeley who has suggested that the position of the Prime Minister in Britain today is immeasurably 'more potent than that of the American President'.[1]

This view of the Prime Minister's power has been challenged by a number of writers. Mr J. P. Mackintosh, for example, after examining the practical working of recent governments in his study *The British Cabinet* states: 'This is not Prime Ministerial Government because the Prime Minister can in exceptional circumstances be removed, and he will collapse if deserted by his colleagues and his party.' Mr G. W. Jones writes: 'A Prime Minister who can carry his colleagues with him can be in a very powerful position, but he is only as strong as they will let him be.'[2] Professor Anthony King suggests that most British writers really know little about the Presidency of the U.S.A. and that the tendency to compare the British Prime Minister with the American President is unhelpful. He quotes Mr Harry Truman as saying that 'the principal power that the President has is to bring people in and try to persuade them to do what they ought to be doing, without persuasion. That's what I spend most of my time doing. That's what the powers of a President amount to.'[3]

It is almost certainly true that the power of the Prime Minister is greater today than it was in the past, for the influence of the office has grown alongside the influence of government itself. It is doubtful, however, if he can be described as all powerful. Any Prime Minister, however outstanding, has only a limited amount of time and energy; moreover, he is not the only person with power in the Government or the party; there are others who have ideas and wills of their own. The Prime Minister can be regarded as being at the centre of a vortex of political forces with demands and pressures coming in from every side – from colleagues in the Government, Parliament, political parties, pressure groups, and other bodies. The extent to which he can conciliate and harness these pressures and super-impose on them his own policy and priorities will determine to a large extent the success or failure of his term in office.

In 1938, Professor Laski referred to the Prime Minister as being 'more than *primus inter pares* but less than an autocrat'. This description still applies but a realistic and meaningful assessment of the Prime Minister's

[1] H. Berkeley, *The Power of the Prime Minister* (Allen and Unwin, 1968).
[2] G. W. Jones 'The Prime Minister's Power' in Rose (ed.), *Policy Making in Britain*, p. 328.
[3] A. King (ed.), *The British Prime Minister* (Macmillan, 1969), pp. viii–xv.

power must be arrived at by considering not only his relationship to the Cabinet alone but his place in the structure of government as a whole.

The Role of the Monarchy

Britain is a constitutional monarchy; to quote the much used adage 'the Queen reigns, she does not rule'. In the historical development of our pattern of government the Monarchy has adapted itself to successive social and political changes in such a way that, although divested of its formerly extensive power, it still occupies an important place in the political system and in our national life.

The power of the Crown to act without consulting Parliament is referred to as the Royal Prerogative. In theory the scope of this prerogative is vast. The Queen appoints the Prime Minister and dissolves and summons Parliament; she opens and closes sessions of Parliament and the Royal Assent is required to complete the legislative process. Declarations of war, treaties with other countries and the granting of self-government to dependent territories are executed by the Crown. As the 'Fountain of Justice' the Queen appoints judges and dispenses mercy; criminal cases are conducted in her name. As the 'Fountain of Honour' she creates peerages and awards other titles and decorations. She appoints Bishops of the Church of England. The Queen is the Head of the Armed Forces and officers receive the Queen's commission; the nation's fighting ships are Her Majesty's ships. She is Head of the Commonwealth and is received by Heads of States in foreign countries. She has weekly meetings with the Prime Minister and is entitled to 'encourage, warn and advise' him on affairs of State.

In practice, of course, these powers are largely formal and decisions are made on the advice of the Prime Minister and other members of the Government. Thus, the Queen's Speech, although read by the Queen in person, is written by the Prime Minister. The prerogative of mercy is exercised on the advice of the Home Secretary. The arrangement whereby the actions of the Government are nominally done by the Queen has, from the point of view of the Government, considerable political advantages for it allows important decisions to be made without subjecting them to the glare of publicity which might well affect the outcome of negotiations. This practice, however, does not affect the matters from being raised afterwards in Parliament, where the Government must answer for its actions.

The Queen and the Royal Family also have a significant place within the wider political culture. The Queen's presence in the ceremony and pageantry associated with the great occasions of State reflects her role as the symbol of the continuity of government; she is, in a sense, the personal embodiment of the idea of the State. The crown and the robes exemplify the stability of our system of government. As Ian Gilmour observes: 'Modern societies still need myth and ritual. A Monarch and his family

123

supply it; there is no magic about a mud-stained politician.'[1]

The role of the Monarch in Britain presents a marked contrast to similar institutions in other Western countries. The remaining monarchies of Western Europe, for example, are much less august and royal than our own. In republics like Western Germany the Head of the State is an elected President; in the U.S.A. the political leader and the constitutional head are combined in the office of President. Each of these patterns have their advantages and disadvantages and they represent the outcome of historical and constitutional development in the countries concerned.

In modern Britain the division between pomp and power is clear-cut and relationships between the Queen and the Government proceed smoothly and without friction. There are, however, one or two areas of great political importance where the extent of the Royal prerogative is still unclear. These concern the Queen's functions in relation to the dissolution of Parliament and the appointment of the Prime Minister.

There is no longer any doubt that Parliament cannot be dissolved by the Queen contrary to the wishes of the Prime Minister. This question arose during the controversy over Irish Home Rule in 1913. At this time some Conservative leaders and distinguished constitutional lawyers, including A. V. Dicey and Sir William Anson, argued that the King should dissolve Parliament in order to allow the electorate to decide whether or not the measure to establish the Irish Free State should be proceeded with. King George V personally took the view that an election would be desirable and urged the Prime Minister, Mr Asquith, to request a dissolution. The Prime Minister declined and no election was held. The predominance of the Prime Minister in this matter was confirmed in 1918 when Mr Lloyd George, who wanted to continue the Coalition Government after the end of the war, requested King George V to dissolve Parliament. The King had strong reservations about this, but the Prime Minister's view prevailed and an election was held. The Sovereign retains the right to express an opinion on the wisdom or unwisdom of holding an election at a particular time but this can have no more than a persuasive influence on the Prime Minister's decision.

Appointing the Prime Minister
The extent of the prerogative in the appointment of a Prime Minister is now much clearer than was formerly the case but some doubts still remain. Where circumstances are 'normal' there is no problem. Both of the major parties now have a formal procedure for electing their leaders, and if the leader dies or resigns a fresh election is held. After a general election the Queen simply sends for the leader of the party winning the most seats. The Conservative Party did not adopt its present arrangements for selecting a leader until 1965 and the absence of a carefully defined procedure produced difficulties in 1957 and again in 1963 which, in the

[1] I. Gilmour, *The Body Politic* (Hutchinson, 1969), p. 313.

124

first case at least, involved the Queen in what some commentators allege to be dubious party manoeuvrings.

Sir Anthony Eden, because of ill-health, resigned as Prime Minister in 1957. It was widely forecast in the press that he would be succeeded by Mr R. A. Butler, who had acted as deputy for the Prime Minister in his absence. Mr Eden did not name his successor to the Queen and we have no knowledge of what other advice, if any, was given to her. The Queen consulted Sir Winston Churchill and Lord Salisbury, in their roles as elder statesmen of the Conservative Party, and they supported Mr Macmillan. The Chief Whip, Mr Heath, sounded opinion among back-benchers and reported on his findings. There appears to have been some substantial support for Mr Butler, and the choice clearly lay between these two. Sir Winston Churchill and Lord Salisbury asked Cabinet Ministers individually for their opinions and the Ministers appear to have been overwhelmingly in favour of Mr Macmillan. The Queen then appointed Mr Macmillan as Prime Minister.

In 1963, Mr Macmillan, who was ill, announced that he intended to resign. On this occasion there were a number of contenders for the leadership but Lord Hailsham and Mr R. A. Butler seemed to have the best prospects of being chosen. There was a period of considerable activity throughout the whole of the party but eventually Lord Home emerged from the 'processes of consultation' as the final choice. This decision was reported to rest on a kind of negative choice in that there were less objections to him than to alternative candidates. Mr Macmillan then nominated Lord Home.

In these cases a clear distinction must be made between the actions of the Sovereign and those of the political parties involved. It is constitutionally important for the Queen to maintain an attitude of strict impartiality between personalities and parties and to steer clear of involvement in the internal disagreements of any political party. Neither the 1957 nor the 1963 events would have occurred if there had been a straightforward method of electing Conservative leaders.

Difficulties may still arise in a situation where no one party has a clear majority in the House of Commons after an election or where a Government in office which is dependent upon the votes of a second party loses the confidence of the House. A serious case arose in 1931 when the minority Labour Government was dependent upon Liberal support. Britain was in the throes of a severe economic crisis and the Government was faced with the prospect of introducing cuts in unemployment benefits which would not be supported by Labour and Liberal M.P.s. According to the account given by Lord Morrison, the Prime Minister, Mr Ramsay MacDonald, assented to the Cabinet's view that the Government should resign and the King was notified accordingly.

The King, however, on the advice of Mr MacDonald brought into consultation Mr Stanley Baldwin, the Leader of the Conservative Party, and Sir Herbert Samuel, the acting Liberal Leader. Mr Lloyd George, the Leader of the Liberal Party, was ill and afterwards disagreed with his deputy's action. Sir Herbert Samuel suggested that Mr MacDonald should be invited to continue as Prime Minister of a National Government and Mr Baldwin agreed that he would co-operate in this. The King invited Mr MacDonald to form such a Government and his surprised colleagues were advised of this. The understanding reached with the King was that Parliament would be dissolved as soon as the economic crisis was over. Only a handful of Labour M.P.s supported the new Government and in the election which followed Labour representation in the Commons dropped from 288 seats to 52. Lord Morrison's view is that the King 'would have been wise to have ascertained what was likely to happen by inquiry of one or more Labour Privy Councillors'. He believes that the King 'received bad advice and that he himself made a mistake in accepting it'.[1]

It is difficult to foresee the future course of events but it is clear that the Sovereign may still have an important part to play in the British system of government. In the choice of Prime Minister and other important matters the Queen would be advised by her private secretary who is expected to be well versed in constitutional matters. In cases of uncertainty she would presumably consult appropriate senior members of the Privy Council who have held high government office.

The Privy Council
The Privy Council is the Queen's Council of State and all of its members are appointed by the Queen on the advice of the Prime Minister. There is no fixed number for its composition and its present membership of over 300 includes the Royal Family, the Archbishops of Canterbury and York, the Speaker of the House of Commons, all Cabinet Ministers and ex-Cabinet Ministers, the Lords of Appeal and retired High Court Judges; and a number of high ranking Ambassadors and prominent public figures from both Britain and the Commonwealth. Members are entitled to be addressed as the 'Right Honourable'.

The Privy Council meets as a body on the marriage or death of the Sovereign. All members must take an oath of secrecy; in the case of Cabinet members this extends to meetings of the Cabinet. The quorum is three and most of its work is done by a few Cabinet Ministers who meet in the Queen's presence.

Nowadays its functions are largely formal. The Privy Council is the channel through which various Crown appointments are made. It gives immediate effect to decisions of the Cabinet by issuing Proclamations or Orders-in-Council. Many Government Departments were originally established as Committees of the Privy Council: thus the present Department of Education evolved from the committee which was set up in 1839

[1] Morrison, *Government and Parliament*, pp. 91–4.

to supervise the money spent on public education. From time to time special committees are set up when this method is deemed to be more satisfactory than the use of the machinery of the House of Commons. For example, in 1957 a small committee was established for the purpose of inquiring into the tapping of telephones.

The Judicial Committee of the Privy Council forms part of the country's legal structure and functions quite separately from its other work. It is staffed by legal dignitaries and deals with appeals from Commonwealth Courts, Ecclesiastical Courts and the Disciplinary Committee of the General Medical Council.

The Privy Council provides another example of an institution which, throughout the course of history, has adapted itself to changing political circumstances. It continues to play a useful part in the machinery of government.

10   The House of Commons

The essential distinction between Government and Parliament must be emphasised. These two great institutions fulfil contrasting and complementary functions.

J. A. G. Griffith *The Commons in Transition*

If we assume that a Government is in being, what are the functions the House must perform? There is the ventilation of grievance. There is the extraction of information. There is the business of debate, with the attempt, through debate, to sustain public interest, and to educate it, in the significance of what is being done.

Harold J. Laski *Parliamentary Government in England*

The Supremacy of Parliament

The doctrine of the Sovereignty or Supremacy of Parliament asserts that Parliament (including the Queen, the Lords and the Commons) is the supreme law-making body. No other body can make regulations without its authority; it can repeal any existing laws, it can extend its own life and only in matters of interpretation can its authority be questioned by the Courts. No Act of Parliament, however, can limit the actions of future Parliaments. Erskine May states: 'The constitution has assigned no limits to the authority of Parliament over all matters and persons within its jurisdiction. A law may be unjust and contrary to sound principles of government; but Parliament is not controlled in its discretion, and when it errs, its errors can only be corrected by itself.'[1] Although Parliament can, in theory, legislate for any thing that is 'not naturally impossible' it is, in practice, limited by the values of its own members, to the connection between the Government and the party to which its members belong, and the activities of pressure groups and public opinion.

Functions

The functions of Parliament, and more particularly those of the House of Commons, have been variously described in a number of classical statements including those of Walter Bagehot (in *The English Constitution*), H. J. Laski (in *Parliamentary Government in England*), and Lord Eustace

---

[1] Sir T. Erskine May, *The Law, Privileges, Proceedings and Usages of Parliament*, 16th edn (Butterworth, 1964), p. 28.

Percy giving evidence before the Select Committee on Procedure, 1931. Basically, the functions of Parliament as a whole are those of making decisions on the government of the nation and criticising the way in which these decisions are administered. This involves decisions on the raising of money and the nature and level of public expenditure. It means that issues have to be debated, Ministers questioned and that statutes and regulations must be subjected to scrutiny. In the process of discharging these responsibilities the wider public, largely through the media of press and television, becomes aware of the actions and deficiencies of the machinery of government and of at least some of the activities of individuals and groups who seek to influence its decisions.

Remembering that the Government monopolises the legislative programme and that M.P.s are organised on a party basis, the main functions of the House of Commons can be listed as:

(i) supporting (or opposing) the Government;
(ii) maintaining a constant and searching criticism of the Government and governmental administration;
(iii) ventilating grievances;
(iv) making a major contribution to the legislative process;
(v) debating issues of major political importance;
(vi) raising taxation and authorising public expenditure.

In recent years some critics have spoken of the declining power of Parliament. While it is undoubtedly true that the political centre of gravity has moved more and more towards the Prime Minister and the Cabinet, the influence of the House of Commons on the process of government is considerable. When opposition to a particular measure is sufficiently widespread, it can affect substantial amendments or even cause them to be withdrawn. Parliament can also make or break a Minister by showing its appreciation of his experience and skill or by exposing his incompetence. This is what Professor Laski called 'the selective function of the House – by which is meant that subtle psychological process by which one member makes a reputation and another fails to make one, with its consequential repercussions on the personnel of Government'.[1]

Parliamentary privilege
In the ceremonial which forms part of the opening of every new Parliament the Speaker claims 'the ancient and undoubted rights and privileges of the Commons'. In the contemporary setting the most important privileges are:

(i) immunity from actions in the courts in respect of words spoken in the House;
(ii) the right to decide on its own constitution;
(iii) the right to regulate and control its own proceedings;
(iv) the right to uphold the dignity of Parliament;

[1] H. Laski, *Parliamentary Government in England* (Allen and Unwin, 1938), p. 144.

(v) power to punish both M.P.s and persons outside of the House for breach of privilege or contempt.

Erskine May summarises the position in the following terms: 'Parliamentary privilege is the sum of the peculiar rights enjoyed by each House collectively as a constituent part of the High Court of Parliament, and by members of each House individually, without which they could not discharge their functions, and which exceed those possessed by other bodies and individuals.'[1]

The 'ancient' privileges still formally requested include freedom from arrest, freedom of access to the Sovereign, and the favourable construction of its proceedings. The need for these arose in the early days of Parliament when deliberate attempts were made to interfere with the freedom of M.P.s and the activities of the House and Members needed to be protected from arbitrary arrest by the Sovereign. None of these has any practical significance today. The well-known Civil Rights M.P. from Northern Ireland, Miss Bernadette Devlin, was recently accused of offences arising from civil disturbances. She was convicted and served her prison sentence, returning to Westminster early in the autumn of 1970.

The House guards jealously those privileges which are necessary to ensure its effective functioning but is deeply conscious of the need to avoid giving the impression of retaining powers which are unnecessary or unjustifiable.

When a question is raised involving a possible breach of privilege it is the Speaker's function to rule as to whether or not there is a *prima facie* case. If he decides that there is, the matter is considered by a Committee of Privileges which is made up of M.P.s. An interesting case arose in 1965 involving Dr A. E. P. Duffy, a Labour M.P., who then represented Colne Valley. Dr Duffy, speaking at what he thought was a private meeting in his constituency, alleged that some Conservative M.P.s were 'half-drunk and disgusting to look at' during a censure debate in the House.

These remarks were reported in the press and Dr Duffy was subsequently found guilty of gross contempt of the House and a breach of its privileges. The Committee of Privileges recommended that in view of a letter sent to it by Dr Duffy, no further action be taken. In his letter, Dr Duffy said: 'I had no wish to impugn the reputation of Parliament. On the contrary, I was moved throughout, as I am now, by an anxiety to uphold its prestige and to this end I unreservedly withdraw any remarks which may be construed to the contrary.' In submitting its report to the House, the Committee quoted precedents involving similar cases. It stated: 'Words or writings reflecting on the House, and on members of the House, have constantly been punished upon the principle that such acts tend to obstruct the House in the performance of its duties by diminishing the respect due to it.' In 1947 a Labour M.P., Mr Garry Allighan, was punished by expulsion from the House after the Committee of Privileges had ruled

[1] Erskine May, *Parliament*, 16th edn, p. 42.

130

that articles which he had written, in which it was alleged that M.P.s had disclosed information from party meetings to newspapers, were injurious to the House.

The Speaker

The Speaker occupies a most important position in Parliament. He is Chairman of the House of Commons and acts as its representative in many public ceremonials. The Speaker has usually been chosen by inter-party agreement between Front Bench representatives, but there was a contest in 1951, and in 1970 vociferously expressed dissatisfaction with this arrangement after the retirement of Dr Horace King may well result in wider consultation in the future. Angry back-benchers forced an election by nominating Sir Geoffrey de Freitas as a rival to Mr Selwyn Lloyd, the Front Bench nominee. Sir Geoffrey was an unwilling candidate and Mr Selwyn Lloyd was elected by 294 votes to 55. The Speaker continues in office for the life of a Parliament but is normally re-elected if he wishes to continue. He receives a substantial salary and, on retirement, is awarded a pension and a peerage. On appointment, the Speaker, in effect, ceases to be party political because he has to serve the House as a whole. There was for some time a tradition that the Speaker's constituency was not contested at general elections but in recent years this has not always been observed. Parliament has not yet found a satisfactory way of dealing with the situation in which an elected member assumes this essentially non-partisan office.

The procession of M.P.s to the Chamber each day is led by the Speaker, who is prededed by the Sergeant-at-Arms bearing the Mace and followed by his Chaplain and his Secretary. Having arrived at the Chamber he presides over 'Prayers' before the official business begins. He discharges his duties as chairman without the aid of a bell or gavel and because he possesses an extensive knowledge of Standing Orders and the traditions and customs of the House which is respected by the Members, the proceedings are carried on without incident for the greater part of the time. It is his job to call upon M.P.s to speak; he must therefore know all Members and their special interests and be careful to see that minority groups and back-benchers are allowed a reasonable opportunity to contribute. Privy Councillors, however, are given precedence in debates.

Before major debates both Government and Opposition inform the Speaker which of their 'front-benchers' they wish to have called; other Members must 'catch the Speaker's eye' before they are allowed to speak. Back-benchers frequently find great difficulty in being called and some become so frustrated that they stop trying. One newly elected Member in the present Parliament waited hopefully for $5\frac{1}{2}$ hours to 'get in on' a major debate but in the end left the chamber with the speech still in his pocket.

The day to day business of the House is arranged between representatives of the party leaders with the co-operation of the Speaker; these

131

discussions are referred to as being conducted 'behind the Speaker's Chair'. The Speaker has extensive powers to deal with recalcitrant Members: refusal to comply with the Speaker's instructions in the conduct of debate can result in an order for the member to leave the Chamber; if a Member is 'named' for unruly behaviour it is customary for a Motion to be moved that the Member be suspended for a given period. In theory at least he also has the power to order the imprisonment of an M.P. or a member of the public who attempts to disrupt the proceedings of the House.

If the Speaker is absent from the House, the Clerk advises the House accordingly and the Chairman of Ways and Means or, in his absence, the Deputy Chairman of Ways and Means, takes the chair and is invested with all the Speaker's powers until the next meeting of the House.[1] The Speaker also nominates a panel of experienced M.P.s who act as Chairmen of Standing Committees.

The Speaker's duties include: giving decisions on whether or not to allow debates on matters of urgency; accepting or rejecting motions for the ending of debates; the certification of 'Money' bills; and acting as intermediary between M.P.s and the Sovereign in formally fulfilling the Members' right of access. It is his responsibility to bear in mind at all times the wellbeing of the House and its members.

The Speaker, along with other members, is advised by the Clerk of the House. The Sergeant-at-Arms, an official appointed by the Crown, attends him and enforces the orders of the House.

The Whips

All parties in the House of Commons, Conservative, Labour and Liberal alike, have a group of officials known as Whips who are responsible to the party Leader for ensuring that the work of the parliamentary party runs as smoothly as possible. They are appointed by the Leaders from among Members of the House belonging to their party. The term was first used by Edmund Burke in 1769 making an analogy with fox-hunting where 'whippers-in' rounded up hounds which had strayed from the pack.

Government Whips are paid by virtue of holding nominal offices. The Government Chief Whip is Parliamentary Secretary to the Treasury and his deputy and assistants are junior Lords of the Treasury. Since 1965, Opposition Chief Whips in both the Commons and the Lords have received payment for their services. Although the Government Chief Whip is not a member of the Government, the importance of his position is signified by the fact that he sits on the right of Ministers on the Front Bench. Many prominent Ministers have previously served their party in this role; the present Prime Minister, Mr Heath, was for a time Conservative Chief Whip.

[1] Although the Committee of Ways and Means was abolished in 1967 (see ch. 12), the offices of Chairman and Deputy Chairman of Ways and Means still exist. See, e.g. List of Principal Officers and Officials of House of Commons for 12 July 1971.

The Whips from each party work together in arranging the business of the House in accordance with the wishes of the party leaders. There is a great deal of 'give and take' in settling the details; these and other procedural matters are spoken of as being arranged 'through the usual channels'. When the 'usual channels' break down, they break down with a vengeance, as was the case in the consideration of the Industrial Relations Bill in the Spring of 1971 when every clause was resisted by the Labour Party, resulting in all-night sittings and endless divisions.

The Whips act as intermediaries between the Leader and back-benchers, their job in this respect being to see that the Leader is aware of the feelings and reactions of M.P.s, in turn advising them on the Leader's wishes and problems. They are in a unique position to assess a Member's worth and promise and see that claims to preferment are not overlooked. When Government majorities are small they undertake responsibility for 'pairing' Members who wish to be absent from the House to ensure that the relative voting strengths remain unaltered. They nominate M.P.s to Committees and to some extent can arrange for Members who so wish to 'catch the Speaker's eye' in certain debates. Members, therefore, make their wishes known to the Whips.

The Whips send out weekly to Members a memorandum outlining the business to be considered in the following week. This indicates by a system of underlining the importance attached to a particular debate: a 'three-line' whip means that a division is likely and attendance is essential; a 'two-line' implies the matter is important but not vital; one-line indicates that attendance, as always, is desirable but no fuss will be made if the Member is absent. The Whips have the responsibility of ensuring that there is always a quorum in the House and that, in divisions, the maximum vote is registered in support of their party's point of view.

On many, if not most matters, things run smoothly but occasionally an individual M.P. or a group of Members refuse to comply with the Whip's instructions. When this occurs the Member is 'disciplined' and in the last resort the Whip is 'withdrawn', either for a short period or indefinitely. The latter circumstance is most serious because it could well result in the termination of a political career. Members, therefore, do not lightly refuse to comply with the Whip's requests.

The degree of discipline exercised by the Whips varies in accordance with different parliamentary circumstances and sometimes according to the policy of the person holding office as Chief Whip. Thus a Government with a large majority, as the Labour Government had in 1945, can afford to be more lenient than a Government with a small majority such as Labour had in 1950–1 and 1964–6. In a survey of M.P.s carried out by *The Observer* in 1963, 81 per cent of Conservatives and 70 per cent of Labour M.P.s who answered the questions took the view that party discipline in the House was 'just about right'.

The Whips' job is a difficult but important one because the efficient working of the House and the morale of M.P.s rests to a great extent upon their faithfulness and skill. The Whips are sometimes seen as the embodiment of a rigid party orthodoxy which has stifled individuality in Parliament, but they are in the main hard-working M.P.s who are doing their best to give effect to the policies which their respective parties are trying to pursue.

The Chamber

The Chamber of the House of Commons, which was destroyed by enemy action on 10 May 1941, was described by Dr Eric Taylor as having 'a cosy appearance which was enhanced by the deep overhanging galleries all around the room, and by the fact that all the available floor space was packed with seating of the traditional pew-like variety. It was essentially a chamber which lent itself to close debate, repartee, intervention, rejoinder, rather than sounding rhetoric.'[1]

The new House was designed to preserve all the 'essential features' of the old. The old chamber provided seats for 346 of the membership of 615 in 1941, the new chamber has seating accommodation (including the side galleries) for 437. The number of Members is currently 630 and this will be again increased to 635 when the proposals of the Boundary Commission come into effect at the next general election. This restriction on seating capacity is deliberate. As the House of Commons *Guide to visitors* puts it: 'the House is not a forum for set orations; its debates are largely conversational in character; and for many of them – highly specialised in theme, or of a routine nature – few Members are present, being engaged on other Parliamentary duties in the Palace of Westminster. Thus, a small and intimate Chamber is more convenient. Conversely, on great occasions, when the House is full and Members have to sit in the gangways, or cluster round the Speaker's Chair, at the Bar and in the side galleries, the drama of Parliament is enhanced, and there is, as Sir Winston Churchill once put it, "a sense of crowd and urgency".'

Most members of the public do not appreciate the vast amount of time spent by M.P.s in both formal and informal activity directly connected with their parliamentary duties. When not in the Chamber they may be engaged in party meetings, standing committees, study groups, or meeting experts, dignitaries or visitors. As one M.P. put it to the present writer: 'It is possible to have a long and busy day without ever going into the Chamber.' At weekends and in the recesses M.P.s are expected to be available for political and public engagements in their constituencies.

When the House is in session the Speaker sits at the head of the Chamber and below him is the Table of the House at which sit three Clerks. On opposite sides of the table are two despatch boxes and at the end rests the Mace, the symbol of Royal authority. At the other end of the Chamber the Sergeant-at-Arms sits, wearing the traditional Sword. On the Speaker's

[1] E. Taylor, *The House of Commons at Work* (Penguin, 1970), pp. 13–14.

right is the Government Front Bench (or Treasury Bench) and on his left
the Opposition Front Bench. Front Bench members have the privilege of
using the despatch boxes when addressing the House. The Galleries above
the Chamber provide some accommodation for visitors. (See figure 4.)

Voting is often done simply by acclamation (i.e. expressions for or

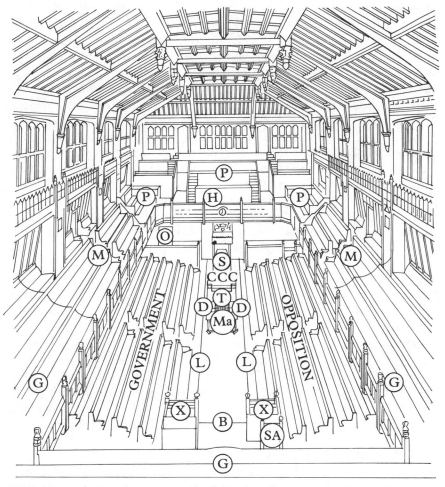

Figure 4. Chamber of the House of Commons
Source: *A Guide for visitors to the House of Commons*

KEY: S—Mr Speaker. P—Press Galleries. H—*Hansard* Reporters. O—Govern-
ment Officials' Box. C—Clerks of the House (when the House goes into Committee,
Mr Speaker leaves the Chair, and the Chairman sits in the chair of the Clerk of the
House, which is the one on the left). T—Table of the House. D—Despatch Boxes.
Ma—Mace (when the House goes into Committee, the Mace is put 'below the
Table' on hooks). L—Lines over which Members may not step when speaking from
the Front Benches. B—Bar of the House. X—Cross Benches. SA—Sergeant-at-
Arms. M—Members' Galleries. G—Public Galleries.

against a particular proposal are given verbally). When, however, a division is called for M.P.s 'divide' by giving their votes to a 'teller' in the appropriate Lobbies – the 'Ayes' going to one lobby, the 'Noes' to another. This method of voting frequently comes under criticism as being time-wasting and archaic.

Members' conditions

Facilities for Members are woefully inadequate and progress in making improvements is extremely slow. Until quite recently most M.P.s worked under incredibly uncomfortable conditions but now all or most who wish to have the facility have a desk somewhere in the vicinity of the House and access to a shared telephone. Until recently no financial allowance was made for secretarial assistance but the Select Committee on House of Commons Services, in its Sixth Report of the 1968–9 session, recommended that 'provision should be made at public expense for secretarial assistance or an allowance to meet the cost of up to a maximum of one full-time secretary per member'; in December 1969, it was announced that M.P.s would be able to claim an allowance for secretarial assistance of up to £500 a year. The Select Committee also recommended that M.P.s should be allowed free trunk calls, and that they should be allowed to send all letters on public business free. In a speech made in 1971, Mr William Whitelaw, the Leader of the House, said that M.P.s today worked harder, were at Westminster for longer hours, and had fewer outside resources than their predecessors; he also added: 'I have to admit that the House of Commons is a daunting place for any of those who seek to make any changes whatsoever.'

It has been remarked that British M.P.s have the worst conditions of any legislature in the Western world; certainly they compare unfavourably with American Congressmen and with the Members of the Federal Parliament in West Germany. The style of the buildings and the spaciousness of the public rooms are doubtless appreciated by Members but they offer small compensation for working conditions which appear sometimes to make the effective discharge of their duties very difficult indeed.

M.P.s and Ministers' salaries

M.P.s were first paid in 1912 when all members not in receipt of salaries as Ministers or officers of the House were awarded a salary of £400 per annum. In 1924 they were allowed free rail travel between London and their constituencies and in 1946 this was extended to cover travel between M.P.s' homes and Westminster. In 1937 the amount paid in annual salary was raised to £600, in 1946 to £1000 and in 1964 to £3250.

The first comprehensive pensions scheme for M.P.s and dependents was introduced in 1965. At present, members pay £150 per year into the fund and the Exchequer contributes a similar amount. Members who have served in the House for ten years or more receive a pension of £600 at the

136

age of 65 or on ceasing to be an M.P., if they retire later than this. The amount paid increases to £900 after fifteen years and by £24 per year in Parliament beyond this. These pensions are kept under review and are increased from time to time.

The Prime Minister receives £14 000 a year, the Lord Chancellor, as chief law officer, £14 500 (i.e. £500 more than the Prime Minister). Ministers in charge of departments receive £8500 per annum; Ministers of State between £5625 and £7625; Parliamentary Secretaries and Under Secretaries of State get £3750 and Private Parliamentary Secretaries are unpaid. The Speaker's salary is £8500 per annum.[1]

At the end of November 1970, a scheme to avoid the embarassment which is caused to M.P.s in requesting increases in their own pay was published by Mr Douglas Houghton, the chairman of the Parliamentary Labour Party, in his Private Member's Bill. The Bill was backed by Mr John Silkin, a former Chief Whip in the Wilson Government, Mr Robin Turton (Conservative) who is Father of the House, and Mr Geoffrey Lloyd (Conservative) who entered the House of Commons in 1931. Mr Houghton proposed the establishment of a review body of between five and seven members, none of whom shall be a member of either House. It was proposed that they should be appointed by the Prime Minister after consultation with the Leader of the Opposition. The new body would keep under review the salaries, allowances, expenses, and pensions of M.P.s and such other conditions of M.P.s' service as the review body thinks fit. Provision was made for the Prime Minister to refer any of these matters to the review body and must report any such reference to the Commons.

The review body would have to act on the principles of
(i) *Service*: Payments offered to M.P.s should not be so high 'as to include any element of luxurious living' but should recognise that parliamentary service 'calls for and should be willingly accorded a measure of personal sacrifice'.
(ii) *Pay*: It should not be so low as to deter people for financial reasons from entering or remaining in the House, and should allow the man with no external means 'to discharge the proper expenses of conscientious and efficient membership of that House, and to live at a level consistent with the dignity of the service'.
(iii) *Reports*: The review body would have to report at intervals of not more than two years, and the reports would have to be published and laid before both Houses of Parliament.

The support for this measure brought a swift response from the Government and on 4 December 1970, Mr William Whitelaw, the Leader of the House of Commons, announced that the Government would set up an independent review body which would look at parliamentary pay, allowances, expenses and pensions, once in the course of each Parliament. This body will also deal with the payment of members of the boards of

[1] These scales were substantially increased in December 1971.

nationalised industries, the judiciary, and other senior appointments which are made by the Government.

Custom and tradition

In the procedure of the House a considerable number of ancient customs and traditions are adhered to, even though many of these have nowadays little or no practical utility. Some Members, perhaps the majority, prefer to retain these customs because, they claim, they provide part of the colourful and impressive pageantry of Parliament which symbolises its long history and gives reminders of the successful outcome of its battles with the Crown. They believe that the ceremonial characteristic of the British Parliament is inextricably interwoven with the continuity and stability of our system of government. Other Members and observers have no patience with what they regard as so much 'mumbo-jumbo' and suggest that it would be much better to have modern buildings, a streamlined procedure and up-to-date facilities for both M.P.s and servants of the House. This, in their view, would enhance the efficiency of Parliament and improve the quality of much of the work which it undertakes. A few of these traditions and customs are now outlined.

While in the Chamber, M.P.s must refer to their colleagues not by name but as the Honourable Member for a named constituency. If the Member referred to is a former serving officer in the armed forces, he must be referred to as the Honourable and Gallant Member for —; Queen's Counsel are addressed as Honourable and Learned Members. The argument used for the retention of this practice is that the need to identify the Member being addressed necessitates a pause which will allow a cooling of temper should this be necessary whereas the use of mere names would not. When a 'point of order' is raised during a division this is done by an M.P. placing a top hat on his head. As few M.P.s nowadays wear top hats, a few collapsible versions of this headgear are placed at strategic points in the chamber. When an M.P. is speaking from the floor of the House in the space between the Front Benches he must not put his foot over the red line in the carpet, for to do so immediately raises shouts of 'Order! Order!' The reason is that in former days M.P.s carried swords and when words failed to persuade there was a tendency to use more forceful methods. The lines were inserted to lay down limits of physical proximity between the opposing groups.

When the House adjourns, usually after the adjournment debate at 10.30 p.m., cries of 'Who goes home?' resound through the lobbies. This dates from the time when it was advisable for M.P.s to return to their residences in groups in order to avoid the attention of foot-pads lying in wait in the dark London streets, and suitable parties were organised before setting off. Before the House goes into one of its rare secret sessions, cries of 'Mr Speaker, I spy strangers' are uttered and the public galleries are then cleared to leave only M.P.s and officials in occupation of the Chamber.

138

The Speaker, before taking office, makes a show of reluctance to assume the chair and Members go through the motions of dragging him there. This is done to remind Members and onlookers of the days when to take this job was much less attractive than it is today. The House of Lords is referred to as 'another place' and when the Royal Assent is being given to a Bill, the Gentleman Usher of the Black Rod summons M.P.s to the House of Lords. When all are assembled the Royal Assent is given in Norman French with the words 'La Reyne le veult' (The Queen wishes it). A financial Bill is assented to with 'La Reyne remercie ses bons sujets, accepte leur benevolence et ainsi le veult.' (The Queen thanks her good subjects, accepts their benevolence and thus wishes it.)

When an M.P. wishes to terminate his association with the House, he does not resign in the ordinary way but has to apply for the office of Steward or Bailiff of Her Majesty's Chiltern Hundreds, or of the Manor of Northstead. These are fictitious 'offices of profit under the Crown' acceptance of which automatically disqualifies the holder from membership of the House of Commons.

Length of sessions

It is customary to speak of *a* Parliament lasting for the duration of time between one general election and the next, e.g. we can speak of the 1945–50 Parliament. The life of Parliament is, under the terms of the Parliament Act, 1911, limited to five years, but the actual time is shorter than this. Parliament can, in exceptional circumstances, pass special legislation to extend its own life; thus the Parliament elected in 1935, because of the Second World War, lasted until 1945. Each Parliament organises its business in yearly sessions, normally running from October to October, which end in *prorogation*. Business not completed in one session cannot be carried over into another. Parliament *adjourns* for the recesses at Christmas, Easter, Whitsun and Summer. The Summer recess runs from late July or early August until October when Parliament reassembles for a few days until it is prorogued; each session normally lasts for between 160 and 170 days.

A new session opens with the Queen's Speech, which is read by the Queen herself from the Throne in the House of Lords, or, when she is unable to be present, by the Lord Chancellor. M.P.s are ceremonially summoned by Black Rod to the Bar of the House of Lords to hear the Speech and then they return to the Commons to debate its proposals. The Queen's Speech is composed by the Government and it sets out its programme for the forthcoming session.

Programme

Since 1945, the normal hours for sitting have been 2.30 p.m. until 10.30 p.m. on Mondays to Thursdays, and from 11 a.m. to 4.30 p.m. on Fridays, although the House frequently suspends Standing Orders and sits much later than this. In each session of the 1955–9 Parliament the average length of the sitting in each of the four sessions was less than 8 hours. In the 1959–64 Parliament the average for each of the five sessions was between 8 and 8½ hours. In the 1966–7 session arrangements were made on an experimental basis for morning sittings to be held from 10 a.m. to 1 p.m. on Monday and Wednesday mornings with the afternoon meetings ending at 10 p.m. on each day from Monday to Thursday. The average length of the day for that session was 9 hours 50 minutes. The morning sessions, which began in December 1966, were discontinued in October 1967. The total time available for the House is frequently criticised by some Members, who suggest that Parliament could without undue inconvenience meet for an additional fifty days or so in each Session.

Although regular consultations between Government and Opposition are held and much is done to meet each other's requests in relation to the issues to be discussed, the final determination of the timetable rests with the Government. About half of the total time available is taken up with Government legislation but the Opposition are allowed 29 days in each session during which the topics to be debated are initiated by them and not by the Government. These were styled officially as Supply Days when the Opposition was, in theory, criticising the Government's financial Estimates, but, in practice, they were used to initiate a debate on any subject which the Opposition wished to raise. Opposition Days, which are still referred to by M.P.s as supply days, can now be taken in half-days if desired, and spread throughout the whole of the session. Sixteen Fridays in each session are devoted to Private Members' Bills and four to Private Members' Motions. Occasional half-days are also allocated for this purpose.

On Mondays to Thursdays the daily timetable normally follows the following pattern:

2.30 Prayers. (Conducted by the Speaker's Chaplain.)[1]

2.35 Private Business after Prayers. (This includes matters which can be disposed of quickly, e.g. motions for writs for by-elections, unopposed Private Bills, the presentation of petitions.)

2.45 Questions for Oral Answer.

3.30 Miscellaneous Matters. (This again is devoted to business which can be disposed of quickly, e.g. introduction of new Members, Ministerial Statements, questions of privilege, personal statements by M.P.s, requests to raise matters of 'urgent public importance'.) At the Commencement of Public Business. (Matters considered under this heading include the presentation of Public Bills for formal first reading, Government Motions relating to the arrangement of

---

[1] The Second Report from the Select Committee on Procedure for the Session 1969–70 recommended that, in order to allow more time for questions, the House should meet at 2.20 p.m. instead of 2.30 p.m. on Monday to Thursday. This proposal has not been implemented.

140

business), and (on Tuesdays and Wednesdays only) Motions for leave to bring in a Bill under the 'Ten Minute' Rule.

3.45 Orders of the Day. (This, in effect, is the agenda for the main business of the day which includes debates on legislation and other motions.)

7.30 Possible interruption of public business to deal with 'prayers' against statutory instruments.

10.00 Debate on the Adjournment. (The Motion 'That this House do now adjourn' is used to provide M.P.s with an opportunity to raise grievances and to make criticisms of the Government. On one day per week the topics to be discussed are chosen by the Speaker from a list submitted by Members, otherwise topics are initiated by M.P.s who have been successful in a fortnightly ballot. The procedure normally is that the M.P. concerned makes a short speech which is replied by the appropriate junior Minister.)

10.30 House adjourns.

An Order Paper is prepared for each day which sets out the business to be considered. It includes the text of all questions to be asked, a list of Bills and Motions to be considered (see appendix III).

The proceedings are conducted in accordance with Standing Orders, and 'the practice of the House', which is the description used to refer to the conventions and traditions which have been built up over a long period. Erskine May's *Law, Privilege, Proceedings and Usage of Parliament*, which is regularly revised by the Clerk of the House, provides the recognised authorative work in this field. The official record of proceedings, which includes a verbatim record of all contributions and details of all decisions reached, is published daily in *Hansard*. All M.P.s are entitled to a free copy.

Her Majesty's Opposition

It is open to all M.P.s not in the Government to contribute to the critical function of Parliament but it is in the nature of our political system that the discharge of this role will be systematically organised by the Opposition. The importance of the existence of a cohesive opposition was legally recognised in the Ministers of the Crown Act, 1937, which provided for the payment of a salary, in excess of the basic M.P.'s salary, to the Leader of Her Majesty's Opposition. The Act defines the Leader of the Opposition as 'that Member of the House of Commons who is for the time being leader of the party in opposition to Her Majesty's Government having the greatest numerical strength in the House'.

Because Parliament is the arena for a struggle between two main groups competing for the electorate, the Opposition is, in effect, offering itself as an alternative Government and this means that its activities have to be constructive and not merely obstructive. During the Debate on the Queen's Speech at the first Session of Parliament following the general election,

141

1970, Mr Wilson said: '...Her Majesty's Opposition will not be tempted to censure and negative opposition for opposition's sake. That is not good for Parliament. It is not good for democracy. Opposition, no less than Government, must follow a theme consistent, comprehensive, based on priorities, and subject to a single unifying approach, bringing together every aspect of government, foreign affairs, defence, financial, economic, social, industrial policies. We shall wait for each new development of policy, wait watchfully and keenly, but we shall not rush into condemnation for the sake of it.' During the 1964–6 Parliament when the Conservative Party was in opposition, Sir Edward (now Lord) Boyle, writing in *The Observer* suggested that – 'effective Opposition activity must be reasonably sustained and consistent...fitful opposition is always weak opposition, and strong action by the Opposition Front Bench will never impress if it seems to arise, not spontaneously, but from the result of back-bench insistence'.

There is between the parties an underlying consensus of the role of Parliament and the place of the Opposition within it. The practice of consulting on the timetable has already been mentioned, and in addition to the Opposition Days and the right to choose the subjects to be debated in the reply to the Address from the Throne, facilities are provided for Votes of Censure. It is customary for the Chairmanship of the important Public Accounts Committee to be given to an Opposition Member and Opposition M.P.s are represented on all Committees in proportion to their strength in the House.

In these and other aspects there is co-operation as well as conflict. In a limited number of matters, e.g. royal marriages, some aspects of defence and foreign relations, the Prime Minister will as a matter of courtesy keep the Leader of the Opposition informed or he may occasionally consult him before taking action. At times of extreme difficulty, e.g. in war or crisis, when an indication of national unity is important, the Opposition may publicly identify itself with the actions of the Government as was done when Ian Smith unilaterally declared the independence of Rhodesia in 1965.

Parliamentary Questions

Question Time is the occasion when the back-bencher has an opportunity of publicly taking part in the work of Parliament. Question Time comes virtually at the beginning of the day's business when the Chamber is fuller than it is normally likely to be for the rest of the day; press reporters are in full attendance and reports appear either in the evening papers or on the following day. It provides one of the few occasions when M.P.s are free of the Whips. Questions are not asked by M.P.s in the Government and the Leader and Deputy Leader of the Opposition seldom submit this type of question.

Erskine May lays down that: 'Questions addressed to Ministers should relate to public affairs with which they are officially connected, to proceedings in Parliament, or to matters of administration for which they are responsible.' Each Member can put down only two questions each day for oral answer, these being 'starred' on the Order Paper, but the number for *written* answers is unlimited; written answers also appear in Hansard. At least two days notice must be given, e.g. an M.P. must hand his question into the Table Office before 2.30 p.m. on Tuesday if he wishes it to appear on the Order Paper on Thursday.

To quote this rule, however, may give a false impression as to the speed with which a starred question can be answered. Only the Prime Minister has regular weekly times, his ques   ns being at 3.15 p.m. on Tuesdays and Thursdays. Questions for other Ministers are grouped by reference to the Departments for which they are responsible and they answer questions addressed to them on a rota system; an Order of Questions is published at about monthly intervals giving the order in which Ministers will answer questions on given days. Thus, on one day the Home Secretary, say, will be first in the Ministers down to answer questions; he is not down to answer again until 7 or 8 days later when he is fourth in the answering order and he will not be first in order until a lapse of another three to four weeks. All of this becomes important when it is realised that 150 or more questions for oral answer may be put down on any one day and of these there is only time to answer between 35 and 45.

The number of starred questions varies from day to day or from session to session but the average since the end of the war is about a hundred. If a member's question is not reached, a written answer is given unless he demands an oral answer, in which case the question must be re-submitted.

All the questions are printed in full on the Order Paper and when a particular question is reached the Speaker announces the name of the Member who is to ask the question, and the Member simply says 'Number 21, Sir', or whatever the number of the question is, and the Minister gives his answer. The M.P. concerned must ask his question personally and if he is not in the Chamber the question falls. A limited number of 'Supplementary' questions may be asked at the Speaker's discretion. These are frequently designed to embarass the Minister and in the cut and thrust which follows the manifestation of quick thinking and parliamentary skill, or the absence of these qualities, enhances or depresses the parliamentary reputation of those involved.

The Minister, however, comes to the House well-armed. The majority of questions are designed to probe into governmental policy and administration, and it is the job of the Civil Service to furnish all necessary information. A file is prepared on each question which will contain all relevant facts and a draft answer; it may also contain notes on the questioner and hazard guesses as to likely supplementary questions. There is no doubt that parliamentary questions cause Ministers to give personal consideration to the issues raised.

In recent years M.P.s have made much more use of Questions put down for written answer. At least part of the reason for this is the difficulty which Members experience in having 'starred' questions answered within a reasonable time. It is perhaps not generally appreciated that the bulk of starred questions are asked by a minority of Members. The Fifth Report of the Select Committee on Procedure for the 1966–7 Session shows that seventeen Members submitted nearly a quarter of all the questions put down and more than half of the questions were received from seventy Members.

Questions may be asked for a variety of reasons. An M.P. may have been dissatisfied with replies to letters to a Minister on a constituency matter and therefore wishes to press him publicly; others may be making individual or concerted efforts to harry the Government. Some Members may simply be seeking information which they cannot otherwise obtain and others, it must be admitted, are more concerned with the publicity received in the weekly papers in their constituency than with the actual issue raised. Question time may also be used by the Government to make an announcement on a minor policy matter (e.g. testing of motor vehicles) or to give publicity to something it has done which might otherwise pass unnoticed. Like other aspects of Parliamentary life it has both serious and less serious aspects. Sometimes there is a determined probe designed to remedy a genuine grievance or problem. Sometimes it is just an elaborate exercise in point scoring. Serious questions are taken seriously and there is no doubt that Question Time is one of the major forces which helps to keep Ministers on their toes in an effort to ensure that when the activities of their Departments are exposed to public view, they are seen in the most favourable possible light.

It was once said, one hopes not entirely seriously, that the ideal answer to a parliamentary question is 'brief, appears to answer the question completely, if challenged can be proved to be accurate in every word, gives no opening for awkward "supplementaries", and really discloses nothing'.[1] In December 1965, a Conservative Member, Mr P. Blaker, asked the Prime Minister if a speech about European unity made by the Foreign Secretary, Mr Michael Stewart, represented the policy of the Government. Mr Wilson replied 'Yes'. He was then asked a supplementary question to which he replied: 'Entry into the E.E.C. is not open to us in existing circumstances and no question of fresh negotiations can arise at present. We shall work with our E.F.T.A. partners through the Council of Europe, and through W.E.U., for the closest possible relations with the Six consistent with our Commonwealth ties.' No further questions were asked on this by Conservative M.P.s because, although Mr Wilson had not said so, the reply he had given was a direct quotation from the Conservative election manifesto of 1964 and the Conservative questioners were doubtless well aware of this.

[1] Quoted in J. Harvey and L. Bather, *The British Constitution* (Macmillan, 1964), p. 127.

144

Legislation

All proposals for legislation must be put into the form of a Bill, the drafting normally done by Parliamentary Counsel. Before it becomes law, a Bill must be approved by both the House of Commons and, subject to the provisions of the Parliament Acts of 1911 and 1949, the House of Lords, and receive the Royal Assent. The last requirement is nowadays purely formal.

Bills fall into three main classes:

(1) PUBLIC BILLS

These are Bills which affect the whole community and they are normally introduced by the Government as a result of election pledges, successful pressure by outside organisations, Reports of Royal Commissions, Select Committees, the needs of Government Departments, etc., or to deal with some important matter requiring Government regulation. Some Bills must be introduced by the Government annually as part of the ongoing process of government as, for instance, in the case of the Finance Bill and the Consolidated Fund Bill. Public Bills may, however, also be introduced by Private Members but whereas most Government Bills pass into law, very few Private Members' Bills do.

(2) PRIVATE BILLS

These differ from Public Bills in that they affect a section of the community only and not the public as a whole. They deal with personal matters, special groups of people, or the concerns of a particular locality or undertaking. These again may be introduced as Private Member's Bills. Included in this category also are Provisional Order Confirmation Bills which are introduced by the Government to delegate certain powers to local authorities to grant the use of land for various purposes.

(3) HYBRID BILLS

These are brought in as Public Bills but they have the characteristics of Private Bills in that they principally affect a particular section of the community. Thus, the Bank of England Bill introduced by the Labour Government in 1946 to bring about government control of the Bank affected the interests of the then shareholders in the Bank.

Bills may originate in either House but in practice all controversial Bills originate in the Commons. The speed at which a Bill can pass through the various stages of consideration varies. Standing Orders in both Houses regulate the general pattern but these can, if considered necessary, be suspended. The time taken also depends on such factors as the length and complexity of the Bill, the extent to which its proposals are opposed by the Opposition and Government back-benchers, etc. The procedure for Private Bills, Hybrid Bills and Provisional Order Confirmation Order Bills, although the same in principle, differs from that for Public Bills. The details which follow relate only to Public Bills introduced by the Government.

Much activity takes place long before a Bill is formally presented in the

145

House of Commons. The practice varies in accordance with the objects of the intended legislation, but nowadays a large number of them will require consultation with outside interests. Thus before a Bill dealing with industrial relations is introduced there will be consultations and negotiations with employers organisations and the trade unions. A Bill to introduce changes in the educational system would necessitate discussions with Local Authority Associations and teachers' unions. A 'White Paper' may be published setting out the Government's general intentions; thus, before the Bill to appoint a Parliamentary Commissioner for Administrations with employers' organisations and the trade unions. A Bill to intro-2767) which explained the reasons for this decision and the role which the Government visualised the Commissioner would play in our system of government. Sometimes a 'Green Paper' which sets out *alternative* possibilities is issued. When the Bill is finally prepared it is substantially in the form which the Government hopes will be approved. Because the Government commands a majority in the House and can, if necessary, use a three-line Whip to ensure the support of M.P.s in the Government Party, the most that M.P.s can normally hope to do is to amend the details. This, however, is not invariably the case because Bills are sometimes withdrawn as was the case with the Peerage and Industrial Relations Bills introduced by the Labour Government in the 1966–70 Parliament. Sometimes a bill may be drastically altered as in the case of the Race Relations Bill, 1965.[1]

The process of legislation proper begins with the First Reading. This is a pure formality designed, as it were, to put the Bill 'on the stocks', the stage formerly employed of requesting leave to introduce a Bill having now been dispensed with. The major debate on principles takes place at the Second Reading. This stage is usually taken on the floor of the House but this is not always the case. Thus, unless ten Members object, Scottish Bills go before the Scottish Standing Committee, and now any Government Bill can be sent to a Standing Committee for the second reading if the Minister responsible for the Bill so desires and less than twenty Members object. The Committee Stage follows when the Bill is taken clause by clause. Amendments may be made either by the Government itself or by other Members; all amendments must be approved by the majority of the Committee. This is followed by the Report stage when the Bill is formally reported to the House. Here again amendments may be moved. The Third Reading is then taken; until recently the practice was that the Bill as a whole (as amended) was again discussed but no further amendments could be made; but since November 1967 the Third Reading is now ordinarily taken without debate.

At the same time provision was made for certain second readings to be taken in Committee and for the Report Stage to be similarly dealt with and it is now therefore possible for a Bill to go through all the stages without

[1] See K. Hindell, 'The Genesis of Race Relations Bill' in Rose (ed.), *Policy Making in Britain.*

ever appearing on the floor of the House. The Bill finally goes to the House of Lords where a similar procedure is followed. If it is approved in the Lords then it receives the Royal Assent. It then becomes an Act of Parliament and forms part of statute law.

Each of these stages is formally represented as having a definite purpose viz: first reading – announcement; second reading – examination of principles; Committee and Report – amendment; third reading – final debate; but it must be said that the practice is rather different to the theory and the actual procedures are not always so tidy. Thus the clause by clause examination at the Committee stage allows a reiteration of the justification and objections heard in the second reading[1]; the Report stage has sometimes given rise to a regurgitation of the Committee stage with the same Members who took part in the earlier stage speaking again.[2]

Because of the enormous pressure of legislation and the rule that all the stages of legislation must be completed in the session in which it is initiated, the Government has to take steps to curtail discussion which, in some cases, would otherwise be carried on indefinitely. The procedures used for the curtailment of discussions are various. Firstly there is the routine 'closure'. Under Standing Order No. 29, it is open to any Member to move 'that the question now be put'. If the Speaker allows the motion a vote is taken immediately and if it is carried the debate ends. The motion is normally, in practice, moved by the Government Chief Whip. In Committee, methods referred to as the 'guillotine' and the 'kangaroo' are employed. The effect of the guillotine is to cut off debate at a time fixed in advance; clauses which have not been discussed by that time are put to the vote without discussion. When the kangaroo is used a number of clauses are 'jumped over', only selected clauses which are regarded as the most important being discussed and the rest are voted on without discussion.

The partial streamlining of the legislative process, brought about by the changes introduced in 1967, were part of a kind of *quid pro quo* agreement between the Government and the Opposition. The Government's concern was to speed up the passage of important legislation and it wanted the House to approve the simplification of the various stages of the passage of Bills as outlined above, the introduction of morning sittings and the use of the guillotine after two hours of debate. These were agreed to in exchange for concessions which would be helpful to the Opposition and back-benchers in general. These included a greater flexibility in the use of 'Supply' days, amendment of Standing Order No. 9 to allow debates on 'matters of urgency' more readily, and a widening of the Statutory Instruments Committee's terms of reference. As we have already seen the arrangements for morning sittings were soon discontinued but the other changes are still operative. In spite of the new arrangements Professor

[1] J. P. Mackintosh, *The Government and Politics of Britain* (Hutchinson, 1970), p. 123.
[2] B. Crick, 'Whither Parliamentary Reform?' in *The Commons in Transition* (Fontana, 1970), p. 255.

Crick believes that procedure on legislation is still a patchwork quilt with remarkably little shape or pattern, and that no important conceptual breakthrough has been made.[1]

Private Members' Bills

The opportunities open to a back-bencher to air a grievance or publicise a point of view include the avenues of Question Time, adjournment debates, bills under the 'ten-minute' rule and Private Members' Bills and motions.

An M.P. who has been successful in a ballot and seriously wishes to introduce a bill usually has a hard row to hoe. For every successful bill there are dozens of others which have fallen by the wayside and unless he has the tacit support of the Government his efforts are almost certainly doomed to failure; his 'turn' may never be reached and, if it is, his bill might well be 'talked out'. If it gets a second reading and it goes on to the Committee stage, it may take a long time to emerge. Unless he is extremely fortunate, therefore, both Government good will and personal persistence are required. A good example of this is provided by the Obscene Publications Bill, originating with the Society of Authors, which was introduced by Mr Roy Jenkins, M.P., in 1954. The first attempt was unsuccessful but on two subsequent occasions it was re-introduced by other M.P.s. Finally it received a second reading and would in the normal course have gone to Committee where it might well have been submerged by more pressing business. It did, however, receive tacit support from Mr R. A. (now Lord) Butler, the then Home Secretary, who arranged for it to be considered by a Select Committee. This committee reported in 1958 and the Bill became law in 1959, five years after it had been first introduced.[2] This case illustrates the fact that the Private Member's Bill procedure provides an avenue for dealing with issues which Governments are unlikely to sponsor themselves. In this category are Mr John Parker's Legitimacy Bill, introduced in the 1958–9 Session, and Mr Leo Abse's Sexual Offences (No. 2) Bill, dealt with in 1967.

One of the most frequently cited Private Member's Bills to become law was the Matrimonial Causes Act, 1937, which had been introduced by Sir Alan Herbert. Another well-known success is that of Sydney Silverman, M.P., who devoted much of his parliamentary career to the abolition of hanging. His Bill on Capital Punishment passed through the Commons but was rejected by the Lords; in the following session the Government introduced its own Bill and this passed into law. As indicated in chapter 5, many of the Private Member's Bills which do reach the Statute Book have originated in pressure groups outside of the House.

During the 1969–70 Session a major success was achieved by Mr Alfred Morris, M.P., whose Bill designed to improve facilities for the chronically

---

[1] Crick, 'Whither Parliamentary Reform?', p. 266.
[2] For a fuller account, see A. H. Birch, *The British System of Government* (Allen and Unwin, 1967), p. 224.

148

sick and disabled was given precedence by the Government in the last few days of the Parliament and which received the Royal Assent on 29 May 1970. (See appendix IV.)

Committees

The House of Commons, like any other large assembly, delegates some aspects of its work through Committees. The amount of delegation in the British Parliament is, however, much smaller than in other legislatures and whether or not those that do exist are used to the best possible advantage is a matter for frequent discussion among M.P.s and academics. There are two main types of Committee; one group is directly connected with the legislative process and the other with various matters of scrutiny of and inquiry connected with the process of government.

As we have seen, various stages of Bills may be considered either by a Committee of the Whole House or by a smaller committee. The Committee stage of most Bills is taken in a Standing Committee. There are eight of these Standing Committees, labelled as A, B, C, etc., each being composed of 20 to 50 M.P.s, the proportion from each party being determined in relation to its representation in the House. A chairman is appointed for the whole of the session but the rest of the membership fluctuates in accordance with the subject matter of the Bill being considered at any particular time. This arrangement has the advantage of making use of the specialised interest and knowledge of Members but it introduces the corresponding disadvantage of a lack of continuity. The proceedings in the Standing Committees are modelled on those of the House as a whole; the Front Benches are represented and the Whips are present. A Government defeat in a Committee, however, does not prejudice the position of the Government in the House itself. One of the Standing Committees is primarily concerned with Private Members' Bills and one deals with Bills relating to Scottish affairs. Additionally there exists a Scottish Grand Committee and a Welsh Grand Committee. In the legislative process use is made of joint Committees made up of M.P.s and peers which deal with the Committee stage of non-controversial legislation.

Many M.P.s have substantial interests outside of the House, e.g. in business, journalism and the law, and they are not keen to attend the standing Committees which meet in the mornings. The work involved, therefore, falls on the shoulders of a relatively small number of M.P.s, probably ranging between 70 and 200 who, in the main, make up the 'full-time' members of the House.

The committees concerned with aspects of legislation are quite different in nature from those concerned with scrutiny and inquiry. The function of the latter, which are known as Select Committees, is to probe into the subject of their inquiry and to report their findings to the House. The Select Committees are of two main types, viz:

    (*a*) they may be *ad hoc* bodies which are set up to enquire into a specific matter which is causing concern and where a report is required fairly quickly,

(b) they may be sessional committees which enquire into the work of a particular Department, which we will refer to as 'specialist' committees; or a particular field of activity which cannot always be related to a particular Department, which will be referred to as 'subject' committees.

Some Select Committees, like the Public Accounts Committee, the Statutory Instruments Committee, and the important Committee of Privileges, are well-established, but since 1966 there have been new developments which have proved to be extremely controversial and the pattern which will eventually emerge has yet to be determined.

Developments in the period 1966–70 will perhaps more readily be understood if an outline is given of some of the main sessional Select Committees which existed in 1966. Reference has already been made to the Select Committees on Procedure in other sections of the book, and the examples quoted will give an indication of the kind of tasks which it undertakes. The Select Committee on House of Commons Services has been mentioned earlier in this chapter in connection with M.P.s' allowances and working conditions; this committee generally assists the Speaker in running the day-to-day business of the House and concerns itself with the issue of *Hansard* and other official publications; it is also responsible for Members' catering facilities and has executive power in the discharge of this function.

The former Select Committee on Estimates examined the estimates of Government expenditure and subjected them to the kind of detailed investigation which was not possible in the House of Commons.[1] The Public Accounts Committee, which was first appointed in 1861, probes into details of government expenditure and can summon officials to give personal explanations to aid it in its task. It is made up of fifteen members and its Chairman is a prominent member of the Opposition. The Comptroller and Auditor-General attend the meetings and its findings are reported to the House. The Select Committee on Nationalised Industries, which was set up in 1956, looks into the working of the various publicly owned industries. It was seen as a means of providing for some degree of public accountability without making it necessary to interfere in matters of day-to-day management of the industries concerned. In the 1966–7 Session, for example, it studied the Post Office and British European Airways and made various recommendations.

The Select Committee on Nationalised Industries provides an example of the kind of body which a number of M.P.s and academics interested in the reform of Parliament wished to have extended to cover all spheres of Government administration. This group was anxious that Select Committees should have the opportunity of probing to find out what was happening inside Government Departments, investigating the practical effect of

[1] Now replaced by the Expenditure Committee p. 224 (see below).

Government policies, conducting inquiries outside of the House where this was felt to be necessary, taking account of the representations of pressure groups and public opinion and publishing their findings for the information of the House and the wider public. It was felt that this type of procedure would provide the kind of scrutiny and appraisal that was generally lacking in the existing procedure and give an opportunity to back-bench M.P.s to develop specialised interests and to involve themselves much more constructively in the work of government.

In 1966 two new 'specialist' Select Committees were set up on an experimental basis, the intention being that two departmental committees would be set up each year until all aspects of domestic policy were subject to scrutiny. It was felt that the establishment of Committees for defence and foreign affairs would create special difficulties and these aspects of government were not included in the scheme. One was to be concerned with the work of the Department of Agriculture, Fisheries and Food and the other with Science and Technology. The Agriculture Committee looked into the question of British agriculture and the European Economic Community, and the Science Committee reported on the Nuclear Reactor Programme, and other matters. It soon became evident, however, that there was a fundamental difference of view between the Government and the members of the Committees on the extent of their powers and the way in which these should be discharged. This is best illustrated by the relationship between the Government and the Agriculture Committee. The Government felt unable to supply it with official correspondence about the staffing of the British Delegation to the E.E.C. in Brussels and raised objections to the Committee holding sittings in Brussels. This Committee was notified that it would cease to function in December 1969 but strong representations were made and it was eventually wound up in February 1969. The Government was also very concerned by the request of the Select Committee on Nationalised Industries to investigate the Bank of England and the Committee was not allowed to investigate the formulation of monetary policy or the execution of exchange control.

The Select Committee on Science and Technology was reappointed session by session until the dissolution of Parliament in 1970. The place of the Agriculture Committee was taken by a Committee to consider the activities of the Department of Education and Science and the Scottish Education Department; it examined the role of Her Majesty's Inspectors of Schools and went round the Universities holding public sittings in an effort to establish the causes of student unrest. In November 1968 an additional 'Subject' Committee was set up to consider the operation of the Race Relations Act, 1968, and the admission of immigrants to the United Kingdom. Early in 1969 Committees were appointed to look into Scottish Affairs and Overseas Development. A Committee was also appointed to review the work of the Parliamentary Commissioner for Administration.

John P. Mackintosh, M.P., a former Professor of Politics and a member of both the Procedure Committee and the Agriculture Committee, argued in an article in *The Times*, 13 March 1969, that the Agriculture Committee was replaced by the Scottish Committee simply as a sop to Scottish Nationalists. He concluded that 'instead of ending this Parliament with an established range of investigatory committees covering the key sectors on internal administration and with a solid body of Labour and Conservative M.P.s convinced by experience of the value of this work, an incoming government will inherit a run-down experiment which, if its leaders desire, can be quietly dropped'.

In October 1970 a report on *Select Committees of the House of Commons* set out the incoming Conservative Government's proposals for a future Select Committee structure which was intended to serve as the basis for a debate in the House.[1] These proposals hinge on recommendations made in a special report of the Select Committee on Procedure for the 1968–9 Session. This recommended that the Estimates Committee should be changed to a Select Committee on Expenditure which would have a General Sub-Committee of sixteen members and eight further Sub-Committees, each having nine members; these would be neither 'subject' nor 'departmental' but 'functional' and their Order of Reference would be to consider the activities of Departments of State concerned with named functions (e.g. Education, Science and the Arts) and the Estimates of their expenditure presented to the House and to examine the efficiency with which they are administered.

It was visualised that the General Sub-Committee would scrutinise the projections of expenditure in the public sector as a whole, guide the work of the Committees generally and co-ordinate the inquiries undertaken with the work of other Select Committees. The tasks of the functional Sub-Committees would be:

   (i) to study the projected expenditure of Departments related to the field of its inquiry and report on major changes and variations in policy and on progress made by the Departments in clarifying objectives and priorities;

  (ii) to examine the financial implications of policy objectives and assess the success of Departments in attaining them;

 (iii) to enquire into departmental administration and the effectiveness of management.

Because the new Expenditure Committee, unlike the existing Estimates Committee, 'would not be barred from considering the policy behind the figures, there would be occasions when it would be appropriate for Ministers to give evidence before it, as they have done before the Specialist Select Committees'. The Special Report of the Select Committee had also recommended that the Public Accounts Committee and the Select Committee on Nationalised Industries should be retained and that these should function alongside the proposed Expenditure Committee.

[1] Cmd. 4507: *Select Committees of the House of Commons* (H.M.S.O., 1970).

The Government accepted the view that it would be desirable to have five year projections of expenditure instead of formally looking only a year ahead and submitted that a system of Select Committees on these lines would 'provide an effective machinery of scrutiny without in any way impairing the responsibility of Ministers to Parliament or detracting from the importance of proceedings on the Floor of the House'.

In January 1971 the House agreed that the Estimates Committees should be replaced by an Expenditure Committee whose function would be 'to consider how, if at all, policies implied in the figures of expenditure and in the estimates may be carried out more economically, and to examine the form of the papers and the estimates presented to this House'. The Committee is to consist of forty-nine members to be nominated at the beginning of each session of whom nine shall form a quorum. The Committee has powers to appoint sub-committees and to refer to them any of the matters coming within the jurisdiction of the Expenditure Committee. The Committee appointed a Steering Sub-Committee and six functional sub-committees to cover the following fields:

Public Expenditure (General)
Defence and External Affairs
Trade and Industry
Education and Arts
Employment and Social Services
Environment and Home Office

There seems little doubt that the revised arrangements will, within their limits, prove to be a more satisfactory method of working than the previous arrangements. (See chapter 12.)

Conclusion

The Government dominates the parliamentary timetable and its measures are debated on party lines but, as Professor Hanson has pointed out, 'M.P.s perform some of their most valuable work when they put party behind them, as for instance in the select committees where deliberation and reports cut across party lines.'[1] The opportunities of private Members in terms of legislation are limited but their role in general criticism is of great importance.

This should not be taken to suggest that the M.P.'s role within his parliamentary party is that of a mere cipher. The internal party meetings of M.P.s are very important; both the Parliamentary Labour Party and the Conservative 1922 Committee meet regularly and back-benchers use this opportunity to voice their views and criticisms; neither Front Bench can afford to ignore signs of widespread discontent. The business of the House of Commons is complex and M.P.s necessarily adjust their behaviour to the particular activity in which they are engaging. The debate on the efficiency of the parliamentary machine seems likely to continue, but the

[1] A. H. Hanson, *Governing Britain* (Fontana, 1970), p. 83.

basic division of labour between Government policy and criticism is not in dispute; as Sir Ivor Jennings observes, it is 'the function of Government to govern and of the House of Commons to criticise'.[1] Much of the argument is not about intention but effectiveness. The British Parliament has a long and eventful history which reflects the process of social change in the country at large; similarly, its present problems and conflicts mirror those in the wider society which it exists to serve.

[1] I. Jennings, *Cabinet Government*, 2nd edn (Cambridge University Press, 1951), p. 449.

11 The House of Lords

The Lords provides for tired statesmen and superannuated M.P.s a dignified and now remunerated refuge.

Ian Gilmour *The Body Politic*

Introduction

Bicameral legislatures are a strongly entrenched feature of political democracies, but a few countries, including New Zealand, Israel, Norway and Denmark, provide exceptions to the general pattern. The existence of a second chamber stems either from the continuance of a historical tradition or from considered choice. In countries with federal systems of government such as the United States and Australia, representation in the upper chamber is territorially based with each state electing representatives as provided in the constitution. In Britain the situation is markedly different.

Some who favour the continuance of a second chamber in Britain claim that the House of Lords undertakes the necessary task of delaying legislation which runs counter to the 'will of the people' or which it deems to be hasty and ill-conceived. Others, perhaps more realistically, believe that it makes a substantial contribution to the smooth working of government by undertaking work for which the House of Commons cannot find sufficient time. Whatever the validity or otherwise of these claims, it must be recognised that there is nothing which a second chamber does which could not, if it were so desired, be undertaken by parts of a reconstituted first chamber which was given responsibility to discharge the relevant functions.

The British House of Lords differs from second chambers in other systems in that it still has a largely hereditary basis. It is this feature, which results in a built-in Conservative bias, that has bedevilled discussions about the role of the second chamber in the British system of government. Clearly any proposals for change should be related both to the functions of the chamber and to its composition; these two functions cannot sensibly be separated because the nature of the work it is required to do determines the type of individuals who are required to undertake it. Failure to consider the two together will inevitably result in a blurring of the important issues involved.

The Conservative party, because of its history and traditions, is less offended by the existence of the hereditary element than other groups, but even the Labour Party has had a curiously ambivalent attitude towards the reform of the House of Lords. In answer to the question: 'Why does the House of Lords endure?', Professor Crick replies: 'The "Second Chamber" endures because the work it does is extremely useful to the House of Commons. The House of Lords endures because the Conservative Party has a political interest in retaining a connection between the Order of Peerage and the membership of the House of Lords, and because the Labour Party has had no better idea of how to find enough people to do the work.'[1]

Before examining this suggestion further it will be helpful to look at the composition of the House of Lords in more detail.

TABLE 28   *Composition of the House of Lords, 1901–68*

	1901	1930	1960	1968
Lords Temporal				
Hereditary peers	517	686	833	858
Irish peers	28	18	1	—
Scottish peers	16	16	16	—
Lords of Appeal	4	7	8	10
Life peers	—	—	24	168
Lords Spiritual				
Bishops and archbishops	26	26	26	26
Totals	591	753	908	1062

Composition

Table 28 gives an indication of the way in which the composition of the House has changed in the course of this century.

A hereditary peerage of the United Kingdom carries with it the right to a seat in the House of Lords. These include holders of titles created in the peerage of England before 1707 and in the peerage of Great Britain from 1707 to 1801. There have been no new Scottish peerages since the Act of Union in 1707. Until 1963 it was the practice for the Scottish peers, at the beginning of each new Parliament, to elect sixteen of their number to sit in the Lords. The Peerage Act of 1963 enabled all Scottish peers to be admitted to membership, which resulted in an increase from sixteen to thirty-one. The position of the Scottish peers is complicated by the fact that a high proportion hold English titles as well. Those with English titles are eligible for membership as of right; it is those with Scottish titles only who are affected by the new legislation. Until the creation of the Irish Free State (now the Republic of Ireland) in 1922, Irish Peers were entitled, under the Act of Union, 1800, to elect twenty-eight representative members to sit in the House of Lords. The last of the Irish peers who had

[1] B. Crick, *The Reform of Parliament* (Weidenfeld and Nicholson, 1968), p. 105.

been elected for life before the secession died in 1961. The Peerage Act of 1963 allows Irish Peers to become candidates at parliamentary elections in any constituency in the United Kingdom and to vote at parliamentary elections. This group was previously excluded from elections in constituencies in Northern Ireland.

It will be seen that the number of the 'Lords Spiritual' has remained constant at twenty-six members. This group includes the Archbishops of York and Canterbury, the Bishops of London, Durham and Winchester and the twenty-one senior bishops in order of their appointment. The Lords of Appeal in Ordinary are legal dignitaries appointed under the terms of the Appellate Jurisdiction Acts to perform judicial functions in the House of Lords. They are entitled to sit for life and this right continues even if they resign their judicial office. They receive a substantial salary as long as they perform their judicial duties.

The Peerage Act, 1958, made provision for the creation of Life Peers and Peeresses who are entitled to sit in the Lords but who do not pass on this right to their heirs as is the case with hereditary peers. The object of this legislation was to provide a more balanced representation of the parties in the upper House and to provide a group of members, both men and women, who would actively contribute to its work; this was the first occasion upon which women were allowed to sit in the Lords. The changes did not, however, affect in any way the entitlement of the hereditary peers. The legislation was introduced by the Conservative Government and opposed by the Labour Party on the grounds that it only tinkered with the problem; the Labour Party, however, did not put forward any alternative proposals. The number of life peers and peeresses has increased steadily since the Act was introduced and by 1971 the total exceeded 200.

In 1957, a few months before the passage of the life peerage legislation, arrangements were made for a daily 'attendance allowance' to be paid to those peers who take part in the work of the House of Lords. This was initially at the rate of three guineas (£3.15) per day but it was raised to four and a half guineas (£4.72½) in 1964, and to six pounds ten shillings (£6.50) in 1969.[1] Travelling expenses are payable in addition to the attendance allowance.

Following the case of 'the reluctant peer', Anthony Wedgwood Benn (see chapter 3), a Conservative Government also passed the Peerage Act, 1963. This allowed hereditary peers a year in which to disclaim their titles and so become eligible for membership of the Commons. The act provided for future heirs to disclaim an inherited title within twelve months, but for sitting M.P.s this period was reduced to one month. The disclaimer is exercised for the life of the individual concerned and it does not affect the subsequent devolution of the peerage. Under the same statute peeresses in their own right became eligible to sit in the Lords and to surrender their titles on exactly the same terms as all other peers.

[1] Daily attendance allowance was increased to £8.50 in December 1971.

Attendance

At the present time over one thousand individuals are legally eligible for a seat in the Lords. If they all attended this would give Britain the largest second chamber in the world; in practice, however, this huge membership is only nominal and only a small proportion take an active part in its work.

Recently steps have been taken to ensure against the possibility, real or imagined, that the 'backwoodsmen' will descend upon the House and swamp it with their power to vote on some issue which might be of concern to them. In the 1945–50 Parliament, 217 peers did not attend a single session and the largest recorded attendance was 288. In 1958 a Select Committee reported that 561 peers had never attended or had attended for less than ten sittings. In that year the House of Lords adopted standing orders by which those peers who did not habitually attend could be 'granted leave of absence' for the whole or part of a session. By the end of the year leave of absence was granted to 234 peers out of a total of 880.

In 1963 the Lords agreed that peers must reply to a Writ of Summons which was to be deposited for them in the House. Failure to reply and take the Oath within one month was deemed to be equivalent to an application for leave of absence until the end of the session. In the Session 1961–2, 324 (59 per cent) of the total membership of the House attended between 1 and 20 sittings and only 39 (7 per cent) attended more than 100 days in a session of 115 days.

P. A. Bromhead notes that for the whole period between 1919 and 1958 the average number voting in divisions was 80.[1] In the session 1954–5 the average daily attendance was 92; in the session 1966–7 it was 192, and in 1969–70 it was 235 and in 1970–1 it reached 265. It is clear, therefore, that the scale of attendance is increasing and there is evidence that by far the most active groups are life peers and peeresses, and hereditary peers of first creation.

Appointment

Peers are appointed by the Crown on the recommendation of the Prime Minister. The Opposition can and does make nominations which are, if approved, proposed to the Sovereign by the Prime Minister. Lord Home, who introduced the Life Peerages Bill for the Government, said in the House of Lords during the debate on 3 December 1957, that the Prime Minister 'would when appropriate seek the advice of the Leader of the Opposition', one purpose of the Bill being 'to enable the Socialist point of view to be put more effectively'.

Membership of the House of Lords is used by both the major parties as a means of honouring former Prime Ministers, Ministers, M.P.s and distinguished supporters. It is now customary for Prime Ministers to be offered an earldom; this was accepted by Mr Attlee but refused by

[1] See P. A. Bromhead, *The House of Lords in Contemporary Politics* (Routledge, 1958), pp. 31–8 for analysis of attendance and contributions to debates.

Sir Winston Churchill on the grounds that he did not wish to prevent his children from seeking membership of the House of Commons.

The Prime Minister's power of patronage in the creation of peerages also provides a convenient means of persuading an M.P. to move to the Lords and thus provide a vacant seat in the Commons for a Minister defeated in a general election. A high proportion of life peers are former Members of Parliament. A peerage can also be conferred upon an individual whom it is desired to bring into Parliament in order to serve as a Minister or in some other capacity.

Not all individuals who are made peers are active in political life but they can frequently be identified as being in support of one party or the other. Among the well-known people who have been honoured in this way in the post war period are the former West Indian cricketer, Sir Leary Constantine, Sir Eric James, who was, at the time of his appointment, High Master of Manchester Grammar School, Mr Ted Willis, the playwright, and Sir Laurence Olivier, the actor. The fact that during the period of the Labour Government, from 1964–70, no hereditary peerages were conferred by the Prime Minister, Mr Wilson, is of considerable constitutional importance. Up until the time of writing none have been conferred by Mr Heath.

The Bryce Conference
The classic statement of the functions of the House of Lords is contained in the report of the Conference on the Reform of the Second Chamber which met in 1917.[1] They are listed in the following terms:

(i) The examination and revision of Bills brought from the House of Commons, a function which has become more needed since...the House of Commons has been obliged to act under special rules limiting debate.

(ii) The initiation of Bills dealing with subjects of comparatively non-controversial character which may have an easier passage through the House of Commons if they have been fully discussed and put into well considered shape before being submitted to it.

(iii) The interposition of so much delay (and no more) in the passing of a Bill into law as may enable the opinion of the nation to be adequately expressed upon it. This would be specially needed as regards Bills which affect the fundamentals of the Constitution or introduce new principles of legislation, or which raise issues whereon the opinion of the country may appear to be about equally divided.

(iv) Full and free discussion of the large and important questions such as those of foreign policy, at moments when the House of Commons may happen to be so much occupied that it cannot find sufficient time for them. Such discussions may often be all the more useful

[1] Cmd. 9038: *Conference on the Reform of the Second Chamber* (H.M.S.O., 1918).

if conducted in an Assembly whose debates and divisions do not involve the fate of the Executive Government.

The Lords at work

The deliberations of the House of Lords proceed at a much more leisurely pace than those of the House of Commons. Peers sit for about 120 days in each session as opposed to 160 or more days for M.P.s. The Lords meet each day from Monday to Thursday, usually from 2.30 p.m. to 6 or 7 p.m. The quorum is three as against forty in the Commons. Debates are much more informal than in the Lower House and there is no closure, so that every peer who wishes to speak has an opportunity of doing so.

The Lords have few rules or standing orders governing debates. Lord Morrison states: 'The Lord Chancellor who is also Speaker of the House and sits on the Woolsack, has but little controlling power over debate, his duty being substantially confined to putting the question on all Motions which are submitted to the House and collecting the voices or stating the results of divisions. Moreover, he freely takes part in debate, moving to the place he occupies in the House as a peer, as opposed to the Woolsack which he occupies as Speaker. The Woolsack is technically outside the House.'[1] Speakers taking part in the debate do not address the chair but speak to the House as a whole. The order of speeches is agreed through 'usual channels'. The legislative work of the House of Lords can be divided into three categories:

(i) Non-controversial bills are introduced in the Upper House and detailed work is done on these before they are passed to the Commons, which under modern conditions is always short of time for legislation. This work requires a painstaking approach and a concern for details; it may for many members be dull but it is of considerable importance. Normally this aspect of legislation does not occasion political controversy. Much of the work is on 'consolidating' Bills such as the Companies Act of 1947, during the passage of which 400 amendments were dealt with at the Committee stage. There is also an arrangement whereby Private Members' Bills can in certain circumstances be initiated in the Lords. This was the case, for example, with the Indecent Advertisements (Amendment) Act and the Riding Establishments Act, both of which received the Royal Assent in 1970.

(ii) The Upper House amends legislation initiated in the House of Commons. Again an excellent example is provided from the spate of legislation which was dealt with in the 1945–50 Parliament. The Bill which formed the basis of the Transport Act, 1947, was large and complex and had been very badly drafted. Professor Crick who discusses the passage of this Bill in considerable detail in his *Reform of Parliament* records that because of the pressure of other

[1] Morrison, *Government and Parliament*, 3rd edn, p. 185.

legislation, it received inadequate discussion in the Commons; 31 clauses, 5 schedules, and nearly 200 Government amendments were not discussed. When the Bill was returned to the Commons over 242 amendments had been made by the Lords, over 200 of these being drafted or 'agreed' amendments. In commenting on this episode *The Times* observed that 'if a revising chamber did not exist it would have been necessary to invent one'. In 1971 the complex and controversial Industrial Relations Bill, consisting of 150 clauses and 8 schedules, received extensive scrutiny in the Lords because of the 'guillotine' imposed in its stormy passage through the Commons. During this period the House sat for an average of eight hours a day instead of its customary four.

(iii) The House of Lords fulfils an important role in the examination of Private Bills and Provisional Order Bills. It is this legislation which enables local authorities and other corporate bodies, such as universities, to undertake development work which cannot be done without parliamentary sanction. Hearings and inquiries are frequently necessary for this purpose and these are quite often held at some distance from London. Peers who undertake this work are sometimes required to travel to the provinces.

Debates on what the Bryce Conference referred to as 'the large and important questions' usually take the form of a Motion 'to move for papers'. The peer who raises a particular issue normally has some specialised knowledge of the subject; he makes his statement, and an appropriate Minister in the Lords will voice the Government's view. Divisions on these debates are rare and they usually end with the original speaker asking leave to withdraw the Motion. When this is done the Official Report of the proceedings will read: 'Motion for Papers, by leave, withdrawn.'

Matters raised sometimes deal with such important topics as defence, foreign policy, economic affairs, the liberty of the subject, social services and social problems; on other occasions the issues raised are of minor importance only. Speeches made are frequently less partisan than those in the Commons. Occasionally the standard of debate is very high but often contributions are trivial and dull. Professor Crick has observed: 'The House shines in dealing with matters that the Commons can give little time to; it is mostly dull and often downright embarassing...on the "great issues" which constantly engage the Commons.'[1]

The House of Lords also acts in a judicial capacity as the Supreme Court of Appeal in both civil and criminal matters, but this work is nowadays divorced from its other functions. Apart from the force of tradition there seems to be no reason why it should not be practically and constitutionally separated from the Lords.

The judicial function is exercised by the Law Lords who are the Lord Chancellor, the Lords of Appeal in Ordinary, ex-Lord Chancellors and

[1] Crick, *The Reform of Parliament*, p. 120.

161

other peers who have held high judicial office (e.g. those who have been Lords of Appeal, Judges of the Supreme Court or of the Court of Session in Scotland). Since *O'Connell*'s case in 1844 it has been a convention that no lay peer shall take part in the judicial work of the House. Three Law Lords must be present to hear appeals.

The House still decides on disputed claims to the peerage. The former right of peers to be tried by the House of Lords, instead of in the ordinary courts, was abolished by the Criminal Jurisdiction Act, 1948.

Powers of delay

The House of Lords' power to hold up legislation was reduced first by the Parliament Act, 1911, and again by the Parliament Act, 1949. When a Liberal Government came into office in 1906 it became clear that some limitation on the power of the Lords would have to be imposed.[1] Between 1906 and 1910 eighteen out of 213 Government Bills failed to pass into law; not all were rejected outright but several were so drastically amended that they were abandoned.

The dispute was brought to a head in 1909 when the Finance Bill was rejected by the Lords. Parliament was dissolved and the Liberals were again elected in the general election of January 1910. An attempt was then made to reach agreement between the major parties on the question of the Lords' delaying powers but this failed and the Prime Minister, Herbert Asquith, was required to face a general election for the second time in a year. He made it clear to the King, however, that if re-elected he would, if necessary, exercise the prerogative of creating peers to ensure that 'the decision of the country' was not thwarted. Mr Asquith was again successful in the election of December 1910 and, after some hesitation, the Lords bowed to his threat and the Parliament Bill was passed in 1911.

The Parliament Act, 1911, took away the power of the Lords over 'Money' Bills (i.e. those dealing with the raising or spending of public money). The Speaker was given the responsibility of deciding whether a particular Bill was a Money Bill or not. Money Bills could be neither amended nor rejected and were to become law on receiving the Royal Assent regardless of the Upper House. Over Bills other than Money Bills the Lords were to retain only a suspensive veto of two years duration.

The present position, under the terms of the Parliament Act, 1949, is that if a Bill is passed in two successive sessions by the Commons, and is rejected in each session by the Lords, it may then be presented for the Royal Assent provided that one year has elapsed between the second reading in the first session and the third reading in the second session. This means, in effect, that the House of Lords has a suspensory veto of only nine months.

The second of these Parliament Bills was twice rejected by the Lords and became law under the provisions of the Parliament Act, 1911, as

[1] See Mackenzie, *English Parliament*, p. 185.

162

discussed above. The Lords retain the power of veto over Private Bills and on any Bill to extend the life of Parliament.

Towards reform

The preamble to the Parliament Act, 1911, had stated the intention 'to substitute for the House of Lords as present constituted a second chamber constituted on a popular instead of hereditary basis'. It was recognised, however, that this change could not immediately 'be brought into operation'. In the sixty years or so since this declaration was made little progress has been made towards its realisation.

The Conservative Party has not been eager to make any radical change and the Labour Party, having for the most part left behind the abolitionist proposals of its early days, has not displayed a serious determination to embark upon a root and branch reform. The various proposals considered since 1911 are illuminating and the more important of these will be examined before drawing attention to other possibilities that attempt to view changes in the composition and functions of a second chamber in relation to the work of the House of Commons.

The all-party Bryce Conference in 1917, which has already been referred to, proposed that the Second Chamber should consist of two elements:

(i) 246 members elected by M.P.s. For this purpose M.P.s would be arranged into 13 geographical areas on the basis of the constituencies which they represented and would vote using the method of proportional representation with a single transferable vote;

(ii) 81 peers to be elected from existing peers by a Joint Committee of both Houses.

It was suggested that the Second Chamber should be elected for twelve years with one third of its membership retiring every four years. It was argued that this would prevent the possibility of sudden change and that, under this procedure, the membership of the chamber would always include people with a long experience of public affairs. No action was taken to implement these recommendations.

When the Labour Government put forward the Parliament Bill in 1947 (which was to become the Parliament Act, 1949), an attempt was made to reach an interparty agreement on the problems raised by the House of Lords. Accordingly a conference of party leaders was arranged and in the meantime consideration of the Bill was suspended. These talks broke down because 'the Government Representatives and the representatives of the Official Opposition considered the difference between them on the subject of powers was fundamental and not related to the length of the period of delay'.

The difference on the question of delay was in fact reduced to a matter of three months. The Conservatives were prepared to accept a delay of eighteen months, or twelve months from the date of the third reading in

163

the Commons but the Labour Party insisted on a period of nine months from the third reading. But, as the Official Statement of the party leaders made clear, the vital disagreement was more fundamental than this.

In spite of this, however, the parties did reach agreement on a number of important matters affecting the future development of the second chamber, and issued an 'agreed statement' which made reference to the following points:

(1) The Second Chamber should be complementary to and not a rival of the Lower House. Reform should be based on a modification of its existing constitution as opposed to the construction of a new type based on some system of election.

(2) The revised constitution should secure as far as practicable that there will not be permanent majority for any one party.

(3) A Hereditary Peerage should not by itself constitute a qualification for admission to a reformed chamber.

(4) Members who would be styled 'Lords of Parliament' should be appointed on grounds of personal distinction or public service. They might be drawn from Hereditary Peers or Commoners who would be created Life Peers.

(5) Women should be eligible for membership.

(6) Provision should be made for the inclusion of certain descendants of the Sovereign, certain Lords Spiritual and the Law Lords.

(7) Some remuneration should be payable to members in order that people without private means should not be excluded.

(8) Peers who were not Lords of Parliament should be entitled to stand for election to the Commons and to vote.

(9) Some provision should be made to exclude members who neglect or become unfitted to perform their duties.[1]

It will be seen that these recommendations are far from revolutionary in tone and scope. In some cases they stake a claim for the continuance of the existing pattern (e.g. inclusion of the Lords Spiritual and descendants of the Sovereign) but in others there was some considerable advance (e.g. the recognition that the possession of a hereditary peerage should not by itself constitute a claim for membership and the establishment of the principle of remuneration).

The scope of the Peerage Acts of 1958 and 1963 has already been noted and it will now be convenient to look at the proposals on the reform of the House of Lords which were introduced by the Labour Government in 1968.

Labour Government's proposals 1967–9
In the autumn of 1967 a proposal to 'reduce the power of the House of Lords and eliminate its hereditary basis' was included in the Queen's Speech. It appears that this was largely due to the efforts of Mr Richard

[1] Cmd. 7380 (H.M.S.O., 1948).

Crossman, the then Leader of the House of Commons who had been impressed by the statement of Lord Carrington, the Conservative Leader in the House of Lords, made in a routine Lords debate that the House of Lords would 'only be able to use its delaying powers once'. Press reports of the period suggest that Mr Crossman persuaded a sceptical Labour Cabinet that it might be possible to reach an agreement with the Conservatives on Lords Reform and thus save a good deal of time and trouble in Parliament. Accordingly in November 1967, a group of prominent Privy Councillors from all three parties began meeting together charged with the task of hammering out a basis of reform which would prove generally acceptable. The Committee was made up of Mr Crossman, Mr Roy Jenkins, Lord Longford and Lord Shackleton representing the Labour Party; Mr Reginald Maudling, Mr Iain Macleod, Lord Carrington and Lord Jellicoe from the Conservative Party; and Mr Jeremy Thorpe and Lord Byers for the Liberal Party.

There seems little doubt that the main impetus in the group came from Mr Crossman and Lord Carrington, who were able to overcome the scepticism of their respective colleagues and by June 1968 the talks had, in the words of Lord Carrington, 'all but reached agreement'.

This harmony was severely jolted when, on 18 June 1968, the House of Lords rejected a statutory instrument extending sanctions against Rhodesia which had been laid by the Government. The repercussions of this political protest by the Conservative peers was far reaching. It is virtually certain that Mr Heath, the Leader of the Opposition, had been warned of the possible consequences by the Shadow Cabinet but he refrained from taking action in advance presumably to avoid dissension in the Conservative Party and because he wished to continue harassing the Government which was at the time having some difficulty with its back-benchers. The action on the statutory instrument would not, in fact, have had any serious effect as the Government simply had to renew the order and Lord Carrington had made it clear publicly that the Conservative peers would not reject it a second time. The Rhodesian sanctions were, therefore, not in jeopardy but the action of the Conservative peers triggered off a series of events which were to damn the prospects of a further instalment in the reform of the Lords.

It was alleged in the press that the incident provided an opportunity for the Prime Minister to revive the morale of the Parliamentary Labour Party and he announced in the House of Commons that the inter-party talks would be scrapped and promised early legislation on 'a comprehensive and radical' reorganisation of the Second Chamber which would not be bound by the compromises reached in the talks.

In view of what followed it is important to realise that many Labour M.P.s had been unsympathetic to the inter-party talks because they felt that they should have been consulted on the issue and they were worried about the nature and extent of the compromises which had been made.

165

When the White Paper on reform was issued in November 1968, it became clear that the Government's proposals were in fact much the same as the 'package deal' agreed in the all-party talks. Now, however, the Government had the problem of getting legislation through the House of Commons in the face of opposition from both Conservatives and some of its own back-benchers.

The essence of the Government's proposals was that the size of the Lords should be reduced from a notional membership of over 1000 to a working chamber of about 230, all of whom would be peers of first creation. The possession of a hereditary peerage would no longer give entitlement to membership. Although hereditary peers would continue to have the right to speak they would have no vote unless they were included in the group of seventy or so hereditary peers to be granted qualifying life peerages. The numbers of the Lords Spiritual would be reduced from 26 to 16. The Lords' power to reject statutory instruments would be abolished. The delaying powers on legislation would be amended in such a way that the possibility of veto during the final session of Parliament before a general election would be removed.

The White Paper was greeted with horror by the Conservative traditionalists and derision by the hard-core of Labour back-benchers. The Government nevertheless proceeded with its proposals and the Parliament (No. 2) Bill was introduced in November 1968. The difficulties of translating this into legislation were immediately apparent. The Government had to depend on the votes of Labour M.P.s, forty-five of whom had expressed their intention of resisting the Bill. The 'normal channels' of communication had completely broken down and the Bill was subjected to a sustained 'filibuster' which in the end forced the Government to withdraw the Bill in order to save itself from embarrassment. The Bill was in effect defeated by an unholy alliance of the Tory right and the Labour left. Mr Wilson sourly remarked that some members of his party derived 'more satisfaction from continuing to contemplate the indefensible' than from realistic efforts to reform the Second Chamber.

The future

In speculating about the future of the Second Chamber two things need to be taken carefully into account. The first of these is the recognition that the functions of the Upper House are inseparably related to those of the Lower House and reform of the former cannot sensibly be examined without reference to the latter. Secondly, that although all-party agreement on this issue may be desirable, it may in practice be impossible to achieve. It is unlikely that the Conservatives will agree to a wholesale removal of the hereditary peers from government and equally unlikely that, in the end, Labour will settle for anything less. Sooner or later it may be necessary for a Government, and presumably a Labour Government, to fulfil the dictum that 'the duty of a Government is to govern' and to act unilaterally.

What then should be the general direction of change? Assuming the continued existence of a second chamber, and few M.P.s nowadays question this, certain basic requirements are clear:

(i) The Second Chamber must be complementary to and not in opposition to the Lower House. It is for this reason that the Bryce Conference rejected proposals for an elected second chamber, the feeling being that this procedure might produce a body which would attempt to rival the Commons.

(ii) In order to continue and to extend its role in supplementing the work of the House of Commons (and perhaps providing a forum for a more detailed study of the nature of present and future problems) it would require between 100 and 150 members who could devote themselves to this work on a more or less full-time basis. This implies that able men and women must be carefully selected and adequately remunerated for their services.

Professor Crick has made some interesting and highly relevant observations on these problems. He suggests that the question of delaying powers should be settled by removing them. On the question of the composition of the Second Chamber he recommends that life peers should continue to sit but the Writ of Summons to hereditary peers be discontinued. The House, he suggests, should also have added to it a hundred or so new style 'Lords of Parliament' who would be appointed and salaried. These would be people experienced in law, central and local government, and from a variety of professions and occupations, who would be willing to serve for a fixed period. They should, he believes, be given statutory tenure for an agreed period, and their previous occupations and pension rights etc. should be safeguarded. This Professor Crick considers would introduce a valuable principle of horizontal mobility which is a feature normally absent in our society. The procedure for nominating Lords of Parliament 'could well be institutionalised into an All-Party Selection Committee (not necessarily composed of members of either House)'.[1]

Such far-reaching changes as these may be a long time in coming. In the meantime it seems likely that the existing House of Lords will not seriously challenge the power and authority of the House of Commons and that it will continue to be 'restrained – except on rare occasions – by an apologetic awareness of the anachronism of its own existence'.[2]

---

[1] Crick, *The Reform of Parliament*, ch. 6.
[2] N. Beloff, 'Lords bring Wilson in from the cold', *The Observer*, 1968.

12 Government and Finance

Finance is not something apart from policy but an expression of it. By deciding what to do in other spheres, the House largely decides by inference what it is to do in the financial sphere.

H. J. Laski *Parliamentary Government in England*

Principles and practice

Parliament's financial procedures still bear the stamp of their historical development. The principle that the 'redress of grievances must precede supply', which was developed under the Normans, still colours the methods employed to regulate taxation and government spending. Theoretically, the raising of revenue and the pattern of expenditure are still largely separate issues, and different procedures are used to operate and supervise them. In practice, the two are closely related and one cannot sensibly be considered without reference to the other. The criticism sometimes made that the financial procedures used by Parliament are ill-suited to the present-day level of expenditure has considerable substance because, in spite of recent changes, existing practices do not differ radically from those used before the massive expansion of government services.

The budget is one of the main weapons in a Government's armoury because it is this machinery which is used to determine and to effect changes in the economy and to arrange the pattern of social spending. Through the budget, social policies are translated into the language of financial burdens and priorities of spending; if we are to understand its political significance, therefore, the budget must be analysed in this light.

Leaving aside for the moment the differing approaches of the rival political parties, it must be recognised that the underlying principles of national finance were developed over a long period of time, each being the result of a particular episode in history which has more or less adapted successfully to meet the needs of modern government. These principles can be summarised as follows:

    (i) Parliament must consent to the authorisation of public expenditure and the imposition of taxes.

168

(ii) All grants of public money and proposals for taxation must be initiated by a Government motion.

(iii) The process must begin in the House of Commons and, after due consideration by Members, be approved in the form of an Act of Parliament.

(iv) Money may only be spent by the Government in pursuance of the purpose for which it was originally approved by Parliament.

(v) Financial business must be conducted through a single fund known as the Consolidated Fund, or the Exchequer Account.

(vi) Each financial year must be separate and self contained. At the end of the year departments must forfeit any surplus and account for any deficit.

(vii) Certain payments, when voted, do not require approval from year to year and are referred to as 'charges on the Consolidated Fund'. These include either payments of an essentially contractual nature, e.g. interest on the National Debt, or for services which it is desired to make manifestly free of any suggestion of political control, e.g. annuities to members of the Royal Family, salaries of High Court judges, the Speaker, the Leader of the Opposition, etc.

In finance, as in other matters, the dominant position is held by the Government. The view that the House of Commons controls finance is nowadays completely unrealistic; 'redress of grievances' amounts to little more than the opportunity for the Opposition to debate major issues of policy and, to a lesser extent, for back-benchers to draw attention to matters of concern to themselves and their constituents; 'control' in effect means the provision of facilities for criticism and the public exposure of deficiencies and abuse. The main responsibility for sustained scrutiny falls, in reality, not upon the House of Commons as a whole but upon the Expenditure Committee (which replaced the Select Committee on Estimates in 1971) and the Public Accounts Committee. In 1903, the Select Committee on National Expenditure pointed out that an assembly of more than 600 M.P.s influenced by party loyalties was not the best 'instrument to achieve a close and exhaustive examination of the immense and complex estimates' and that divisions were nearly always decided by 'a majority of members who had not listened to the discussion'. The position today is little different from that commented on seventy years ago. As Professor Crick puts it: 'control means influence, not direct power; advice, not command; criticism not obstruction; scrutiny, not initiative; publicity not secrecy'.[1]

Parliament's financial procedures are complicated and an indication of how these procedures operate can best be given by looking first at the role of the Treasury and then examining the preparations for the budget.

[1] Crick, *The Reform of Parliament*, p. 80.

The Treasury

The Treasury still occupies a key position in British Government. The nominal head of the Treasury is the Prime Minister, who holds the office of First Lord of the Treasury, but the actual responsibility for the work of the department rests with the Chancellor of the Exchequer, who is the Second Lord of the Treasury. At present other Ministers in the department include Chief Secretary, Parliamentary Secretary, Financial Secretary and Minister of State, all of whom are members of the Government. Government Whips hold nominal office as Lord Commissioners of the Treasury.

The Treasury has close contacts with other government departments connected with industry, trade and finance and with the Bank of England and the Central Statistical Office. The Chancellor is also head of the Board of Inland Revenue and the Board of Customs and Excise. The Treasury must concern itself not only with the administration of internal financial procedures but also with the wider considerations of international finance. It deals with matters affecting productivity, the balance of payments, gold reserves and exchange control policy. Its responsibilities for internal finance include supplying data and making calculations on all matters relevant to the budget, the raising and repayment of loans, and the policy of the Bank of England. It scrutinises the estimates of other departments and ensures that the sums voted to them by Parliament for current expenditure are not exceeded and are applied to the objects specified by Parliament.

Between 1964 and 1969 some of the most important functions of the Treasury were taken over by the Department of Economic Affairs, under the leadership of the then Deputy Prime Minister, Mr George Brown (now Lord George-Brown), which assumed responsibility for formulating the general objectives of economic policy and the co-ordination of the work of other departments in an effort to achieve these objectives. This new department produced a National Plan for economic development in 1964 and a further one in 1969. It attempted to establish national policy for prices and incomes operated through a Prices and Incomes Board and encouraged regional development through a Regional Development Council. When the Department of Economic Affairs was wound up in 1969 its functions were again placed under the control of the Treasury.

The Budget

As Anthony Sampson observes: 'The core of the Treasury's traditional role is the annual ritual of the budget. The Treasury's year revolves round the budget as shops revolve around Christmas: the process begins months beforehand – preparing estimates for the departments, calculating the effect of taxes, working out priorities for future spending.'[1] The budget is

[1] A. Sampson, *Anatomy of Britain Today* (Hodder and Stoughton, 1969), p. 301.

normally presented to Parliament in April because the financial year runs from 1 April to 31 March. It is nowadays much more than a mere annual accounting exercise. In the words of the Plowden Report: 'The budget is seen, not as a simple balancing of tax receipts against expenditure, but as a sophisticated process in which the instruments of taxation and expenditure are used to influence the course of the economy.'[1]

The actual presentation of the budget is preceded by a series of White Papers dealing with the overall economic situation which provide the basis for the particular fiscal proposals which will be subsequently introduced. The budget speech, which covers the whole range of expenditure on social services, defence, subsidies, etc., and income derived from a variety of sources, is always delivered to a full house. The Chancellor first comments on the accounts for the past year; he then gives details of the Estimates for the forthcoming year. He analyses the current economic situation, particularly in relation to the balance of payments, and comments on the level of employment, etc. The actual details of his proposals for taxation come last in the speech. The necessary budget resolutions are then approved, and under the provisions of the Provisional Collection of Taxes Act, 1968, become immediately effective.

The budget debate usually lasts for five or six days and when this is completed the Finance Bill, which incorporates the budget proposals, is introduced. The debates on the Finance Bill take up 15 days and the Bill must receive its second reading within 20 days of the budget debate. Until recently the Committee stage was always taken in a Committee of the Whole House but in the 1966–7 Session it was taken 'upstairs' instead of on the floor of the House. This procedure was objected to by the Opposition and some obstructive tactics were employed. In 1968–9, a compromise was reached under which the bulk of the Bill goes 'upstairs' but a limited number of the more controversial issues, selected by the Opposition, are taken on the floor of the House. This has resulted in an improved situation in that the bulk of the Members need not concern themselves with technical details and the Government gets its business through more quickly. The various stages of the Finance Bill have to be completed by 5 August.

Early in 1967 the pretence that the Committee of Supply was directly discussing financial matters was officially dropped and the Committee was abolished, its functions being transferred to the House as a whole and the 29 'Supply' days are now recognised simply as 'Opposition' days. Later in the same year the Committee of Ways and Means, which had dealt with revenue matters, was also abolished. The terminology of 'Supply' and 'Ways and Means' is still generally used, e.g. proposals for authorising taxation and the payment of monies into the Consolidated Fund are couched in the form of 'Ways and Means' resolutions; the 'Opposition' days are still referred to as 'Supply' days (see chapter 10).

[1] Cmd. 1432: *The Control of Expenditure* (H.M.S.O., 1961).

The Estimates

In the autumn (usually in November) each department is required to submit its estimates for the forthcoming financial year to the Treasury and the scrutiny covers the period up to February. The procedure and mode of presentation of the Defence Estimates is different from the Civil Estimates. In the Civil Estimates, each separate item is scrutinised, but for the Defence Estimates a total sum is fixed and this is apportioned according to overall defence requirements and needs of the various services. The estimates are presented to Parliament in February, the Civil Estimates being introduced by the Financial Secretary to the Treasury and the Defence Estimates by the Minister of Defence. The necessary expenditure is approved by Parliament (in traditional terms 'Supply' is granted) in the form of two Consolidated Fund Bills, the first one being approved in March and the second later in the year (usually July) as one of the last acts of the parliamentary session.

The first Consolidated Fund Bill provides for:

(i) 'Votes on Account' for the early part of the forthcoming financial year which are sums designed to provide the money which departments must have until the full estimates are approved in July.

(ii) Technically, the granting of money for the pay of officers and men for the armed services. In fact this is used as is necessary by the defence department pending approval of the full Estimates. This can be done because sums under the Defence Estimates (but not the Civil Estimates) can be transferred from one 'vote' to another, a process known as *virement*.

(iii) Excess Votes to cover deficits incurred in the previous financial year.

(iv) Supplementary Estimates to cover items omitted in current estimates.

The later Consolidated Fund Bill, known as the Appropriation Bill, approves the Estimates as a whole and regularises all adjustments which have been made. It 'appropriates' all the estimates (including those approved in March) to their specific purposes in accordance with the principle enunciated at the beginning of this chapter.

The former Select Committee on Estimates, working through sub-committees, directed its attention to different departments successively, and its comments on current estimates served mainly to suggest future alterations. Professor A. H. Hanson described it as '*de facto* a collection of specialised sub-committees, engaged in investigations which hover somewhat uncertainly on the ill-defined borderline between policy and administration, and concerned with finance only to the extent that, within the areas it happens to be investigating, the maintenance of efficient financial control is an essential constituent of economic policy-implementation'.[1] The new Expenditure Committee (described in chapter 10) is designed

[1] 'The House of Commons and Finance' in *The Commons in Transition*, p. 47.

TABLE 29   *National Revenue and Expenditure. Financial Year 1969–70*

Revenue		Expenditure	
	£ million		*£ million*
Taxation		*Supply Services*	
Income Tax	4 899.9	Defence	2 204.5
Surtax	255.4	Government and Exchequer	55.2
Profits tax	2.1	Commonwealth and Foreign	305.3
Corporation tax	1 686.5	Home and Justice	265.1
Capital gains tax	126.8	Transport, Trades and Industry	2 815.9
Death duties	365.5	Agriculture	385.8
Stamp duties	120.2	Local government, Housing and	
Special charge	19.7	Social Services	5 042.5
		Education and Science	450.8
Total:	7 476.1	Museums, galleries and the arts	17.2
		Public buildings and common	
Customs and Excise		services	281.2
Beer	450.5	Smaller departments	21.8
Wines and spirits	413.2	Miscellaneous	28.1
Tobacco	1 143.0	Customs and Excise	37.2
Hydrocarbon oils	1 310.7	Inland Revenue	105.8
Protective duties	226.2		
Purchase tax	1 111.6	Total:	12 016.4
Betting	119.1		
Temporary charge on imports		Debt interest	512.8
(debit)	1.1	Payments to Northern Ireland	251.9
Other	1.3	Other expenditure	41.0
Import deposits	188.2	Surplus transferred to National	
Less export rebates	10.2	Loans Fund	2 444.4
Total:	4 952.5		
Motor vehicle duties	416.7		
Selective employment tax	1 888.1		
Interest and dividends	92.4		
Broadcast receiving licences	101.2		
Other receipts	339.6		
Total:	15 266.6	Total:	15 266.6

Source: *Annual Abstract of Statistics 1970*, pp. 295–8.

to meet many criticisms of the Select Committee on Estimates and its terms of reference and method of working will probably result in more stringent scrutiny and analysis than has been the case in the past.

Government expenditure now runs at about fifteen thousand million pounds per annum and the bulk of this is derived from taxation. The general pattern of revenue and expenditure is shown in table 29. Direct taxes, such as income tax, surtax and estate duty are assessed and collected by the Inland Revenue and indirect taxes, e.g. purchase tax, entertainments tax, customs duties on goods entering the country, and excise duties on beer and spirits, are charged and collected by the Customs and Excise. Additional sources of revenue include receipts from the Crown Lands amounting to one and a half million pounds a year, profits tax, death duties, motor vehicles taxes, etc., and proceeds from borrowing.

As we have seen, payments from the Consolidated Fund are of two types, viz. Supply Services or Consolidated Fund Services. All payments are authorised by the Comptroller-General: on his instructions payments for Supply Services are transferred from the Bank of England to the Paymaster-General's account. Payments under the Consolidated Funds Services are made by the Treasury or the Bank of England acting on its behalf. Because revenue and expenditure is not spread evenly through the year, short term government borrowing is sometimes necessary. This, however, is kept to a minimum: day-to-day borrowing can be covered by the Bank of England and use can be made of money in government funds such as the National Insurance Fund.

Longer term borrowing involves substantial amounts, and the total money owed in the repayment of loans is known as the National Debt, which has risen from £650 million in 1913 to a current figure of some £30 000 million. Loans have been used to pay for expenditure on the prosecution of wars and, particularly since 1945, on the construction of capital works in the form of roads, schools, hospitals, etc.

Control of expenditure

The difficulties of exercising a comprehensive and penetrating control of expenditure have already been referred to. The general scrutiny by M.P.s is exercised in debates in the whole House and the examination of the more technical aspects is undertaken in the Standing Committee; the Comptroller and Auditor-General has to approve and examine all accounts and report to the House; the detailed scrutiny is undertaken by the Public Accounts Committee.

The office of Comptroller and Auditor-General dates back to 1866. He is appointed by the House of Commons and is removable only by an Address of both Houses of Parliament. This, along with the fact that his salary is charged on the Consolidated Fund emphasises his independent position. His main tasks are to ensure that the Treasury demands on the Consolidated Fund are strictly in accordance with the Appropriation Act and to ensure that expenditure by the various departments is in accordance with the specific votes approved by Parliament. His reports to Parliament form the basis of the work of the Public Accounts Committee whom he assists in its work and by whom he is encouraged to report any irregularities, waste or extravagance. He is assisted by a staff of 500 civil servants who have experience of audit work.

The Public Accounts Committee (the composition of which was discussed in chapter 10) is appointed at the beginning of each session. Its function is to examine the 'accounts showing the appropriateness of the sums granted by Parliament to meet public expenditure'. This committee receives the Comptroller and Auditor-General's report and meets for about thirty half-days during the session. It is one of the committees with the highest prestige and its findings are taken with the utmost seriousness in the Treasury and the departments being investigated. It has the power to examine accounts, call for documents and receive personal explanations and observations from officials. The accounts are, of course, examined retrospectively and its examinations are always in arrears, but through its work irregularities have been exposed and improvement in accounting methods implemented. The best way to obtain an understanding of its method of working is to make a first-hand examination of the verbatim reports of its proceedings. An example of its mode of working is given in appendix V.

One of the significant achievements of the Public Accounts Committee occurred in 1967 when it was revealed that the costs of defence expenditure had been excessively high and the Ferranti electronics firm had made huge and unjustifiable profits from a government contract. The firm agreed to repay a large proportion of these profits to the Government. The contract had been made by the Ministry of Civil Aviation but the report of the Public Accounts Committee showed that there had been quite inadequate supervision by the Treasury, millions of pounds having been authorised by civil servants without any proper check on their methods of costing.

In the article previously quoted Professor Hanson wrote: 'If effective criticism of the Government's financial policy is to be effectively made, two things are needed, viz. (1) a decision to break with the practice of looking at expenditure year-by-year, since major expenditure commitments are nowadays made, in effect, for varying periods of years ahead and (2) the bringing together in *one* procedural exercise, of the two processes which are still kept rigidly separate – the authorisation of expenditure and the raising of resources, whether taxation or by loan.'

A recent Government Green Paper went some way towards meeting these proposals.[1] It took account of the Plowden proposals and recognised the archaic nature of some of the procedures. Thus, it submits that the present 'Vote on Account' should be replaced by a clause in the Appropriation Act 'enabling the Government to spend in the period beyond the end of the financial year and before the next Appropriation Act a stated proportion of the sums voted for the current financial year'. While proposing that the Estimates and Supply procedure should be left substantially unaltered, the Green Paper also proposed that annual White Papers rather than Estimates' documents would 'provide Parliament with a satisfactory basis for the kind of discussions of policy for which Supply Days have been increasingly used'. These White Papers, it was suggested, would contain an analysis of expenditure proposals for three years ahead and in some cases for five years ahead and link these to a projection of resources available in terms of existing rates of taxation. This procedure, which has now been implemented, will allow debates to be conducted with much more realism than was previously the case when data was restricted to a single year.

The Select Committee on Procedure had also been giving consideration

[1] Cmd. 4017: *Public Expenditure, a New Presentation* (H.M.S.O., 1969).

to the methods of examination and control of public expenditure by the House of Commons and it published a special report in July 1969.[1] This report distinguished three stages in the scrutiny of expenditure, viz:

  (i) discussion of the Government's expenditure strategy and policies;
 (ii) examination of the means (including new methods of management) being adopted to implement strategy and to execute policies, as reflected in annual estimates of expenditure;
(iii) retrospective scrutiny of the results achieved and the value for money obtained on the basis of annual accounts and related information...

As far as the procedural arrangements of the House of Commons in relation to these stages, was concerned, the Select Committee recommend a two-day debate in November on the Government's annual expenditure White Paper; this would be without prior examination by a Select Committee but would be supported by a medium-term economic assessment. It was proposed that the annual cycle of events outlined earlier would then run on until the following November, with a Select Committee pursuing inquiries and publishing reports of their findings in time to allow consideration by the Government and the House of Commons before the next expenditure debate in the autumn. The Committee also proposed the establishment of a Select Committee on Expenditure to replace the Select Committee on Estimates and as we have seen, this proposal has been implemented.

Although these developments have been generally welcomed as important steps in the desired direction some critics remain unconvinced that they deal effectively with the basic problem of satisfactorily relating financial procedures to the other functions of the House of Commons.[2]

[1] Special Report from the Select Committee on Procedures, Session 1968–9, H.C. 51.
[2] See e.g. P. Jay, 'Public Expenditure and Administration', *Political Quarterly*, vol. 41, no. 2, June 1970.

13 Government Departments

Upon what principle are the functions of Departments to be determined and allocated? There appear to be only two alternatives, which may be described as distribution according to persons or classes to be dealt with, and distribution according to services to be performed.

Report of the Machinery of Government Committee, 1918

Structure and organisation

Britain is a highly centralised country and although there is considerable devolution of responsibility, the key decisions are made in the central departments of government based in Whitehall. The relationship between departments and Parliament rests on the principle of ministerial responsibility. Ministers have final responsibility for the work of a department and they, in turn, are subject to the decision of the Cabinet which is collectively responsible to Parliament.

The internal organisation of departments varies but all are essentially hierarchical. Above and beyond the official hierarchy is the authority and influence of the Prime Minister and the Cabinet. This suggests an image of small elite groups of politicians hovering over a series of departmental pyramids and in an important sense the impression is valid. There is a danger, however, that it may also suggest a situation in which there is little or no communication between the various components of the overall structure and this is far from being the case. F. M. G. Willson observes: 'Whitehall is not fairly represented as a collection of pyramids, even if it is stressed that there is close contact between their apices. It is better thought of as a honeycomb, in which there is constant movement between cells horizontally as (well as) vertically, – though it is important to note that horizontal movement between departments is always at similar levels – thus Assistant Secretaries deal with Assistant Secretaries and Senior Executive officers with their counterparts, but principals in one department do not deal with Under Secretaries in another department.'[1]

Before looking at the various departments in more detail it is necessary

[1] F. M. G. Willson, 'Policy Making and Policy Makers' in Rose, *Policy Making in Britain*, pp. 363–4.

TABLE 30 *Ministers and Government Departments, 1971*

Functional grouping	Department	Minister in charge	Other Ministers
Finance	The Treasury	(Prime Minister and First Lord)*† Chancellor of the Exchequer*	Chief Secretary Finance Secretary Minister of State
Trade and Industry	Department of Trade and Industry	Secretary of State for Trade and Industry and President of the Board of Trade*	Minister for Trade Minister for Industry Minister for Aerospace 3 Parliamentary Under-Secretaries
	Department of Employment	Secretary of State for Employment*	Minister of State 2 Parliamentary Under-Secretaries† Minister without Portfolio (with responsibility for Industrial Relations Bill in House of Lords)
	Ministry of Agriculture, Fisheries and Food	Minister of Agriculture, Fisheries and Food*	Parliamentary Secretary
Social Services and Amenities	Department of Health and Social Security	Secretary of State for Social Services*	Minister of State 2 Parliamentary Under-Secretaries
	Department of Education and Science	Secretary of State for Education and Science*	Paymaster-General (with responsibility for Arts) 2 Parliamentary Under-Secretaries
	Department of the Environment	Secretary of State for the Environment*	Minister for Housing and Construction Minister for Transport Industries Minister for Local Government and Development 4 Parliamentary Under-Secretaries
	Ministry of Posts and Telecommunications	Minister of Posts and Telecommunications	

Functional grouping	Department	Minister in charge	Other Ministers
Legal and National	Home Office	Secretary of State for Home Department*	2 Ministers of State Parliamentary Under-Secretary
	Lord Chancellor's Office	Lord Chancellor*	
	Law Officers' Department	Attorney-General Solicitor-General	
	Lord Advocate's Department	Lord Advocate Solicitor-General for Scotland	
	Scottish Office	Secretary of State for Scotland*	Minister of State 3 Parliamentary Under-Secretaries
	Welsh Office	Secretary of State for Wales*	Minister of State
	Privy Council Office	Lord President of the Council (and Leader of the House of Commons)*	
Defence and External	Foreign and Commonwealth Office	Secretary of State for Foreign and Commonwealth Affairs	Chancellor of Duchy of Lancaster (with responsibility for Common Market negotiations)* Minister for Overseas Development Minister of State Parliamentary Under-Secretary
	Ministry of Defence	Secretary of State for Defence*	2 Ministers of State 3 Parliamentary Under-Secretaries
Machinery of Government	Civil Service Department	Prime Minister*† and Minister for the the Civil Service	Lord Privy Seal (and Leader of the House of Lords) Parliamentary Secretary†
	The Cabinet Office	Prime Minister*†	

* Indicates Member of the Cabinet.
† Indicates that individual is listed more than once.

to distinguish between the various types of department; these can conveniently be divided into three main groups:

(a) Ministers or Departments of State which are responsible to Parliament through a Minister.

(b) Special departments such as the Cabinet Office which are responsible to the Prime Minister.

(c) Subsidiary or satellite departments such as the Board of Inland Revenue and the Social Survey Department.

The principal departments responsible to Parliament make their own arrangements for the organisation of work, and although this varies there is a discernible basic pattern based on a hierarchy of authority and a compartmentalisation of functions. The important division at the senior level is between the politically appointed Minister and the permanent officials who are civil servants. Typically, a department will be headed on the political side by a Secretary of State or other Minister in charge, assisted by Ministers of State and Junior Ministers. The Permanent Secretary (or Permanent Under-Secretary when the Minister holds the title of Secretary of State), is assisted by one or more deputy secretaries and assistant secretaries. Usually major departments have a principal finance officer and a senior official responsible for organisation and management. Many departments have their own legal advisers and maintain an information division. Some departments maintain a regional organisation and some, which have continuous dealings with the general public, have local offices in all parts of the country.

Table 30 indicates the present organisation of the major departments of state as they existed in 1971. These are grouped according to the nature of their principal functions but it should be noted that this is not an official government nomenclature. Table 30 may usefully be compared with Table 31 which lists the main government departments as they existed in 1964.

The Conservative Government elected in 1970 took the view that 'government departments should be organised by reference to the task to be done or the objective to be attained, and that this should be done on the basis of the division of work between departments rather than, for example, dividing responsibility between departments so that each one deals with a client group'.[1] The implementation of this principle has resulted in a reordering of responsibility for functions between the departments previously dealing with trade and industry, aviation supply, the environment and education. The special position of the Scottish Office and the Welsh Office (see chapter 15) is not affected by the adoption of this functional division, although the principle does apply in the division of work within their departments.

The principal functions of the major departments are to assist the Minister in the preparation of legislation and estimates; to effect smooth

[1] Cmd. 4506: *The Reorganisation of Central Government* (H.M.S.O., 1970).

180

TABLE 31 *Government Departments, 1964*

Functional grouping	Department
Finance	The Treasury
	Paymaster-General's Office
Trade and Industry	Ministry of Economic Affairs*
	Board of Trade
	Ministry of Labour
	Ministry of Power
	Ministry of Agriculture, Food and Fisheries
	Ministry of Technology*
	Ministry of Land Resources*
Social Services and Amenities	Department of Education and Science
	Ministry of Health
	Ministry of Pensions and National Insurance
	Ministry of Housing and Local Government
	Ministry of Works and Buildings
	Postmaster-General's Department
Legal and National	Home Office
	Lord Chancellor's Department
	Law Officers' Departments
	Scottish Office
	Welsh Office
Defence and External Relations	Foreign Office
	Commonwealth Relations Office
	Colonial Office
	Ministry of Overseas Development*
	Ministry of Disarmament*
	Ministry of Defence and Aviation*

* Indicates departments newly created in 1964.

working relationships between the department and the Cabinet, Parliament and other departments; and to supervise the implementation of legislation and regulations that cover matters for which the department is responsible. The following summaries of the work of selected departments will serve to indicate the nature of some of the main fields of government activity.[1]

The Treasury
Despite recent changes, which are discussed below, the Treasury still occupies a central role in government administration and it was, at least until recently, referred to as the 'department of departments'. Details of its part in the financial procedures were given in chapter 12 and in this section we are mainly concerned with its wider responsibilities. The fact that the Prime Minister is First Lord of the Treasury is indicative of the department's importance. The actual extent of the Treasury's wider powers has ebbed and flowed in the period since the Second World War

[1] See *Britain: an Official Handbook*, current edn (H.M.S.O.).

181

but its primacy of place in the spectrum of governmental administration has not been seriously questioned.

In 1964 the Department of Economic Affairs was created by the incoming Labour Government, and this took over the major part of the Treasury's responsibility for economic planning and co-ordination. This took from the Treasury an important source of power and authority, but when the Department of Economic Affairs was wound up in 1969 it was decided to return responsibility for economic planning to the Treasury.

Until recently the Treasury held responsibility for the general control of the Civil Service and for the staffing of the various departments. In 1968, however, the Government accepted a recommendation of the Fulton Committee on the Civil Service that this function should be transferred to a newly created Civil Service Department. The Fulton Committee took the view that 'the central management of the Service is not, under modern conditions, an appropriate function of the central finance department'.[1]

The Civil Service Department

The office of Minister for the Civil Service is held by the Prime Minister but the day-to-day work of the department is supervised by another senior Minister, at present the Lord Privy Seal. The Permanent Secretary in the department is head of the Civil Service.

Since 1968 this department has had responsibility for Civil Service personnel, including recruitment, pay and promotions. The department is also responsible for promoting the development of administrative and managerial training and provides a management consultancy service which all departments are encouraged to make use of. The Civil Service Commission, which is the recruiting body for the civil servants, forms part of the department but care is taken to ensure that its independence and impartiality are maintained.

The Home Office

The Home Office was created in 1872. The department is headed by the Secretary of State for the Home Department who is usually referred to as the Home Secretary. The Home Secretary is generally responsible for the maintenance of law and order through the whole of Great Britain and for various matters relating to safety and public welfare.

The chief matters falling within the Home Secretary's responsibility are: the police forces; the treatment of offenders and juvenile delinquents; the organisation of magistrates' courts; various aspects of the administration of criminal justice; the law relating to the conduct of parliamentary and local elections; the control of firearms, explosives and dangerous drugs; immigration control and the naturalisation of aliens; problems of racial integration; and matters connected with British nationality and citizenship of the United Kingdom and Colonies.

[1] Cmd. 3638: *The Report of the Committee on the Civil Service* (H.M.S.O., 1968).

The Home Secretary advises the Sovereign in the exercise of the royal prerogative of mercy and is the avenue through which petitions are presented to the Queen. He also acts as the channel of communication between the Governments of Northern Ireland, the Channel Islands and the Isle of Man.

The Foreign and Commonwealth Office

This department headed by the Secretary of State for Foreign and Commonwealth affairs has been developed by bringing together the previously separate Foreign, Commonwealth and Colonial Offices. In 1970 the Ministry of Overseas Development was also brought under its wing (see below).

The Foreign and Commonwealth Office acts as the channel of communication between the British Government and the Governments of foreign and Commonwealth countries in all matters affecting international and Commonwealth relations. It makes arrangements for the Government to be represented in the United Nations organisation, the North Atlantic Treaty Organisation and other international bodies. It is also responsible for ensuring that the interests of British subjects in foreign countries are safeguarded, the promotion of British trade interests and the explanation of the Government's policy overseas.

The department supervises the discharge of the Government's responsibilities in respect of both dependent territories and associated states in the Commonwealth. In the case of the former it is mainly concerned with agreements on defence and external affairs, but in the latter it retains responsibility for the existing pattern of government and for actively assisting progress towards self-government and self-determination in the territories concerned. From time to time it has serious problems to cope with in this respect; in recent years for example it has had to cope with the unilateral declaration of independence in Southern Rhodesia and disturbances in Anguilla.

The Government recognise that the management of overseas aid is a function distinct from the general conduct of foreign affairs and have decided that development work in the unified department will form a separate functional wing under the direction of a Minister of Overseas Development.

Reorganisation of Government departments 1970

Some departments such as the Treasury and the Home Office have a long and continuous history, others are recent creations. The pattern of departments is likely to alter with different Governments and even with the same Government at different stages in a relatively long period of office. Thus, in 1964, the Labour Government introduced a Ministry of Economic Affairs, a Ministry of Technology, a Ministry of Land and Resources, and a Ministry of Overseas Development. Some of these departments were modified during the period 1964–70 and those which remained when the Conservatives came into office at the end of this time disappeared as a result of amalgamation and reorganisation.

A. H. Hanson and M. Walles, in discussing this kind of development, observe: 'There has been a continuous process of creation, fission, fusion and transfer, rapid at some times, slower at others. The resultant changes are to be largely explained by the expansion of the functions of government, by the development of new areas of policy (e.g. social security; economic planning) and the disappearance of old ones (e.g. India), and by the fluctuations in the degree of emphasis accorded from time to time to different fields of administration.'[1]

What Hanson and Walles have called the 'fission–fusion' process can be illustrated by the reorganisation of departments effected by the Conservative Government in 1970. The principal changes introduced were:

(*a*) The establishment of a new Department of Trade and Industry based on the functions of the Board of Trade, some of the functions of the Ministry of Technology, and responsibilities for monopolies, mergers and restrictive practices transferred from the Department of Employment and Productivity – the last being re-named as the Department of Employment. The objective of the new unified department is 'to assist British industry and commerce to improve their economic and technological strength and competitiveness'. Its responsibilities include both the public and private sector of industry. The services provided include export promotion services, export credits, and a wide range of services notably for small and medium-sized firms, and the encouragement of industrial research. Related to these is the Departments' responsibility for the industrial aspects of regional policy.

The Government believed that the unifying of this field of policy would *inter alia*, have, the advantage of avoiding 'an unreal dichotomy between "internal" and "international" aspects of commerce and industry' and have special advantages in the context of the possibility of Britain's entry into the European Economic Community.

(*b*) A Department of the Environment formed by bringing together the Ministry of Housing and Local Government, the Ministry of Public Works and Buildings and the Ministry of Transport under one Secretary of State. The Government took the view that: 'Because these functions interact, and because they give rise to acute and conflicting requirements, a new form of organisation is needed at the centre of the administrative system.' The Government believed that this unification of functions would place the central government in a better position to deal with the re-organisation of local government.

(*c*) The establishment of a new Department of Health and Social Security to coincide with the integration of the personal social services, including welfare, child care and some aspects of health, effected at local

[1] Hanson and Walles, *Governing Britain*, p. 119.

184

authority level in England and Wales by the Local Authority Social Services Act, 1970, consequent upon the recommendations of the Seebohm Committee.

This part of the re-organisation involves the transfer of child-care responsibilities in England, formerly exercised by the Home Secretary to the new department. The Home Secretary retains his responsibilities in relation to juvenile courts and the problems of juvenile delinquency because they are regarded as 'integral to his overriding responsibility for protecting the public and ensuring the rights and liberties of the subject'.

The Government have also commissioned a study to determine which parts of the machinery of government need to remain in London and which might be re-located outside.[1]

Co-ordination

The machinery of central government, taken as a whole, involves a vast and complex field of organisation. This inevitably presents problems of co-ordination and communication between its various personnel and units, and a variety of means have been developed to cope with these problems.

The Cabinet, Cabinet Committees and the Cabinet Secretariat, by the very nature of their responsibilities, have the need for co-ordination constantly in mind, and it seems likely that the newly established central policy review body (discussed in chapter 9) will make an important contribution towards this end. These centralising procedures are, however, by themselves, insufficient.

At the Civil Service levels there exists a network of inter-departmental committees, some of which are continuing bodies and others are formed on on an *ad hoc* basis, which maintain contacts between related departments and broaden the experience and knowledge of those who are members. The part played by the Treasury in both its financial and wider role is also relevant here, and the establishment of the Civil Service Department will almost certainly have an effect upon inter-departmental relationships both at formal and informal levels.

In the post-war period several attempts have been made to bring about better co-ordination in government by the appointment of co-ordinating Ministers, sometimes figuratively or pejoratively referred to as 'overlords'. In 1951, Mr Churchill appointed Lord Woolton, the Lord President of the Council, as co-ordinator of the Ministries of Food and Agriculture; Lord Leathers was made Secretary of State for the co-ordination of Transport, Fuel and Power; and Lord Cherwell, the Paymaster-General, was given responsibility for the oversight of scientific research and development.

This move was unpopular with M.P.s, and initially there was some confusion about the extent of the 'overlords' power, concern being expressed

[1] Cmd. 4506.

about who was to be responsible for answering questions in Parliament. This matter was clarified by Mr Churchill who, in an announcement in the House of Commons, said: 'The co-ordinating Ministers have no statutory powers. They have, in particular, no power to give orders or directions to a Minister...the existence and activities of these co-ordinating Ministers does not impair or diminish the responsibility to Parliament of the Departmental Ministers whose policies they co-ordinate.' This assurance on accountability and the benefits claimed for the organisational innovation did little to lessen the confusion of the arrangement and the experiment was abandoned in 1953.

More recently the tendency has been not to renew the idea of co-ordinating Ministers but to bring about a much greater degree of unification of departments with related functions. This development provides an excellent example of the 'fusion' aspect of the 'fission–fusion' process. Thus, in Mr Wilson's premiership, the three formerly separate service departments for the Navy, the Army and the Air Force, were integrated into a Ministry of Defence; the Ministry of Pensions (which had been merged with the Ministry of National Insurance in 1953) took over the work of the National Assistance Board and became the Ministry of Social Security in 1968; the Commonwealth and Colonial Offices had previously been merged and these were joined with the Foreign Office to form a unified department dealing with overseas affairs in 1968. In 1969 the Ministry of Technology took over the work of the Minister of Power and the responsibilities relating to industry exercised by the Board of Trade; and a new department of Local Government and Planning assumed responsibility for a wide range of functions including housing, local government, transport and regional planning. A glance at Tables 30 and 31, together with the observations already made on the reorganisation of government in 1970, will show that the process of integration has now been even further developed.

Special advisers

From time to time, experts from the universities, the business world and elsewhere are brought into government departments to advise Ministers. Those so engaged occupy a sometimes uneasy position midway between the political heads of departments and their senior civil servants.

In the case of the Labour Government of 1964–70, Mr Brian Lapping speaks of these appointments in the context of 'the building up of a small group of ministers' friends to scrutinise and if necessary to oppose the permanent officials' line'. Of the industrialist Mr Fred Catherwood, and the two *Financial Times* correspondents, Mr Sam Brittan and Mr Michael Shanks, brought into the Department of Economic Affairs by Mr George Brown, he writes: 'The idea behind their appointments was that they would enable the democratically elected ministers to overcome the

186

resistance of civil servants, by finding ways round the cloistered mandarins' obstructive arguments.'[1]

Perhaps the best known of these advisers during this period were Dr Thomas (now Lord) Balogh from Oxford and Professor Kaldor from Cambridge. Both were Hungarian immigrants and both had an important influence on aspects of the policy and administration of the Labour Government. Professor Kaldor was adviser to Mr James Callaghan during his time as Chancellor of the Exchequer and his schemes for a capital gains tax and selective employment tax were introduced by the Government. Dr Balogh came into the Cabinet Office with a special brief on Overseas Development but in fact acted as personal adviser to the Prime Minister.

Well-known academic economists who have advised earlier Conservative administrators include Lord Robbins, Sir Roy Harrod and Professor Paish. In June 1970, Mr Heath, the Prime Minister, announced that Mr Richard Mayjes, the marketing co-ordinator of Steel International Petroleum Co. had been appointed as adviser to the Prime Minister and the Government. He will lead a team of 12–14 'imported' businessmen who will be particularly concerned with problems of organisation and management in the top levels of central government administration. Mr Mayjes observed, when questioned by reporters about his appointment, 'We shall be a group of businessmen looking at specific things. We shall use our managerial skills to analyse and investigate government departments and say if things need doing differently.' The group included Mr D. Raynor (Marks and Spencer), and Mr R. Hutton (Hambro's Bank).

Advisory bodies
Many government departments are assisted by advisory councils or committees which number upwards of 1000 in all. These are established by Ministers to obtain information, advice and assistance from interested individuals and organisations; in particular, they enable departments to become aware of the views of important bodies of opinion in relation to government policy and administration as, for example, in ascertaining reactions to proposed legislation. In this respect they provide one of the main agencies through which contact between the Government and well established interest or pressure groups is maintained.

The most important of these include bodies such as the National Production Advisory Council on Industry, the Economic Planning Board, the Central Health Services Council, the Air Transport Advisory Council, the Central Advisory Council for Education and the Central Housing Advisory Committee. There are also a whole range of smaller and sometimes highly specialist bodies ranging from the Committee on the Preservation of Wooden Vessels to the Bee Keepers' Advisory Committee. Some of the latter have executive as well as advisory functions as in the case of the

[1] Lapping, *Labour Government 1964–70*, pp. 206–7.

Ancient Monuments Board and the Historic Buildings Council.

The size and membership of the bodies varies, but in the most influential it is now a well established principle that the relevant interest groups should be adequately represented. The National Joint Advisory Council, initially attached to the Ministry of Labour, consisted of 17 representative of the British Employers Confederation, 17 members nominated by the T.U.C. and 6 from the nationalised industries; its function was 'to advise on matters in which employers and workers have a common interest, and to provide for closer consultation between government and organised industry'. The National Advisory Council for the Motor Manufacturing Industry, which was attached to the Board of Trade, met under the Chairmanship of the Permanent Secretary and comprised: 3 Government representatives (from the Board of Trade, Ministry of Transport and Ministry of Supply), 7 employers' representatives appointed on the recommendation of the Society of Motor Manufacturers and Traders, 2 of the organisation ex-officers, 4 trade union representatives and 1 'independent' member. The task of this body was: 'to provide a means of regular consultations between the Government and the motor manufacturers on such matters as the location of industry, exports, imports, research design and the progress of the industry'[1].

The number and range of government advisory bodies has grown tremendously in the course of this century. Before 1914 these were very few, in 1939 there were about 200; at present there are nearly 1000. J. D. Stewart observes: 'For the government, consultation has become a necessity and by government one means not merely the ministers. For most of the consultation takes place well below that level and well below the permanent secretaries of departments.'[2]

Royal Commissions and similar bodies

In addition to the advisory bodies discussed above the Government appoints various *ad hoc* bodies to make detailed investigations into selected areas of policy and to make recommendations for its consideration. These bodies include Royal Commissions and Departmental Committees.

Royal Commissions have been appointed since the fourteenth century but they were not often used as tools of inquiry until the nineteenth century. They can be divided into two main categories. Firstly, there are those which are permanent or which exist over a relatively long period of time; examples of 'permanent' bodies include the Royal Commission on Historical Monuments and the Royal Fine Arts Commission; 'semipermanent' Royal Commissions have included those on Crofter Colonisation (1888–1906), Sugar Supply (1914–21), and Awards to Inventors (1919–35, 1946–56). Secondly, there are the Royal Commissions which are appointed to look into matters upon which the Government feels it

[1] Beer, *Modern British Politics*, pp. 338–9.
[2] Stewart, *British Pressure Groups*, p. 7.

188

TABLE 32   *Royal Commissions, 1957–66*

Subject	Chairman	Year appointed	Year reported or terminated
Doctors' and dentists' remunerations	Sir Harry Pilkington	1957	1960
Local government in Greater London	Sir Edwin Herbert	1957	1960
The police	Sir Henry Willink	1959	(1) 1960
			(2) 1962
The press	Lord Shawcross	1961	1962
The penal system	Lord Amory	1964	1966
Trade unions and employers' associations	Lord Donovan	1965	1968
Prices and incomes	Mr Aubrey Jones	1965	1967
Medical education	Lord Todd	1965	1968
Tribunals of inquiry	Lord Justice Salman	1966	1966
Local government in England	Lord Redcliffe-Maud	1966	1969
Local government in Scotland	Lord Wheatley	1966	1969
Assizes and Quarter Sessions	Lord Beeching	1966	1969

requires detailed information and advice. Table 32, which gives brief details of the Royal Commissions appointed between 1957 and 1966, indicates the range and variety of topics covered in these investigations.

Royal Commissions are normally made up of between five and twenty members who work on a part-time basis, fitting in meetings and the reading of papers as best they can. Members are chosen individually on the basis of their knowledge, expertise and capacity for judgement and not as the representatives of interested groups. They have clerical, secretarial, and specialist help provided by the Civil Service.

There does not appear to be any hard and fast rule which determines whether a particular enquiry will be referred to a Royal Commission or a Committee appointed by a Minister; a Royal Commission tends to have a higher prestige but it cannot be said that the decision to refer a matter to one or the other is made on the importance of the topic to be investigated.

Investigating Committees appointed by Ministers are more numerous

TABLE 33   *Select List of Topics Investigated by Departmental Committees, 1961–6*

Subject	Chairman	Year appointed	Year reported
Higher education	Lord Robbins	1961	1963
Decimal currency	Earl of Halsbury	1961	1963
Renumeration of Ministers and M.P.s	Sir G. Lawrence	1963	1964
Housing in Greater London	Sir M. Holland	1963	1965
Port, transport, industry	Lord Devlin	1964	1964
Aircraft industry	Lord Plowden	1964	1965
Local authority personal services	F. Seebohm	1965	1968
Prison security	Earl Mountbatten	1966	1966

Subject	Chairman	Year
Bribery of Ministers of the Crown or other public servants in connection with the grant of licences, etc.	Sir J. Lynskey	1948
Allegations of improper disclosure of information relating to the raising of the Bank Rate	Lord Parker	1957
Allegations that John Waters was assaulted on 7 December 1957 at Thurso and action taken by Caithness police in connection therewith	Lord Sorn	1959
The circumstances in which offences under the Official Secrets Act were committed by William Vassall	Lord Radcliffe	1962

than Royal Commissions but they are very similar in structure and proceedings and have often been concerned with subjects of comparable importance. Investigating bodies appointed by Ministers are variously described as departmental committees, inter-departmental committees and working parties. Table 33 gives brief details of some matters recently investigated by bodies of this kind.

The reports of both Royal Commissions and Departmental Committees embody findings on facts, and conclusions. The report of a Royal Commission is formally addressed to the Sovereign and reports of other Committees are addressed to the Minister or Ministers who appointed them. Where members disagree, they may submit a minority report or a note of dissent. The reports are popularly referred to by the name of the Chairman, e.g. the Report of the Committee on the Civil Service published in 1968 is referred to as the Fulton Report.

Tribunals of Inquiry
Tribunals which fall into a different category to those discussed in chapter 19 are from time to time appointed by the Government to investigate matters involving allegations of serious misconduct or other offences by Ministers or public officials. These are set up under the Tribunal of Inquiry (Evidence) Act, 1921, which provides that upon a resolution of both Houses of Parliament on a matter of urgent public importance a tribunal may be appointed by the Sovereign or by a Secretary of State with all the powers of the High Court as regards examination of witnesses and production of documents for the objective investigation of facts. Table 34 gives a representative list of inquiries by Tribunals, concentrating on those which have been held since the Second World War. The political effects of some of these inquiries are discussed in chapter 9.

The wider framework
Government departments are at the centre of a huge and complex administrative network. Some have regional and local offices scattered throughout

the country, some discharge certain functions through the medium of local councils, others again have a close and continuing link with public corporations or other government enterprises.

The scale is vast and the Civil Service alone has grown at least twenty-fold in the last hundred years. The sheer size of the government machine, however, makes it impossible for a Minister to be aware of the bulk of the day-to-day activities for which he bears responsibility and he is therefore dependent upon civil servants in his department for information and assistance not only on routine matters but on the data which play a significant part in policy making. The nature of this relationship and the organisation of the Civil Service is discussed in the next chapter.

14   The Civil Service

How far do the defects of the Service arise from the character of the relationship between itself, Parliament, and the public; that is to say, how far are they the inescapable consequences of our democratic system of government (in which case we may have to endure them), or how far are they remediable by changes in organisation and control?

Mr W. J. Brown, M.P., from a speech in the House of Commons, 28 January 1943

Introduction

The term civil servant is applied to employees of the Crown who do not hold political or judicial office and whose salaries are paid wholly and directly out of money voted by Parliament. This description is usually applied to non-industrial staff attached to government departments in the United Kingdom and overseas. Altogether, these groups number nearly 500 000, about one third of whom are women. Basically, the function of civil servants is to assist Ministers in the discharge of their public and parliamentary duties. They work under the direction of Ministers but they are servants of the Crown; informally, at least, they have security of tenure and their employment by the Crown normally continues regardless of changes in the Government.

The Home Civil Service is distinguished from the Diplomatic Service, which is a separate, self-contained service numbering some 6200 in all, which provides staff for the Foreign and Commonwealth Office and for diplomatic and consular posts abroad. This service has its own career structure, but the various levels generally correspond in status and salary with similar ranks in the Home Civil Service.

Historical development

The Civil Service of today has its origins in changes which were brought about in the nineteenth century. The widespread existence of corruption, incompetence and jobbery which then existed in the government service led to demands for reform, and eventually Sir Charles Trevelyan and Sir Stafford Northcote were asked to investigate and make the necessary recommendations.

Their 'Report on the Organisation of the Permanent Civil Service' was

192

issued in 1855. In this they put forward four major recommendations which were designed to provide for the systematic recruitment of able applicants to the government service and to ensure that, as far as possible, effective use was made of those appointed. It was proposed that:

(a) Recruitment should be by examination.

(b) A clear distinction should be made between 'intellectuals', destined for 'superior situations' and 'mechanicals', who would occupy 'lower-class appointments'.

(c) The service should be unified by the adoption of uniform salary grades and the acceptance of the principle that civil servants could be transferred from one department to another.

(d) Promotion should be by merit rather than by seniority.

These recommendations are generally referred to as the Trevelyan–Northcote principles. Civil Service Commissioners were appointed to conduct the examinations, but it was not until 1870 that the reforms were substantially implemented.

Following the Reorganisation Report of the National Whitley Council in 1920, the basic division into two classes was replaced by a four-fold division, each class being recruited by examination and distinguished by the level of education reached. The four classes were named Administrative, Executive, Clerical and Clerical Assistant; the first were likely to be university graduates; the second, 18-year-old leavers with a Higher School Certificate (corresponding to 'A' Levels); the third, 16-year-old leavers with School Certificate (corresponding to a group of 'O' levels in basic subjects). Promotion from one class to another was initially very rare. Entry to the Administrative Class was by either or both of two methods. Method 1 involved an interview and a written examination of five papers based on university syllabuses in a wide range of subjects; Method 2 involved spending two days of interviews accompanied by psychological tests and assessment of approaches to problem situations followed by a selection board. The second method was most frequently employed after the Second World War and the first method was finally dropped at the end of 1970.

These classes make up the bulk of the non-manual Home Civil Service, but with the gradual extension in the sphere of government activity a widening body of professional, scientific and technical personnel have been appointed. The Second World War created a new flexibility in recruitment which led to the waiving of age limits and the acceptance of approved qualifications in lieu of examination. Large numbers of temporary civil servants were recruited to man new and extended departments and these included appointments at the higher as well as the lower levels. Not the least significant among these senior appointments was a number of university dons who included two future Labour leaders in the persons of Hugh Gaitskell and Harold Wilson.

Pre-Fulton structure

The duties and numerical strengths of the various classes as they existed in 1969 are given below. The numbers presented include the equivalent grades in the Diplomatic Service.

(i) The Administrative Class numbers about 3900. The duties of officers in this group include advice to Ministers, major contributions to the formulation of policy, the co-ordination and improvement of government machinery and the general administration and control of government departments. This group is frequently referred to as the Higher Civil Service.

(ii) The Executive Classes (General and Departmental) number some 84 000. These classes are responsible for the day-to-day conduct of government business within the framework of established policy (e.g. the higher level work of accounts and revenue collection). It must be stated, however, that the work done by some officers in the high levels of these classes is difficult to distinguish from that performed by corresponding grades in the Administrative Class.

(iii) The Specialist Classes (General and Departmental) number about 120 000. They include accountants, architects, doctors, economists, engineers, lawyers, librarians, statisticians, surveyors and a variety of scientific officers. Other technically qualified personnel, e.g. drawing office staff, are included in this group.

(iv) The Clerical Classes (general and departmental) are made up of about 191 000 officers who undertake the routine work of departments, e.g. preparation of accounts, keeping of records, handling of claims in accordance with prescribed rules, and the summarisation and annotation of documents. The personal secretaries of senior officers and officers who are responsible for the supervision of defined areas of internal work are included in this group.

(v) The Typing and Machine Operating Classes, numbering about 41 000.

(vi) The Messengerial Class has some 27 000 members and, in addition to messengers, includes office-cleaners, 'paper-keepers', etc.[1]

To these must be added the various divisions of Her Majesty's Inspectorate which are attached to individual departments. These include, *inter alia*, factory inspectors attached to the Department of Employment and schools inspectors linked with the Department of Education and Science.

Praise and Criticism

At different times and from different sources the Civil Service has received both high praise and damning criticism, the most serious criticism having centred on the higher civil service.

By any standards this group constitutes an elite. The Sixth Report of

[1] This description is based on *Britain, 1970* (H.M.S.O.), pp. 61–2.

the Select Committee for the Session 1964–5 shows that of those successful in direct entry to the administrative class, between 1957 and 1963, no less than 85 per cent came from the universities of Oxford and Cambridge, 6 per cent were from London University and 8 per cent from Scottish and other universities. It should be noted, however, that the *Official Handbook for 1970* records that of the total composition of this class in 1969, about 40 per cent was made up of individuals who had been promoted from the executive class or specially recruited at a mature age.

When the first majority Labour Government was elected in 1945, there was considerable speculation as to how the upper echelons of the Civil Service would respond to the demands made by the newly appointed Ministers who were determined to implement a policy of public ownership and comprehensive social welfare. Mr Herbert (later Lord) Morrison who had served in the 1929–31 Labour Government and who, as leader of the House of Commons between 1945 and 1950, bore the main responsibility for organising the passage of a heavy legislative programme, paid the following tribute in 1954: 'From a long and varied experience of the British Civil Service in Home Departments and in the Foreign Office and as a co-ordinating Minister, I have in general formed a high opinion of the energy, ability, resourcefulness and incorruptibility of our Civil Service. The belief among some of the public and even some Members of Parliament that civil servants do not work in harmony with Ministers, I have hardly ever found to be justified.' He adds, 'the British Civil Service is loyal to the Government of the day. The worst that can be said of them is that sometimes they are not quick enough in accustoming themselves to new ideas...'[1] The tenor of this assessment is confirmed by J. P. Mackintosh, who has experience both as a Professor of Politics and a Labour M.P. In 1970, he wrote: 'The post-war governments, both Labour and Conservative, have shown that a Minister with coherent, workable policies and reasonable energy and capacity can get loyal co-operation from his or her civil servants.'[2]

In February 1966, a Committee was set up under the chairmanship of Lord Fulton to examine the structure, recruitment, training and management of the Home Civil Service.[3] In January 1967, the Labour Party published a document approved by its National Executive Committee which was prepared for submission to the Fulton Committee. This put forward views quite different to those quoted above and made serious criticisms of the higher civil service; in particular, it expressed grave concern about the methods of secrecy and the alleged withholding of information from Ministers.

The document stated: 'At times it almost seems that the whole structure of British Government is designed to protect the policy-making functions

[1] Morrison, *Government and Parliament*, pp. 344–6.
[2] Mackintosh, *Government and Politics of Britain*, pp. 147–8.
[3] See Cmd. 3638: *Report of the Committee on the Civil Service* (H.M.S.O., 1968).

of government from public scrutiny.' It also said the information is withheld from the minister either 'because it might lead him to support policies which the department does not (or does not yet) approve of, or even because it is being done in preparation for a future Government of a different political colour.' It adds: 'Inter-departmental Committees of officials are a particularly effective way of undermining the authority of Ministers. The Minister may not be consulted until the officials have arrived at an agreed compromise.' The statement also put forward the view that Ministers, on taking office, should have power to appoint up to four personal assistants who would have direct access to him and to all information in his department. They would take no part in decision making but would act as an extra pair of eyes, help him with policy formulation and keep him in touch with relevant developments in other departments.

The report submitted twenty-two recommendations for the reform of the Civil Service including the need for greater integration within the service, a broader basis of recruitment, a greater mobility of officials, more dynamic management and a new career structure to give scientists and engineers a greater influence in the decision-making process.

The Labour Party document was, of course, only one of the many submissions made to the Committee on the Civil Service whose report was supplemented by five volumes of evidence.

The Fulton Report

The Fulton Committee reported in 1968, and although this recognised the existence of 'exceptionally able men and women at all levels' and spoke of 'the integrity and impartiality' of the Civil Service as a whole, the Committee took the view that the Service generally had 'not kept up with changing tasks' and that basically it was 'a nineteenth-century institution trying to deal with a twentieth-century situation'.

The report listed six aspects of the structure and procedures of the Service which, in its view, worked to the detriment of its existing and future responsibilities. These points were expressed in the following terms:

(1) The Service is still essentially based on the philosophy of the amateur (or 'generalist' or 'allrounder') and this is most evident in the administrative class which holds the dominant position in the Service.

(2) The present system of classes in the Service seriously impedes its work. (The detailed position being that there were 47 general classes and more than 1400 departmental classes.)

(3) Scientists, engineers and other specialist officers are too frequently not given the responsibilities, authority and opportunities which they deserve.

(4) Too few civil servants are skilled managers. Few of the administrative class think of themselves as managers, partly because they have not received adequate management training.

(5) There is too little contact between the Service and the community.

196

(6) Career planning covers too small a section of the Service, being restricted mainly to the administrative class. Nor is there encouragement and reward for individual initiative and objectively measured performance: for many civil servants, especially in the lower grades, promotion depends too much on seniority.

The Committee made a number of recommendations, the majority of which have been put into effect. The most important of these were:

(i) The traditional dominance of the Civil Service by the Treasury should be ended and responsibility for the Service as a whole should pass to a new Civil Service Department responsible to the Prime Minister. The Permanent Secretary of this department would be the Head of the Civil Service.

(ii) The tradition of the 'gifted amateur' should be ended and there should be a development of greater professionalism among both specialists and administrators. This would involve, for administrators, specialism in particular areas (e.g. economic–financial or social welfare) and, for specialists, more training in management and opportunities for greater responsibilities and wider careers.

(iii) The existing class system, which does not correspond with the realities of the Service's work, should be abolished and replaced by a unified grading structure.

(iv) Much more attention should be paid to training. A Civil Service College should be established to provide major training courses in administration and management and a wide range of short courses and conduct research into problems of government machinery and policy.

(v) Much more attention should be paid to career management. All civil servants should have the opportunity to progress as far and as fast as their talents and appropriate training will allow.

(vi) There should be greater flexibility in transfer between the Civil Service and industry. This would be achieved by temporary appointment for fixed periods, short term changes of staff, and freer movement out of the Service.

The traditional characteristics of anonymity and secrecy were touched on in the Report and it was recommended that the Government should set up an inquiry to make recommendations for getting rid of unnecessary secrecy. They also stated that the convention of anonymity should be modified and civil servants, as professional administrators, should be able to go further than now in explaining what their departments were doing, at any rate in so far as concerns managing existing policies and implementing legislation.

Assessment

Since the publication of the Fulton Report there has been much argument as to the validity of its recommendations, the extent to which, if implemented, the fundamental character of the Civil Service and its place within the British system of government will be altered. It has been argued on the one hand that changes were unnecessary and on the other that the proposals were either too faint-hearted or irrelevant.

Thus Lord Simey, a member of the Committee and Professor of Social Service at Liverpool University, wrote a dissenting note which suggested that 'necessary reforms could be obtained by encouraging the evolution of what is basically the present situation . . .'. J. P. Mackintosh remarks: 'In general the Fulton Committee's critique is overdone, in that it is attacking a caricature of the service which was never wholly true and certainly under-estimates the changes that had taken place since the late 1950s.' This writer considers that the Civil Service is moulded chiefly by the doctrine of ministerial responsibility and all that flows from it including secrecy, anonymity and isolation from the wider community, and concludes: 'The Fulton Committee was not, by its reference, allowed to look at relationships with parliament but, as a result, it blamed the service itself for many characteristics imposed upon it by virtue of this relationship.'[1] Others, however, believe that the charges ushered in as a result of the Fulton Proposals will, when fully implemented, effect a radical transformation in the existing pattern of the Civil Service.

The argument that to a large extent the Civil Service *modus operandi* must reflect the fundamental principles of our systems of government is a valid one. But this does not necessarily mean that its efficiency cannot be enhanced by ensuring that the most able occupy the influential positions and by adopting up to date techniques of management and administration. Given the limitations of the system, there seems to be no reason why the Fulton proposals should not make a significant contribution to the development of a Civil Service which is conscious of modern needs and trained to the highest level of competence.

The implementation of the Fulton proposals which were accepted by the Government has been fairly rapid. The Civil Service Department came into operation in November 1968; a Civil Service College was opened in June 1970 and a greatly extended training programme has been introduced throughout the Service; a merger of the administrative, executive and clerical classes up to and including assistant secretary level was announced with effect from 1 January 1971; a project is at present in hand to absorb all posts at and above the level of Under Secretary and equivalent grades into a unified pay and grading structure.

Restrictions on political activities

In pursuance of the tradition of the political neutrality of the Civil Service a system of rules has been developed and designed to ensure that political bias does not affect the work of its members especially in their dealings with Ministers and the general public.

No restrictions are imposed upon the right of civil servants to vote in

[1] Mackintosh, *Government and Politics of Britain*, pp. 151–2.

parliamentary and local government elections. The extent to which the individual civil servant, however, is free to engage actively in political work is determined by the nature of the responsibility he holds in the Service. Generally the situation is that the higher his position in the administrative hierarchy, the greater is the restriction imposed.

Civil Servants can, in this respect, be conveniently divided into three categories. There is first, a 'politically free' group who are at liberty to be engaged in all kinds of local and national political activity, the only important restriction being that if they wish to become parliamentary candidates they must resign their appointments before nomination day on the understanding that if they are not elected they will be reinstated in their jobs within a week of the declaration of the election result. This group is made up mainly of those employed in the industrial grades and those who do routine jobs in the non-industrial grades (e.g. messengers). Secondly, there is an 'intermediate' group who are free, subject to the acceptance of the need for discretion and the granting of permission by the department concerned, to take part in most activities *except* parliamentary candidature. This category includes clerical and typing classes together with certain specialist groups such as experimental officers and draftsmen.

Lastly, there is a 'politically restricted' group which is not allowed to take part in *national* political activities. This group includes members of the Professional, Scientific and Technical grades and the Executive and Administrative Classes in the pre-Fulton classification. 'Departments are encouraged to permit members of this group to engage in local political activities to the maximum extent consistent with the reputation of the service for political impartiality, having regard to the nature of the duties of the officer concerned and the extent of contact with the public that his duties involve. Where permission is granted it is subject to a code of discretion and to the obligation to notify the department of election or co-option to a local council.'[1]

The Government's attitude generally is that the political views of civil servants are not a matter for official concern. There are, however, some Civil Service duties in which secrecy is regarded as being vital to national security and in these cases the Government takes the view that it is justifiable to exclude from employment in its service anyone whose loyalty and reliability in this respect is in doubt. It is for this reason that anyone who is known to be a member of, or actively associated with or in sympathy with, the Communist Party or Fascist organisations, or who is liable to be a security risk for any other reasons, is not employed in certain jobs.

Ministers and Civil Servants

In assessing the work of the Civil Service it is necessary to underline the important distinction between questions about routine efficiency and

[1] *Britain*, 1970, p. 65.

issues concerning the distribution of power between elected Ministers and those appointed permanent officials who make up the administrative class. In theory Ministers make policy decisions which it is the function of the Civil Service to implement, but clearly the actual process of decision making is more complex than this. Mr Peter Shore, who was a Minister in the Wilson Government presented this relationship as one between 'temporary politicians' (i.e. Ministers) and 'permanent politicians' (i.e. higher civil servants) and suggested that 'even the most ruthless Ministerial will and the sharpest Ministerial cutting edge can be frustrated and blunted if they come into conflict with the conventional wisdom of Whitehall'.[1]

The present Head of the Civil Service, Sir William Armstrong, has said: 'The chief danger to which politicians and Ministers are open to is not, as is supposed, that obstructive bureaucrats will drag their feet in implementing their schemes, but that their own optimism will carry them into schemes and policies which will be subsequently seen to fail and which attention to the experience and information available from the Civil Service might have avoided.'

It is difficult, if not impossible, to make a hard and fast judgement on this matter. As Anthony Sampson has observed: 'It is in the dark forests between policies and their execution, between dreams and realities, between doctrine and its application, that the trails of the investigator finally become hopelessly lost; the Member of Parliament, the journalist and even the historian has to admit that the truth will never fully emerge.'[2] It does seem likely, however, that the problem varies in accordance with the actions and attitudes of the individuals principally involved. The earlier discussion (chapter 10) on strong and weak Ministers is relevant here but a strong Minister who is also adept at personal relationships is likely to get better co-operation from civil servants and others than one who does not possess this quality.

Conclusions

Members of the Civil Service at lower levels in the hierarchy are to a large extent bound by traditions and practices developed over a long period of time, which spring, at least in part, from the need for parliamentary accountability. Delay and incompetence there may sometimes be, but of the fundamental incorruptibility of the Civil Service there is no doubt. There is no room for complacency, but in view of the many criticisms which are levelled at the Civil Service it is important to take into account the Fulton Commission's view that 'the country does not recognise enough how impressively conscientious many civil servants are in the personal service they give the public. It is of high importance that these and other qualities should be preserved.'

[1] P. Shore, *Entitled to Know* (MacGibbon and Kee, 1966).
[2] A. Sampson, 'The New Mandarins', *The Observer*, 28 February 1971.

15   Delegation and Devolution

The proper duty of a representative assembly in regard to matters of administration is not to decide them by its own vote, but to take care that the persons who have to decide them shall be the proper persons.

John Stuart Mill *Considerations on Representative Government*

Much of our social and economic legislation covers so vast and detailed a field that no statute, however cumbrous, could possibly provide for all contingencies. Some power of ministerial variation or interpretation is obviously necessary, subject to the attention of Parliament being drawn to what is being done.

L. S. Amery *Thoughts on the Constitution*

Introduction

The scope of government is vast and the machinery of public administration is complex. Since the end of the nineteenth century Parliament has placed in the hands of subsidiary law-making bodies, government departments, statutory bodies and a variety of other agencies, a host of responsibilities and powers which range from the making of law to the management of industrial and commercial concerns. We have already examined the nature of central government departments and the field of local government will be looked at in the next two chapters. In this chapter consideration will be given to the following topics:

(i) The special position of Northern Ireland, Scotland, Wales, the Channel Islands and the Isle of Man.
(ii) Delegated Legislation.
(iii) Public Corporations.
(iv) Other *ad hoc* Bodies.
(v) Regionalism.

The common factor in all these aspects of government administration is that each of them is characterised by some form of devolution or delegation. The extent to which the bodies concerned are responsible to Parliament for the functions discharged varies; in some cases there is close scrutiny, in others the degree of autonomy is considerable.

201

Northern Ireland, Scotland, Wales, the Channel Islands and the Isle of Man

The United Kingdom is made up of England, Wales, Northern Ireland and Scotland. The United Kingdom Parliament has authority over all four countries but the mode of government, to a significant extent, takes into account their different historical developments and special circumstances.

In 1922, the twenty-six counties of Southern Ireland became a fully independent country now known as the Republic of Ireland. The Government of Ireland Act, 1920, gave an appreciable degree of autonomy to the province consisting of the remaining six counties of Northern Ireland. It established a bicameral legislature, consisting of a Senate and a House of Representatives, which is located at Stormont, near Belfast; this has responsibility for nearly all domestic affairs, including agriculture, health, education and local government, but not for the conduct of external affairs.

Normally the United Kingdom Parliament does not interfere in the internal government of the province but in 1969 it intervened strongly in an effort to control widespread civil disorder.[1] Troops were sent out and have remained there since that time. The law in Northern Ireland is derived from and is similar to English Law but it has a separate judiciary. Northern Ireland elects twelve M.P.s to sit in the United Kingdom Parliament.

In order to deal with the special circumstances of Scotland and Wales the Government has established what are in effect regional Ministries under the direction, respectively, of a Secretary of State for Scotland and a Secretary of State for Wales. The Scottish Office is situated in Edinburgh and deals with the work of those central government departments whose functions need not be completely uniform throughout the whole of the United Kingdom. The Welsh Office, situated in Cardiff, had until recently a less comprehensive responsibility than its Scottish counterpart in that, for example, the administration of education and health was the responsibility of London based departments. In the reorganisation of government effected in 1970, responsibility for primary and secondary education and child-care functions were transferred to the Secretary of State for Wales and administrative arrangements were made to ensure that the Welsh Office would in future share in the urban programme of grants to areas of acute social deprivation. Scotland's legal system and educational system are markedly different from those in the rest of the United Kingdom.

The Channel Islands and the Isle of Man are included in the British Isles but are not part of the United Kingdom, their status being that of Crown dependencies. Both territories have a special relationship with the United Kingdom which stems from their proximity to the mainland and their long-standing connections with the Crown. Her Majesty's Government is responsible for their defence and international relations and for

---

[1] Because of continued disturbances, it was decided in March 1972 that the Stormont Parliament should be suspended for one year. During this time the province will be ruled direct from Westminster and a Secretary of State for Northern Ireland has been appointed.

certain services, such as posts and wireless communications, they are for all practical purposes regarded as part of the mainland. They have their own legislative assemblies, with power to legislate subject to the approval of the Queen-in-Council; and their own courts from which an appeal lies direct to the Judicial Committee of the Privy Council. The Isle of Man legislature is bicameral; the upper house, known as the Legislative Council, is appointed and the lower house, the House of Keys, is elected. Joint sessions of both houses form the Tynwald Court. The legislations of Guernsey and Jersey are known as the States. The States of Guernsey also legislates for the adjoining islands of Alderney, Sark, Herm and Jethou.

Delegated legislation

Under the doctrine of the Sovereignty of Parliament, only Parliament itself, or bodies which Parliament has specifically empowered so to do, can make laws which are binding upon all citizens. When Parliament formally delegates some part of its law-making function to another body we refer to the ensuing laws, rules or orders, etc., as delegated or sub-ordinate legislation. The main agencies of delegated or subordinate legislation are Ministers and local authorities. For example, a local council is empowered to make 'by-laws' to regulate the use of its parks by the general public; and under the Companies Act, 1948, the Lord Chancellor was empowered to make 'general rules for carrying into effect the objects of this Act so far as relates to the winding-up of companies in England'.

The discussion in this section will focus mainly upon the role of Ministers and government departments in this connection but it may be noted that the term delegated legislation also includes Orders in Council issued by the Privy Council under statutory authority (but not under the Royal Prerogative as this is regarded as original legislation), the by-laws made by bodies such as the Thames Conservancy Board or British Rail, and the rules made by professional bodies like the Law Society or the General Medical Council.

Although there has been a marked increase in the volume of delegated legislation in the present century, and especially since 1945, there is nothing new in the principle or its application. The report of the Com-mittee on Ministers' Powers, 1932 (the Donoughmore Committee), gives examples of delegated legislation dating from the Tudor period onwards.[1] Thus the Poor Law Amendment Act, 1834, authorised the Poor Law Commissioners 'to make and issue all such Rules, Orders and Regulations for the Management of the Poor, for the Government of Workhouses and the Education of children therein, and for carrying this Act into effect in all other respects as they think proper'. In 1875, the Commissioners for Stamp Duties were given power 'to do acts necessary for putting into force duties imposed on horses and carriages'. The growth of delegated legislation has accompanied the extension of the powers and

[1] Cmd. 4060: *Report of the Committee of the Ministers' Powers* (H.M.S.O., 1932).

responsibilities of government in the change from a *laissez-faire* society to a welfare state.

Delegated legislation assumes a particular significance in war-time or times of national emergency when far reaching powers may be given to the Executive to enable them to act without delay. The Emergency Powers Act, 1920, Section 2, paragraph 10, for instance, reads: 'When a proclamation of emergency has been made, and so long as the proclamation is in force, it shall be lawful for His Majesty in Council, by order, to make regulations for securing the essentials of life to the community, and more regulations may confer or impose on a Secretary of State or other Government departments, or any persons in His Majesty's service or acting on His Majesty's behalf, such powers and duties as His Majesty may deem necessary for the prevention of peace, for receiving and regulating the supply and distribution of food, water, fuel, light, and other necessities, for maintaining the means of transit or locomotion, and for any purposes essential to the public safety and life of the community, and make such provision essential to the powers aforesaid as may appear to His Majesty to be required for making the exercise of those powers effective.'

Legislation such as this involves *sub-delegation* of powers, i.e. the making of rules of one kind or another for which the authority is not the 'parent' Act but another subordinate law. The rules made in this way are sometimes at two, three, or more removes from the original statute. Under the Emergency Powers (Defence) Act, 1939, Defence Regulations were made which gave power for the making of Orders; from these Orders stemmed Directions; and finally, under the Directions, Licences were issued.

Delegated legislation, like Administrative Tribunals (see chapter 19) is an area of activity which has caused great concern to constitutional lawyers who saw this as further evidence of the encroachment of the Executive on the liberty of the subject and felt that civil servants were assuming too much of the power which properly belonged to the elected representatives in Parliament. Notable among these critics in the inter-war years were Lord Hewart who wrote *The New Despotism*, published in 1929, and Sir C. K. Allen, the author of *Bureaucracy Triumphant*, published in 1931. 'The old despotism, which was defeated,' wrote Lord Hewart, 'offered Parliament a challenge. The new despotism, which is not yet defeated, gives Parliament an anaesthetic. The strategy is different, but the goal is the same. It is to subordinate Parliament, to evade the courts, and to render the will or caprice of the Executive supreme.' While writers such as these had an enormous impact in legal, academic and political circles, as is evident from the setting up of the Committee on Ministers' Powers to investigate both delegated legislation and administrative tribunals, there were other writers who felt that they had grossly exaggerated the nature and scale of the problem. Professor H. J. Laski, for example, stated: 'An irresponsible Lord Chief Justice, like Lord Hewart, an academic lawyer whose hatred of change is even greater than his persuasive rhetoric, like

Dr C. K. Allen, are only the best-known names in a dramatic rearguard action that has been fought for many years now against a phantom army of bureaucrats lusting for power which has never had any existence outside the imagination of those who warn us of impending doom and disaster.'[1] It is probable that the true situation lies somewhere between these two extremes and it is perhaps sensible to recognise the importance of the issue without exaggerating its practical significance.

The Committee on Ministers' Powers, which reported in 1932, concluded that the existence of delegated legislation was a practical necessity in modern times and that there was no serious danger of domination by the Executive because of its use. 'The power has been delegated by Parliament', stated the Report, 'for various reasons, because for instance, the topic involved too much detail, or because it was technical, or because the pressure of other demands upon Parliamentary time did not allow the necessary time to be devoted by the House of Commons to a particular Bill.' The Committee did, however, criticise some aspects of the situation which then existed, particularly in relation to the procedure and extent of Parliamentary control of delegated legislation. The recommendations which it made to remedy defects in this respect were not taken up until toward the end of the Second World War when the country had experienced an avalanche of subordinate legislation, the possible continuation of which began to disturb a number of M.P.s of all parties. The nature of the changes made as a result of this concern will be considered in more detail later in this chapter but it will be convenient to look first at the arguments for the use of subordinate legislation and the advantages which it is claimed ensue from its use.

A full statement of the reasons for delegated legislation was recently made by the Speaker's Counsel in a memorandum submitted to the Select Committee on Procedure of 1966–7.[2] This stated that the device of delegated legislation:

(i) relieves Parliament of the minor details of law making, the important province of Parliament being to decide material questions affecting the public interest;

(ii) allows Parliament to act quickly when this is necessary and when prior publication of details would be prejudicial to the intention of the Act, e.g. the fixing of import duties;

(iii) allows expert assistance to be given in dealing with highly technical matters, e.g. trade marks, patents, designs, licences, poisons, legal procedures, etc., before detailed rules are promulgated;

(iv) enables government departments to deal with unforeseen circumstances that may arise in the introduction of comprehensive schemes of reform;

(v) provides flexibility in giving powers to change regulations to meet

[1] H. J. Laski, *Reflections on the Constitution* (Manchester University Press, 1951), p. 42.
[2] H.C. 539: *6th Report of the Select Committee on Procedure* (H.M.S.O., 1967).

new circumstances without the need for an amending Bill;

(vi) provides the means to ensure the safeguarding of the national interest in times of war and emergency.

In 1944 the House of Commons set up a Select Committee on Statutory Rules and Orders (later to become the Select Committee on Statutory Instruments), whose function it was to determine whether the special attention of the House should be drawn to a particular rule or order on any of the following grounds: (a) that it imposed a charge on public revenue; (b) it contained provisions excluding it from challenge in the events; (c) it appeared to make unusual or unexpected use of powers conferred by the statute under which it was made; (d) that it purported to have retrospective effect although the parent Act does not provide authority for this; (e) that there appeared to have been unjustifiable delay in publishing or laying it before Parliament; (f) that there had been unjustifiable delay in notifying the Speaker when an instrument had come into operation before being laid before Parliament, and (g) that for many reasons its form or purport calls for elucidation. This body became generally known as the Scrutiny Committee.

The setting up of the Select Committee was followed by the passing of the Statutory Instruments Act in 1946. This provided that the general term Statutory Instrument was to be applied to the variety of rules and orders which had hitherto existed and prescribed the procedure for numbering, printing, publication, citation and laying these instruments before Parliament. All Statutory Instruments must now be published by Her Majesty's Stationery Office and be available on payment, to interested members of the general public. The Act laid down three distinct procedures for the presentation of Statutory Instruments to Parliament; the mode to be used in each case being specified in the Act providing for the relevant measure of delegation. These are:

(1) Instruments which come into effect after simply being laid. In these cases Parliament is not required to take action and the object is mainly to publicise the Instrument. The procedure is normally used only for minor matters.

(2) Those which are laid before each House for a period of 40 days (excluding vacations) during which time the Government must find time for it to be approved by affirmative resolution in both Houses.

(3) Statutory Instruments which are laid before both Houses for 40 days and which become operative automatically in the absence of a successful 'prayer' to annul it. Under this procedure, which is the most used of the three methods, instruments can be rejected but not amended. The difficulty for M.P.s, however, who wish to seek the annulment of a particular provision is to have time found to hear their case for although prayers are regarded as 'exempted' business they are by no means always fitted into the 40-day period in spite of the Government's efforts to find time. In the period from February 1968 to February 1969, for instance, out of 54 prayers put down, 21 were debated within the 40-day period, 12 were

debated after the expiry of the period, 2 were withdrawn and 19 were not debated. It should, however, be noted that prayers are almost invariably defeated because the Government usually attaches importance to the passage of Statutory Instruments and it is likely that the Whip will be imposed.

The implementation of this Act together with the working of the Scrutiny Committee and the fact that Courts can declare an order which exceeds the powers conferred by its parent Act to be *ultra vires*, has meant, to most informed observers, that the procedures for delegated legislation are now adequately controlled. Furthermore, pressure groups play an important part at all stages; they are likely to be consulted in the framing of the delegated legislation as appropriate, either directly or through the numerous advisory bodies, and they will in any event draw the attention of M.P.s to Statutory Instruments which adversely affect their interests.

Overall it seems that it would be easy to exaggerate the problems of delegated legislation. The whole procedure is now routinised, adverse reports by Scrutiny Committees are rare, and only a handful of members actively concern themselves with prayers of annulment. As Professor Laski observed in the book referred to earlier that: 'after the brief debate on the prayers it is the rarest possible occurence for the very member who moves it to refer to the matter again...he turns to other matters which he almost certainly regards of outstandingly greater importance'. It is worth noting, however, that prayers against Statutory Instruments do provide an additional means whereby an Opposition can harass a Government, if it is so inclined.

With ever increasing pressure on the parliamentary timetable the need for delegated legislation is in the future likely to become even greater.

Public Corporations
Both Parliament and local authorities are representative bodies whose members are answerable and responsible to the electorate. There are, however, numerous, non-elected, *ad hoc* bodies which fall midway between government departments responsible to a Minister and local councils, and these make up what has been called the 'intermediate' area of government. Prominent in this field are the public corporations such as the B.B.C. and those industries which were nationalised early in the post-war period, e.g. the National Coal Board and the Gas Council. Table 35 indicates briefly the development of publicly owned industries between 1900 and 1970.

Although the ideas of state control and nationalisation are normally associated with the Labour Party, from which the philosophy of public ownership and control has stemmed, it can be seen from Table 35 that this form of administration is by no means limited exclusively to Labour. Thus, the National Government implemented Herbert Morrison's plans by establishing the London Passenger Transport Board in 1933. It is true,

TABLE 35 *Development of Nationalised Industries, 1900–70*

1909 Port of London Authority
1926 Central Electricity Board, established to regulate central distribution of electricity
1933 London Passenger Transport Board
1946 The Bank of England
1946 *Civil Aviation:* British Overseas Airways Corporation (B.O.A.C.); British European
      Airways (B.E.A.); British South American Airways (absorbed by B.O.A.C. in 1949)
1947 *Public Transport*
      (a) Transport Act, 1947, established British Transport Commission and provided that:
           (i) Docks and Inland Waterways; (ii) Hotels; (iii) Railways; (iv) London Transport;
           (v) Road Haulage; (vi) Road Passenger Transport should be administered by
           executive boards
      (b) Transport Act, 1953, denationalised Road Haulage
      (c) Transport Act, 1962, abolished B.T.C. and six executive boards and replaced them
           by separate corporations for Railways, London Transport, Docks, Waterways, and
           a Transport Holding Company
      (d) Transport Act, 1968, created the National Freight Corporation and a National Bus
           Company
      (e) Control of London Transport transferred to Greater London Council in 1969
1947 *Electricity*
      (a) Electricity Act, 1947, set up British Electricity Authority in place of Central
           Electricity Board
      (b) Electricity Act, 1957, set up Electricity Council and Central Electricity Generating
           Board. The twelve area Electricity Boards became financially autonomous
1948 Gas Council and twelve Area Gas Boards
1949 *Iron and Steel*
      (a) Iron and Steel Act, 1949, established Iron and Steel Corporation (Vesting date
           1 January 1951)
      (b) Iron and Steel Act, 1953, denationalised the industry and set up Iron and Steel
           Board
      (c) Iron and Steel Act, 1967, re-nationalised the industry
1954 U.K. Atomic Energy Authority
1969 Post Office became a public corporation instead of being run as a government department

Source: Based on D. Butler, J. Freeman, *British Political Facts 1900–1968* (Macmillan, 1969),
ch. XII.

---

however, that public ownership runs counter to the basic tenets of the
Conservative Party, and successive Conservative Governments have taken
steps to abolish or decrease the area of state control, and in the case of
iron and steel and road haulage have implemented a programme of
denationalisation. The Conservative Government elected in 1970 did not
proceed with the Bill to nationalise the docks which had been prepared by
the Labour Government; it decided, as a matter of policy, to break the
monopoly on routes which had been held by the Air Corporations by
allocating these to privately owned airways; it has also disposed of various
publicly owned subsidiary undertakings such as the travel firm of Thos.
Cook and Sons, the State-owned public houses in Carlisle and other
enterprises. An unprecedented event occurred early in 1971 when the
Conservative Government announced its intention of nationalising the
major part of the important industrial firm of Rolls Royce, which had run
into unsurmountable financial difficulty in connection with the supply of

the R.B. 211 aeroplane engine to the American firm of Lockheed. Legislation was passed which enabled a Government-owned company, Rolls Royce (1971) Limited, to be set up to take over the undertaking and to give powers to the Government to sell its interests in the company if it so desires.

In discussing nationalised industries, J. A. G. Griffith and H. Street have observed: 'The common characteristic is that they control industrial or commercial undertakings which supply commodities or facilities, on payment, to the general public.'[1] Public Corporations may then be defined as semi-autonomous public bodies established to manage and control a particular industry or service. Professor A. H. Hanson has outlined the major characteristics of the public corporation in the following terms:

(i) it is wholly owned by the State even though it may raise all or some of its capital by the issue of bonds to the public;

(ii) it is created by special law and is not subject – except to such extent as may be prescribed – to ordinary company law;

(iii) it is a body corporate, i.e. a separate legal entity which can sue and be sued, enter into contracts, and acquire property in its own name;

(iv) it is independently financed, obtaining its funds by borrowing either from the Treasury or from the public, and deriving its revenues from the sale of its goods and services;

(v) it is exempt from the forms of parliamentary financial control applicable to government departments;

(vi) its employees are not civil servants and are recruited and remunerated on terms and conditions that the corporation itself determines.[2]

Altogether about 10 per cent of the total national labour force is employed in nationalised industries. Their managing boards and staffs are appointed on the basis of relevant experience and competence; and statutes relating to the appointment of members of the boards of the fuel and power and transport corporations, for example require the Minister to appoint 'persons appearing to him to be qualified as having experience of and having shown capacity in industrial, commercial and financial matters, applied science, administration or organisation of workers'. Among the best known of the men who have been chairmen of nationalised Boards are Lord Beeching, an outstanding businessman who was Chairman of the British Railways Board from 1963 to 1965 and Lord Robens, a former Labour M.P., who was Chairman of the National Coal Board from 1961 to 1971.

The management of the industry is in the hands of the Board and not the Minister, but it is not completely autonomous. The existence of ministerial control (see below) does in some instances generate friction

[1] J. A. G. Griffith and H. Street, *Principles of Administrative Law*, 2nd edn (Pitman, 1957), p. 273.
[2] A. H. Hanson, *Nationalisation: A Book of Readings* (Allen and Unwin, 1963), p. 13.

between the Government and the Board which cannot always be amicably resolved, and it may finally result in the resignation or dismissal of the Chairman.

The general pattern of the relationship between the Boards of nationalised industries and Parliament can be summarised as follows:

(1) The Minister appoints and has the power to dismiss the Chairman and Members of each Board. He has power to give general directions as to how the industry shall be run but does not interfere in day-to-day management. Boards are normally required to provide the Minister with any information, statistics or financial accounts which he may require. The practice in general is that the Minister responsible is kept fully informed of important developments and all major policy decisions are reached in consultation with him. Formal directives are, therefore, rare.

(2) As far as financial matters are concerned, the usual statutory requirement is for the Board to conduct its business so that its accounts are in balance taking one year with another. Some of the corporations are self-supporting and realise quite considerable annual profits; others receive Exchequer grants to enable them to discharge their responsibilities effectively. Financial targets are agreed with the Minister.

(3) Government has to answer in Parliament for its policy concerning the nationalised industries. Opportunities for parliamentary discussion are afforded by debates, especially the debates on the Annual Reports and Accounts for each industry, and parliamentary questions. The Minister is only responsible for answering questions concerned with general policy and not with matters of day-to-day administration. The Select Committee on Nationalised Industries plays a most important role in highlighting problems affecting the developments of the public corporations.

Many problems of the nationalised industries remain unresolved. Firstly, there is the question which hinges on whether they should be regarded as services which should contribute to national welfare regardless of cost or should be viewed first and foremost as commercial undertaking. Secondly, there is the problem of public accountability and the need to achieve a balance between complete freedom of operation and

TABLE 36 *'Ad hoc' Bodies with responsibilities in the Scottish Highlands*

Highlands and Islands Development Board (including the Highland Transport Board)	Twenty-Four District Salmon Fishing Boards
	Area Gas Board
Crofters Commission	Commissioners of Northern Lighthouses
Three Agricultural Executive Committees	Nature Conservancy
White Fish Authority	North of Scotland Hospital Board
Herring Industry Board	Water Boards
North of Scotland Hydro-Electricity Board	Scottish Special Housing Association
Forestry Commission	Ancient Monuments Commission
Scottish Tourist Board	Countryside Commission
Red Deer Commission	

Source: J. P. Mackintosh, *Devolution of Power* (Penguin, 1968), p. 26.

detailed supervision. Thirdly, there is the problem of establishing satisfactory and reliable criteria for evaluating efficiency in the public owned industries and comparing this with the efficiency of industries in the private sector. Finally, there is the extreme difficulty of ensuring that consumer interests of these monopoly services are properly protected. The statutes setting up the corporations made provision for Consumer Councils of one kind or another in each industry or service, but it is generally agreed that the methods used for this purpose at present are far from satisfactory.

Other 'ad hoc' bodies

Apart from the public corporations discussed in the previous section, there are numerous other *ad hoc* bodies ranging from the Gaming Board to the Regional Hospital Boards; from the Race Relations Board to the Decimal Currency Board and from the Independent Television Authority to the White Fish Authority. Because of the extreme variety of these bodies as regards origin, composition, function and degree of ministerial control, it is extremely difficult to make meaningful general comments upon them. In Sir Arthur Street's words: 'Like the flowers in Spring, they have grown as variously and profusely and with as little regard for conventional patterns. They are even less susceptible of orderly classification...a new species often suggests a new genus.'[1] Generally the area is not so well documented as in the case of the nationalised industries and advisory bodies and any observations made are purely tentative.

J. P. Mackintosh has identified nearly twenty different groups which have responsibilities in the Scottish Highlands and even these do not seem to include all those which have some concern in the area.[2] (See table 36.) It will be observed that this list includes two bodies which are public corporations and others which can be considered under the heading of Royal Commissions and Advisory Bodies. He also reports that a parliamentary question as to the number of *ad hoc* bodies was returned unanswered on the grounds that there were so many and the decision as to which to omit was too difficult.

If we leave out of account the nationalised industries and bodies which are wholly or mainly advisory, the remainder generally exercise regulatory or administrative functions, sometimes covering the country as a whole, sometimes a regional or smaller area. In some cases they will have been set up because it was felt that an *ad hoc* body was better suited to the purpose than a government department or because the existing pattern of regional organisation or local government did not lend itself to the efficient discharge of the responsibilities involved. In so far as common characteristics can be attributed to these bodies it is worth noting that:

    (i) they are usually appointed by the Minister and are in greater or lesser degree responsible to him;

[1] Quoted in Griffith and Street, *Principles of Administrative Law*, p. 275n.
[2] J. P. Mackintosh, *Devolution of Power* (Penguin, 1968), pp. 25–6.

(ii) the composition of the Boards or other governing bodies normally includes representatives of the industrial and professional groups from the relevant fields;

(iii) their function is to control, regulate, administer or encourage particular activities or services;

(iv) in the majority of cases is a need for special expertise and technical knowledge;

(v) they are generally outside of the immediate area of party politics.

Some writers, e.g. J. P. Mackintosh and Peter Self, have linked the development of this vast complex of unrelated *ad hoc* bodies (including especially some of the post 1945 public corporations) with the unsatisfactory pattern of local government and the absence of democratically constituted regional bodies. They suggest that, had more viable local and regional government units existed, they would have been able to exercise many of the functions which were in fact allocated to the less democratic special purposes organisations.[1] It seems likely, however, that for the foreseeable future the public corporation for major industries and services will remain and it must be said that for many of the peripheral services the *ad hoc* arrangement seems to function satisfactorily.

Regionalism

Regionalism is a term which lends itself to a variety of interpretations. For some it refers merely to the existence of the offices of central government departments situated in various centres throughout the country which have responsibility for certain aspects of administration within a defined regional area. For others it embodies the idea of a high degree of self-government by elected regional assemblies. Unlike the vast majority of other advanced countries, the United Kingdom has (apart from the special case of Northern Ireland) at present no intermediate level of government in the latter sense, but it does have, at least in embryonic form, a pattern of regional administration.

During the Second World War England was divided into ten regions and Regional Commissioners were appointed for each region. These officials were responsible for the provision and maintenance of civil defence and also had authority to exercise *all* powers of government should the war situation make this necessary. To assist co-ordination the various government departments adopted a regional pattern of organisation and a number of co-ordinating boards and committees were set up in each region. The office of Regional Commissioner was discontinued on the cessation of hostilities.

During the Labour Administration of 1945–51 the regional organisations of central government departments was continued and, to some extent, developed. In an effort to improve and strengthen co-ordination between

[1] See Mackintosh, *Devolution of Power* (Penguin, 1968) and P. Self, *Regionalism* (Fabian Society, 1949) and p. 233 of present volume.

SCOTLAND

Edinburgh

Newcastle

NORTHERN

YORKSHIRE
AND HUMBERSIDE

NORTH-WEST   Leeds

Manchester

EAST MIDLANDS

Birmingham   Nottingham

EAST ANGLIA
(Offices in
London)

WEST
MIDLANDS

WALES

Cardiff
Bristol

London

SOUTH-EAST

SOUTH-WEST

OFFICES OF ECONOMIC PLANNING
COUNCILS AND BOARDS

Figure 5.   Economic Planning Regions

213

departments in the regions the Government divided England into nine 'Standard Regions' to which all departments were required to conform unless convincing reasons to the contrary were given, and the departments were brought together by the establishment of co-ordinating committees such as the Distribution of Industry Panel and Regional Building Committees. The regional administrative areas of other government bodies did not, however, coincide with the standard regions; for example, England was divided into fourteen hospital regions and the gas industry had ten area boards.

When a Conservative Government regained office in 1951 much less emphasis was placed upon regional organisations. This policy continued throughout the fifties and although the number of civil servants working in the regions did not decrease, much less attention was paid to regional planning and co-ordination and much more of the decision taking process was undertaken at the centre.

In the 1960s the tendency to centralisation was reversed and the emphasis was again placed on regional development. This change of attitude was in part caused by an increasing recognition that planned development would be necessary to lessen the degree of relative social and economic deprivation being experienced in some areas. The new orientation was further strengthened in the period following the return of a Labour Government in 1964.

In 1965, Great Britain was divided in ten Economic Planning Regions (see figure 5), each having an advisory Economic Planning Council consisting of twenty-five to thirty part-time members, appointed by the Minister on the basis of their knowledge and experience of the region, and an Economic Planning Board, consisting of senior civil servants representing the main government departments concerned with aspects of planning in the respective regions. England was divided into eight regions – Northern, North-West, Yorkshire and Humberside, West Midlands, East Midlands, East Anglia, South-West and South-East; Scotland was given its own Council and Board; Wales was to have a Welsh Council supported by an Economic Planning Board which was to be concerned with both economic and social affairs in Wales. Additionally, the Government of Northern Ireland set up an Economic Council comprised of representatives of both sides of industry and other interests. Because government departments in Northern Ireland already had responsibility for planning it was not thought necessary to set up special planning boards for the province.

The function of the Regional Economic Planning Boards is to co-operate with the Regional Economic Planning Councils, which are typically made up of councillors, trade union officials, businessmen and university representatives, in developing long-term strategies for development in the respective regions. The formulation of these strategies involves an examination of all the functions affecting development, including the distribution

214

of population, industry and employment, etc. Sub-regional studies of areas with particular problems are being made.

It is difficult as yet to assess the success or otherwise of these bodies. A cautionary note is sounded by Brian Lapping who writes: 'Several members of the councils, including one or two of their chairmen, expressed dissatisfaction with the way this form of regional involvement in government was working. They complained that their advice was ignored, that since they were appointed rather than elected they had no standing to make public protest at the government treatment of their suggestions, that the staff who were supposed to work for them gave first loyalty to departments in Whitehall through which their future promotion could be obtained.'[1]

An indication of the ideas of those who take the view that what is needed is a series of regional Parliaments can be obtained from a study of J. P. Mackintosh's recent book, *The Devolution of Power*. He proposes a pattern of nine Regional Councils in England, and Assemblies in Scotland and Wales which are elected for three years, with each having 'a Prime Minister and Cabinet, the latter consisting of about eight ministers, a possible division of portfolios being development, finance, health, housing, agriculture, education, police and fire services and the arts and amenities. Ministers, unlike members, would have to be full-time and paid a proper salary.'[2] Above these regional bodies would be the central government and below them a second tier of local authorities designed by the regional assemblies themselves to meet the special needs and circumstances of particular localities.

It is not easy in this context to forecast what the future may hold. One problem would seem to be that in contrast to the cases of Scotland and Wales some of the proposed regions have no natural, historical or social unity, and it is difficult to create real communities of interest in given regions by legislative action. An embryonic form of intermediate government does, however, exist, and any consideration of the revised pattern of government will doubtless benefit from the experience of this and take it into account in any recommendations which are made. This whole question is now being examined by a Royal Commission on the Constitution, under the chairmanship of Lord Crowther, which was set up in December 1968, to look at 'the present functions of the central legislature and government in relation to the several countries, nations and regions of the United Kingdom'.

[1] Lapping, *The Labour Government, 1964–70*, p. 201.
[2] Mackintosh, *Devolution of Power* (Penguin, 1968), p. 200.

16 The Structure of Local Government

The areas of many existing authorities are outdated and no longer reflect the pattern of life and work in modern society. The division between counties and county boroughs has prolonged an artificial separation of big towns from their surrounding hinterlands for functions whose planning and administration need to embrace both town and country. There are too many authorities and many of them are too small in area and resources to support the operation of services to the standards which people nowadays have a right to expect. The present division of responsibilities between authorities is, in some fields, confusing and illogical.

Local Government in England Government White Paper 1971

The scope of local government

Local councils, under the direction and control of the central government, have responsibility for a wide range of functions which play a vitally important role in modern life. Collectively, they are responsible for nearly all non-university education, housing, highways and street lighting. They look after various aspects of the health of mothers and children, the old and the sick. They provide sporting and recreational facilities, art galleries, museums and libraries. They are concerned with police and fire services and have responsibility for a vast variety of other functions.

The report of a Royal Commission on Local Government published in 1969 stated: 'The importance of local government lies in the fact that it is the means by which people can provide services for themselves; can take an active and constructive part in the business of government; and can decide for themselves, within the limits of what national policies and local resources allow, what kind of services they want and what kind of environment they prefer.' The Commission also emphasised that: 'Local government is the only representative political institution in the country outside Parliament; and being, by its nature, in closer touch than Parliament or Ministers can be with local conditions, local needs, local opinions, it is an essential part of the fabric of democratic government.'[1]

The Commission, however, after three years of study reached the conclusion that the present structure of local government does not fit the

[1] Cmd. 4040: *Report of Royal Commission on Local Government in England 1966–1969*, vol. I (H.M.S.O., 1969), pp. 10–11.

pattern of life and work in modern England. It took the view that the system needs to be drastically overhauled if the aims of democracy and efficiency are to be realised. In order to assess the significance of this conclusion we will look briefly at the development of local government and compare the existing pattern with that proposed by the Royal Commission and alternative proposals introduced by the Government early in 1971.

Historical development

England has a long tradition of local government stretching back to Saxon times. The enormous transformation in our society which we refer to as the Industrial Revolution revealed the inability of the then parishes and boroughs to cope with the acute social problems which arose. It was not until the nineteenth century, with the passing of the Poor Law Amendment Act in 1834 and the Municipal Corporations Act in 1835, that the fore-runners of present-day local councils began to emerge.

The development was, however, complicated and erratic. The powers given to the elected councils under the Municipal Corporations Act were severely limited, and special *ad hoc* authorities were established to deal with specific social problems. Thus, the Board of Guardians dealt with poor relief and the School Boards were responsible for the provision of elementary education. Under the provisions of the Public Health Act of 1872, the country was divided into urban and rural sanitary districts and each district was required to appoint a medical officer of health and a nuisance inspector. A year earlier the Local Government Board had been created as a government department with responsibility for the supervision of all local government matters. From then on the development was relatively rapid.

In 1882 a further Municipal Corporations Act reformed the organisation of the Boroughs and a number of alterations were made in their powers and duties. The Local Government Act of 1888 created County Boroughs from the larger towns and Administrative Counties from the ancient counties. Councils were elected for each of these areas. In 1894 Urban and Rural Councils replaced the former sanitary authorities, and Parish Councils were brought into being. Under the Education Act of 1902 the School Boards were abolished and responsibility for education was transferred to the county councils and county boroughs. Similarly, in 1929, the poor law functions, hitherto exercised by the Board of Guardians were transferred to the major authorities.

In 1919 the Local Government Board was abolished and a Ministry of Health was set up which was given responsibility for the supervision of all matters concerned with local government. (These powers were transferred to the Ministry of Housing and Local Government in 1951.)

The Local Government Act of 1933 codified the constitution and powers of the six types of local authority which still exist outside of London. These are: County Boroughs, County Councils, Non-County Boroughs,

217

Urban Districts, Rural Districts and Parishes. The 1933 Act set out clearly the structure of the various authorities, their membership and election arrangements, the officers to be appointed and the financial arrangements. Although important changes in the responsibilities of these authorities have been made since that time, the general pattern and mode of working in local government, for the time being at least, remains the same.

Because London is the capital and forms part of a vast conurbation, the pattern of local government for this area has always been treated exceptionally, and the London Government Act of 1939 modified and clarified the respective responsibilities of the London County Council and the Metropolitan Borough Councils. In 1964, the L.C.C. and the Metropolitan Boroughs were replaced by the Greater London Council and the London Boroughs. For historical reasons the City of London maintains its special identity. It is responsible for a wide range of services but has a constitution quite different from that of other local authorities. Figure 6 outlines the existing structure in England and Wales and table 37 gives an indication of the functions exercised by each type of authority.

Types of authorities

The county borough councils, which provide local government services for towns and cities, are 'all-purpose' authorities; they are 'major' authorities and are solely responsible for all local government services in their areas. The position of county authorities is more complicated.

The county council is also a 'major' authority and provides some services such as education for the whole of its area, other services being provided by 'minor' authorities. Thus, urban district and non-county (or municipal) borough councils are responsible for housing, cemeteries and

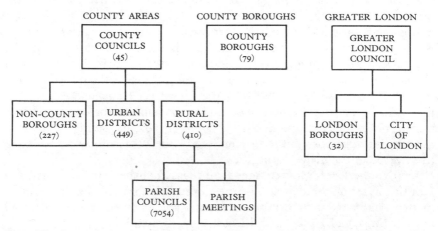

Note: The figures in brackets denote the numbers of each type of authority (in 1966 for Parish Councils and 1968 for the remainder).

Figure 6. Structure of Local Government in England and Wales

218

other functions; these bodies make up the second part of a 'two-tier' system.

Other areas in the county form part of a 'three-tier' system involving a parish council, a rural district council and the county council. Each of these provides different but complementary services, and the elector votes in three different elections.

There is no doubt that this division of function between the different authorities produces many problems and conflicts. County councils and county borough councils frequently clash over policies on education, boundaries, and town and country planning. Parish councils with street-lighting functions need to work closely with rural district councils who are engaged in building housing estates within the parish if repeated digging up of pavements is to be avoided when lighting standards are being erected. Tenants who are evicted from houses which are the property of urban district or rural district councils become the responsibility of the county council welfare department and here again the problems arising can become acute if the officials are not constantly alive to the need for co-operation and liaison.

TABLE 37   *Functions of Local Authorities*

Type	Functions	
County Boroughs	Public baths	Libraries, museums and art galleries
	Care and adoption of children	Police
	Cemeteries	Roads and bridges
	Education	Sanitary services
	Entertainment	Shops inspection
	Fire brigade	Town and country planning
County Councils	Ambulances	Maternity and child welfare
	Civil defence	Roads and bridges
	Education	Remand homes
	Fire brigade	Town and country planning
Non-County Boroughs and Urban Districts	Allotments	Housing
	Baths	Libraries and museums
	Cemeteries	Parks
	Entertainments	Sanitary services
	Food inspection	Shops inspection
Rural Districts	Building control	Street lighting*
	Housing	Roads (delegated)
	Parks*	Town and country planning (delegated)
	Sanitary services	
Parish Councils	Allotments	Mortuaries
	Cemeteries	Parks
	Footpaths	War memorials

* Sometimes provided by Parish Councils.
Note: (1) The examples given are indicative only as local variations are numerous. (2) Many adjoining police forces are now amalgamated.

TABLE 38   *Population Statistics of Selected Minor Authorities**

	Non-county boroughs	Urban districts	Rural districts
Population of largest authority	100 470	123 230	86 390
Population of smallest authority	1 630	1 700	1 490

* Population figures quoted are for mid-1968.
Source: *Report of Royal Commission on Local Government in England*, vol. I, p. 333.

It must be realised that, geographically, county boroughs are situated within the county area but, administratively, they are quite independent of the county council. There is some sharing of facilities, for instance in the use of secondary schools and technical colleges, and some neighbouring authorities co-operate in the provision of major services by forming 'joint-boards'. Police forces are being amalgamated to cover areas wider than that of single county and county borough areas as part of a drive to combat crime more effectively.

Discrepancies in population and areas
The official descriptions of some of the local government units are now in some cases a misnomer. The areas covered by many rural districts are no longer actually rural; some, indeed, are heavily urbanised as in the South Yorkshire coalfield.

There are enormous variations in the population and areas of the various types of authority. The county boroughs range from Birmingham, with a population of 1 074 980, to Canterbury, which has 32 790 inhabitants. Birmingham covers an area of 80 square miles and Bootle only 5 square miles. In the county areas, Lancashire has a population of nearly $2\frac{1}{4}$ million and covers an area of 1614 square miles; Rutland has only 29 680 inhabitants and its area is 152 square miles. The largest and smallest populations of non-county boroughs, urban districts and rural districts are given in table 38.

In the case of the 10 000 or so parishes into which the rural districts of England and Wales are divided no less than thirteen have no inhabitants at all and others have populations of well over 30 000. Over half of the parishes automatically qualify for a parish council because they have a population of 300 or more. About one-third of the remainder have opted to have a parish council and have received the necessary permission from the county council. Parishes which have no parish council hold a parish meeting which normally assembles twice each year.

Greater London
To complete the pattern of local government in England and Wales we must return to the arrangements adopted for the Greater London area. It has already been noted that in 1964 the London County Council (L.C.C.)

220

and the Metropolitan Boroughs were replaced by the Greater London Council (G.L.C.) and the London Boroughs.

The former L.C.C. covered an area of over 100 square miles and was responsible for services such as education and health. The lower tier councils, the metropolitan boroughs, provided housing, libraries and other services. A Royal Commission on Local Government in Greater London reported in 1960 and the present structure resulted from this. The G.L.C. covers over 800 square miles and provides services for about 8 million people. Its boundaries encompass the whole of Middlesex (apart from two small areas which were allocated to other counties) and parts of Surrey, Kent, Essex and Hertfordshire.

The G.L.C. has responsibility for traffic control and main roads. It supervises drainage and has overall control of planning. The new London Boroughs deal with a variety of services including housing. Education was also transferred to the boroughs except that responsibility for education within the old L.C.C. area was retained by the G.L.C., and the Inner London Education Authority was established for this purpose.

The arguments for introducing the change were that the G.L.C. area corresponded much more closely to the actual geographical, economic and social boundaries of London and that the increased size and wealth of the new boroughs would enable them to provide more efficient and more economic services.

The proposals, which were introduced by a Conservative Government, met with considerable resistance. The old L.C.C. had been a Labour stronghold and Labour members of the council and their supporters were loath to let this sphere of influence fall into their opponents' hands. There was resistance too by a number of the metropolitan boroughs who felt that they would lose their identity under the new arrangements. The neighbouring counties who would lose land, population and rateable value to the G.L.C. also expressed objections. In the event the Conservative Government allowed some of the outlying (and predominantly Conservative) areas to opt out and thus lessened the prospect of Conservative domination of the new G.L.C. Labour won the first election for the new body but subsequently lost control to the Conservatives.

Ian Gilmour, M.P., makes the following evaluation of the changes affecting the Greater London area: 'With the abolition of the L.C.C. in favour of a Greater London Council...the government of London became less archaic than local government in the rest of the country, but the area was still the wrong size and the fundamental manner of government was left unaltered.'[1]

Councillors and Aldermen
In most cases membership of local authorities is by popular election, and when elected each councillor serves for three years. The exception is in

[1] Gilmour, *The Body Politic*, p. 329.

borough councils and county councils where one quarter of the members are aldermen who are elected by the councillors and who serve for a period of six years. The office of alderman provides the only existing case of indirect election which exists in the British system of government.

The theory lying behind the existence of the aldermanic system is that it provides an avenue of representation for individuals who have a valuable contribution to make to the community but who do not wish to face the hurly-burly of an election campaign. Actual practice is generally far removed from this and the aldermanic elections are in fact important features in the struggle between the parties competing for control of the council. Sometimes the winning party takes all the vacant aldermanic seats; in other cases they are allocated in accordance with the relative party strengths of the elected councillors. The individuals elected are often either sitting members of the party in power whose seat is fairly certain to be won again at the resulting by-election, or sometimes the place is given to party stalwarts who have failed to win a seat at the election. Generally there is little or no prospect that an aldermanic seat will be given to a non-party man.

A further argument is that the office of alderman helps to preserve continuity on the council. The same argument applies to those councils where a third of the membership retires annually (see below). In neither case does this argument fit the political reality. Continuity, the desirability of which is open to question, is as often as not maintained by the re-election of retiring members. By analogy with the Civil Service and the central government, a sound argument could be put forward for the case that it is the duty of the council officials to maintain any necessary continuity. In any event, urban district councils, rural district councils and parish councils do not have aldermen.

The office of alderman was introduced under the Municipal Corporations Act of 1835 in order to conciliate the ancient chartered corporations whose members were not keen to engage in elections. The existence of the office is, therefore, an anachronism. Proposals for change are frequently resisted by those actively engaged in local government but the impression is that this resistance is not based on logical grounds and that it stems consciously or unconsciously from a desire to retain positions which are felt to confer status. All local authorities have the power to co-opt members to various committees and this procedure would seem to make adequate provision for using the special knowledge and skills of those individuals who are willing to serve the community in a more specialised role.

The Royal Commission which reported in 1969 recommended that the office of alderman should be abolished because it 'blurs the principle of democratic control by the people's elected representatives'.

Constitution and election
If a person is qualified to vote in a general election, he or she is also entitled

222

to vote in a local election. An individual can only be registered once in the same area, but until the passing of the Representation of the People Act, 1969, he may also have been able to vote and stand for election in another area by reason of a property qualification. Up to the time of this legislation eligibility for election to a particular local council was based on any one of three criteria; candidates had to be (i) registered as a local government elector for the area in which he wished to serve, or (ii) occupy as owner or tenant any land or other premises in the area for the twelve months before nomination, or (iii) have lived there for one year.

The Labour Government's Representation of the People Act, 1969, abolished the non-resident qualification for the local government franchise and for membership of local authorities but the latter provision was to be short-lived. The Conservative Government elected in 1970 passed the Local Government (Qualification of Councillors) Act, 1971, which restored the property qualification for those wishing to stand but whose residence is outside of the boundaries of the local government area concerned. It also introduced a new qualification which enables individuals whose principal place of work has been within the area for twelve months prior to the time of nomination to stand as local government candidates. It must be emphasised that these provisions are concerned with council membership and not with voting qualifications. This legislation principally affects the memberships of councils of cities and large towns where it is not un-common for some members to live outside of the areas of the councils on which they serve. Thus, at the end of 1970, 24 council members in Birmingham, 18 in Manchester, 14 in Nottingham and 11 in Leeds lived outside of the town boundaries. It does not seem likely that there will be any significant change in the composition of councils under the existing structure and it is extremely difficult to visualise what the situation in this respect will be like when the new pattern of local government comes into operation in 1974 (see below).

Candidates in local elections do not have to put up a deposit, as in parliamentary elections, but there are legal restrictions on election expenses. Currently the amount allowed for each candidate is £30 plus 5p for every six electors; a higher amount is payable for candidates in G.L.C. elections.

Elections for county councils are held triennially in April. All councillors retire at the same time and those who wish to continue as members must seek re-election. Half of the aldermen, who have completed a six-year span of office, must also retire. After the election the councillors and aldermen choose a chairman, normally from among their members, who holds office for one year. There is a marked tendency in some authorities however, for the person chosen to be re-elected and to continue in office for the whole of the three-year period.

In boroughs and non-county boroughs, elections are held in May. The general pattern is for one-third of the council to retire annually. A mayor is elected and he holds office for one year. The law provides that mayors need not be members of the council but the usual practice is for the councillors and aldermen to choose them from within their own members. The wisdom of holding annual elections is frequently debated; they certainly add to the administrative cost and make the control of the council uncertain from year to year. Additionally there is a tendency for this system to confuse a substantial section of the electorate. It is perhaps worth adding here that some boroughs are referred to as cities. City is simply a title of honour conferred upon a town. The mayors of cities are usually given the title of Lord Mayor.

In the case of urban districts and rural districts provision was made in the Local Government Act, 1933, for elections to be held on the same basis as in boroughs (i.e. one-third of the membership retiring annually), but if the Council decide by a two-thirds majority to hold an election for the full membership every third year this arrangement is adopted. Parish council elections are held trienially. All authorities have power to appoint a chairman from outside of their own numbers but in practice rarely do so.

Functions

Some powers conferred upon local authorities by Parliament are obligatory and the councils concerned must provide the relevant services. Thus counties and county boroughs are required to provide primary and secondary education. Failure to make the necessary provision will result in the service being provided by the government itself; the local authority, however, would be required to meet its normal share of the cost. An instance of default by a local authority occurred in 1954 when Coventry City Council refused to organise civil defence services as required by Parliament. The basis of this authority's non-compliance was that the type of service local authorities were required to provide would be useless in the event of nuclear war. The Home Office, which was the government department responsible, using its powers under the relevant legislation, organised the required defence force in Coventry, and the city council was required to foot the bill. Eventually the council agreed to comply.

Although Parliament lays down general requirements on the provision of services the local councils have some degree of flexibility in the manner in which the requirement is fulfilled, although the extent of the flexibility allowed may vary from time to time. In the provision of secondary education, for instance, the type of schools (grammar, secondary modern, comprehensive, etc.) was for a long time left to the discretion of local authorities. Before the general election of 1970 a Labour Government had made arrangements to compel all authorities to adopt a comprehensive system of secondary education, but after the election the policy was reversed by the incoming Conservative Government. Those councils which are responsible for housing must take into account local needs, but the councils concerned have considerable freedom in deciding the number

224

and type of houses to be built, the rents to be charged and whether or not they should be sold to tenants. Some would argue that in this instance the degree of freedom permitted is too great and that in some cases the provision made does not properly meet local needs.

Other powers are permissive, that is, councils can use them if they wish to do so. Thus under the provisions of the Local Government Act of 1948 certain local authorities can provide entertainments of a specific kind. Whether or not this is done in a given locality will be a matter for the decision of the local councils concerned. Some Acts of Parliament are 'adoptive' and in these cases a more elaborate procedure is necessary before a local authority can assume the powers covered by the legislation. Examples of this type of legislation include the Burial Acts, Public Libraries Acts and the Baths and Wash-houses Acts.

Local authorities can also provide services which are not covered by general Acts of Parliament if these can persuade Parliament to pass the necessary legislation. When this is done the powers apply only within the area of the local authority on whom they have been conferred. Sometimes these 'local' or 'private' acts deal with a specific matter; in other cases they give power to deal with a variety of matters not covered by ordinary legislation. A good example of this type of legislation is provided by the West Riding County Council General Powers Acts, 1948–70. The 1964 Act, for example, confers upon the W.R.C.C. and on minor local authorities within its area certain additional powers in relation to industry, lands and highways, local government improvement and the health and finances of the county. Part II of the 1970 Act enables the authority to raise money abroad and by 'bills' or 'bearer bonds' if it so desires. Some local authorities obtain powers to provide special undertakings; thus, Doncaster controls the racecourse where the St Leger is run and Hull runs its own telephone service. Manchester City Council has recently unsuccessfully promoted a Bill to introduce a local lottery.

It must be emphasised that a local authority has to have legal authority for everything it does. To go beyond these powers renders the councillors who made the decision liable to penalties in the form of a surcharge, i.e. they are required personally to refund the moneys which have been spent without proper authorisation. A minor example of this occurred in 1963 when the councillors of Castle Donnington were required to refund the cost of two telegrams sent to President Kennedy and to Krushchev during the Cuban crisis appealing for a peaceful settlement to the dispute.

Officials and staff

All local authorities are required by law to appoint certain senior officials. Exact requirements vary between one type of authority and another but the larger authorities must have a Clerk (or Chief Officer), a Treasurer, a Surveyor and a Medical Officer of Health. Some appointments are subject to confirmation by a central government department but in general

225

local government officers are appointed at the discretion of the council concerned.

The principal officer is responsible for the co-ordination and supervision of the work of the council as a whole and for seeing that the policy determined by the council is put into effect. Other chief officers are responsible for the work of their particular departments.

Traditionally, the clerks of the larger authorities have been lawyers, and in the majority of cases this still applies. Some interesting changes, however, have recently been made. Newcastle City Council made the experiment of appointing as its chief officer or City Manager, as the post was designated, a highly paid business executive from the Ford Motor Company. Basildon appointed an industrial relations manager from the National Coal Board as its town manager. The Treasurer of Cumberland was appointed as the Town Clerk of Oxford City Council and was the first treasurer in Britain to be appointed as the principal officer of a major authority. The National and Local Government Officers Association has claimed that because the town clerk's job is becoming increasingly managerial, it should be open to candidates from all professions within the local government service. The Institute of Municipal Treasurers and Accountants went further than this. They recommended that the post of 'chief administrative officer' should be open to 'appropriately qualified persons in local authorities and also outside local government'.

The relationship between Chairmen of Committees in local councils and their officials presents problems somewhat similar to the relationship between Ministers and senior civil servants. Theoretically the division of responsibility is that councillors are responsible for policy and officials with administrative and managerial matters. But this distinction is not always easy to make and friction sometimes arises. The problem is related to the whole question of the pattern of local government administration which some observers consider to be outmoded.

The committee system
Full meetings of councils, to which all members are invited, are held once a year to elect a chairman (or mayor) and vice-chairman and to decide the membership of committees. Additional full meetings are held at regular intervals, e.g. monthly or quarterly, to consider and debate committee reports.

The day-to-day work of the council is conducted by the various committees and the officers responsible to them. The clerk or chief officer, or one of his staff acts as secretary to the committees and will prepare the necessary agendas, minutes and reports. The chairman of a committee occupies a powerful and responsible position because, conventionally, his duties go far beyond the regulation of discussion. He is expected to be well informed on his particular field and to act as spokesman for the committee.

Broadly, a committee's work consists of:

(i) considering any special matters referred to it by the full council and, where necessary, reporting back;

(ii) supervising the work of those officials and departments for which it is responsible;

(iii) making decisions on matters arising from the powers which have been delegated to it. Nearly all committees, except the Finance Committee, can co-opt individuals from outside the council to assist them in their work.

The precise arrangements made to allocate the work of the council varies with the size and type of the authority concerned, and there are many local variations. Local authorities are required by law to appoint certain committees. Thus, those authorities which are concerned with education and the administration of the Children's Acts must appoint an Education Committee and Children's Committee. Boroughs which have a separate police force must have a 'Watch' Committee.

Most committees are 'Standing' Committees, i.e. those which deal with the ongoing work of the council. In contrast to the Standing Committees are 'Special' Committees. These are set up to deal with special tasks, e.g. centenary celebrations. When the work is completed the committee is dissolved.

Standing Committees likely to be appointed by a typical borough council include: Finance, Housing, Highways, Education, Planning, Libraries, Cemeteries and Parks Committees. In large authorities the work of committees is sometimes further divided into sub-committees. For example, a County Council Education Committee might have responsible to it Staffing, Primary, Secondary, Further, Building and Courses Sub-Committees. The relationship of sub-committees to the council is analogous of that of its 'parent' committee to the full council.

Generally the decisions of sub-committees are subject to the approval of a full meeting of the council and committees cannot themselves raise money by way of rates or borrow money. In practice this financial restriction does not present problems and the approval of most of the committee's day-to-day work is a formality. Committee reports presented to the full council often go through 'on the nod'.

The advantages of the committee system are usually cited in something like the following terms:

(i) it allows members to specialise and make economic use of the time which they have available;

(ii) it encourages 'democratic' control of the work of officials;

(iii) it enables the work of the council to be completed expeditiously;

(iv) matters requiring decision by the full council can first be considered by a smaller body with more detailed knowledge.

The disadvantages frequently quoted are:

(i) it takes away authority from the council as a whole and places it in the hands of small groups;

(ii) it prevents full and open debate of important matters, the Press rarely being admitted to committee meetings;

(iii) it gives councillors too much power over the details of administration, e.g. it is suggested that many matters which are delayed until a committee meets could perfectly well be dealt with by an official;

(iv) co-ordination of the various activities is made difficult.

The Maud Committee on the Management of Local Government which reported in 1967 took the view that the committee system was seriously outdated.[1] Some local authorities have taken steps to streamline their committee systems and have given careful consideration to the question of the desirability of delegating more decisions to officials.

The question of giving salaries to chairmen of committees in the larger authorities has frequently been raised but no decision has been reached on this. In a paper submitted to the Maud Commission, Professor J. A. G. Griffith outlined a detailed scheme. He suggested that in order to attract competent personnel, salaries for full-time committee chairmen in larger authorities should range from £2000 to £4000 a year. At present councillors and aldermen who have to take time off from their employment can claim a loss of earnings allowance but there is a maximum amount which can be claimed for each day and it is quite possible for the member concerned to be out of pocket when he is engaged in council work.[2]

Finance

The total expenditure of all local authorities in England and Wales in the financial year 1967/8 amounted to nearly six thousand million pounds. Because the issue of the local rates figures so largely in local election campaigns, it is not generally appreciated that the income received from the government grants is now greater than that received from rates. Table 39 shows the main sources of income for local authorities in England and Wales for the financial year 1967–8.

Local authorities can, subject to certain conditions, raise loans for buying land, providing buildings and plant, and fulfilling other responsibilities.

Rates are a form of local tax which are levied on houses, buildings and industrial premises. A value is placed upon each unit to be assessed which is known as the rateable value. Valuation lists are prepared by the Inland Revenue every five years. The occupier of the property is then responsible for paying each year the rate fixed for each pound of assessable value. Thus a house which has a rateable value of £100, in a year at which the rate was fixed at 75p for each £ would be required to pay £75 in rates (100 × 75p).

---

[1] Cmd. 4267: *Report of Committee on the Management of Local Government* (H.M.S.O., 1967).

[2] Most larger councils make a special allowance to the person holding office as Mayor. Here again, however, the amount allowed is likely to be inadequate for a Mayor who devotes all or the greater part of his time to official duties.

228

TABLE 39   Income of Local Authorities in England and Wales, Financial Year 1967–8

	(£1 000)
Capital receipts	1 537 355
Rates	1 323 388
Government grants	1 591 016
Repayments on account of private improvements	12 236
Housing (rents, etc.)	472 061
Trading services	
Water supply	101 102
Passenger transport	96 829
Cemeteries and crematoria	5 662
Harbours, docks, piers, etc.	54 784
Others (including estates, ferries, markets and civic restaurants)	52 323
Miscellaneous (including tolls, fees, rents and interest)	391 108
Total	5 637 864

Source: Ministry of Housing and Local Government as presented in *Annual Abstract of Statistics*, 1970, p. 322.

Rates are 'collected' by county boroughs, non-county boroughs, urban districts and rural districts. The task of these 'rating authorities' is to 'make' and 'levy' rates as required. County councils and parish councils submit these requirements to the appropriate rating authorities: thus, a parish council, for this purpose, works in conjunction with a rural district council and the county council collects its 'share' from all non-county, urban and rural district councils within its area.

The central government requires local authorities to provide certain services and makes decisions which affect the income of local authorities which is derived from rates. Thus no rates are payable in respect of agricultural land, and until the passing of the Rating and Valuation Act of 1961 only 50 per cent of the normal rates were paid for property connected with industry and freight transport. The Act also provided for only 50 per cent, instead of 100 per cent, to be paid for rates on property occupied by registered charities. The total rateable value of some local authority areas is relatively very low and the government has to give correspondingly greater aid in order that a reasonable level of local services can be maintained.

Until 1966, the three main forms of government grant were:

(1) *General Grants*. These were introduced in 1958 when the former 'percentage' grants for education, fire service, public health and other functions, were abolished. The block-grant could be spent at the discretion of the council as it was not tied to particular services. The amount given to local authorities was based on a 'basic' grant which took into account the size of the population and the number of children in the area concerned, and a supplementary grant, which allowed for the number of old people, the school population, density of population and other factors. There was considerable controversy when this system was first introduced. Some

229

argued that it would allow local authorities greater flexibility in the provision of services and strengthen the principle of local discretion, others claimed that it would encourage niggardly councils to 'cut-back' on important services.

(2) *Percentage Grants.* These were retained for some services and were paid in respect of police, roads and other services. The police grant was 50 per cent, and in the case of roads and bridges the grant made was related to the council's expenditure on new roads and the upkeep and improvement of older ones. Grants ranging between 20 per cent to 75 per cent have been paid for different types of work.

(3) *Rate-Deficiency Grants.* These were the grants paid to local authorities which had a low income from rates. The amount paid was related to the authority's overall pattern of expenditure.

This system of government grants was altered by the Local Government Act, 1966. The general and rate-deficiency grants were replaced by rate-support grants. The principle here is that the Minister first decides what total of government money should be allocated to local government, then the total of all specific grants other than the special subsidies for housing are deducted. The sum which remains is the total available for rate-support grants and it is allocated to local authorities in accordance with three basic elements:

(a) *Needs* element, which takes into account the size and age compositions of the population in the particular area, educational requirements and road mileage. The main recipients of this grant are county councils.

(b) A *resources* element, which is dependent upon the extent to which the product of a 1p rate in the area falls short of the standard rate. The basis of this element is similar to that of the former rate-deficiency grant.

(c) The *domestic* element which is determined by ministerial regulation. Rating authorities must pass on benefits from this to ratepayers in the form of rate reductions.

All local authority expenditure is subject to audit by the District Auditor, who, as the representative of the Minister of Local Government and Development, conducts a thorough examination of all accounts. Any expenditure which has not been properly authorised can be 'surcharged' to the members of the Council.

The financial arrangements of local authorities are characterised by thorough preparation of estimates and strict control of expenditure. Each department prepares its forecast of expenditure well in advance of the forthcoming financial year and these forecasts are carefully scrutinised by the Finance Committee. When the various competing claims are considered a decision is finally made which will have to take into account the amount of the rate which will be levied.

230

Supervision and control

Local authorities are subject to strict control both by the central government and the courts of law. Control, therefore, is both ministerial and judicial. Some aspects of this have been referred to in earlier sections of this chapter, but the general position can be summarised as follows.

Before a local authority can act in a number of matters the consent of the Minister, operating through his department, must be obtained. A random sample of measures requiring ministerial consent might include: the introduction or amendment of a by-law, a proposal to increase burial charges, the building of a new estate of council houses, the building of a new secondary school, the appointment of a chief constable. All loans must be sanctioned and the Minister must be satisfied that the amount it is required to raise is reasonable and that the proceeds will be properly applied.

In authorising grants of various kinds the Minister must be satisfied that the services provided are satisfactory and in the last resort grants can be withdrawn. Many statutes make provision for the central government to provide services if a local authority fails to discharge its responsibility effectively. Government departments, under the relevant legislation, make detailed regulations, covering a multitude of matters, and these regulations have the force of law. These range from the level of services to be provided to the detailed procedures which must be followed. Further control is exercised by the existence of the District Auditor and Government Inspectors who are required to report any irregularity or deficiency.

Local authorities are corporate bodies and are subject to judicial control. They must not act *ultra vires*, i.e. they must not go beyond their legal powers. If the public at large is adversely affected by an authority's actions, various forms of redress are available. Thus, in a number of statutes affecting the functions of local government provision is made for an appeal to the courts if a person feels that his rights are infringed. For instance, a local authority may make a demolition order and the owner of a house may feel that this order is not justified and, if so, he may exercise a right of appeal. If a private person receives injury through the neglect of the authority to do its duty, he may be able to claim damages in compensation for the injury. Sometimes statutes make specific provision for this contingency, in others the courts have interpreted statutes in such a way as to allow an action for damages.

The question of extending the powers of the Parliamentary Commissioner for Administration to cover local government matters has been seriously mooted, and specific proposals for this development were made by the Labour Government in 1970. It is interesting to note that the Stormont Government made provision for the appointment of an 'ombudsman' for local government in Northern Ireland where, of course, the circumstances are quite different to those in England and Wales. In 1971 a White Paper setting out the Conservative Government's proposals

231

for the reorganisation of local government in England (see below) the view was expressed that: 'The machinery of the Parliamentary Commissioner for Administration does not necessarily provide a model to be followed closely for the investigation of complaints alleging maladministration in local government.' The Government, however, are conscious of the need for improved arrangements for investigating citizens' complaints, and have stated that they 'intend to begin discussions with representatives of existing authorities with a view to introducing new arrangements at the same time as local government reorganisation becomes effective'.[1]

Control by central government

The existence of these controls from time to time excites controversy. Clearly a local councillor can be expected to have local knowledge but he cannot always be expected to see the needs of the country as a whole. It is the responsibility of the central government to ensure that discrepancies in the provision of services between one area and another are not too great. Furthermore the central government has the responsibility for ensuring that money raised from the public by taxation and rates is lawfully and sensibly spent. The problem of public accountability is a thorny one, for accountability, by its nature, implies caution, and procedures which are foolproof are, inevitably, more time consuming than those which are not subject to strict supervision. Both central government departments and the officers of local authorities need to be on guard against any tendency to establish or perpetuate procedures which are needlessly restrictive. It is the function of M.P.s, councillors and all who are interested in the efficiency of government, constantly to seek for improvement in administrative methods.

The Minister responsible for local government, Mr Peter Walker, has indicated that it is the intention of the present Government to reduce the degree of control by central departments. Referring to the Government's intention to introduce a new pattern of government (see below) Mr Walker said, in March 1971: 'I intend to examine every way in which Whitehall interferes with local government so that interference is reduced to the absolute minimum from the time the reform takes place.' Following this statement, Mr F. Stephenson, president of the Institute of Municipal Treasurers, observed: 'I find it difficult to think of the important areas where the Government would be prepared to do this. I think there are minor areas which cause irritation and double administration where reform is possible, but control will continue over much of the work of local authorities so that the Government can keep control of the national economy.'

The need for reform

Whatever the strengths of local government in England and Wales, and

[1] Cmd. 4584: *Local Government in England. Government Proposals for Reorganisation* (H.M.S.O., 1971).

232

certainly there are many councils, large and small, which do an excellent job, there is little doubt that, taken as a whole, the system falls a long way short of perfection. Indeed, it is clear that the present situation frequently creaks under the burdens which are placed upon it and the need for reform has long been apparent. During the period since 1945 numerous attempts to overhaul the system have been made, but not until the last year or two have any firm decisions been taken.

The failure to bring about radical structural change at the end of the Second World War had more deep-seated effects on the British system of government than is generally appreciated. The claim has been made that one of the reasons why important services, such as hospitals, gas and electricity, were transferred to public corporations and other bodies set up by the government in the immediate post-war period, is that the structure of local government was unable to meet modern administrative demands.[1] Whatever the reason, the powers of local authorities were drastically reduced and government control over the remaining functions was increased.

In 1945 a Boundary Commission was set up. This had power to adjust local government areas but it had no authorisation to deal with functions. It produced voluminous reports, but it did not succeed in altering a single boundary and it was finally wound up of its own volition in 1949. The Commission itself pointed out that it could not produce a workable scheme if its powers were limited to boundary changes alone. It argued that it needed powers to deal with functions and to create new types of local authorities to suit local needs.

In 1958 two new Local Government Commissions were established, one for England and one for Wales, to carry out a somewhat similar exercise. Only in the sprawling conurbations which were termed Special Review Areas, which included Tyneside, the Black Country, the West Riding of Yorkshire, Greater Liverpool and Greater Manchester, were they given powers to deal with functions as well as with boundaries. The English Commission was more successful than the 1945 body and some changes were implemented, although some of the proposals made aroused fierce controversy. The Welsh Commission, in its 1962 report, said: 'Boundaries cannot reasonably be divorced from functions or from finance . . . That we were not permitted to reconsider the redistribution of functions was, we believe, a serious mistake and a disservice to Wales.' The Minister concerned rejected these proposals, as had the Minister in 1945.

The English Commission was dissolved in 1966 and a new full-scale Royal Commission was set up to make a comprehensive investigation. Its terms of reference were: 'to consider the structure of Local Government in England, outside Greater London, and to make recommendations for authorities and boundaries, and for functions and their division, having

[1] See P. Self, *Regionalism* (Fabian Society, 1949).

233

regard to the size and character of areas in which they can be most effectively exercised and the need to sustain a viable system of local democracy'. Sir John (later Lord) Redcliffe-Maud was appointed as Chairman. A further Commission, with Lord Wheatley as Chairman, was appointed to scrutinise Scottish local authorities. Wales was not covered by either Commission; the reason for this was that, in consultation with a cross-section of Welsh councils, a working-party of officials had almost completed a review of local government in Wales.

The 'Maud' proposals

The Maud Commission reported in June 1969. It proposed that England should be divided into eight 'provinces' each of which would have a provincial council. The eight provinces would be divided into fifty-eight 'unitary' areas, covering both town and country areas, which would be responsible for all services; additionally, in order to cater for the special circumstances of the Birmingham, Liverpool and Manchester conurbations, these three areas would form 'Metropolitan' Councils and each would have a second tier of smaller metropolitan district councils (22 in all). The key functions of the metropolitan authorities would be planning, transportation and major development. The main functions of the metro-

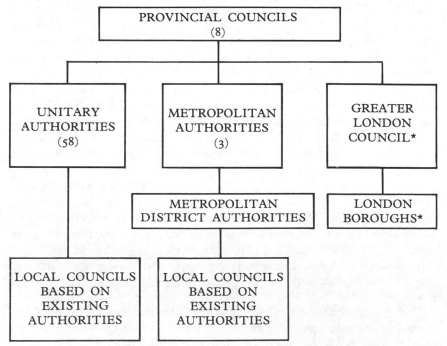

*The structure in Greater London was outside of the Commission's terms of reference but it has been included here for the sake of completeness.

Figure 7. The Maud Commission Proposals on the Structure of Local Government in England

234

politan districts would be education, the personal social services, health and housing. The Provincial Councils would be indirectly elected by the unitary and metropolitan areas (including, in the south-east, the Greater London authorities), and would also have co-opted members. They would concentrate on the provincial strategy and planning framework within which the main authorities would operate. Unitary and metropolitan authorities would be elected in the normal way.

It was also proposed that within the unitary areas, and wherever they were wanted, within the metropolitan areas, *local* councils should be elected to represent and communicate the wishes of cities, towns and villages in all matters of special concern to the inhabitants. The only *duty* of the local council would be to represent local opinion, but it would have the *right* to be consulted on matters of special interest to its inhabitants and it would have the *power* 'to do for the local community a number of things best done locally, including the opportunity to play a part in some of the main local government services on a scale appropriate to its services and subject to the agreement of the main authority'. The structure proposed by the Maud Commission is presented in diagram form in figure 7. These proposals were supported by 10 of the 11 members of the Commission. The remaining member, Mr Derek Senior, presented a long and detailed minority report advocating the adoption of the principle of 'city-regions'. This minority view appeared as Volume II of the Commission's Report.

The Labour Government almost immediately accepted the majority report in principle and promised legislation on this in the mid-1970s. In February of 1970 it issued a White Paper on local government reforms which followed the main lines of the Maud recommendations, but with some important changes. Firstly, the Government proposed to increase the number of metropolitan areas from 3 to 5, West Yorkshire and South Hampshire being added to Maud's SELNEC (South-East Lancashire and North-East Cheshire), the West Midlands, and Merseyside. The 'unitary' or 'single-purpose' authorities were correspondingly reduced to 51. Secondly, the Labour Government took the view that, in metropolitan areas, education and rating should be the responsibility of the metropolitan, not the district council. Thirdly, the White Paper proposed that the unitary authorities should delegate some of their duties to district committees on which members of local councils would sit as of right.

The Labour Government also decided not to act on the Commission's proposals for the eight provincial councils until the Crowther Commission on the constitution had reported. It stated that it intended to consult local councils about the frequency of elections and changes in the rules disqualifying council employees from seeking election. It was not convinced by arguments in favour of paying a salary to councillors, but it believed that expense allowances ought to be substantially improved. It proposed the establishment of ten or more Local Commissioners of Administration to investigate complaints of maladministration.

The future

These, like all other proposals for reform, aroused great controversy among local authorities and the Local Government Associations. In the event, the Labour Government failed to win the general election in 1970 and the incoming Conservative Government, which was pledged to the introduction of a two-tier system, scrapped the previous Government's plans and its own proposals were published in February 1971.[1] The pattern proposed for England, excluding Greater London, provides for a two-tier system to be adopted throughout the whole of the country but with differences in the division of function between the 'county' and 'district' authorities in the 'metropolitan' areas which are designated as (i) Tyneside and Wearside, (ii) Merseyside, (iii) Greater Manchester, (iv) West Yorkshire, (v) South Yorkshire, and (vi) the West Midlands. (See figure 8.) The main local government functions will be divided between the two types of authorities as follows:

(a) *All County Councils*

Planning: plan making; development control (strategic and reserved decisions); acquisition and disposal of land for planning purposes, development or redevelopment

Highways, Traffic and Transport

Housing: certain reserve powers, e.g. for over-spill

Building regulations

Weights and measures

Food and drugs

Clean air

Refuse disposal

Environmental health

Museums and art galleries

Parks and open spaces

Playing fields and swimming baths

Coast protection

Police

Fire

(b) *All District Councils*

Planning: most development control; acquisition and disposal of land for planning purposes; development and redevelopment

Housing: housebuilding; housing management; slum clearance; house and area improvement

Refuse collection

Environmental health

Museums and art galleries

Parks and open spaces

Playing fields and swimming baths

Coast protection

[1] Cmd. 4584: *Local Government in England* (H.M.S.O., 1971).

236

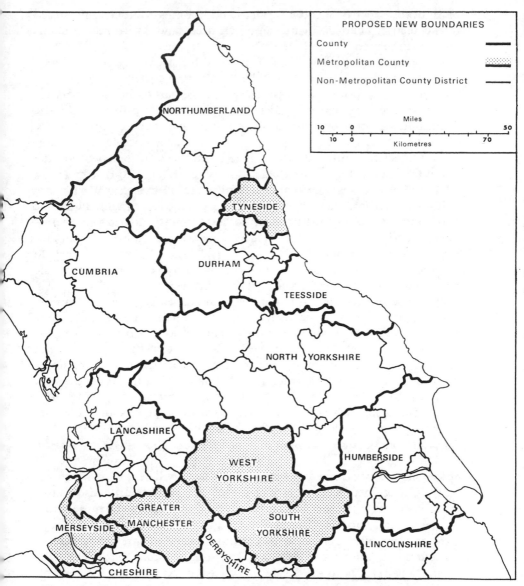

PROPOSED NEW BOUNDARIES

County

Metropolitan County

Non-Metropolitan County District

Miles

Kilometres

NORTHUMBERLAND

TYNESIDE

CUMBRIA

DURHAM

TEESSIDE

NORTH YORKSHIRE

LANCASHIRE

HUMBERSIDE

WEST YORKSHIRE

GREATER MANCHESTER

MERSEYSIDE

SOUTH YORKSHIRE

DERBYSHIRE

LINCOLNSHIRE

CHESHIRE

Figure 8. New local government areas in the northern half of England as proposed by the Local Government Boundary Commission Designate in April 1972.

(c) Education, personal social services and libraries will be administered by the district councils in metropolitan areas and by county councils outside of the metropolitan areas.

Where the same function is shown in both lists (e.g. parks and open spaces) this indicates that there will be 'concurrent powers' exercisable by both types of authority. The Commission will be part of the machinery for keeping local government areas and electoral divisions up-to-date. It is the Government's intention to introduce a Bill to give effect to these changes in the 1971–2 session of Parliament, by which time a number of consultations with existing authorities will have taken place. It is hoped that the new authorities will take over their responsibilities on 1 April 1974.

Under these plans many towns, which are at present 'all-purpose' authorities, will lose their separate identities and will be merged with the surrounding rural and urban areas to form county districts or metropolitan districts. It seems likely that in some areas the proposals will give rise to protracted struggles between the rival political parties in efforts to gain control of the new councils, and that the problems of reallocating the senior staff of existing authorities will be considerable.

The Government suggests that in many instances the future units might be styled 'boroughs' as in the case of the metropolitan districts and districts in county areas which will be the direct successors to existing boroughs. The Government also intends to 'seek ways in which the office of mayor and other traditional attributes and dignitaries of boroughs can be retained, as well as special honours granted to particular towns – including the style "city" and the right of the Mayor of certain cities to the title "Lord Mayor" '.

The Government has taken the view that the report of the Crowther Commission must be available before taking decisions on the constitution of any regional bodies and the range of functions they might exercise in relation to central and local government. Parish councils outside of the metropolitan counties are to be retained and these will have certain powers, but the Government has expressed the view that neighbourhoods or small communities within larger built up areas might preferably be represented by non-statutory bodies. Overall, the reorganised system 'will be founded upon the organisations of the existing authorities and will preserve wherever possible the loyalties attaching to ancient units of local government'.

Questions relating to the financing of local government are to be dealt with by the Government at a later stage. In a further White Paper, the Government also accepted the principle of a two-tier system of local government for Scotland which was recommended by the Wheatley Commission, but with considerable differences on how the tiers should be divided. It proposes (a) eight regional authorities (the Highlands, North-East, East, South-East, Borders, Central, West and South-West) which will have responsibility for 'strategic' services including planning, industrial development, roads, education, social work, the police and fire services, (b) forty-nine district authorities which will have responsibility

238

for local planning, urban development, building control, housing and environmental health, except in the Highlands, Borders and South-West where local planning and building control will be regional responsibilities. The intention lying behind this latter provision is to avoid the creation of district authorities in the more remote parts of the country which have to be unduly extensive in area merely to support minimum planning staffs. Orkney and Shetland, exceptionally, are to be single tier 'all-purpose' authorities. The Government's pattern for Scotland compares with the structure of seven regions and thirty-seven districts proposed by the Wheatley Commission.

Proposals for Wales were published in a consultative document. The pattern proposed is that Wales should be divided into seven new counties and thirty-six district authorities. The counties will be responsible for education, strategic planning, personal social services, highways and fire services. The district council will be responsible for housing, aid to industry, some planning and coast protection, refuse collection and disposal, clean air, parks, playing fields and public baths, burial and cremation and markets. Cardiff will continue to be a city and the capital of the principality but will become part of a new district authority including Penarth and parts of the adjoining rural districts.

On the day following the publication of the Government's proposals, the editorial in *The Guardian* dismally observed: 'The Maud report was both emphatic and convincing on the disadvantages of two-tier systems and the advantages of placing all local authority functions (which are usually inter-acting and inter-related in one way or another) in one set of hands. It pointed out that the most effective bodies in the present systems are the all-purpose county boroughs. The Maud philosophy, therefore, was to develop the county borough style, but extending it to take in the rural hinterland which surrounds urban centres. Mr Walker goes in the opposite direction, abolishing all county boroughs in favour of a new set of two-tier counties. On past experience, this is to exchange the more efficient for the less efficient.'

The Maud Commission in its report had stated that: 'The pattern and character of local government must be such as to enable it to do four things:

To perform efficiently a wide range of profoundly important tasks concerned with the safety, health, and wellbeing, both material and cultural, of people in different localities.

To attract and hold the interest of its citizens.

To develop enough inherent strength to deal with national authorities in a valid partnership.

To adapt itself without disruption to the present unprecedented process of change in the way people live, work, move, shop, and enjoy themselves.'[1]

Once the new pattern of local government is established, it is likely to last for a long time: whether or not it will succeed in fulfilling the objectives specified by the Maud Commission remains to be seen.

[1] Cmd. 4040: vol. I, p. I.

17 Local Government at Work

The value we shall get from time and money spent on local government will ulti-
mately still depend on the calibre and humanity of councillors and their staff, on the
way they organize their work, and on the degree of mutual understanding they
achieve between themselves and the communities they serve.

Royal Commission on Local Government in England, 1969

Why local government?

In the previous chapter consideration was given to the structure of local
government in England and Wales. The main purpose of this section is to
examine in more detail the way in which the system actually operates by
asking such questions as: Does local democracy really fulfil its professed
objectives? How much interest does the electorate take? From which
sections of the community are councillors selected? How far does party
politics come into it?

Firstly, it must be pointed out that the task of government could be
carried out quite effectively without the existence of a local government as
we know it today. Many government services are provided locally which
have no connection at all with local councils. The Department of Health
and Social Security and the Department of Employment, for example,
have offices scattered throughout the country which provide facilities and
exercise supervision in the localities for which they are responsible. In
other cases, services are provided by public corporations such as the
National Coal Board and the Post Office; others are administered by
regional boards as in the case of the hospital service. Sometimes local
authorities merely act as agencies for the central government, as for
example in the collection of motor taxes, and have no say whatsoever in the
policies pursued. If it were so desired all government services could be
provided by one or another of these methods and the need for local
authorities as such would disappear. The continuance of elected local
authorities is, therefore, a decision based on a choice between alternatives.
The local government pattern is chosen and maintained for some services
because it is believed that in a democratic society it is desirable to have
some degree of involvement on the part of citizens in the various localities.

240

Some of the arguments advanced, however, greatly exaggerate the degree to which the present system of local government contributes to the practical working of democracy and L. J. Sharpe suggests that defenders of the idea of local democracy often make claims which cannot easily be substantiated.[1] In evaluating these arguments it is worthwhile to ask questions such as: how far do local councils encourage local interest and participation in the administration of services? To what extent do they offer a training ground for the politically active? Do they really bring different social groups together? Are they able to ensure that local needs are actually taken into account?

The electors

Although only a few empirical studies have been made it seems fairly certain that knowledge about local government on the part of the electorate as a whole is very limited indeed. Few electors know the name of their local councillor, and in a survey carried out in Newcastle under Lyme in 1958 a quarter of those interviewed had not heard of the impending election a week before polling day. In a survey conducted by the National Association of Local Government Officers, published in 1957, only 6 per cent of those interviewed claimed to have attended a council meeting. Compared with a general election, when between 75 per cent and 85 per cent of the electorate have usually voted, turn-out in local government elections is relatively low, the proportion voting ranging roughly between 30 per cent and 50 per cent with an average turn-out of about 40 per cent. Voting turn-out tends to be greater for smaller authorities than for larger authorities, and is generally higher in rural district areas than in urban areas. There are also very considerable regional differences. In 1961 the lowest turn-out was in the rural district of Adminster in which only 9.9 per cent of the electorate voted; the highest was in the urban district of Amlych (Wales) which had a turn-out of 97 per cent.

A recent study of the County Borough of Reading undertaken by Dr Roy Gregory supports the view that local issues have little effect on the outcome of local elections. The results of local elections tend much more to follow the trends of opinion in relation to national issues. 'With one possible exceptions', he writes of the Reading elections between 1945 and 1967, 'the very few results that were out of line with the national movement of opinion do not seem to be associated with local issues and controversies; and what is by common consent the most celebrated local controversy since the war does not seem markedly to have affected the local results.' The controversy referred to was that arising from the Labour group's decision in 1958 to build an expensive swimming pool. Dr Gregory observes that this reaction to national rather than local events poses 'a genuine problem for the theory of local democracy'. On one hand the realisation that local voting does not closely coincide with the Labour

[1] L. J. Sharpe, *Why Local Democracy?*, Fabian Tract no. 361 (Fabian Society, 1965).

group's actions might encourage them 'more readily to pursue necessary but unpopular policies. On the other hand, for those who believe that elections and their prospect play an important part in maintaining responsiveness at the local level, the outlook is most discouraging.'[1]

Social background of councillors

Membership of local authorities in many areas is far from being representative of the population as a whole. L. J. Sharpe carried out an investigation into the social class composition of three county borough councils and three county councils. Generally the results show that extent of middle-class representation on the local authorities concerned is much greater than the size of this group in the population as a whole.[2] Blackpool council was 90.5 per cent middle-class as against 24.5 per cent in its population as a whole. The corresponding figures for Chester were 48.8 per cent and 17.4 per cent. The Cornwall County Council was 100 per cent middle-class

TABLE 40   *Social Class of Councillors*

		Elected councillors in study areas				M.P.s	
Registrar-General's social class	Total adult pop. in 1961 (%)	All (%)	Lab. (%)	Con. (%)	Lib. (%)	Lab. (%)	Con. (%)
I	3	11	9	14	21	25	32
II	16	40	28	58	58	38	66
III	50	39	48	26	17	30	2
IV	22	7	11	2	2	7	—
V	8	3	4	—	2		

Source: L. J. Sharpe, *Voting in Cities* (Macmillan, 1967), p. 311.

in composition, although in the county as a whole the working-class population was 74.7 per cent. The council membership in Durham, on the other hand, was 77.4 per cent working-class which compares with 89.2 per cent working-class in its population as a whole. It seems likely that the history and tradition of particular areas still has a considerable impact.

L. J. Sharpe and his colleagues made a detailed study of eleven towns in the 1964 borough elections, these were Durham, West Hartlepool, Wolverhampton, Oxford, Southampton, Exeter, Torquay, Bristol, Chester, Leeds and Bradford. The overall analysis of the results shows that, as is the case in other areas of political leadership, local councillors in the areas studied were drawn disproportionately from higher social groups than the general population which they represent (see table 40).[3]

[1] R. Gregory, 'Local Elections and the Rule of Anticipated Reactions', *Political Studies*, vol. I, no. I, March 1969.
[2] L. J. Sharpe, 'Elected Representatives in Local Government', *British Journal of Sociology* (1962), pp. 189–208.
[3] L. J. Sharpe, *Voting in Cities* (Macmillan, 1967), pp. 311–12.

It should be noted, however, that in this respect councillors appear to be more representative than Members of Parliament. Table 40 also shows that the Labour councillors are more representative than Conservative and Liberal councillors. Further evidence from L. J. Sharpe's study shows that in all political parties a higher proportion of candidates successful in the election was drawn from social classes I and II than from candidates in social classes III, IV and V. The main explanation of this success, at least in the case of the Conservative candidates, appears to be that the candidates concerned are more likely to be selected for the safer and more hopeful seats.

M.P.s and local councils

A fairly high proportion of M.P.s have had experience of local government. Conservative M.P.s who have served on local authorities include some 35 per cent of their membership in the House of Commons and about 45 per cent of Labour M.P.s have been councillors before entering Parliament. Once elected, however, very few on either side are able to maintain their membership of the local authority with which they have been connected. This results in a situation in which, in terms of membership, local politics in Britain are much more sharply separated from national politics than in most Western democracies. A number of well known national politicians can, however, be closely associated with local government in the urban areas. Both Joseph Chamberlain and Neville Chamberlain were Lord Mayors of Birmingham. Clement Attlee was Mayor of Stepney and Herbert Morrison was for many years leader of the Labour group on the London County Council. The late Mrs Bessie Braddock, M.P.'s connection with Liverpool City Council over many years provides a notable exception to the general rule.

Duration of council membership

Bealey, Blondel and McCann's study of Newcastle under Lyme shows that, at least in the borough which they investigated, the average political career of candidates is short. In the years between 1932 and 1962, 305 candidates stood for election to the borough council and this group engaged in an aggregate of 672 fights and uncontested elections. The average number of elections was therefore 2.23. Twelve of this sample had been elected as aldermen at the beginning of the period; of the remaining 29.3, over two-fifths appear to have contested an election only once; 55 stood four times or more and 51 contested three elections. It is clear from this study that in Newcastle under Lyme just over one hundred people constituted the hard core of the personnel engaged in local campaigns over a whole generation.[1]

In his study of political life in Glossop published in 1959, Professor Birch writes: 'During the past thirty years there has been a marked reduc-

[1] F. Bealey, J. Blondel and W. P. McCann, *Constituency Politics* (Faber, 1965), pp. 299–300.

tion in the number of people willing to stand for election, so that in practice the parties spend more of their time trying to find suitable candidates than deciding who shall be nominated from a number of applicants.' He notes that, in 1955, the Conservative party was unable to nominate a single candidate, although over thirty people had been approached.[1] It must be emphasised that both in continuity of service on the councils and the availability of candidates respect there are very considerable local variations. In some areas there are no lack of candidates, in others it is difficult to find anyone willing to stand. Generally it can be said that people are more likely to offer themselves as candidates when the prospect of success in the election is extremely good. This means that in some areas there are plenty of Conservative candidates and few from the Labour Party, in other localities the situation is reversed.

Party politics

A number of references have already been made to the fact that much of the activity in some local authorities is connected with party politics, but thus far no detailed comment on this has been made. There are still many electors and commentators who bemoan the fact that party politics intrudes upon local government affairs, the basis of this argument being that the administration of essentially local services should not be the subject of inter-party disputes. This, however, seems to be an unrealistic premise. We have already seen (chapter 1) that the activity of politics arises from disagreements about the use of resources and the policies which should be pursued and that it cannot be decided in advance which matters will become political matters. Disagreements arise from differing values, beliefs and attitudes and quite frequently these differences are reflected in the policies of the major rival parties. The provision of houses and schools is as likely to arouse as much controversy at the local level as the scale of defence and the level of social services does at the national level. For good or ill, political party battles are fought in connection with local authorities and the nature of these must be examined. It must, however, be said that controversial issues at local level are much more likely than Parliamentary disputes to cut across party allegiances.

First of all it must be stated that there is nothing new in the existence of party politics in connection with local authorities. Party politics in many cities goes back to the first half of the nineteenth century but although, in the cities and larger towns, councillors wore political labels this did not necessarily mean that all the councils in these towns were the subject of 'party-control' in anything like the modern sense. Local government in Birmingham was conducted on party lines from the time that Joseph Chamberlain became Mayor in 1873. The first elections to County Councils in 1888 were reported according to party composition, and the London County Council from its inception was organised on a political

[1] A. H. Birch, *Small Town Politics* (Oxford University Press, 1959), pp. 114–15.

party basis. Since the formation of the Labour party in 1906 there has been a gradual extension of party politics in local government especially in urban areas, but as many as half of the rural districts and the majority of parish councils are still conducted on what is, superficially at least, a non-party basis. It is not, however, true as is sometimes said that party organisation is unknown in parish councils. In the relatively densely populated parishes in the Yorkshire coalfield, for example, elections are fought on the same party lines as in the adjacent boroughs.

'Party politics' in local government means different things in different places. In some areas one party is virtually certain to have a majority on the council, in others support may be divided fairly evenly between two or more parties. Having been elected on a party label, councillors may act with a fair measure of independence or they may be subject to strict control by the party organisation. Regardless of these local differences the major parties themselves have differing attitudes about the way in which their members should conduct their affairs in the local councils, the Labour party having a stronger tradition of concerted activity than either the Liberal or Conservative parties. The way in which the existence of local political organisations affects the actions of councillors and the degree to which they owe allegiance to them varies tremendously in different localities. The Labour party retains its name in local politics, as usually does the Liberal party and candidates normally fight elections under the official banners. Conservatives and anti-Labour organisations which, in terms of personnel and support, can be regarded as Conservative, include Progressives, Moderates, Anti-Socialists, Owner Occupiers and Citizens; some 'Independents' are genuinely independent and others are likely to be Conservatives in all but name.

At the local level as well as the national level it can be argued that the effect of party politics has been to bring stability and coherence to government and to provide the elector with clearly defined choices. It is likely, however, that the personalities of candidates play a much larger part generally in local elections than is the case in national elections; this does not, however, necessarily prevent individuals from losing seats in periodical 'swings' from one party to another which sometimes reflect dramatically the electorate's response to national events. The often expressed desire to have genuinely independent councillors in local government is open to the same arguments as the claim for non-party M.P.s in the House of Commons (see chapter 4). Opponents of the party system in local government, as well as suggesting that political programmes are inappropriate in this sphere, claim that party politics has led to a decline in the quality of councillors and that it produces unnecessary divisions in the community. Both of these claims are, however, open to challenge. If there has been a decline in the quality of councillors this is by no means limited to those who are party representatives. It seems likely that party politics in local government has come to stay and it is more realistic to consider ways in which the operation of this system can be improved than merely to resent its presence.

Party systems in local government

The way in which party politics operates in the actual conduct of local councils varies considerably between one area and another. A fairly sophisticated analysis of the workings of party systems in local government has recently been put forward by J. G. Bulpitt.[1] This scheme involves a basic division between *positive* and *negative* party systems. In negative party systems, the prevailing atmosphere is anti-party political; this may be because two or more party groups form only a minority of the total council membership, or because the parties, although possessing a majority membership of the council, do not accept responsibility as parties for running the authority. In a *positive* party system, the parties' representatives form a majority of the council membership and they accept responsibility as parties for their activities in the council. Chairmanships of committees and other important offices will be allocated on a party political basis. At election time the parties are likely to put forward co-ordinated statements of policy. 'Positive' systems are further subdivided into one-party, primary and secondary party systems.

J. G. Bulpitt quotes both Salford and Sale as examples of one-party systems. In Salford the idea of government and opposition groups pervaded all the activities of the council. The Labour group took all the committee chairmanships and deputy chairmanships and all the aldermanic places. Only one Conservative proposal had been approved by the council in the period since the war. It was within the Labour group itself that many important issues had to be settled. Sale had been controlled by the Conservative party continually since 1946; only once between 1946 and 1960 did the Conservative membership fall below twice the size of all other groups in the council. The Labour and Liberal groups were small and loosely organised. The main differences in the council were between the older and younger Conservative members. The Conservatives dominated the whole character of the council and its activities. Outside of the council a powerful owner-occupiers' association watched the activities of the council and actively intervened on the question of council-house rating assessments. The distinctive party attitudes between these two groups can be seen in Salford's decision to expand the 'direct works' department and in the large-scale purchase of land for council purposes and, in Sale, the decision to cut the number of houses built by the council and the abolition of the rate subsidy to the housing revenue account.

The *primary* system applies when the various groups on a council are tightly organised and officers and issues are contested on party lines. The *secondary* system applies when, although elected on party labels, the

[1] J. G. Bulpitt, *Party Politics in English Local Government* (Longmans, 1967). See especially pp. 104–30.

246

various groups are not so continuously and consistently divided on party lines. Bulpitt describes how in Middleton and Macclesfield the Labour groups followed a strict interpretation of the party standing orders for Labour groups and the political temperature in the council chamber was high; these authorities are therefore categorised as primary party systems. In Manchester and Rochdale, by contrast, the temperature of political party debate was low and the parties were agreed on practically all major lines of policy. The distribution of chairmanships, etc., generally followed an agreed pattern, and no party group was strictly disciplined. Although these authorities were *formally* organised on a political basis the degree of political conflict was relatively low and they are, therefore, described as *secondary* party systems.

In considering situations where one party has a monopoly of the areas, it is important to recognise that conflicts frequently take place within the party organisation. It seems that politics, like nature, abhors a vacuum.

The Newcastle under Lyme study by F. Bealey and his colleagues, previously mentioned, gives some fascinating glimpses of the activities of local parties and their relationships with the council and the electorate in both the borough and the rural district of Newcastle under Lyme. In the case of the borough it shows that Labour's unbroken spell of power over a long period had tended to separate the council members from their rank-and-file supporters, and especially from their voters. Relying on traditional support, many of the Labour councillors became unheedful of public opinion. Because of the dissatisfaction of council-house tenants, however, a storm blew up and this had the effect of forcing the Labour councillors to take a much more active interest in the views and wishes of the electors.[1]

Professor A. H. Birch's study of political life in Glossop referred to above also provides an illuminating picture of the relationship between the council, its members, the political parties and the electorate in that locality. Glossop, in Bulpitt's terminology, would be classified as having a secondary party system in the council. Professor Birch relates how, although the members were elected under party banners, the influence of their affiliations in the council once elected were difficult to trace. 'The Liberals', he writes, 'do not believe that their council members should be tied to any particular policy and they do not hold caucus meetings and frequently disagree during debates; the Labour members still hold caucus meetings but no binding decisions are taken there and it is quite common for Labour Councillors to be on opposite sides during council debates.'

The author of the Glossop study also points to an interesting divergence of viewpoint between the older council members who have lived in the locality for a long period and the younger members who include many newcomers to the area among their numbers; this is a difference which cuts across party affiliations. The older, Glossop-born councillors defended the right to conduct affairs as they had always done, even though this appeared

[1] Bealey, Blondel and McCann, *Constituency Politics*, pp. 384–5.

to be rather muddled, whereas the younger newcomers favoured a much more businesslike approach. Exchanges in the council chamber were direct and uninhibited, one group for example, described their critics as 'a bit stupid' and 'just like ostriches with their heads in the sand'.[1]

The details of elections and voting behaviour described in this study are very revealing. In Glossop it was the practice for the Labour and Liberal parties not to put up the full quota of candidates in each ward so that the elector had typically to cast his votes among four candidates – two Conservative, one Labour and one Liberal. Analysis of election results showed a marked reluctance on the part of the electors to cast both votes for the two candidates from a single party. Thus, in 1953, in one ward one Conservative candidate obtained 1136 votes and the other 776. Also, many of the electors used only one of their votes, following the practice known as 'plumping'. The figures for 1949, for example, showed that 7510 electors voted (i.e. a total of 15 020 possible votes in all), but the total number of votes cast was only 11 324. This means that 3696 out of the 7510 voters used only one of their votes. This report again emphasises that, in local elections, the personalities of the candidates are likely to weigh fairly heavily in the minds of most voters.[2]

Local government associations

Two further matters need to be mentioned in this section. The first is concerned with the organisation of the staff of local authorities and the second with the associations formed to represent the interests of the various types of local authorities.

The main trade union of local government officers and clerical staff is the National and Local Government Officers Association, which has recently become affiliated to the Trade Union Congress. The less-skilled employees are members of the National Union of Public Employees, the National Union of General and Municipal Workers or the Transport and General Workers Union. Rates of pay and conditions of service are governed by the recommendations of Whitley Councils on which the local authorities and the trade unions concerned are represented.

Associations exist for each kind of local authority. These include the Associations of Municipal Corporations, the County Councils' Association, Urban District Councils' Association, Rural District Councils' Association, and the National Association of Parish Councils. These bodies provide information and advice for their members and generally represent the interests of their particular group of authorities. They are consulted by the Government on local government matters and occupy a powerful place as major pressure groups. There is some danger that these groups wield too much power when proposals for the reorganisation of government are under consideration. The associations, because they are made up

[1] Birch, *Small Town Politics*, pp. 120–2.
[2] Birch, *Small Town Politics*, pp. 113–14.

248

of members and officials of existing authorities, have a vested interest in the continuance of the present pattern. The interests of the associations are not necessarily coincident with the interests of the electors or with the views of groups which are not committed to the existing pattern. In any gathering of members of local authorities there is usually a fairly ready agreement on the need for change. There is, however, much more difficulty in securing agreement on specific proposals which affect the power and prestige of the authorities with which they are associated.

Conclusion

Although the limitations of the existing structure of local government have been emphasised, the importance of its role in the political system should not be minimised. Despite the existence of strong central control some local authorities have impressive records of achievement and have done much to improve standards in the locality concerned.

International comparisons tend to work in favour of at least some aspects of the British system. Ian Gilmour writes: 'It is probably less corrupt than in most countries. It is also an impressive witness to the tradition of voluntary service.'[1] Interest and participation on the part of the mass of the electorate may be low but the councils can on occasions provide a forum for criticism of and pressure on the central government and not infrequently they reflect at the local level the kind of conflict of interest which characterises the parliamentary scene.[2]

[1] Gilmour, *The Body Politic*, p. 331.
[2] Details of a number of studies on the working of individual local authorities are given in the section on further reading.

Part 4   State and Citizen

---

18   The English Legal System

> No one ever sat down and drafted the English legal system. There was no moment of time at which it came into existence, and no document which set out what it was to be.
>
> Peter Archer *The Queen's Courts*

Introduction

It must first be explained that much of what follows applies only to England and Wales, for although the United Kingdom is a unitary state, there is no single body of law which applies throughout the whole of the country. Scotland has a legal system different in many respects from that of England; the law of Northern Ireland also is substantially different from that which applies in England. In spite of these differences, however, a good deal of modern legislation does apply throughout the whole of the United Kingdom.

In any society provision must be made to ensure that the behaviour of one individual or group does not unduly interfere with the freedom of others. Much social behaviour in Britain is regulated by the law enacted by Parliament, but Statute Law covers only part of the complex provision for the regulation of personal behaviour and additional legal rules are included in a body of law which has been developed by the courts themselves called the Common Law. The courts exist to interpret the law where doubt exists, to try offences which are alleged to have been committed under statute law and to settle a vast variety of disputes between individuals and groups. Where applicable the courts order punishment or obtain redress for wrongs which have been suffered. The legal system also provides for appeals from lower courts to higher courts in an effort to ensure that wrong decisions by the courts themselves are corrected. Law, however, slowly changes in response to changing social needs and Parliament can repeal or amend old laws and make new ones and the common law can extend its scope to embrace new developments and unforeseen circumstances.

In his famous book on *Jurisprudence*, Sir John Salmond states 'law consists of principles recognised and applied by the state in the administration of justice'. Justice, however, is an abstraction concerned with notions

250

of right and wrong, fairness and unfairness, rights and repression, equality and inequality, which the law makers in their wisdom or unwisdom normally attempt to embody in the rules which they prescribe. The Courts can only administer the law as it is written, however, and if the law is thought to be unjust, they must be party to the injustice until such time as the law is altered. To quote Sir John Salmond again: 'the law consists of the rules recognised and acted on by courts of justice'.

English law is distinguished from other systems of law by a number of features which include: the absence of a comprehensive legal code; a reliance on the common law as the basis of the system; the independence of the judiciary; the division of the legal profession into two branches; the use of the *accusatorial* procedure and its presumption of innocence. Some of these characteristics are discussed further below.

In the English system everyone is presumed to know the law, in spite of the actual impossibility of being able to do this, and ignorance of the law is no excuse. This latter aspect is expressed in the maxim *Ignorantia juris, quod quisque scire tenatur.* (Ignorance of the law, which every man is presumed to know, excuses no man.)

Sources of Law

(1) COMMON LAW

Before a centralised system of government had evolved in England offences were tried in local courts by the Lords of the Manor, and over a period of time a body of law based on custom and tradition gradually grew up. In the twelfth century the King's justices were sent out to all parts of the country 'on Assize' and they tried cases, basing their decisions on similar cases tried at earlier times. Because of the central guidance and direction which developed from this practice more uniformity in the administration of the law was introduced and *precedents* (decisions by judges in superior courts which must generally be followed by other judges) were more firmly established. In the thirteenth century these decisions began to be recorded and so came to be recognised as integral parts of the law.

The common law is judge-made law and this remains the solid foundation of the English legal system and the provisions of common law are taken fully into account by Parliament in the enactment of statutes. It is important to notice that the success of this development has been dependent on the calibre of the judges and the independence which they have been afforded. From time to time particular provisions or related sections of the common law are supplanted by statute law. This allows undesirable developments to be checked, substantial clarifications to be made and affords the opportunity of codification. Thus, the Property Acts of 1925 greatly simplified the law relating to land and the Sale of Goods Act, 1893, modified the law relating to the field described in the title of the legislation. The common law at one time dealt with a number of criminal matters but nearly all important aspects of this have been superseded by statute law.

(2) EQUITY

In the fifteenth and sixteenth centuries many people who had suffered wrongs of one kind or another complained that they were not getting justice from the common law courts and this situation was made worse by the fact that the procedures used did not provide remedies for some wrongs. They, therefore, appealed to the King as the 'Fountain of Justice' and eventually certain matters came to be dealt with by the Chancellor in the Court of Chancery, so that by the end of the eighteenth century a whole new system of rulings came into existence.

The Supreme Court of Judicature Acts of 1873–5 provided that the two systems of common law and equity would be administered together and that, where there was conflict between the two, equity was to be the dominant principle. Equity, in the words of Maitland, must be regarded as 'supplementary law, as a sort of appendix or gloss added to our code, at every point presupposing the existence of common law'. Its effect generally is to make the common law more *equitable* than it would otherwise have been.

(3) STATUTE LAW

This is the law made by Parliament following the procedure outlined in chapter 10. The doctrine of the parliamentary supremacy applies here as elsewhere and if there is conflict between common law and statute law the latter prevails. Legislation consists of some 3000 statutes and the delegated legislation which stems from this.

Civil Law and Criminal Law

In both the content of law and the procedures followed a distinction must be made between *civil* offences and *criminal* offences.

(i) *Crimes* are regarded as being offences against the community as a whole because they represent threats against its interest and security. In criminal cases *prosecutions* against the *accused* are brought in the name of the sovereign (so that the title of the case would be *Regina* versus so-and-so); the expenses of the *trial* are borne by the State; and punishment for convicted persons is by fine or imprisonment. The death penalty for murder was suspended for a period of five years in 1965 when the Murder (Abolition of Death Penalty) Act substituted a mandatory life sentence. In 1969 it was decided by Parliament that abolition should be made permanent.

(ii) *Civil disputes* arise between one individual or corporate body and another. In these cases the person making the complaint (the *plaintiff*) against another (the *defendant*) brings a *suit* or *action* against him which is settled by a properly constituted court. The State does not enter into the case except to act as umpire in the dispute. The arrangement for the

252

payment of the costs of the *hearing* are made by the judge, the successful *party* normally, but not necessarily, being awarded costs. The object of civil *proceedings* is to gain redress in the form of either restitution of rights or property or to claim damages in the form of pecuniary compensation. The main branches of civil law are Contract, Tort and Trusts.

Some courts are concerned with civil matters only and some with criminal matters; others again have both civil and criminal jurisdiction. For some offences there is a *double liability* in that the court may both inflict *punishment* and award *compensation* to the person wronged; this could apply, for instance, in a criminal court where a person is found guilty of malicious damage. In other cases, however, the person wronged must choose between civil and criminal remedies. Thus a person who has been subject to common assault or battery may institute either criminal or civil proceedings but not both. A person convicted for this offence in a criminal court cannot be sued in a civil court for the same act.

In criminal cases prosecutions, once begun, cannot be withdrawn; in civil cases they can, and often are, withdrawn, provided that neither party objects. Many civil cases are in fact settled 'out of court' (see below).

Personnel of the law

The English legal profession is divided into two branches: *barristers-at-law* and *solicitors* of the Supreme Court. Both are referred to as lawyers.

(1) *Barristers* must have passed the 'Bar' examinations and be members of one of the four Inns of Court: the Inner Temple, Middle Temple, Lincoln's Inn and Gray's Inn. The Inns are under the direction of senior barristers known as 'masters of the bench' and each Inn has the power to admit an appropriately qualified member by a 'call to the Bar' and to *disbar* a member for professional misconduct. Barristers have the right of audience in any court but appear normally only in superior courts. They do not communicate direct with the general public but are 'briefed' through a solicitor. Judges and other legal officers are appointed from their number. A barrister of ten years' standing may apply to 'take silk' and become a Queen's Counsel (Q.C.). This gives him considerable status in the profession and when he appears in court he must be assisted by a junior counsel. Most of the higher judicial offices are filled from the ranks of Queen's Counsel.

(2) *Solicitors* qualify by completing a period as an articled clerk and passing the Law Society examinations. They are then 'admitted' to the profession and receive a certificate to practise from the Master of the Rolls. The solicitor maintains contact with clients and usually works in partnership with other solicitors. Solicitors have the right of audience in Magistrates Courts, County Courts and the new Crown Courts.[1] Only a minority

[1] See pp. 257–8, 263–6. Solicitors sometimes appear before quarter sessions whose jurisdiction is to be transferred to the new Crown Court. The solicitors right of audience in the Crown Court is governed by Section 12 of the Courts Act, 1971.

of solicitors are engaged in the work of advocacy, i.e. representing clients in the court; more often the solicitor's role is to 'brief' barristers for cases in courts where solicitors do not have the right of audience or to be occupied in legal work which does not involve appearance in the courts such as the preparation of wills or mortgages.

The division of the legal profession into two branches reflects a historical development in which barristers have been regarded as the superior group. Attempts by the Law Society, which is the professional organisation of solicitors, to obtain the right of audience in the higher courts and to become eligible for more senior judicial appointments have met with only limited success. Until quite recently it was extremely difficult to transfer from one branch to the other, but arrangements have now been made which greatly facilitate such transfers.

LEGAL OFFICERS AND COURT OFFICIALS

It will be convenient here to set out brief details of the leading dignitaries in the legal hierarchy, who are referred to from time to time in this chapter and elsewhere in the book. The various courts mentioned in the descriptions are discussed more fully below:

(i) *The Lord Chancellor.* In addition to his political duties as a senior member of the Government and Speaker of the House of Lords, the Lord Chancellor is responsible for the machinery of the courts and makes or advises on various judicial appointments. He is responsible for the appointment of Justices of the Peace. He reviews, when necessary, the more serious proceedings of courts martial, appoints chairmen of some administrative tribunals (see chapter 19) and supervises various offices concerned with legal practice and procedure. He presides over the House of Lords when exercising its judicial functions and over the Judicial Committee of the Privy Council. He also appoints the members of the Law Commission. His salary is £14 500 per annum of which £10 500 is paid in respect of judicial duties and £4000 as Speaker of the House of Lords.

(ii) *The Law Officers of the Crown* are:

(a) *The Attorney-General,* who is the legal adviser to the Government and represents the Crown in court cases. He is a barrister, an M.P., and a member of the Government appointed by the Prime Minister.

(b) *The Solicitor-General,* who is the deputy to the Attorney-General. The title is deceptive because he must be a *barrister*. He also is an M.P. and a member of the Government.

(iii) *The Director of Public Prosecutions,* who is an appointed civil servant who may be either a solicitor or a barrister of ten years' standing. He works under the direction of the Attorney-General. He, or members of his department, prosecute in serious criminal cases and in cases referred to him by government departments, e.g. prosecutions under the Official Secrets Act.

254

(iv) *The Lord Chief Justice*, who is head of the Queen's Bench Division of the High Court. He spends much of his time presiding over the Court of Criminal Appeal and the Divisional Court of the Queen's Bench Division. He takes precedence over the Master of the Rolls and the President of the Probate, Divorce and Admiralty Division.[1] His salary is £10 000 per annum.

(v) *The Master of the Rolls*, who is the senior judge in the Court of Appeal and is responsible for the rules of the Law Society and for admitting solicitors. He ranks next to the Lord Chief Justice.

(vi) *The President of the Probate, Divorce and Admiralty Division*, who is the senior judge in this division. He ranks next to the Master of the Rolls.

(vii) *Masters and Registrars of the Supreme Court.* There is a Master of the Queen's Bench Division, a Master of the Chancery Division, and in the Probate, Divorce and Admiralty Division, officials who perform the duties of masters are known as Registrars. Their work is largely concerned with various legal questions arising before the parties to a case appear in court. In the Queen's Bench, these 'interlocutory matters' are decided 'in Chambers'. An appeal from the decisions made by a Master may be made to the judge but these are in practice rare. Masters and Registrars of the Supreme Court are appointed by the Lord Chancellor, the Master of the Rolls, and the President of the Probate, Divorce and Admiralty Division, dependent upon the division and the nature of the work which is allocated to them.

(viii) *The Lord Justices*, who are judges of the Court of Appeal.

(ix) *The Lords of Appeal in Ordinary*, who are the Law Lords who sit in the House of Lords and who play a major role when the House exercises its judicial functions.

Judges

The independence of judges is a cardinal feature of the British system of government. All judges are appointed by the Crown for life and their salaries are charged to the Consolidated Fund as a token of their freedom from interference. They may only be removed from office by an Address to the Crown by both Houses of Parliament. Judges cannot be sued for defamation in respect of words uttered in court. The Prime Minister nominates the Law Lords, and the Lord Justices of Appeal, the Lord Chief Justice, the Master of the Rolls, the President of the Probate, Divorce and Admiralty Division, but in making these appointments there is little doubt that he is guided by the Lord Chancellor. The Lord Chancellor recommends the appointment of the ordinary judges of the High Court, who are known as *puisne* (literally, younger) judges. He will also be responsible for the appointment of Circuit judges to serve in the Crown Court and County Courts and the metropolitan and other stipendiary magistrates.

[1] References to the present divisions of the High Court (and to Quarter Sessions and Assizes) should be read in the light of the impending changes discussed below. See pp. 257–8, 267.

The wisdom of allowing judges to continue in the discharge of important judicial functions at relatively advanced age is often questioned. Another accusation is that judges are steeped in their own traditions and easily become out of touch with the development of modern life, more particularly in their understanding of the way of life of lower income groups and the younger generation. Judges of the High Court, however, are held in high regard and their integrity and incorruptibility is a feature much commented on by foreign observers, and any assessment must take account of both the merits and demerits of our system. As R. M. Jackson has observed: 'Complacency is a dangerous thing. So is indiscriminate disparagement. Our machinery of justice is likely to continue much in its present form for some years, and improvement is more likely to occur by investigation of its actual working than by apology or abuse.'[1]

Juries

A jury in England or Wales consists of twelve persons, except in County Courts when the number ranges from seven to eleven. Most householders aged between 21 and 60, whether men or women, are liable for jury service (those selected are marked 'J' on the electoral register) and if called they are legally compelled to serve. People in certain occupational groups, e.g. doctors, can claim exemption.

Juries in civil cases are increasingly rare but the Master may order a jury trial if he considers it appropriate. As Peter Archer remarks: 'It is the criminal law, where personal liberty is felt to be more particularly at stake, that the principle of the jury trial is still inviolate.'[2]

It is important to notice that a jury is independent of both the judiciary and the executive. In criminal cases, the accused person can have up to seven jurors changed without having to give reasons; this is known as a 'peremptory challenge'. Others can be changed if sufficiently good reasons are advanced. Once jurors have been 'sworn' they must not communicate with others about the case under consideration and they are themselves protected from interference. It is an offence to assault, threaten or attempt to corrupt a juryman before or during a trial. The Juries Act, 1949, authorised payments in respect of jury service and all persons who are summoned and attend court are now entitled to draw travelling and subsistence allowances and to receive compensation for loss of earnings at rates which are revised from time to time.

Until recently it was necessary for verdicts of juries to be unanimous, but under the Criminal Justice Act, 1967, majority verdicts of 10–2 were authorised for criminal cases. The Courts Act, 1971, extended this provision to juries in civil cases where these are still used.

In cases where a jury is appointed it is the practice for the judge to 'sum

---

[1] R. M. Jackson, *The Machinery of Justice in England*, 2nd edn (Cambridge University Press, 1967), p. 236.
[2] P. Archer, *The Queen's Courts* (Penguin, 1963), p. 175.

up' for the instruction of the jury and for the jury to decide the verdict on the basis of the evidence presented. The judge decides questions of law and the jury determines questions of fact. The judge instructs the jury on what is relevant to the case and what is irrelevant. When there is no jury, which is the situation which normally applies in civil cases, there is a panel of not less than three judges. The senior judge gives the decision of the court together with the reasons for it; the other judges present are also entitled to add their comments.

Recent legislation affecting structure of courts

Description of the courts other than the magistrates' court and the county court (see below) is complicated by the fact that the existing structure will be substantially changed when the Administration of Justice Act, 1970,

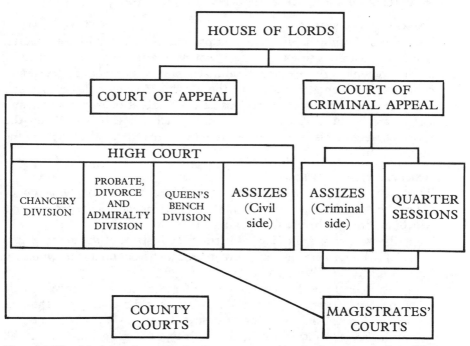

Note: (1) The Administration of Justice Act, 1970, provides for the reorganisation of the High Court on the following basis:

HIGH COURT			
CHANCERY DIVISION	FAMILY DIVISION	QUEEN'S BENCH DIVISION	
		ADMIRALTY COURT	COMMERCIAL COURT

(2) The Courts Act, 1971, provides for assize courts and magistrates' courts to be replaced by a single Crown court.

Figure 9. English Courts of Law

257

and the Courts Act, 1971, are fully implemented. Both of these Acts form part of the ongoing process of modernising the law and the courts. Some of the resulting changes will necessarily be brought about in piecemeal fashion; the relevant provision of the Courts Act reads: 'This Act shall come into force on such date as the Lord Chancellor may by order in a statutory instrument appoint, and different dates may be appointed for different provisions of this Act, or for different purposes.' Figure 9 presents the system of courts as they have existed over a relatively long period of time and indicates the main changes which will in due course be made. Further details of this legislation are given as appropriate when the various courts are discussed in the following sections. Criminal and civil courts are considered separately although, as will be seen, they do not all exercise exclusively jurisdiction of one kind or the other. Courts function as courts of 'first instance' or 'appeal', or both.

CRIMINAL COURTS

The courts of criminal jurisdiction at present include magistrates' courts, which deal with less serious offences; courts of quarter sessions; courts of assize (including the Central Criminal Court which acts as the assize court for the London area), and the Crown Courts in Liverpool and Manchester, which try more serious cases. Trials at quarter sessions and assizes are by jury. About 98 per cent of all crimes come within the jurisdiction of magistrates' courts and only 2 per cent are dealt with in the higher criminal courts.[1]

MAGISTRATES' COURTS

These are also known as Courts of Petty Session and, wrongly, as Police Courts because the police play a prominent part in many of the proceedings which are brought before them. They are of two types:

(i) Those comprised of lay magistrates or Justices of the Peace (J.P.s) of whom there are at present 19 250 throughout the whole of England and Wales.

(ii) Those in Inner London and some large cities, which have a single paid or *stipendiary* magistrate. At present there are 34 of these in London and only 11 in other cities.

Criminal cases which come before both types of magistrates' court fall into three categories:

(a) 'Summary' offences which can be dealt with by the magistrates themselves.

(b) Some more serious offences which may be tried either in the magistrates' court or by a jury at assizes or quarter sessions. These cases can be heard in the magistrates' court if the accused person so wishes after he has been informed of his rights. The fact that if convicted in a jury trial the penalties are stiffer than in the

[1] For a general survey of the working of English criminal law, illustrated cases, see: F. T. Giles, *The Criminal Law* (Penguin, 1954).

magistrates' court may well influence the choice.

(c) The preliminary hearing of indictable offences. (Indictable offences are more serious offences triable before a jury, where the charges are preferred in writing.) The object of these proceedings is to see if there is sufficient evidence for the case to be heard by a higher court. The charge may be either dismissed or committed to quarter sessions or assizes.

The jurisdiction of magistrates' courts includes matrimonial proceedings for separation and maintenance orders, adoption, affiliation and guardianship orders. They also have jurisdiction in respect of matters such as 'nuisances' under the Public Health Acts. Committees of magistrates have quasi-administrative responsibilities in relation to applications for the licensing of public houses, clubs and betting shops, the performance of stage plays, extensions of shopping hours, etc. Applications from the police to remand persons in custody pending the preferment of charges are considered by the magistrates.

Magistrates' courts (other than those manned by stipendiary magistrates) normally consist of between two to seven Justices of the Peace but certain offences, e.g. drunkenness, can be dealt with by one J.P. sitting alone. They are advised by a Clerk to the Justices who is a qualified barrister or solicitor whose function is to inform them on points of law and procedure. In the more populous areas two or more courts usually sit simultaneously. The maximum penalty for any summary offence is detailed in the statute creating the offence; for indictable offences triable summarily (category (b) above) a court of petty sessions cannot inflict a sentence of imprisonment longer than six months or a fine of more than £100 or both. If, however, the magistrates consider that a penalty on the maximum of this scale is insufficient for a particular offence they may refer the accused person to quarter sessions for sentencing. Stipendiary magistrates, who must be barristers of seven years' standing, sit alone and function as both judge and jury; they can award slightly higher penalties than the lay magistrates.

Most prosecutions for minor criminal offences are brought by the police and are conducted by a solicitor retained by the police, a police inspector or other police officer. Both barristers and solicitors have the right of audience but legal representation is the exception rather than the rule. Proceedings are normally relatively informal, the accused and the witnesses being allowed to tell their stories in their own way. The aim of the magistrates' courts is to get justice done swiftly and cheaply and in most cases it succeeds in doing this.

Appeal from the magistrates' court at present lies to the quarter sessions on either the conviction or sentence of a person who pleaded not guilty. In the higher court the entire case is reheard. There is also an appeal to the high court on conviction or acquittal on points of law only; this is open to both defence and prosecution.

Frequent criticisms of the system of magistrates' courts include: the manner in which J.P.s are appointed, their lack of training, anomalies in sentencing and the non-deterrent effect of small sentences, and the possibility of undue influence on the part of the Clerk and the police. A Royal Commission on the Justices of the Peace, with wide terms of reference, was appointed in 1946; its report, which was published in 1948, gives an authoritative account of the development of the system up to that time.[1] One important feature of this was that nearly all individuals and bodies which gave evidence agreed that the system of lay justices should continue. The Justices of the Peace Act, 1949, following the recommendations of the Royal Commission, made provision for schemes of instruction in the principles and practice of law for lay justices.

A Royal Commission on the Selection of Justices of the Peace which reported in 1910 found that magistrates appointed in county areas were largely Conservative because of the politics of the Lord Lieutenant who had responsibility for recommending their appointment. The report of this Commission recommended that the Lord Chancellor should set up advisory committees in counties and in boroughs with separate commissions of the peace and this proposal was implemented. From that time, selection of J.P.s was more broadly based than hitherto although the circle from which recruits are taken still appears to be unduly limited. The position now is that magistrates are appointed by the Lord Chancellor on the recommendation of local advisory committees. In county areas this committee is under the Chairmanship of the Lord Lieutenant. Members of the advisory committee are themselves appointed by the Lord Chancellor. The membership and proceedings of the committees function on the basis of secrecy. The name and address of the secretaries of advisory committees are available from the Clerk of the County Council or the Town Clerk, depending on the area covered by the committee.

Although a leaflet published by the Lord Chancellor's Office in 1969 states that its purpose was 'to explain to the public how Justices of the Peace are appointed', the details of how this is done remains obscure. According to the leaflet, 'Any person or organisation may recommend a candidate for appointment', and 'political views are neither a qualification nor a disqualification for appointment'. 'Although the only age condition is that a person shall not be over 60 years of age on first appointment, it is desirable that all Benches should contain a proportion of younger magistrates, men and women in the thirties and forties.'

In the 1960s, the Labour Government introduced changes which were designed to broaden the basis of recruitment, but it is difficult to calculate the extent to which these measures have been successful. Until 1966, although there was a statutory duty for training to be provided, it was not obligatory for magistrates to attend. From 1966 it became compulsory for new J.P.s to undertake training courses designed to enable them 'to under-

[1] Cmd. 7463: *Report of the Royal Commission on Justices of the Peace* (H.M.S.O., 1948).

stand the nature of their duties, to obtain sufficient knowledge of the law to follow normal cases, to acquire a working knowledge of the rules of evidence and to understand the nature and purpose of sentences'.

Although no detailed analysis has been made of the social background and political affiliations of J.P.s it seems fairly clear that a high percentage of lay magistrates are drawn from the body of people active in local politics and the suspicion remains that appointments are, or have until quite recently been, decided by a process of political bargaining in the advisory committees. It appears also that some advisory committees have local rules affecting appointments which are determined by factors such as whether or not employers will release certain groups of employees for service on the bench.

Publicity has recently been given to the fact that instructions have been issued to advisory committees by the Lord Chancellor to the effect that M.P.s and their party agents cannot be appointed as J.P.s for the areas in which their duties in these respects are performed unless they agree to resign these offices on appointment as J.P.s. Speaking to the Magistrates' Association in the autumn of 1971 the Lord Chancellor, Lord Hailsham, said that this ban had been imposed 'because they are particularly vulnerable to political pressure in difficult decisions'. Referring to the time when he himself had been an M.P. he added: 'A sizeable number of my visitors and correspondents had business in the courts and sometimes both sides wrote to me or came to see me about the same case.' A spokesman from Transport House stated that many protests had been made against this ruling, and observed that the Chairman of a Conservative Association was often more important than the secretary, but that the former was not required to resign on appointment as a J.P.

The procedure for the appointment of Justices of the Peace still seems to be most unsatisfactory and the most pressing need appears to be for more openness in the selection process. Perhaps one solution would be for advisory committees to be established whose composition is made public and to make it clear that nominations from all individuals or organisations are welcome and will be carefully considered. To say this is not to decry the sense of service and competence of the majority of existing lay magistrates, it is merely to emphasise the importance of having a wider field of recruitment than exists at present and of ensuring that, as far as possible, justice is not only done but seen to be done.

There seems to be little doubt that on the grounds of expense alone the present system of lay magistrates will continue into the foreseeable future. In 1971 it was estimated by the Lord Chancellor's office that to introduce stipendiary magistrates throughout the country would cost in the region of £2 million a year. At least 300 new stipendiary magistrates would be needed if such a change were to be made at present and this would place an impossible strain on a legal profession that is already understaffed. The present Lord Chancellor, Lord Hailsham, is strongly in favour of retaining lay magistrates; in a speech delivered in 1971 he said: 'What justices lose in professionalism, they gain in local knowledge; what they lose in speed, they gain in humanity.'

QUARTER SESSIONS
Each county at present has a Court of Quarter Sessions which must meet at least every three months and sit for the number of days required to deal with the cases outstanding. In fact, they are held much more frequently than this and a committee under the chairmanship of Mr Justice Streatfeild, which reported in 1961, recommended that 'Quarter Sessions' should be empowered to sit as and when necessary. This recommendation, along with others, was adopted in the Criminal Justice Administration Act, 1962, although the title of Quarter Sessions remained. The court consists of two or more lay magistrates sitting with a jury under a chairman who is nowadays usually legally qualified. Ninety-four boroughs have the right to hold their own quarter sessions and here the bench consists of a single official sitting alone without a jury, who is known as the Recorder. He is a barrister of at least five years' standing appointed by the Lord Chancellor. He is frequently a barrister in private practice who sits for a few days each quarter or as required. The clerk to quarter sessions is known as Clerk of the Peace.

The quarter sessions is primarily a criminal court which tries cases more serious than those within the jurisdiction of the magistrates' court but less serious than those triable at assizes. However, it is now legally permissible for county quarter sessions which have a legally qualified chairman to try certain offences which would otherwise be excluded.

As well as being a court of first instance for criminal cases, the Court of Quarter Sessions also hears appeals from civil cases in the magistrates' court. Appeals from criminal cases tried at quarter sessions lie to the Court of Criminal Appeal and thence if necessary to the House of Lords. Subject to certain conditions, a further appeal from its appellate jurisdiction lies to a divisional court of the Queen's Bench. A further appeal in civil cases lies to the Court of Appeal and, with leave either of the Divisional Court or Court of Appeal itself, to the House of Lords.

THE CROWN COURTS
The work of quarter sessions in the areas of Liverpool and Manchester is taken in the Crown Courts. These were set up in 1956 and also deal with assize court work. Each court has a full-time recorder as judge and he sits with a jury.

ASSIZES
Courts of assize are branches of the High Court presided over by judges and are held in county towns and other large towns and cities. The judges go round 'on circuit' three or four times a year, each town being visited at least once on each circuit. After dealing with criminal matters the judges

262

turn their attention to civil cases. Since 1962 there has been more flexibility in the judges' circuit and they go where they are most needed. The procedure whereby high court judges exercise their authority by virtue of the commission of assize allows practising barristers and county court judges to assist them when necessary by appointment as special commissioners.

Assize courts have jurisdiction to try indictable offences and they deal with the most serious and difficult cases; the trial is by judge and jury. Appeals in criminal matters lie to the Court of Criminal Appeal with leave from either the assize court or the Court of Criminal Appeal.

The Courts Act, 1971

The Courts Act, 1971, implemented with some modification the Report of the Royal Commission on Assizes and Quarter Sessions which met under the chairmanship of Lord Beeching during 1966–9. The Act provides that courts of assize and quarter sessions will be replaced by a single Crown Court which will be able to sit anywhere in England and Wales, as the High Court will be able to do for the trial of civil cases. All trials on indictment will take place before the Crown Court, which will also exercise the appellate jurisdiction of quarter sessions.[1]

The judges of the Crown Court will be the High Court Judges and the circuit judges and recorders. Although a majority of the Royal Commission 'inclined to the view that solicitors should be eligible for appointment to the Circuit bench or as recorders', this view was rejected by the Government; in the second reading debate in the Lords, the Lord Chancellor said that he had maintained the *status quo* because the Bill was 'about the structure of the courts and not about the structure of the legal profession'. The Act provides that no person shall be appointed as circuit judge unless he is a barrister of at least ten years' standing or a Recorder who has held that office for at least five years. The judges will sit with justices of the peace in the case of appeals and committals for sentence and 'in such other classes of cases as the Lord Chief Justice, with the concurrence of the Lord Chancellor, may direct'.

The new Circuit Bench will be made up of the county court judges, the full-time judges of the Central Criminal Court, the Recorders of Liverpool and Manchester, the present full-time chairmen and deputy chairmen of quarter sessions and the holders of certain other full-time judicial appointments. The circuit judges will be able to sit in the Crown Court and the county courts and will also, if so requested by the Lord Chancellor, be available to assist the High Court Judges in the trial of civil actions. This arrangement will also apply to a number of part-time recorders to be appointed from the ranks of barristers and solicitors of at least ten years' standing.

The new unified court service will be under the control of the Lord

[1] These changes will come into operation on 1 January 1972.

Chancellor who will be responsible for servicing all the higher courts and the county courts. The provision of accommodation for the Supreme Court and the county courts throughout England and Wales will be taken from local authorities and will become the responsibility of the central government, except in the case of the Central Criminal Court which will remain as the responsibility of the Common Council of the City of London. The problem of accommodation is discussed in the last section of this chapter. These measures have been described by Lord Gardiner as 'the greatest reform in the administration of justice in this century', and very considerable changes, physical, professional and psychological, will have to be made to ensure that the aim of providing more streamlined machinery for the administration of justice is fulfilled.

The Court of Criminal Appeal
The Court of Criminal Appeal was established by the Criminal Appeal Act, 1907. The members of the Court are the Lord Chief Justice and the judges of the Queen's Bench Division. The quorum is three and an uneven number of judges must sit. The court can increase or decrease a sentence imposed by a lower court and can quash a conviction if it decides that a wrong decision was taken in the lower court. The Criminal Appeal Act, 1964, gives the court power to order a new trial if fresh evidence has come to light.

Criminal Proceedings
Criminal law in England presumes that the accused person is innocent until his guilt has been proved to the satisfaction of the jury. The defendant has the right to have a legal adviser to assist in his defence and can apply for legal aid if he is unable to meet this expense. If he is remanded in custody he can be visited by his legal adviser to ensure the proper preparation of his defence.

Criminal trials, apart from those which would endanger the security of the State, are held in public and the rules of evidence, which are concerned with the proof of facts, are vigorously applied; thus, the judge will warn the jury of the danger of convicting on evidence which is uncorroborated.

During the trial the defendant has the right to hear and, normally through his counsel, to cross-examine all prosecution witnesses. He can only be questioned himself if he agrees to be sworn as a witness in his own defence. No inquiry can be made into his character or into past offences unconnected with the one for which he is being tried. The jury alone decides whether he is 'guilty' or 'not guilty'.

The Civil Courts
The main civil courts in England and Wales at present are the County Courts and the High Court. The civil jurisdiction of the magistrates' court was dealt with in the previous section. The assize courts also have a civil

264

side and, although these courts are mainly concerned with criminal matters, important civil actions are heard locally. There are limitations on time, however, and busy assize court judges cannot be expected to hear long and complicated cases which could be more conveniently considered in the High Court. The plaintiff will normally be appropriately advised by his solicitor and the defendant has the right to apply for its removal from the assize courts to the High Court or vice versa. Assize court judges have the jurisdiction of the High Court but in practice only Queen's Bench and divorce cases are heard.

THE COUNTY COURT

The County Court was created by statute in 1846 with the object of providing a method of settling minor civil disputes, much more cheaply than is possible in the High Court where legal costs are invariably substantial. There are nearly 400 of these courts so located that a court within reasonable travelling distance is available to everyone. There are about 100 county court judges who work on a circuit which may be one court or several depending on the work to be done. County court judges, who must be barristers of seven years' standing, are appointed by the Queen, on the advice of the Lord Chancellor.[1] The judge is assisted by a registrar who is a solicitor of at least seven years' standing. By far the greater part of civil litigation in England and Wales is covered by the county court. In 1962, for instance, more than 1 500 000 proceedings were commenced in the county court as against 180 000 in the High Court. Of the cases commenced in the High Court only 2 per cent actually went to trial, 98 per cent being settled 'out of court' by a procedure described below. Solicitors as well as barristers have the right of audience.

The jurisdiction of the county court is extensive, some being 'co-extensive' with that of magistrates' courts (e.g. making orders for the adoption of children) and some being 'concurrent' with that of the High Court. A plaintiff, however, who commences an action in the High Court which falls within the jurisdiction of the county court would, if successful, only recover costs of the order applicable in the county court and would thereby suffer a proportionate financial loss. The case is also liable to be transferred to the county court on the decision of the High Court, with the plaintiff being responsible for costs incurred in the High Court up to that time. Jurisdiction in some cases, e.g. bankruptcy and admiralty cases, is limited to certain courts which are specifically designated for this purpose. On some matters, e.g. cases under the Hire Purchase Acts, it has exclusive jurisdiction. Since 1934, appeals from the county court lie direct to the Court of Appeal.

The general principles of the extent of the jurisdiction of the county court are as follows:

[1] Under the provisions of the Courts Act, 1971, Recorders will be appointed who will act as part-time judges in the County Court.

(i) Actions in a variety of civil cases up to a prescribed amount.

(ii) Actions transferred from the High Court – no limit applies in these cases.

This jurisdiction includes: actions in contract and tort, except libel, slander, and seduction, where the amount claimed does not exceed £750; equity matters such as trusts, mortgages and dissolution of partnerships, where the amount does not exceed £5000; and actions concerning title to land or actions for the recovery of the possession of land where the net annual value for rating does not exceed £400. Other matters dealt with include adoption cases, bankruptcies (in courts duly designated), undefended divorce cases (again in designated courts), cases arising under the Rent Restrictions Acts, and Hire Purchase Acts; and complaints of racial discriminations brought by the Race Relations Board which are dealt with by specially designated courts sitting with two assessors.

Usually, cases are heard by a judge sitting alone, but on infrequent occasions there will be a jury of eight. This might arise, for example, where an action for fraud or defamation is remitted to the county court by the High Court. Peter Archer writes: 'The county court judge must combine the qualities of a High Court Judge and a magistrate. He may be confronted with almost any legal problem which exists for his High Court colleagues. But he has to dispose of a bewildering variety of cases almost with the speed demanded of a magistrate.'[1] Some years ago an actual list of cases heard in one day was submitted by a county court judge to the Committee on Supreme Court Procedure, under the Chairmanship of Lord Evershed, Master of the Rolls. This included: a petition to adopt a child, an application to pay money out of court, eleven judgment summonses, four applications of various kinds, thirteen landlords' claims for possession, an action remitted from the High Court, two other actions, and the dissolution of a partnership.[2]

The registrar occupies an important place in the work of the county court. Like the judge he may be concerned with the work of one court or several. He is responsible for the administration of the court and also exercises judicial functions. Sometimes he sits in open court and decides cases which would otherwise be taken by the judge. Whether he sits in open court or works informally in chambers is decided by the nature of the business in hand. He has power to deal with undefended cases and disputed cases up to a prescribed amount where neither party objects. He may also hear a case as an arbitrator if the parties agree and the judge consents. All the registrar's decisions are subject to review by the judge. It can be seen from the foregoing that the county courts have a vitally important role in the English legal system.

THE SUPREME COURT OF JUDICATURE

The Supreme Court of Judicature which sits in the Royal Courts of

[1] Archer, *The Queen's Courts*, p. 133.
[2] Archer, *The Queen's Courts*, p. 134.

Justice in the Strand is a court of first instance for civil cases and an appellate court. The court is divided into the Court of Appeal and the High Court of Justice, which is mainly staffed by the heads of the division previously described and 65 *puisne* judges. At present the High Court is further divided into three divisions: the Queen's Bench Division, the Chancery Division and the Probate, Divorce and Admiralty Division. The High Court also has original criminal jurisdiction but this, in modern times, is of little practical importance. For the hearing of cases of first instances, the High Court Judges sit singly. Appellate jurisdiction in civil matters is exercised by a Divisional Court of two or three judges or by a single judge of one of the three divisions, as appropriate to the particular case under review, who is nominated by the Lord Chancellor.

Under the existing system cases have been allocated to the three divisions on the following basis:

(1) *The Queen's Bench Division.* This division deals with the bulk of the work in the High Court and is responsible for any cases not specifically allocated to the other two divisions, and deals with all types of common civil actions, e.g. fraud, libel, slander. When complex commercial cases are under consideration a special jury is drawn from the City of London.

(2) *The Chancery Division.* The work of this division is based on the work of the former Court of Chancery which was concerned with equity matters. It embraces partnerships, trusts, bankruptcy, 'specific performance' of contracts, estates of deceased persons where the validity of the will is not in dispute, and the wardship of 'infants'.

(3) *The Probate, Divorce and Admiralty Division.* The common link of the variety of matters dealt with by this division has been that they dealt with branches of the law which have to some extent been influenced by Roman Law. Admiralty matters include collisions, salvage and disputes about insurance and cargoes.

Under the terms of the Administration of Justice Act, 1970, the Probate, Divorce and Admiralty Division of the High Court will be abolished. A new Family Division will be created which will assume responsibility for domestic and matrimonial cases, including cases on guardianship and adoption which are at present dealt with in the Chancery Division. Undisputed wills will be dealt with by the division but disputed wills will be assigned to the Chancery Division. Admiralty cases will be dealt with by separate Admiralty Court which will be established within the Queen's Bench Division.

The Act also provides for the setting up of a separate Commercial Court also to be attached to the Queen's Bench Division. The background to the rules within which this court will operate are both legally and politically interesting. The Bill contained a proposal that the court should be able to sit in private; the reason for this was that business and industrial organisations, presumably because they did not wish to have details of their operations made public, often preferred to have disputes settled in

267

secret by arbitrators and it was hoped that this provision would encourage firms and companies to use the courts as an alternative to this practice. The proposal was approved by the Lords but was defeated in the Commons following intensive pressure by the Bar Council, the Law Society and some opposition M.P.s, all of whom believed that to have the court sitting in private would be contrary to the spirit of justice. This result makes it probable that the practice of referring business disputes to arbitrators will continue.

Appeals from the High Court and (as at present constituted) the civil side of assizes, are heard in the Court of Appeal, and they may, with leave of the court or the House of Lords, go to the House of Lords.

Civil Law-Appeal Courts

The appellate functions of the three divisions of the High Court have already been referred to. The composition and powers of the main civil courts of appeal are outlined below.

THE COURT OF APPEAL. The Court of Appeal comprises the Lord Chancellor, the Lord Chief Justice, the Master of the Rolls and thirteen Lord Justices of Appeal. Three judges sit together, and the court can sit simultaneously in two or more divisions. If an appeal is allowed the court has power to reverse the decision of the lower court, amend it or order a new trial.

THE HOUSE OF LORDS. The House of Lords, sitting as a court, is made up of the Lord Chancellor, ten Lords of Appeal in Ordinary and other peers who have held high judicial office. Lords of Appeal must have had fifteen years at the Bar or two as a Supreme Court judge. For civil matters the House of Lords is the ultimate court of appeal for the whole of the United Kingdom and in criminal matters for England and Wales and Northern Ireland only. The quorum is three, but normally five, and sometimes seven, members sit. Since 1963 its judgments are delivered in printed form and are known as 'opinions'.

THE JUDICIAL COMMITTEE OF THE PRIVY COUNCIL. This body is comprised of the Lord Chancellor, the Lords of Appeal in Ordinary, and all Privy Councillors who have held high judicial office in the United Kingdom. Strictly speaking it is not a court but a committee of the Privy Council and, although it hears appeals from the Prize Courts of the Probate, Divorce and Admiralty Division of the High Court it is not a part of the ordinary judicial system. It hears appeals also from the Ecclesiastical Courts and from Disciplinary Committee of the General Medical Council. It is the court of appeal for courts of the Channel Islands, the Isle of Man and some Commonwealth countries. The Committee usually sits in a room at No. 11 Downing Street. Its judgments take the form of advice to the Queen.

Legal aid and advice

The principle that the law must be open to all is of fundamental importance, and clearly it would be unjust for a person to be without the means to safeguard his interests if he is unable to proceed because he lacks the necessary financial resources. Before the passing of the Legal Aid and Advice Act, 1949, the aphorism, perhaps falsely attributed to Lord Darling, to the effect that, 'The Law, like the Ritz Hotel, is open to all', was frequently cynically uttered. Now, however, provided that certain basic requirements are satisfied, free or contributory legal aid can, in specified cases, be obtained by all persons when the need arises.

The legal aid scheme in England and Wales is run by the Law Society under the general guidance of the Lord Chancellor. It is operated through area committees supported by a network of local committees. The costs of the scheme are met from a Legal Aid Fund, the income of which is derived from Exchequer Grants, contributions from assisted persons and costs recovered from parties in litigation.

In civil cases, applicants for free legal aid must show that the grounds for initiating or defending a claim are reasonable, and certain actions, e.g. libel and slander, are excluded from the scheme. A successful applicant is allowed to select from a panel of solicitors and, if necessary, the solicitor will instruct a barrister. In criminal cases a legal aid order may be made by the court itself if it appears a defendant's means are insufficient to meet the cost of the proceedings. In cases of murder the court is obliged to do this. The court also has the power to order applicants to make a reasonable contribution according to their personal means. The aid in these cases normally consists of representation by a solicitor and counsel assigned by the court.

Oral advice on legal matters is available from practising solicitors in England and Wales and Scotland, free of charge to persons in receipt of social security benefits, and at a nominal cost to others with low incomes for an interview lasting up to half-an-hour. This scheme is also financed from the Legal Aid Fund and is run by the Law Society. There is also a voluntary scheme following a similar pattern in which those seeking advice pay a fee of £2.

Until recently a non-assisted party had difficulty in recovering costs when successful against a party who was in receipt of legal aid. This difficulty has now largely been remedied by the Legal Aid Act, 1964, which provides that, in cases of this kind, the court may make an order for the payment to the unassisted party of a sum out of the Legal Aid Fund to defray the whole or part of his costs.

It has long been argued by constitutional lawyers and others that the absence of legal aid for persons appearing before administrative tribunals (see chapter 19) constitutes a serious injustice. The validity of this criticism has more recently been conceded but not pursued because of restriction on expenditure; the first tangible provision of this kind arises from the Legal Aid (Extension of Proceedings) Regulations, 1970, which extends legal aid to persons appearing before the Lands Tribunal provided, of course, that they are appropriately qualified to receive it. It now seems likely that this type of provision will, in due course, be further extended.

A Small Claims Court?
It has frequently been suggested that a Small Claims Court, in which small-scale litigation would be swift and cheap, should be established because, the exponents of this idea claim, justice has become too expensive a luxury for a considerable number of people who wish to pursue claims for small amounts of money owing to them through breach of contract, personal injury, and other causes. Under the existing system the cost of attempting to recover anything less than £100, it is argued, is virtually prohibitive.

In an attempt to draw attention to this problem Mr Michael Meacher, M.P., in 1971, introduced a Bill under the ten-minute rule providing for the setting up of such a court. His attempt was from the start doomed to failure, but it did provide the opportunity to give the question an airing.

The Coroner's Courts
The office of Coroner originated in the twelfth century and present-day Coroners retain the responsibility for investigating deaths which occur in suspicious circumstances, or from unknown causes, and 'treasure trove'. Coroners are appointed by local authorities and must be barristers, solicitors or medical practitioners of at least five years' standing. They are removable by the Lord Chancellor for established misbehaviour.

When a death occurs which the Coroner has reason to suspect is due to murder, manslaughter or infanticide, or was caused by an accident arising from the use of a vehicle on the public highway, he must summon a party of between seven and eleven members and hold an inquest. In some cases the jury may be dispensed with if the finding of the *post mortem* examination is negative. When an inquest is held it must hear anyone who wishes to give evidence and the Coroner has power to compel the attendance of anyone who may be able to help the inquiry.

If the jury find that the death was caused by murder or other crimes, the Coroner issues a warrant for the arrest of the person named. The Coroner has power to commit him for trial but in practice the accused is brought before a magistrate's court in accordance with the normal procedure for serious criminal offences.

Law reform
A distinction must be made between *substantive* law, which is concerned with individual rights and the remedies available from the courts when these rights are infringed, and *procedural* law, which is concerned with the process through which remedies are granted. As R. M. Jackson has observed: 'When the law works badly it may be possible to effect a cure by

alerting either substantive law or procedural law.'[1] Although the common law can and does develop through the decisions of judges as a result of which precedents are modified or extended to meet new circumstances, it is through statute law that substantial reforms are made. It must be remembered, however, that when the need for reform is accepted the actual implementation of the changes may be delayed for a considerable period because of pressure on the parliamentary timetable.

The main avenues through which proposals for reform are likely to come include the following:

(a) The Law Commission and other Committees established by the Government (these are discussed below).

(b) The Law Society and Bar Association.

(c) Private Member's Bill (see e.g. references to the abolition of capital punishment and changes in divorce law discussed elsewhere in the book).

(d) Various pressure and professional groups, e.g. the Howard League for Penal Reform, the British Academy of Forensic Science, the Married Women's Association.

(e) Royal Commissions, e.g. the Mental Health Act, 1949, was based upon the Royal Commission on Mental Illness and Mental Deficiency, and some of the less controversial proposals in both the Labour and Conservative Bills on the law relating to trade unions are based on recommendations made by the Royal Commission on Industrial Relations.

In 1947 the Statute Law Committee was reconstituted and given the task of considering 'the steps necessary to bring the Statute Book up to date by consolidation, revision or otherwise'. A special branch of the office of Parliamentary Counsel was established to assist in this work. The Consolidation of Enactments (Procedure) Act, 1949, gave additional strength to this arrangement with the result that between 1947 and 1952 no less than thirty Consolidation Acts were passed.

In 1932 a Law Revision Committee was set up by the Lord Chancellor 'to consider how far, having regard to the Statute Law and to judicial decisions, such legal maxims and doctrines as the Lord Chancellor may from time to time refer to them, require revision in modern conditions'. In 1952 this committee was reconstituted as the Law Reform Committee whose function was to consider, 'having regard especially to judicial decisions', what changes were desirable in legal doctrines referred to it. Outside bodies may now make recommendations which the Lord Chancellor may refer to the committee. In the same year a Private International Law Revision Committee was set up and the Criminal Law Revision Committee was established in 1959.

In 1965, largely due to the influence of the Lord Chancellor, Lord Gardiner, who was keenly concerned to make progress in law reform, the

[1] Jackson, *Machinery of Justice*, p. 334.

Law Commissions Act was passed. Under the provisions of this Act, a body of five full-time law Commissioners, with a five-year term of office, was appointed by the Lord Chancellor from the ranks of distinguished practising and academic lawyers. The Law Commission is directed 'to take and keep under review all the law with which it is concerned with a view to its systematic development and reform, including, in particular, the codification of such law, the elimination of anomalies, the repeal of obsolete and unnecessary enactments, the reduction of the number of separate enactments and generally the simplification and modernisation of the law'. The Commission is required to report to Parliament annually.

The first report, issued in 1966, welcomed the growing interest in the work of the Commission and stated: 'Consultation must develop not only with lawyers but with laymen. The grass roots of law reform are to be sought elsewhere than in the field of law.' Of the 632 proposals for reform made to the Commission in its first year of working, 360 came from the legal professions, 151 from the public, 51 from organisations outside of the legal professions, 65 from the legal and general press and 5 from other sources. The fourth annual report, published in 1970, indicates that detailed preparations are being made for major codification in several branches of law.

Problems of accommodation and personnel

The problems of introducing a new court structure are closely connected with those of accommodation and personnel, for the new arrangements can only work successfully if sufficient lawyers and adequate buildings are available. For a long time now the pressure on buildings and legal personnel, particularly barristers, has been acute and the existence of uncertainty about when a case will be heard creates considerable difficulty for lawyers and litigants alike as well as adding substantially to the costs. When Lord Hailsham became Lord Chancellor in 1970, he was confronted with 555 cases to be heard at the Central Criminal Court and 1300 at the Inner London Sessions. There were arrears of 261 cases in Liverpool, and in Birmingham delays in hearing criminal cases were being kept down at the expense of cases in the civil lists.[1] The Lord Chancellor has observed that 'to delay justice is to deny justice' and the Lord Chancellor's staff, in an effort to mitigate the worst effects of this situation, have been searching for public buildings which can be converted to temporary use as law courts. They have found a number of suitable buildings in the London area but have formed the view that the only way to deal with the problem in Birmingham, Leeds and Liverpool, is to build new courts. The Courts Act, 1971, provides for a £10 million building programme spread over ten years to provide facilities for the Crown Courts.

A statement issued by the Law Society in December 1970, which was

[1] Reported in *The Guardian*, 12 November 1971.

272

at least in part designed to press the claim for solicitors to have much wider rights of audience in the courts, drew attention to some disturbing features.[1] They claimed that, because of the acute shortage of barristers, criminal cases are being put into the hands of inexperienced counsel, to the inevitable disadvantage of the defendant. The Society reported that it had received a complaint from the senior prosecuting solicitor to a county council which stated that during 1969 he had delivered 1226 briefs to barristers, of which more than a third were returned, often on the evening of the day before the trial.

Reference was also made in the report to a number of cases in which difficulty had been experienced in making satisfactory arrangements for defendants. In one of the cases, the instructions went to five barristers before being accepted and the barrister who agreed to act had only twenty minutes to absorb them before the trial. 'This was the case of a man of 21 who had spent most of his adult life in prison and who had only been discharged from prison some eight days or so before committing the offence. He was sentenced to a further 12 months.' The Law Society also stated that: 'In Chester, Newcastle, London, and other areas, the practice is growing in Quarter Sessions in legal aid cases of not marking the names of counsel on the briefs at all. They are delivered to a set of chambers, whose clerk tries to find somebody to appear in court. The solicitor in the case has little or no say in who represents his clients.'

The report drew attention to the fact that the system under which barristers operate allows them to withdraw from a case while it is actually going on and hand its conduct over to a junior colleague. This occurs when the barrister concerned is also responsible for a case in another court and the two coincide for part of the time of the hearing. The solicitor's statement mentions that in a recent criminal case the barrister in charge had to leave to appear in another court at a critical stage when his clients were giving evidence. The case had to be turned over to a less experienced man who also had to make the final address to the jury.

Anthony Sampson has written: 'The Law is the most striking example of a profession which has become trapped in its conservatism and mystique. Its proud independence and remoteness have given it magnificent strength as a bastion of liberty and justice; but have also made it totally unsusceptible to pressures of change.'[2] This may be an overstatement but there can be little doubt that, although the English legal system may be amongst the best in the world, there is need for considerable improvement in both substantive and procedural law, in court facilities and procedures and an increase in the numbers of judges and barristers. Only if this is done can the ends of justice be properly served.

[1] Reported in *The Guardian*, 3 December 1970.
[2] Sampson, *Anatomy of Britain Today*, p. 162.

19   Administrative Justice

Our terms of reference involve the consideration of an important part of the relationship between the individual and authority. At different times in the history of this country it has been necessary to adjust this relationship and to seek a new balance between private right and public advantage, between fair play for the individual and efficiency of administration. The balance found has varied with different government systems and different social patterns. Since the war the British electorate has chosen Governments which accepted general responsibilities for the provision of extended social services and for the broad management of the economy. It has consequently become desirable to consider afresh the procedures by which the rights of the individual citizens can be harmonised with wider public interests.

Report of the Committee on Administrative Tribunals and Inquiries, 1957

Clearing the ground

Before looking more closely at the nature and purpose of those bodies known as administrative tribunals and the procedures followed by Ministers in conducting departmental inquiries, it is necessary to make two preliminary points. Firstly, it must be emphasised that, although disputes between the citizen and the State cover the greater part of the area under consideration, we are not exclusively concerned with this problem. A few of the tribunals which will later be listed are primarily concerned not with disagreements between individuals and government departments but with disputes between one individual and another as, for example, is the case in Rent Tribunals and Agricultural Land Tribunals. The function of the State in these cases is to provide machinery other than the ordinary courts of law to settle these disputes. Furthermore, even when a particular problem arises from actions of a government department, the case does not always represent a straightforward clash of interest between one individual and the State machinery; one group of individuals may be aggrieved by a particular proposal but others may benefit from it and wish it to succeed. As Peter Archer affirms: 'the issue is misleadingly stated if it is expressed as a conflict of society against the individual. Society consist of individuals, any of whom may find his interests in need of protection against a government department, while the individual will suffer together with his fellows if departmental policy is unnecessarily obstructed.'

274

Secondly, without wishing in any way to minimise the nature of the problem or to condone administrative excesses which have occurred, it must be said that it is an issue dear to the heart of constitutional lawyers and there is a danger that the scale of the problem may sometimes be exaggerated. To quote Peter Archer again: 'The officials themselves, whose policies are in question, are not usually heartless. Many of them, indeed, have benefited (or suffered) from a legal training, and they are not unaware of the watchful eyes both of the Courts and Her Majesty's Opposition.'[1] The matter was perhaps placed in its correct perspective by Mr R. A. (now Lord) Butler in the House of Commons in 1957, when he introduced the report of the Franks Committee which had spent two years investigating these matters. He said: 'the findings of the Committee are, on the whole, comforting, but unless we are constantly on our guard, these diseases may attack the body politic almost unnoticed, and if they are not resolutely checked at the outset they may eat right into its structure'.

Development of administrative justice
The need for bodies to deal with disputes between government departments and the citizen, and between one individual and another, on questions arising from legislation and related regulations stems from the changes in society which have taken place during the last hundred years or so which are characterised by a decline in *laissez-faire* capitalism and a growth of State intervention into increasingly wide areas of national life. Before 1900, formal disputes between a citizen and the central government were few and those that did arise, and upon which representations were made, were dealt with by the ordinary courts and in some cases by Parliament itself. But as the scale of social legislation increased it became necessary to find new ways of dealing with the ensuing problems because it was not possible for the legal system to cope with them and, in any event, many issues were minor ones quite unsuited to the normal process of litigation. Also it was necessary in the majority of cases to balance the legitimate demands of social policy against individual rights.

The growth of tribunals and inquiries was not a systematic development; machinery was developed on an *ad hoc* basis, the development of each new service bringing new demands. During the inter-war years, great concern at what was alleged to be the ever increasing domination of the executive was expressed by constitutional lawyers and others, and Lord Hewart's famous book entitled *The New Despotism*, which appeared in 1929, was characteristic of this concern. In this it was suggested that Parliament had escaped from *royal* domination only to have it replaced by an *executive* despotism; it challenged hotly the growth of both administrative justice and delegated legislation, regarding both as 'administrative lawlessness' which was inimical to the freedom of the individual. The Committee on Ministers' Powers (the Donoughmore Committee) which

[1] Archer, *The Queen's Courts*, p. 246.

275

reported in 1932 was concerned with administrative justice as well as with delegated legislation.

In recent years there has been much more concern with administrative justice than with delegated legislation. Today an individual is much more likely to be involved in a problem falling within the scope of administrative tribunals and inquiries than he is to appear in a court of law, because so many aspects of life now come within their scope. The building of motorways, the siting of airports, compulsory purchase of land for schools, or slum clearance, may bring us into dispute with a government department, the final decision on our representations or objections resting with the Minister; tribunals exist to deal with disputes arising from patents, social security, health services, industrial injuries, rents and other services with which many citizens at one time or another come into contact. In 1957 the Franks Committee reported that Rent Tribunals had been dealing with 15 000 cases a year and that the annual number of planning appeals was 6000. Between 60 000 and 70 000 cases a year were being heard by National Insurance and Industrial Injuries Local Tribunals.[1]

The Crichel Down Case
A classic case of maladministration, in the form of the 'Crichel Down' affair arose in the early 1950s and the publicity which this occasioned caused decisive action to be taken.

Crichel Down was an area of land in Dorset which was requisitioned by the Air Ministry in 1940 for use as a bombing range. At this time an undertaking was given to the owners, a naval officer and his wife, that they would have the opportunity of acquiring the land again when it was no longer required for military purposes. In 1950, however, the land was transferred to the Ministry of Agriculture. The original owners made a claim to the land and offered to buy it back but the Ministry of Agriculture refused the offer and installed a farmer to run a model farm.

The owners had good political connections and arrangements were made for questions to be asked in Parliament. A political storm ensued and eventually the Minister of Agriculture, Sir Thomas Dugdale, arranged for a public inquiry to be set up. When the findings were published the civil servants concerned were severely criticised and they were transferred to other departments. The Minister resigned and in 1955 a committee, under the chairmanship of Sir Oliver Franks, was established to look into the whole question of Administrative Tribunals and Enquiries.

The Franks Committee
The Committee reported two years later and its recommendations were debated in the House of Commons on 31 October 1957. In discussing the nature and scope of its inquiry the Committee stressed two important distinctions: 'The first is between these decisions which follow a statutory

[1] Cmd. 218: *Report of the Committee on Administrative Tribunals* (H.M.S.O., 1957).

procedure and those which do not. The second distinction is within the group of decisions subject to statutory procedure. Some of these decisions are taken in ordinary courts and some are taken by tribunals or by Ministers after a special procedure.' The Committee were instructed to consider only those cases in which the decision on objections was taken by a tribunal or a Minister after a special procedure, paying particular attention to the procedure for the compulsory purchase of land. The point here is that there were, and are, many matters for which no formal provision in the form of a tribunal or, for example, a public inquiry, exists. All that an aggrieved person can do in these cases, as the Committee itself recognised, is 'to complain to the appropriate administrative authority, to his Member of Parliament, to a representative organisation or to the press. But there is no formal procedure on which he can insist.'

The Crichel Down affair, therefore, which (as the Committee acknowledged) was 'widely regarded as a principal reason' for the appointment of the Committee, fell outside of its terms of reference. The inquiry held in this case was an *ad hoc* inquiry for which there was no statutory requirement. The Report stated: 'It may be thought that in these cases the individual is less protected against unfair or wrong decisions. But we are not asked to go into questions of maladministration which may arise in such cases.' (See below.)

The Committee found it difficult to establish clear principles to guide a decision as to which matters should be decided by a tribunal and which by ministerial adjudicators. It observed: 'Many matters remitted to tribunals and Ministers appear to have, as it were, a natural affinity with one or other method of adjudication. Sometimes the policy of the legislation can be embodied in a system of detailed regulations. Particular decisions, single case by single case, alter the Minister's policy. Where this is so, it is natural to entrust the decisions to a tribunal, if not to the courts. On the other hand it is sometimes desirable to preserve flexibility of decision in the pursuance of public policy. Then a wise expediency is the proper basis of right adjudications, and the decision must be left with a Minister.'

We are thus concerned with two main types of procedures. The first of these are the tribunals (known variously as tribunals, courts, committees, commissions, referees) and the second, ministerial inquiries for which there is an established procedure in the case of dispute. A dispute between an individual and the State authority might, typically, arise in circumstances such as the following:

(a) A teacher has an accident and breaks a leg while playing in a Staff *v.* Boys football match which is held in after-school hours. He claims industrial injuries but this is disputed by the National Insurance authorities. If the teacher presses his claim his case would be considered by the appropriate tribunal.

(b) A new comprehensive school is to be built which requires several acres of land owned by farmers. They refuse to sell, claiming that the price offered is too low and that if the land is acquired, they will be deprived of their livelihood; they enter formal objections. The local authority claims that there is no suitable alternative site and the Department of Education agrees. Because the land must be compulsorily acquired, an inquiry must be held at which the objections of the farmers and others interested in the proposal will be heard. This would normally be held in the locality. The Minister later issues a decision on whether or not the proposals to acquire the land are rejected or confirmed. The only appeal from the Minister's decision is to the High Court on points of law only.

Tribunals are variously constituted. The following example, which describes what happens when a patient makes a complaint against his doctor in general practice, is taken from the Franks Committee Report and describes the procedure which applied at that time. A complaint is first investigated by the appropriate Service Committee of an Executive Council (after the Chairman of the Council has ruled that there is a *prima facie* case.) A Service Committee consists of an equal number of lay and professional members, together with a lay chairman. The Committee reports to the Executive Council its findings on fact and recommendations on action. If the Executive Council considers that the doctor concerned should be removed from its list of general practitioners the Council makes representations to the National Health Service Tribunal. If the Council considers that no action should be taken or that a lesser penalty is called for, both the practitioner and the complainant have a right of appeal against the Council's decision to the Minister whose decision is final. The National Health Service Tribunal consists of two members appointed by the Minister and a legally qualified chairman appointed by the Lord Chancellor. A decision by the Tribunal that a practitioner not be removed is final, but if the Tribunal directs that a practitioner be removed the practitioner has a further right of appeal to the Minister whose decision is final. The Committee observed that this procedure is more concerned with the discipline of doctors than it is with the redress of patients' grievances.[1]

Tribunals
The tribunals examined by the Franks Commission were grouped into the categories listed below. Not all of these bodies still exist but the lists are left unaltered so as to give an indication of the range of bodies concerned.

(1) TRIBUNALS CONCERNED WITH LAND AND PROPERTY. County Agricultural Executive Committees, Agricultural Land Tribunals, Local Valuation Courts, the Land Tribunal, Rent Tribunals.

(2) TRIBUNALS CONCERNED WITH NATIONAL INSURANCE, NATIONAL ASSISTANCE, AND FAMILY ALLOWANCES. National Insurance Local Tribunals, Industrial Injuries Local Tribunals, the National Insurance Commissioner, the Industrial Injuries Com-

[1] Cmd. 218, pp. 43–4.

278

missioner, National Assistance Appeal Tribunals, Family Allowance Referees.

(3) TRIBUNALS CONCERNED WITH THE NATIONAL HEALTH SERVICE. Medical Practices Committee, Service Committees of Executive Councils, the National Health Service Tribunal.

(4) TRIBUNALS CONCERNED WITH MILITARY SERVICE. Military Service (Hardship) Committees, Reinstatement Committees, the Umpire, Conscientious Objectors, Local and Appellate Tribunals, Pensions Appeals Tribunals. (All of these except the last have been affected by the Government's decision to end compulsory national service.)

(5) TRIBUNALS CONCERNED WITH TRANSPORT. Licensing Authorities for Public Service Vehicles and Goods Vehicles, the Transport Tribunal.

(6) MISCELLANEOUS TRIBUNALS. General and Special Commissioners of Income Tax, Compensation Appeal Tribunals, Independent Schools Tribunals.

Industrial tribunals (e.g. the Industrial Court, wages councils, etc.) were excluded from the inquiry because it seemed to the Committee that it was not 'appropriate to examine this aspect of the important relationship between employer and employee in isolation from the many other inter-related industrial questions'.

Since 1957 other bodies have come into being which fall within the scope of this field of study. Notable among these have been the Monopolies and Restrictive Practices Court and the now defunct Prices and Incomes Board.

The arguments for the use of administrative tribunals instead of the law courts, apart from the factors of the overburdening of the courts and the inappropriate nature of the disagreements involved for traditional judicial examination which have already been mentioned are (i) that in administrative tribunals both initial hearings and subsequent appeals (if any) are quicker, (ii) that frequently technical knowledge is needed of a kind that judges cannot be expected to possess, and (iii) that a desirable flexibility of decision which the common law doctrine prejudice would inhibit. Furthermore a tribunal, specialising as it does with a particular type of case, develops an expertise that would otherwise be difficult to achieve. This generalisation, however, may obscure the fact that whereas some tribunals deal with matters which are relatively straightforward others are concerned with quite complex issues.

The Franks Committee, in the words of the then Home Secretary, 'did not find proved any charges of widespread maladministration of justice in these tribunals or proceedings. On the contrary, as its Report states, the Committee found much to commend and many of its recommendations endorse present practices.' The Committee did, however, make a number of criticisms of existing arrangements and put forward ninety-five detailed recommendations. It pointed to the fact that some tribunals used unsatisfactory procedures; they were frequently presided over by people without legal qualifications; applicants were not always given a full and fair hearing and would not be legally represented, and no legal aid was available; proceedings were sometimes unnecessarily conducted secretly; in some cases there was no right of appeal and frequently they failed to publish reasons for their decision.

Relevant principles

To remedy these defects it was proposed that tribunals should discharge their functions in accordance with the principles of openness, fairness and impartiality. The report stated: 'In the field of tribunals openness appears to us to require the publicity of proceedings and knowledge of the essential reasoning underlying the decisions; fairness to require the adoption of a clear procedure which enables parties to know their rights, to present their case fully, and to know the case which they have to meet; and impartiality to require the freedom of tribunals from the influence, real or apparent, of Departments concerned with the subject-matter of their decisions.'

The Committee was concerned that the rules of 'natural justice' should apply to both tribunals and ministerial inquiries. These rules state:

    (i) a man must not be judged in his own cause (e.g. a Minister should not act as both judge and jury in deciding a dispute with his own department);

    (ii) both sides in a dispute must be heard – *audi alternam partem* (e.g. at a tribunal hearing each party must have an adequate opportunity to present its case properly).

These principles were applied in the case of *Spackman v. Commissioners of Public Works* (1885) when Lord Selborne observed that an administrator 'must give the parties an opportunity of being heard, and stating their case and their view. He must give notice that he will proceed with the matter and he must act honestly and impartially and not under the direction of some other person or persons to whom the authority is not given by law.' It is convenient to add here that the Donoughmore Committee had suggested two additional principles of natural justice which are relevant to the theme under consideration, viz. (*a*) that reasons for a decision should be made known to the parties, (*b*) that when a public inquiry is held prior to the Minister's decision the report of the inspector should be made available to the parties heard.

Recommendations

The main recommendations of the Franks Committee were as follows:

(1) TRIBUNALS

    (i) Two Standing Councils on Tribunals, one for England and Wales and one for Scotland, should be set up to keep the constitution and working of tribunals under continuous review.

280

(ii) Chairmen of tribunals should be appointed by the Lord Chancellor. Members should be appointed by the Council on Tribunals.

(iii) All Chairmen of Tribunals exercising appellate functions should have legal qualifications; chairmen of tribunals of first instance should ordinarily have legal qualifications.

(iv) Detailed procedures for each tribunal should be formulated by the Council on Tribunals in the light of the general principles enunciated in the Report. The aim should be to combine an orderly procedure with an informal atmosphere.

(v) Citizens should be made aware of their right to apply to a tribunal.

(vi) A citizen should know in good time before the hearing the case which he has to meet. He should receive a document setting out the main points of the opposing case.

(vii) Hearings before tribunals should be held in public except in cases involving: (a) public security, (b) intimate personal and financial circumstances, (c) a person's personal capacity and reputation.

(viii) The right to legal representation should be curtailed only in the most exceptional circumstances.

(ix) The official scheme of legal aid should be extended to tribunals which are expensive and to final appellate tribunals.

(x) As soon as possible after the hearing, a tribunal should send to the parties a written outline of decision which would set out the decision itself, the reasons for the decision and the rights of appeal against the decision.

(xi) Final appellate tribunals should publish selected decisions and circulate them to lower tribunals.

(xii) There should be an appeal on fact, law and merits from a tribunal to an appellate tribunal except where the tribunal of first instance is exceptionally strong and well qualified.

(2) ADMINISTRATIVE PROCEDURES INVOLVING AN INQUIRY OR HEARING

(i) An acquiring or planning authority should be required to make available, in good time before the inquiry, a written statement giving full particulars of its case.

(ii) The main body of inspectors in England and Wales should be placed under the control of the Lord Chancellor.

(iii) At the inquiry, the initiating authority, whether a Minister or local authority, should be required to explain its proposals fully and support them by oral evidence.

(iv) The code or codes of procedure should be formulated by the Council on Tribunals and made statutory; the procedure should be simple and inexpensive but orderly.

(v) In connection with the compulsory acquisition of land, development plans, planning appeals and clearance schemes, a public inquiry should be held in preference to a private hearing.

281

(vi) The complete text of the Inspector's report should accompany the Minister's letter of decision and be available on request both centrally and locally.

(vii) The Minister's letter of decision should set out in full his findings and inferences of fact and the reason for his decisions.

(viii) In connection with the compulsory acquisition of land, acquiring authorities should notify as early as possible those likely to be affected by their proposals.

Implementation

Nearly three-quarters of the total of ninety-five recommendations were implemented either by administrative action where this was possible, or by the passing of the Tribunal and Inquiries Act of 1958 and other legislation; indeed, in some respects, particularly in relation to the procedure for Enquiries and Hearings, they went beyond them. It was decided to have only one Council of Tribunals, with a special Scottish Committee. Largely on the grounds of the doctrine of ministerial responsibility, government departments retained the right to appoint inspectors and members of tribunals. It was arranged, however, that chairmen of tribunals should be appointed from panels maintained by the Lord Chancellor. The Government could not agree to the award of costs to successful parties in disputes heard by tribunals or to the extension of legal aid.[1] The special position in regard to the acquisition of land by service departments was retained.

Tribunals have always been required, in accordance with the doctrine of *ultra vires*, to act within their powers and to adhere to the rules of natural justice, and nothing in the legislation stemming from the Franks Committee Report interferes with an aggrieved person's right to resort to the Courts. Furthermore, the sets of measures accepted by the Government at this time went a long way towards removing many of the criticisms which had been voiced and made the first step towards the systemisation of administrative justice in Britain.

Case studies

The following case studies, it is hoped, will bring to life some of the principles discussed above. The first of these, which is taken from a local newspaper, deals with an application for a certificate of bad husbandry considered by an Agricultural Land Tribunal in October 1970.[2] The second contains an account of a case which led to the then Ministry of Housing and Local Government being brought to task by the Council on Tribunals; full details of the latter are given in the Council's report to the Lord Chancellor, published in 1966.[3]

[1] See reference to legal aid in previous chapter.
[2] Report condensed from the *Bingley Guardian-Chronicle*, 15 October 1970. Actual names and places omitted.
[3] Reported in *The Guardian*, 10 February 1966.

(I) PROCEEDINGS AT AN AGRICULTURAL LAND TRIBUNAL

A farm in Yorkshire, which consisted of 22 acres of pasture with farm-house and buildings, was leased by the owner to a tenant on a five-year agreement, the tenancy being renewable after this period from year to year on 12 months' notice. The owner's application for a certificate of bad husbandry against the tenant was considered by an Agricultural Land Tribunal sitting in the area late in 1970.

During the course of the hearing the owner, questioned by his own solicitor, said that before letting the farm he had occupied it himself. He stated that he had left the farm buildings in quite a reasonable condition, but when he visited them late in 1968 he felt concerned about the degree of depreciation which he alleged had taken place. He gave details of this in relation to both buildings and fields and stated that during one visit to the farmhouse he had seen some pigs, a sheep, poultry, eight dogs and a cat in the kitchen. Questioned by the tenant's solicitor, the owner agreed that he knew when he let the farm that the tenant had not a lot of capital but he felt that the tenant's background was quite good. The tenant wanted to follow the example of his brother who had started a small farm and done quite well. If he had farmed the place properly, he said, there would have been no need for the tribunal.

The following is an extract from the exchange which took place in the hearing between the tenant's solicitor and the owner:

Question: Did you ask Mr — (the tenant) in June 1968, to give up posses-sion of the farmhouse to your son who was anticipating marriage?

Answer: No, I wanted him to give up possession because I was not satisfied with his farming. In conversation I might have told him my son was going to be married.

Question: Did you tell Mr — there was a house he might apply for in a village nearby and, if he gave up the farmhouse, he could go on farming the land?

Answer: I told him he could leave the animals on the land until he could dispose of them.

Question: Immediately after that you served notice to quit, a year before it was in order according to the agreement?

Answer: I found that out afterwards.

Question: Repairs to the roof were your responsibility under the tenancy agreement but not one penny piece has been spent on landlord's repairs since Mr — took over.

Answer: A lot had been done to the farm a few years before.

Question: When a man starts on a farm with dilapidated guttering and with only £150 capital, and five years later has nearly £2000 capital, he has not done too badly, has he?

Answer: Not bad at all, but it has all been taken out of the farm.

The tenant's answer to the allegations concerning animals in the kitchen was that he had only taken day-old pigs or perhaps chickens in to warm.

283

He also claimed that he had asked the owner about repairs and had been promised that materials would be sent if he would do the jobs himself and that he could have a month's free rent for cleaning up the place. These materials the tenant stated had never been received. He admitted that there might have been 'a bit of obstinacy' about his attitude after this time. In further evidence he gave details of his efforts to maintain milk production and fertility. A chartered auctioneer was called to report on the farm and the level of efficiency and in his view the management of the land had been 'quite satisfactory and up to the average'.

In announcing his decision, the chairman of the tribunal said that they felt that the landlord had given little encouragement to the tenant to improve his holding and that a certificate of bad husbandry would not be issued.

(2) MINISTERIAL INQUIRY INTO PROPOSALS FOR THE REDEVELOPMENT OF PACKINGTON ESTATE

In August 1964, Islington Borough Council applied to London County Council for planning permission to redevelop Packington Estate for residential purposes. When no permission came within the prescribed two-month limit, the Islington Council exercised its right to appeal to the Minister of Housing, who then appointed an inspector to hold a public inquiry.

At the six-day inquiry held in February 1965, opposition to the Islington Council's application was based on the proposition that the site was suitable for rehabilitation and should not be redeveloped. An association of 425 residents of properties surrounding the estate and a firm of surveyors acting on behalf of London and Manchester Insurance Co. Ltd played a leading part in opposing the Council's proposals.

The inspector recommended that the Council's appeal to redevelop the land should be allowed subject to certain conditions. But the Minister, Mr Richard Crossman, made it known on 23 July 1965, that he had decided to dismiss the appeal, though without prejudice to the submission to him of another application.

On 13 October 1965, the Islington Borough Council made a second application and planning permission was granted on 22 November 1965. The objectors were not consulted before this decision was taken; the residents' association and the representatives of the insurance company therefore made a formal complaint and the matter was considered by the Council on Tribunals.

The Council's report to the Lord Chancellor expressed the view that the complainants were treated 'less than fairly' and states that 'openness, fairness and impartiality' – the hallmarks of good administration – are not enough, if they are not all apparent. Two points in particular were brought to the Lord Chancellor's attention. These were:

    (i) misleading phraseology used in the letter from the Ministry of Housing on 23 July 1965;

284

(ii) the Ministry's failure to ensure that the objectors' views on the revised proposals had been heard before the Minister came to his decision on the Islington Borough Council's second application.

The Council on Tribunals did not suggest that the Minister had at any stage exceeded his powers but it did consider that the complainants had real reason to feel aggrieved. The Report emphasised its assumption that the Ministry was correct in suggesting that the second application was substantially different from the first. If, as the complainants maintained, the two applications were substantially the same, the Council considered that 'the complainants have the further grievance that one or other decisions must have been wrong'.

When the matter was discussed in the House of Commons, the Minister, Mr Crossman said: 'I am clear that nothing would have been gained by a second enquiry that would have justified the months of delay. For the Opposition, Mr Boyd-Carpenter, M.P. contended that would be objectors to the revised Islington Scheme had been refused information by the Borough Council on the ground that the matter was before the Minister. This, in Mr Boyd-Carpenter's view, amounted to 'concealment'. Another Conservative M.P. suggested that there might be something of a Crichel Down in the Islington affair; Mr Crossman replied that a day's debate would show that there was not.

Comparisons with foreign systems

British observers who are critical of the present practice of administrative tribunals and inquiries and who feel that the Parliamentary Commissioner's terms of reference are too narrow to make good all existing defects in British procedures point with approval to the system which exists in France.

There the structure of courts is different to the British system in that they are divided into three distinct branches; there is a Criminal Branch, a Civil Branch and an Administrative Branch. At the apex of the hierarchy of the Administrative Branch is the Conseil d'Etat (Council of State) which acts as a general administrative appeal tribunal and is the final authority on administrative matters. It supervises specialist units for military, financial and social service administration and the prefectorial units in the various regions. The Conseil d'Etat has great prestige, and critics claim that the French system provides much more effective safeguards for citizens who wish to complain of maladministration than does the machinery in Britain. Although there are long delays in appeals the expense is small and there is a wide range of remedies available. One of the branches of the German courts also is exclusively concerned with administrative cases.

The Franks Committee gave consideration to two special proposals put to it. Professor W. A. Robson had advocated the establishment of a general administrative appeal tribunal with jurisdiction to hear not only appeals from tribunals and inquiries for which there was an established procedure but also against harsh or unfair treatment in any field not covered by these two sets of machinery.

This was rejected by the Committee on various grounds. Firstly it was considered that a general tribunal would lack the special expertise upon which the rest of the structure was based; secondly, if, in order to avoid this, the proposed appeals tribunal were to sit in several divisions corresponding to the various groups of tribunals, the general effect it was suggested would be very little different to the existing practice and 'the essence of the proposal, a unified appellate body, would be largely lost'. Thirdly, the logical outcome of this proposal would be that two distinct systems of law would be established in that final determination of points of law would be made by the general administrative appeal tribunal in one case but by the superior courts in another. The Committee felt that there were too many evils 'attendant on this dichotomy'.

The Committee also rejected a proposal for the establishment of a new division of the High Court, to be called the Administrative Division. Although this avoided the objection of producing conflicting systems of law, it also brought in the undesirability of having a *general* body hearing appeals from *specialist* bodies. The Committee concluded that the appropriate appeal structure for Britain was, in the first instance, to an appellate tribunal, followed by an appeal to the courts on points of law.

Proposals for a General Tribunal to deal with complaints against discretionary decisions, where there is no specialised tribunal, have been put forward by the British Section of the International Committee of Jurists, generally known as the Whyatt Committee.[1] Professor Crick has argued that a reconstituted House of Lords could form the basis of a Court of Administrative Appeals.[2]

Sweden, Finland, Denmark, Norway and New Zealand all have an Ombudsman, or 'grievance man', who is an official appointed by the legislature to investigate and report on complaints of maladministration. The Whyatt Committee recommended a similar appointment in Britain and in 1965 the Government set out its proposals for this development in a White Paper.[3]

The Parliamentary Commissioner

The White Paper drew attention to the fact that tribunals and inquiries did not cover all cases where a citizen may feel he is suffering injustice as a result of faulty administration, and the task of the official to be appointed, the Parliamentary Commissioner for Administration, would be to fill this gap in the provision for the consideration of grievances.

The view was taken, however, that the terms of reference for the

[1] See: 'Justice', *The Citizen and the Administration: The Redress of Grievances* (Stevens, 1961).
[2] Crick, *Reform of Parliament*, p. 156.
[3] Cmd. 2767: *The Parliamentary Commissioner for Administration* (H.M.S.O., 1965).

Commissioner should be defined in such a way that they would not erode the functions of M.P.s whose traditional role in this respect is to ensure that constituents do not suffer injustice at the hand of government. It was decided, therefore, that the Commissioner would act only at the instance of M.P.s. Complaints must go first to any M.P. who would decide whether or not it should be passed to the Parliamentary Commissioner.

The White Paper stated that, subject to certain exceptions, the field for the Commissioner would be 'the whole range of relationships between the private person and the central Government'. Matters where the dominant considerations are of national or public interest, e.g. foreign relations, the armed services, criminal investigations, were excluded, as were matters concerned with the jurisdiction of tribunals, the prerogative of mercy and the conferment of honours. Most criticisms, however, were directed at local government administration and the complaints connected with the nationalised industries, because it is with these bodies that the ordinary citizen most comes into contact. The White Paper stated that: 'In due course, it may be desirable to consider extending the powers of the Commissioner to deal with complaints of the private citizen against the administrative actions of other public authorities.'

The first Commissioner, Sir Edmund Compton, who had previously been Comptroller and Auditor-General, was appointed in 1967. The procedure to be followed in investigating a complaint referred by an M.P. was that if the Commissioner found that there was substance in the complaint he would inform the Minister concerned. If the matter was then put right he would inform the M.P. who made the complaint and that would be the end of the affair as far as the Commissioner was concerned. If, however, the Department did not adjust the matter to his satisfaction it would be open to him to report the matter to Parliament on an *ad hoc* basis. The Commissioner would work closely with a Select Committee set up for the purpose and report to Parliament annually. In the first 19 months in office (April 1967 to December 1968), 2189 complaints were referred to him. Of these more than half were declared to be outside of his jurisdiction and 180 were not pursued beyond a preliminary investigation. Those remaining were fully investigated and reported upon. One case which received much public attention was the complaint of residents in the vicinity of Heathrow (London Airport) who were subjected to annoyance caused by aircraft.

Conclusion

Some observers take the view that the powers given to the Parliamentary Commissioner are not sufficiently extensive and speak of a 'toothless Ombudsman'; they believe that M.P.s have been too jealous of their right to ventilate grievances and that the Parliamentary Commissioner could have played a much more effective role. Dissatisfaction with the related procedures of administrative tribunals and inquiries is also still expressed.

The Law Commissioners have proposed that a Royal Commission or a similar body should be appointed to enquire further into the whole field of the relationships between the citizen and the administration, and it seems unlikely that any further changes will be introduced until this kind of investigation has been made.

20   The Constitution

What has been achieved is at least an accepted political way of life that the constitution itself now helps to protect, and the longer a constitution has lasted the more it ought, in theory, to be able to withstand political strain. In politics nothing succeeds like success.

Dorothy Pickles *Democracy*

Introduction

The constitution of a modern state is the framework of institutions and practices which determines the basis and mode of government. In most countries except Britain, this general pattern is set out in a document which is referred to as 'the Constitution'. These documents usually include a statement of the orientation and purpose of government as it is conceived by the framers, an indication of the relationship between the various organs of government – the legislature, the executive and the judiciary, and an enumeration of the citizen's rights and obligations. Written constitutions of this kind can normally be amended only by a prescribed, and usually prolonged, procedure.

The American constitution, originally adopted in 1788, for example, is a brief document which, including the amendments, consists of about 6000 words. It begins with a short preamble, which is indicative of its general purpose but has no legal force; this is followed by three articles dealing with the legislative, executive and judicial branches of government respectively; it then continues with a further four articles dealing successively with the position of the States, the modes of amendment, the supremacy of the Federal Government, and the process of ratification. The twenty-five amendments to date are appended.

The preamble reads:

'We, the people of the United States, in order to form a more perfect union, establish justice, insure domestic tranquility, provide for common defence, promote the general welfare, and secure the blessing of liberty to ourselves and our posterity, do ordain and establish this Constitution for the United States of America.'

Article IV, Section I, states:

'All persons born or naturalised in the United States and subject to the jurisdiction thereof, are citizens of the United States and of the State wherein they reside. No state shall make or enforce any law which shall abridge the privileges or immunities of citizens of the United States; nor shall any state deprive any person of life, liberty, or property, without due process of law, nor deny any person within its jurisdiction the equal protection of the laws.'

Since Britain has no written constitution of this kind, it might reasonably be asked whether or not its citizens are at a disadvantage compared with those whose rights are set out in a written document.[1] This does not appear to be the case because it is evident that inclusion in the constitution does not of itself guarantee that they will be granted automatically. Two examples will illustrate this point.

The fifteenth amendment to the American constitution provides that: 'The right of citizens to vote shall not be denied or abridged by the United States or by any States on account of race, colour, or previous condition of servitude' and that 'Congress shall have the power to enforce this article by appropriate legislation.' The limitations on the franchise introduced in several states apply, in theory, to all citizens but in practice are applicable only to Negroes.

Article 125 of the Constitution of the U.S.S.R. recognises the right of free speech and the freedom of the press. With every allowance for possible prejudice on the part of Western news media, it does not seem that very much reliance can be placed upon this assertion.

In Britain the right of free speech and free association is determined negatively rather than positively: in other words, a citizen in the British system has these rights except in so far as they are curtailed by the ordinary law. Thus the right of free speech is restricted principally by the law of defamation and rulings concerning race relations and incitement; the so-called right of assembly is restricted by relevant legislation such as the Public Order Act, 1936.

Neither is durability a universal characteristic of written constitutions. The American Constitution has endured since 1788, but France has had more than a dozen different constitutions since 1789. The most democratic of all constitutions, that of the Weimar Republic, established in Germany in 1919, was overthrown by Hitler in 1933. In Europe, only the Scandinavian countries, together with Belgium, Holland and Switzerland have constitutions which pre-date 1914. The constitutions of 'new' Commonwealth countries (e.g. Nigeria and Ghana) have come and gone within the space of a few years. The strength of a constitution is measured, not in its

---

[1] On 27 October 1970, the Earl of Arran was granted leave to introduce a Bill in the House of Lords which was designed 'to declare the rights and liberties of the subject'. The Second Reading debate was held on 26 November 1970, when the Bill was subjected to considerable criticism by the Lord Chancellor. At the end of the debate the Bill was withdrawn. A similar attempt was made by Mr S. Silkin, M.P., who introduced a Protection of Human Rights Bill as a Private Member's Bill on 2 April 1971: this was 'counted out' when the House was adjourned for the lack of a quorum.

text or format, but in the extent to which it operates successfully, with reasonable stability and continuity.

It must also be emphasised that no written constitution, however lengthy, could possibly contain a complete description of the detailed working of government. Particular ways of doing things become hallowed with time and by no means all of them find their way into the formal description. In this sense even written constitutions give only incomplete accounts, and to begin to understand the way in which American government, for example, works one would have to look beyond the written constitution, to observe how the system operates in practice and examine a variety of conventions, customs, rulings of the Supreme Court, etc.

Furthermore, as Ian Gilmour observes: 'Institutions form only part of the governmental process; that process consists also of a series of interlocking relationships, a set of habits and traditions, a confusion of true and untrue and obsolete ideas, and an amalgam of constitutional conventions, myths and fictions.'[1] The values and purposes of those who make the important political decisions are, in the end, more important than procedural provisions.

The British Constitution

In contrast to the formal constitutions of other systems, the British Constitution consists of a mixture of historic documents, statute law, common law decisions, judicial interpretations, conventions and customs, the law, procedure and privileges of Parliament, and a few classic writings. Although 'the Constitution' has formed the subject of academic works by historians, constitutional lawyers and political scientists, no official attempt has even been made to draw these component parts together in a single document. It must be remembered that the pattern of the constitution changes from time to time and no part of it is inviolate; law affecting the structure and functions of government are made and changed in precisely the same way as those dealing with shopping hours and British Summer Time. An indication of the nature of the various components and the kind of contribution which each makes is given below.

(1) EARLY LEGISLATION AND HISTORIC DOCUMENTS

The famous Magna Carta, 1215, marks an early stage in our constitutional development. Its clauses 'embody a protest against arbitrary punishment and assert the right to a fair trial and to justice which need not be purchased'.[2]

The Petition of Right, 1628, was not a statute but a document setting out the grounds of popular protest to the King. These included: taxation not approved by Parliament, arbitrary imprisonment and other matters affecting the liberty of the subject. The King succumbed to all of these demands.

[1] Gilmour, *The Body Politic*, p. 3.
[2] Wade and Philips, *Constitutional Law*, 4th edn, p. 5.

The Bill of Rights, 1689, which ended the King's supposed powers of suspending and dispensing with legislation without parliamentary consent was a major victory for the House of Commons in its continuing struggle with the Crown.

The Act of Settlement, 1701, not only provided for the succession to the Throne but also established the independence of the judiciary and set the seal upon the principle of constitutional monarchy.

(2) LATER STATUTES

A whole series of later statutes, some of which are discussed elsewhere in the present volume, have contributed to our constitutional development. It is only possible to indicate here some of the most important of these; those listed in table 41, for example, are concerned with some aspects of the franchise; the life of Parliament, the relationship between the Lords and Commons, the composition of the House of Lords, Ministers and Parliament, the legal system, the structure of local government, King Edward VIII's abdication, changes in the special legal position of the Crown and a definition of British nationality.

TABLE 41 *Some Statutes of Constitutional Importance*

Representation of the People Acts, 1832–1949
The Ballot Act, 1872
The Parliament Acts, 1911 and 1949
The Peerage Acts, 1958 and 1963
Ministers of the Crown Acts, 1937 and 1964
The Judicature Act, 1873
The Local Government Acts, 1888–1948
Emergency Powers Act, 1920
His Majesty's Declaration of Abdication Act, 1936
Crown Proceedings Act, 1947
British Nationality Act, 1948

(3) THE COMMON LAW

The development of the common law was discussed in chapter 18. Judicial decisions were given in cases concerned with the Royal Prerogative, remedies available by way of judicial orders and the writ of Habeas Corpus, questions of individual rights and liberties and other matters of considerable constitutional importance. The importance of the contribution made by common law decisions can be illustrated by reference to the principle concerning the immunity of judges. The general rule of common law is that no action will lie against a judge for any acts done or words spoken in his judicial capacity in a court of justice. In *Scott v. Stansfield* (1868) it was said: 'It is essential in all courts that the judges who are appointed to administer the law should be permitted to administer it under the protection of the law independently and freely, without favour and without fear.' *Bushell's Case* (1670) laid down that a similar immunity attaches to the verdicts of juries and the same principle applies to words

292

spoken by the parties in the case, counsel and witnesses. In *Law v. Llewellyn* (1906) it was held that no action lies against a justice of the peace in respect of defamatory words spoken by him when exercising judicial functions.

(4) JUDICIAL INTERPRETATION OF STATUTE LAW

In theory the function of the judge is concerned with an explanation of the meaning of the law, but in practice he has to decide its application in the particular circumstances of the cases which come before him and, by interpretation, he makes law by adding to or subtracting from the scope of the relevant legal provision. The case of *Bradlaugh v. Gossett* (1884), for instance, which upheld the decision of the House of Commons to prevent a member from taking the oath, established beyond any doubt the exclusive right of the House of Commons to regulate its own proceedings without reference to the Courts.

There are numerous cases dealing with allegations that the powers in a given statute have been exceeded, i.e. that the authority concerned has acted *ultra vires*. A good example is provided in the case of the *Attorney-General v. Fulham Corporation* (1921). Under the Baths and Wash-houses Acts, 1846 and 1847, the council had power to establish a wash-house, where people could wash their own clothes. The council decided to install a municipal laundry with modern equipment to which residents of the borough could bring their clothes, the actual washing being done by council employees. Local laundry firms objected to this and individual members of these, as ratepayers, sought an *injunction* to restrain the council from operating a laundry on a business basis. It was held that the council's action was *ultra vires*.

A further illustration can be provided by a consideration of two cases concerned with the Crown's right to dismiss public servants. Generally the rule is that, because the Crown cannot hamper its future action, it has virtually complete freedom of action in this field. Thus in *Dunn v. The Queen* (1896) it was laid down that in the absence of a statutory provision to the contrary (e.g. that regulating a judge's tenure of office), civil servants may be dismissed at the Crown's discretion. In *Reilley v. The King* (1934) however, it was held that the Crown is bound by an express provision, e.g. where a contract is held for a fixed term and the contract makes express provision about the grounds of dismissal.

The fate of a municipal laundry in Fulham or a civil servant's tenure of office may, at first sight, seem to be of limited importance but, as steps in a series of cases which firmly establish important constitutional principles, these cases are of considerable constitutional relevance.

(5) CONVENTIONS

It has already been observed that no set of legal rules can provide completely for every contingency in the growth of a system of government and, inevitably, a variety of practices and procedures are adopted by politicians

293

and others who participate in the process of government to make the system work smoothly. When such a practice becomes firmly established it is referred to as a convention. In this context, Sir Ivor Jennings speaks of 'rules which may be followed as consistently as the rule of law and which determine the procedure which the men concerned with government must follow'.[1] Conventions, he reminds us, imply some form of agreement and he adds that: 'New needs demand a new emphasis and a new orientation even when law remains fixed. Men have to work old law in order to satisfy new needs. Constitutional conventions are the rules which they elaborate.'

Conventions emerge as a need arises: some are sustained for a time and then wither away, others are confirmed by use and become fundamental parts of the system. The best guide to their existence and current importance is to assess the extent of general agreement and the willingness to give legal effect to the practice should the need arise. The need to give legal reinforcement to accepted modes of government, in practice, rarely arises, but the question is well worth asking because it gives a strong clue as to the importance attached to the various practices which are in operation.

Among the more important conventions are included: that the Prime Minister must be a member of the House of Commons; the whole basis of Cabinet government together with the doctrines of individual and collective responsibility of Ministers; that the Government must resign if it ceases to command the support of the House of Commons on major issues; that the Royal Prerogative is exercised on the advice of Ministers, etc.

Many conventions arise in connection with the practice and customs of Parliament, e.g. the impartiality of the Speaker, the selection of an Opposition M.P. as Chairman of the Public Accounts Committee, and the non-participation of lay peers in the judicial work of the House of Lords. The great asset of conventions is that they enable helpful practices to evolve naturally and to be amended if need be without the need for a series of cumbersome legislative measures.

Constitutional lawyers have advanced sophisticated arguments to explain why conventions, which lack the force of law, are adhered to. But the reason that people act in conformity with this seems to lie in the fact that these arrangements, which were designed to meet changing political conditions, were arrived at on the basis of widespread agreement and acceptance and they seem likely to last for so long as they prove satisfactory in making the machinery of government function. In practical terms, the compulsion to work in accordance with the major conventions rests in the beliefs, attitudes and assumptions of the politicians themselves, reinforced, as it generally is, by the pressure of public opinion.

(6) THE LAW AND CUSTOM OF PARLIAMENT

The nature and extent of Parliamentary privilege was discussed in

[1] I. Jennings, *The Law and the Constitution* (University of London Press, 1946), p. 79.

chapter 10. From the right of the House of Commons to control its own proceedings and to maintain its independence and dignity, there flows a number of powers, privileges and immunities which form part of the Constitution.

The bulk of the rules which govern the internal proceedings of the House of Commons are covered by Standing Orders, which themselves form part of the law and custom of Parliament. Some practices, however, are conventional, e.g. certain forms of observance in connection with the Speaker (see above). Other practices, e.g. the arrangement of parliamentary business through the 'usual channels' and 'pairing' arrangements are perhaps better regarded as quasi-conventional in that, although these practices are normally followed, they can be, and sometimes are, broken.

Additionally, it should be noted that although much of the law and custom of Parliament figures largely in the Constitution, nothing in this respect is fixed or immutable; Standing Orders can be suspended, procedures are changed and the 'usual channels' sometimes break down as happened in the consideration of the Industrial Relations Bill in 1971.

(7) CLASSIC WRITINGS

Where constitutional questions arise which are not covered by statute law, judicial proceedings or convention, reference is often made to the works of authoritative writers. Thus in formulating their rulings, Speakers of the House of Commons refer to Sir T. Erskine May's *Treatise on the Law and Privileges of Parliament*, confident in the knowledge that the opinions contained therein will be respected by the vast majority of M.P.s.

Other more general works on government such as Walter Bagehot's *The English Constitution* (1867), A. V. Dicey's *Law of the Constitution* (1855), and Sir Ivor Jennings' *Cabinet Government* (1936) have acquired in political, legal and academic circles a respect which, making due allowance for the times at which they were written, gives them a special place when the nature and functioning of the British Constitution is being considered.

Types of constitutions

There are extremely wide variations between different types of constitutions and even between different constitutions of the same type. It is customary to classify constitutions on a number of criteria in accordance with the nature of their more salient characteristics. Thus a given constitution may be written or unwritten, unitary or federal, parliamentary or presidential, monarchical or republican, rigid or flexible in relation to the ease or difficulty of the amending process. Following these categories, the British Constitution can be said to be unwritten, unitary, parliamentary, monarchical, and flexible; the Constitution of the U.S.A., using the same criteria, is written, federal, presidential, republican and rigid.

As will be clear from what has been said earlier, the British Constitution is *unwritten* only in the sense that the documents and practices upon which it is based have not been brought together into a single, inclusive statement. It is *unitary* in that the whole apparatus of government is regulated from the centre under the authority of one sovereign body. The legislature takes the form of a highly developed *parliamentary* system which occupies the central position in a *constitutional monarchy*. The British system is infinitely *flexible* because constitutional changes are brought about by the use of conventions or by utilising the normal legislative processes.

The American Constitution, in contrast, takes the form of a *written* document which is the overriding source of political authority. The government is *federal* in character, with certain powers being reserved to the Federal government and others being the prerogative of the government of the component States. The U.S.A. has a popularly elected *President* who symbolises the *republican* character of the Constitution. The President is the chief executive and he is dependent upon the Congress, which consists of the Senate and the House of Representatives, for the passing of legislation which will give effect to his policy and programme. The American Constitution is *rigid* in that it can only be amended after prolonged deliberation; Article V of the Constitution reads:

'The Congress, whenever two thirds of both houses shall deem it necessary, shall propose amendments to this Constitution, or, on the application of the legislatures of two-thirds of the several States, shall convene a convention for proposing amendments, which in either case shall be valid to all intents and purposes as part of this Constitution, when ratified by the legislatures of three-fourths of the several states, or by conventions in three-fourths thereof, as one or other mode of ratification may be proposed by Congress...'

It must be emphasised that the use of some of these categories may result in a restricted and even misleading impression of the constitutions to which they are applied if their limitations are not taken fully into account. The limitations of the descriptions 'written' and 'unwritten' has already been referred to and in all cases it can be said that it is the function and not the form that is the important criterion. The distinction between 'flexible' and 'rigid' constitutions has to be approached with caution because it tends to emphasise unduly the formal aspects of the amending machinery, and there may be a temptation to conclude from the differences indicated that one is necessarily superior to the other, whereas in fact all procedural devices imaginable will be of limited consequence if the desire and determination to bring about necessary change is absent. In the U.S.A., for example, the formal procedure for the amendment of the written constitution is cumbersome and time-consuming, but the Supreme Court does, in effect, assume an amending function when it gives a ruling on constitutional issues referred to it and this results in a greater degree of 'flexibility' than would otherwise be the case. Conversely, where constitutional change through the medium of simple legislative action is possible, reform will not ensue unless the will to change in the desired direction is present.

296

It is now necessary to examine further the notions of the 'separation of powers' and the 'rule of law', both of which traditionally occupy a place in a consideration of the fundamental principles of the constitution even though their practical political relevance has been questioned.

The separation of powers

The three organs of government consist of the legislature, the executive and the judiciary. The popular exposition of the doctrine of the separation of powers suggests that, in order to avoid a situation in which no one branch of government obtains a monopoly of power which is almost certain to result in arbitrary rule, the three functions should be kept entirely separate.

It is necessary to note, however, that this popular formulation is erroneous in that it does not accurately reflect the writings of Montesquieu, with whose *L'Esprit de Lois* (1748) the doctrine is commonly associated. Montesquieu did not himself suggest that the three powers should function in such watertight compartments that they do not meet at any point. If this attempt were to be made in a real situation it would prove to be impossible to achieve, for even in the U.S.A. where the doctrine was taken into account in framing the constitution (see Articles I, II and III) there is by no means a strict separation of powers.

In Britain the overlapping and inter-connection of powers, especially in relation to the executive and the legislative, are prominent characteristics. The Cabinet both dominates the executive and monopolises the legislative programme; the Lord Chancellor has links with all three branches; the courts are to all intents and purposes independent but many judicial or quasi-judicial matters are referred to administrative tribunals which are, in essence, the creatures of the executive. J. A. G. Griffith and H. Street contend that, as is popularly conceived, the doctrine 'is so remote from the facts that it is better disregarded altogether'.[1]

The questions raised in this connection, however, will serve to illuminate some important considerations, so it may be helpful to pursue the investigation a little further. E. C. S. Wade and G. C. Philips submit that the separation of powers can mean three different things, viz:

(a) that the same persons should not form part of more than one of the three organs of government, e.g. Ministers should not sit in Parliament;

(b) that one organ should not control or interfere with another in the discharge of its functions, e.g. Ministers should not be responsible to Parliament;

(c) that one organ of government should not exercise the functions of another, e.g. that neither Ministers nor judges should make and amend laws.[2]

[1] Griffith and Street, *Administrative Law*, 2nd edn, p. 17.
[2] Wade and Philips, *Constitutional Law*, 4th edn, p. 19.

These provide more precise meanings than the generalised view discussed above but it can be seen that none of them can be accurately applied to the British Constitution. Indeed the separation doctrine focusses on the wrong criteria. As Sir C. K. Allen has emphasised, it is not separation but mutual restraints that are important and, generally, these have been achieved by the various checks and balances upon the three organs of government which have been developed.[1] J. A. G. Griffith and H. Street observe that 'the real argument is not whether the Executive, for example, is exercising legislative or judicial powers which properly belong to Parliament or to the courts (for no kind of power *belongs* to any particular authority) but whether the power is being exercised by the authority best suited to exercise it and whether the exercise is sufficiently controlled by political and legal action'.[2]

The Rule of Law

The doctrine of the Rule of Law is likewise imprecise but the key concept which is implicit in this is much more directly relevant as a constitutional principle than is the separation doctrine. E. C. S. Wade and G. C. Philips consider that the rule of law 'means that the exercise of powers of government shall be conditioned by law and that the subject shall not be exposed to the arbitrary will of his ruler'.[3]

In considering this doctrine we may usefully turn again to the down to earth analysis made by J. A. G. Griffith and H. Street. These writers point to the important distinction between an idea which is backed by the force of law and one which is merely desirable and wise. The first must be adhered to whether or not it is just or unjust, desirable or undesirable, wise or unwise; the second may have considerable persuasive power but there can be no guarantee that, without the backing of the law, it will have any appreciable practical effect. The rule of law, as it is variously interpreted, may be characterised by one or both of these considerations.

In his *Introduction to the Study of the Law of the Constitution* (1885), A. V. Dicey postulated three meanings for the rule of law, viz:

(i) '. . . the absolute supremacy or predominance of regular law as opposed to arbitrary power. . . a man may be punished for a breach of the law, but he can be punished for nothing else';

(ii) '. . . equality before the law, or the equal subjection of all classes to the ordinary law of the land administered by the ordinary law courts';

(iii) '. . . with us the law of the constitution, the rules which in foreign countries naturally form part of a constitutional code, are not the source but the consequence of the rights of individuals, as defined and enforced by the courts. . .'.

[1] C. K. Allen, *Law and Orders* (Stevens, 1965).
[2] Griffith and Street, *Administrative Law*, 2nd edn, p. 16.
[3] Wade and Philips, *Constitutional Law*, 4th edn, p. 48.

These meanings have been explained and commented upon by E. C. S. Wade and G. C. Philips who conclude that, when allowance is made for altered circumstances and conditions, the rule of law in Dicey's meaning remains a principle of our Constitution. They state however: 'This does not mean that it is a fixed principle of law from which there can be no departure. Since Parliament is supreme, there is no legal sanction to prevent the enactment of a statute which violates the principle of the rule of law. The ultimate safeguard then is to be found in the acceptance of the principle as a guide to conduct by any political party which is in a position to influence the course of legislation.'[1]

Griffith and Street observe that 'the rule of law seems to be at once a deduction and an *a priori* postulate', and go on to discuss two other meanings which are sometimes attached to the idea of the rule of law, both of which are firmly accepted principles of the Constitution. The first of these recognises that the powers of government are derived from statutes and the prerogative and it can only do what it has legal power to do. The second meaning is a corollary to the first in that the law is binding upon the government and until it changes the law, 'it is bound by the law. When it has changed the law, it is bound by the new law.'[2]

The Rule of Law is a phrase which is often used emotively with a meaning which is best suited to support the particular argument that is being advanced. To suggest that there is need for a more precise definition which can be made generally applicable is not to deny the importance of the moral ideas which are implicit in its use.

Government and the governed

Britain's Constitution has developed over a long period of time and the problems which it has had to face are identical with those upon which the framers of more recent written constitutions for political democracies have had to decide. One of the writers of the famous *Federalist* essays (first published 1787–8) which sought to organise support for the American Constitution drew attention to one of the fundamental and recurring problems of government. He said: 'In framing a government which is to be administered by men over men, the great difficulty lies in this: you must first enable the government to control the governed; and in the next place oblige it to control itself.'[3]

In the attainment of this lofty purpose some governments have achieved a high measure of success and some have miserably failed. The most potent factor of political success in this respect is a widespread desire to create and maintain a desire and respect for democratic institutions and a willingness to use constitutional methods to bring about political and social change. Freedom is fragile and it cannot be achieved and maintained

[1] Wade and Philips, *Constitutional Law*, 4th edn, p. 58.
[2] Griffith and Street, *Administrative Law*, 2nd edn, p. 21.
[3] A. Hamilton, *The Federalist*, 'Everyman' edn (Dent, 1926), p. 264.

without commitment, vigilance and effort.

Government is the unavoidable concomitant of social life and, in a democratic society, politics is the means through which the important decisions are made. Because these are human activities there will inevitably be a gap between aims and their fulfilment. It is, therefore, all the more important that the standards of political institutions to be aimed at, the criteria for human welfare which they are designed to serve, and the level of determination to seek these goals, should be correspondingly high. Knowledge of the contemporary political process alone will not bring this about but it can make an important contribution to the armoury of those who accept and are willing to work towards these ends.

Appendices

I General Election Results 1945–70

Date	Winning party	Overall majority	Party	No. of seats won	Total vote (%)	Total Electorate	Total Seats	Total Turn-out	Swing (%)
1945 (5 July)	Lab.	146	Con. Lab. Lib. Others	213 393 12 22	39.9 48.0 9.0 3.1	32 836 419	640	76.1	Lab. 11.3
1950 (20 February)	Lab.	5	Con. Lab. Lib. Others	298 315 9 3	43.5 46.1 9.1 1.3	34 269 770	625	84.0	Con. 2.8
1951 (25 October)	Con.	17	Con. Lab. Lib. Others	321 295 6 3	48.0 48.8 2.6 0.7	34 645 573	625	82.5	Con. 0.9
1955 (26 May)	Con.	60	Con. Lab. Lib. Others	345 277 6 2	49.7 46.4 2.7 1.2	34 858 263	630	76.8	Con. 2.1
1959 (8 October)	Con.	100	Con. Lab. Lib. Others	365 258 6 1	49.3 43.8 5.9 1.0	35 397 080	630	78.8	Con. 1.1
1964 (15 October)	Lab.	4	Con. Lab. Lib. Others	303 317 9 1	43.4 44.1 11.2 1.3	35 892 572	630	77.0	Lab. 3.1
1966 (31 March)	Lab.	97	Con. Lab. Lib. Others	253 363 12 2	41.9 47.9 8.5 1.7	35 966 975	630	75.8	Lab. 2.6
1970 (18 June)	Con.	30	Con. Lab. Lib. Others	330 287 6 7	46.4 42.9 7.5 3.2	39 618 796	630	71.4	Con. 4.7

II   General Elections, Prime Ministers and Governments, 1895–1971

General election	Prime Minister	Complexion of Government	Duration of Government
1900	Marquis of Salisbury	Conservative	1895–1902
	A. Balfour	Conservative	1902–5
1906	Sir H. Campbell-Bannerman	Liberal	1905–8
1910 January/February			
1910 December	H. Asquith	Liberal	1908–15
	H. Asquith	Coalition	1915–16
1918	D. Lloyd George	Coalition	1916–22
1922	A. Bonar Law	Conservative	1922–3
1923	S. Baldwin	Conservative	1923–4
1924	R. MacDonald	Labour	1924
	S. Baldwin	Conservative	1924–9
1929	R. MacDonald	Labour	1929–31
1931	R. MacDonald	National	1931–5
1935	S. Baldwin	National	1935–7
	N. Chamberlain	National	1937–9
	N. Chamberlain	Coalition	1939–40
	W. Churchill	Coalition	1940–5
	W. Churchill	Conservative	1945
1945	C. Attlee	Labour	1945–51
1950			
1951	W. Churchill	Conservative	1951–5
1955	A. Eden	Conservative	1955–7
1959	H. Macmillan	Conservative	1957–63
	Sir A. Douglas Home	Conservative	1963–4
1964	H. Wilson	Labour	1964–70
1970	E. Heath	Conservative	1970–74
1974 FEB	H. WILSON	LABOUR	FEB-OCT
1974 OCT	H. WILSON	LABOUR	
	J. CALLAGHAN	Labour	1974–9
1979 May	M. THATCHER	CONSERV.	

III   Extracts from an Order Paper

Note: This appendix consists of material extracted from the House of Commons Order Paper No. 80 for Tuesday 9 February 1971. The purpose of including this material (the typography of which is similar to the actual Paper) is to indicate the nature of the business conducted on a typical day. The procedures relating to the various forms of business are discussed in the text, especially in chapter 10.

ORDER PAPER

PRIVATE BUSINESS AFTER PRAYERS

THIRD READINGS

1   Berkshire County Council Bill [*Lords*].

2   Bristol Corporation (General Powers) Bill [*Lords*].

SECOND READINGS

(* *Bills to be referred to the Examiners are marked with an asterisk*)

1   British Railways (No. 2) Bill.   (*By Order.*)

2   British Transport Docks Bill.   (*By Order.*)

3   Chichester Harbour Conservancy Bill.   (*By Order.*)

4   City of London (Various Powers) (No. 2) Bill.   (*By Order.*)

   Mr T. H. H. Skeet
       On Second Reading of City of London (Various Powers) (No. 2) Bill,
       to move, That the Bill be read a second time upon this day six months.

*5   D. & J. Fowler Limited and Associated Company Bill.   (*By Order.*)

6   East Sussex County Council (Newhaven Bridge) Bill.   (*By Order.*)

7   Greater London Council (General Powers) (No. 2) Bill.   (*By Order.*)

8   Haringey Corporation Bill.   (*By Order.*)

9   Hertfordshire County Council Bill.   (*By Order.*)

10   Isle of Wight County Council Bill.   (*By Order.*)

11   Kesteven County Council Bill.   (*By Order.*)

12   London Transport (No. 2) Bill.   (*By Order.*)

*13   National Westminster Bank (North Central Finance & Lombard Banking) Bill. (*By Order.*)

14   Oxfordshire County Council (No. 2) Bill.   (*By Order.*)

15   Stockport Corporation Bill.   (*By Order.*)

16   Torbay Corporation (No. 2) Bill.   (*By Order.*)

QUESTIONS FOR ORAL ANSWER
Questions to the Prime Minister (see page 5478) will begin at 3.15 p.m.

*   1   **Dr John Gilbert** (Dudley):   To ask the Minister of Agriculture, Fisheries and Food, whether he will make a statement on the progress of his discussions with the brewing industry with respect to the European Economic Community draft directive on brewing.

★   ★   ★

303

* 97 **Mr Michael O'Halloran** (Islington, North): To ask the Secretary of State for Social Services, if he will now make a further statement about the proposed development of the Whittington Hospital, Archway, London, N.19; when building will commence; and what will be the estimated cost, and the approximate date of completion.

* 98 **Mr Michael Meacher** (Oldham, West): To ask the Secretary of State for Social Services, how many of the 24,000 persons wage-stopped prior to November 1970 have already been removed from the application of the wage-stop as a result of the rise in National Joint Council rates after the local authority manual workers' strike; and how many further persons will be removed from the scope of the wage-stop when the present review is completed.

* 99 **Mr Neil Marten** (Banbury): To ask the Secretary of State for Social Services, on what basis a fair comparison is made between social security benefits in Great Britain and foreign countries.

*100 **Mr Ray Carter** (Birmingham, Northfield): To ask the Secretary of State for Trade and Industry, if he will recommend the appointment of a Royal Commission to examine the function and future of the newspaper industry.

*101 **Mr Patrick Wall** (Haltemprice): To ask the Secretary of State for Trade and Industry, what representations he has received from the home cucumber producer; and if he will take steps to protect the home producer from cucumber imports from Eastern Europe during the British season from mid-March to mid-September.

*102 **Mr Barry Jones** (East Flint): To ask the Secretary of State for Wales, how many trawlers there are in Wales; what are their principal ports; and if he will make a statement on the fishing industry in Wales.

*103 **Mr Barry Jones** (East Flint): To ask the Secretary of State for Wales, if he will make a statement on the 1970 harvest in Wales.

*104 **Mr Leo Abse** (Pontypool): To ask the Secretary of State for the Home Department whether he is aware that the present operation of section 2 of the Official Secrets Act 1911 encroaches upon the liberties of the Press and of private individuals; and whether, in order to reconcile the needs of a free Press with the needs of security, he will refer this section to the Law Commission for review as part of their programme for studying anachronistic laws.

*105 **Mr Leo Abse** (Pontypool): To ask the Secretary of State for the Home Department, whether he is aware of the comments of the trial judge in the recent proceedings taken against the editor of the Sunday Telegraph and others concerning the need to amend section 2 of the Official Secrets Act 1911; and, in order to prevent any proceedings being taken on grounds of breaches of security which could become political trials, what action he intends to take to review and amend the Official Secrets Act.

*106 **Mr Arthur Davidson** (Accrington): To ask the Secretary of State for the Home Department, what proposals he has to amend the Official Secrets Act.

*107 **Mr Peter Archer** (Rowley Regis and Tipton): To ask the Secretary of State for the Home Department, whether he will introduce legislation to amend or repeal section 2 of the Official Secrets Act 1911.

AT THE COMMENCEMENT OF PUBLIC BUSINESS

Notices of Presentation of Bills

1 Mr Denis Howell

SALE OF TICKETS (OFFENCES): Bill to prohibit in certain circumstances the sale or resale of any ticket for entry or admission to any sporting event or entertainment; and for connected purposes.

2 Mr Charles Fletcher-Cooke

CARRIAGE OF GOODS BY SEA: Bill to amend the law with respect to the carriage of goods by sea.

3 Mrs Joyce Butler

ANTI-DISCRIMINATION: Bill to make illegal, and provide for the prevention of, discrimination against women; to establish an anti-discrimination board; and for connected purposes.

ORDERS OF THE DAY AND NOTICES OF MOTIONS

*Those marked thus * are Government Orders of the Day*

* 1 INDUSTRIAL RELATIONS BILL: Committee [5th allotted Day]. [*Progress 2nd February.*]

Clause No. 37 (Action by Commission for promoting settlement of question referred under s. 35).

Amendment proposed, in page 27, line 31, to leave out from the word 'provisions' to the end of the subsection.—(*Mr Harold Walker.*)

Question proposed, That the Amendment be made:—

For Amendments, see separate Paper

* 2 VEHICLES (EXCISE) BILL [*LORDS*]: Second Reading.

* 3 HYDROCARBON OIL (CUSTOMS AND EXCISE) BILL [*LORDS*]: Second Reading.

4 *MR SPEAKER KING'S RETIREMENT*

Mr Patrick Jenkin

That the annual sum of £5,000 be granted to Her Majesty out of the Consolidated Fund of the United Kingdom for payment of an annuity to the Right Honourable Horace Maybray King, lately Speaker of the House of Commons, and that, if Una King, his wife, survives him, the annual sum of £1,667 be granted as aforesaid, for the payment of an annuity to her.

As Amendments to Mr Patrick Jenkin's proposed Motion (Mr Speaker King's Retirement):

Mr Arthur Lewis

Line 1, leave out '£5,000' and insert '£4,000'.

Line 4, leave out '£1,667' and insert '£1,250'.

305

Line 5, at end, add:—
'and both these payments to commence on the date when the Government next increase welfare benefits as paid under the National Insurance Act'.

A Bill is to be brought in upon this Resolution when it has been agreed to by the House

On the Motion for the Adjournment of the House under Standing Order No. 1 Mr Ernest Armstrong proposes to raise the subject of the need to expand educational opportunity in the Northern Region.

PUBLIC COMMITTEES

1	Race Relations and Immigration	9.30	Birmingham
2	Standing Committee A (further to consider the Courts Bill [*Lords*]	10.30	Room 12
3	Standing Committee B (further to consider the Coal Industry Bill)	10.30	Room 10
4	Standing Committee E (further to consider the Industry Bill)	10.30	Room 9
5	First Scottish Standing Committee (further to consider the Education (Scotland) Bill)	10.30	Room 14
6	Standing Committee B (further to consider the Coal Industry Bill)	4.00	Room 10
7	Standing Committee D (further to consider the Land Commission (Dissolution) Bill)	4.00	Room 11
8	Nationalised Industries (to consider Draft Report)	4.00	Room 8
9	House of Commons (Services)	4.00	Room 16
10	Science and Technology: Sub-Commitee B ...	4.30	Room 15
11	Expenditure: Steering Sub-Committee	5.00	Room 6
12	Armed Forces Bill [*Lords*]	6.00	Room 16
13	Privileges	6.00	Room 13

QUESTIONS FOR WRITTEN ANSWER

Questions handed in on Monday 8th February are marked thus ¶

1 **Sir Clive Bossom** (Leominster): To ask the Minister of Agriculture, Fisheries and Food, what discussions he has had with the Belgian and French Governments about exporting British cattle on a dead-weight basis, in view of the concern at the present arrangements for live-weight exports.

2 **Mr David Steel** (Roxburgh, Selkirk and Peebles): To ask the Minister of Agriculture, Fisheries and Food, if he will enumerate all the departmental committees of inquiry or commissions coming under the responsibility of his department and indicate the dates on which these were set up.

IV Case-study of a Private Member's Bill – The Evolution of the Chronically Sick and Disabled Persons Act, 1970

On 6 November 1969, Mr Alfred Morris, Member of Parliament for Manchester, Wythenshawe, won first place in the ballot for the right to introduce a Private Member's Bill in the 1969–70 Session. The Chronically Sick and Disabled Persons Act, 1970, which resulted from this opportunity has been described as 'the Private Member's Bill of the year' and 'the most significant advance in social provision for the long-term sick and disabled made in this or any other country'. This appendix outlines the inception of the Bill and the process of its enactment.

Mr Morris's high place in the ballot meant that he was certain of the chance to have a Bill considered, but that the time for preparation would be exceedingly short as it would have to be published by 26 November 1969, and submitted for a Second Reading on 5 December 1969.* He had first to decide the subject to be introduced, and in this he had no lack of advice and offers of assistance; he was offered no less than 450 ready-made Bills from a variety of pressure groups, and there were doubtless a number of M.P.s who were more than willing to let him ride their favourite hobby-horses. If he had accepted the offer of one of the outside groups he would almost certainly have been supplied with professional drafting assistance, briefs for speeches and secretarial assistance. All of these offers were, however, refused and, in spite of the difficulties of which he was all too conscious, Mr Morris decided to prepare a Bill designed to deal with some of the pressing problems of the chronically sick and disabled.

This was a field in which he had a strong personal commitment, his own father having died of war wounds after a long period of disablement and his wife's mother was severely disabled. 'When a parent is disabled,' says Mr Morris, 'the family is disabled.' Mr Morris's personal experience and his long involvement in politics had given him a deep insight into the needs of the chronically sick and disabled, but to translate the proposals to deal with these problems into the official language of a Bill at such short notice was a mammoth task.

He therefore set down quickly, in the form of a series of resolutions, what he felt personally needed to be done and announced his intention of introducing a Bill on these lines. He then embarked upon a seemingly endless series of consultations with interested M.P.s of all parties and the various organisations promoting the welfare of individuals with physical and mental disabilities. Once underway, the whole operation rapidly 'snowballed'. There was manifest goodwill and encouragement from M.P.s, servants of the House and outside 'interest' groups, and the prospects for the eventual enactment of comprehensive legislation in this field began to look good.

The ramifications, however, were enormous. Personal or written consultations were held with representatives of the Central Council for the Disabled, the Disablement Income Group, the Spastics Society, the National Association for Mental Health, the National Society for Mentally Handicapped Children, the National Campaign for the Young Chronic Sick, the Institute of Child Health, the National Society for Autistic Children, the Muscular Dystrophy Group, the Disabled Living Activities Group, and many other organisations. Also, it soon became clear that, apart from the Treasury, the work of no less than eleven Departments of State would be involved; the provision proposed impinged upon the responsibilities of the Department of Health and Social Security, the Ministry of Housing and Local

* The Second Report from the Select Committee on Procedure for the Session 1970–1 *The Process of Legislation*, (H.C. 538); recommends that a ballot for Private Members' Bills should be held before the summer adjournment in order to give those successful three months to prepare their Bills. It also suggested that M.P.s should be allowed help from government draftsmen.

Government, the Ministry of Transport, the Department of Employment and Productivity, the Post Office, the Department of Education and Science, the Ministry of Public Building and Works, the Ministry of Technology, the Home Office and the Scottish and Welsh Offices. In this exercise co-operation and effective liaison would be all important.

During the twenty days between the announcement to proceed with the Bill and its publication there was a scene of frantic activity involving the sponsor of the legislation and his supporters. Mr Morris and the voluntary organisations were deluged with letters and telephone calls – the Central Council for the Disabled alone received 1100 letters in the space of two or three days; volunteer secretaries and shorthand-typists came into the House to help Mr Morris to cope with an ever mounting volume of correspondence and much midnight oil was burned. People passing through the Lobbies regularly became accustomed to seeing wheel-chairs and other aids for the disabled. Speaking in the Second Reading debate at a later stage, one Member remarked: 'Wheel-chairs have become such a common-place that after the business of the House is complete the police shout, "Who rolls home?".'

The set of resolutions which formed the original basis of the proposals were gradually amended and extended and the pattern of the Bill proper began to emerge. The resulting proposals were very much a co-operative effort. The National Campaign for the Young Chronic Sick, for instance, pressed for a provision to have young long-stay patients in hospital accommodated separately from geriatric patients and resolutions to this effect were included; Mr Jack Ashley, himself a sufferer from acute deafness, submitted proposals for further improvements in welfare services for the deaf and these too were incorporated. The translation of the resolutions into the official language of a Parliamentary Bill was achieved in record time with the expert help of Mr Giles Eccleston of the Public Bill Office and the Chronically Sick and Disabled Persons Bill, consisting of thirty-two clauses, was published on 26 November 1969.

The remainder of its journey through the Commons was marked by intensive effort and a kind of co-operative endeavour rare in the Parliamentary scene. Liaison with the voluntary organisations was maintained through the Central Council for the Disabled which is a federal body representative of the many groups working for different categories of the disabled. It had recently established a Legal and Parliamentary Committee, and this seemed to be the body most appropriate for the conduct of regular face-to-face meetings to deal with problems as they arose. At every stage of the Bill's passage through the House Mr Morris received unstinted help and co-operation from the Government and the various Departments, the responsibility for the many inter-departmental consultations being taken by senior officials of the Department of Health and Social Security. This experience has, it is understood, had the incidental advantage of going some way towards improving the efficiency of inter-departmental machinery in Whitehall.

The Second Reading debate was held on 5 December 1969, when the measures proposed gave rise to expressions of appreciation and support from all Members who spoke and the Bill was welcomed on behalf of the Government by Dr John Dunwoody, the Joint Under-Secretary of State, Department of Health and Social Security. The debate began at 11 a.m. and ended at 3.30 p.m. thus taking up nearly all of the time available on that day. The Bill was agreed to and committed to a Standing Committee.

Standing Committee 'C', which considered the Bill, was made up of 16 Members including the Chairman, Sir Myer Galpern and two Junior Ministers, Dr John Dunwoody (mentioned above) and Mr Reginald Freeson, Joint Parliamentary Secretary, Ministry of Housing and Local Government, and Mr Morris. Nearly all members of the Committee had a special interest in the issues under consideration and eleven of them had spoken in the Second Reading debate. The Committee met

308

on four Wednesday mornings between 11 December 1969, and 4 February 1970, each sitting lasting from 10.30 a.m. to 1 p.m. At each meeting Mr Morris moved a procedure Motion proposing the order in which the various clauses should be considered. This was made necessary by the fact that the Bill was being prepared so hurriedly, and the relevant data on some sections was more advanced than on others. Thus, the relevant section of the official report of the Committee for 17 December 1969, reads:

'*Mr Morris*: I beg to move,

That the Bill be considered in the following order, namely, Clauses 25 and 26, Clause 5 and New Clause 1, Clause 7, Clause 10, Clause 12 and New Clause 3, Clauses 13 to 15, Clause 20, Clause 22, Clause 28, Clause 31, the remaining Clauses, New Clause 2.

I am moving this procedure Motion both to meet the convenience of colleagues in the Committee and organisations outside which are advising hon. Members about various parts of the Bill, and because Departments of State require as much time as possible to give a positive response to the propositions which we are making in the Bill.

Question put and agreed to.'

During the course of the Bill's progress through the Standing Committee Mr Morris and his colleagues held regular consultations with the Parliamentary and Legal Committee of the Central Council for the Disabled and the representatives of other interested groups.

The Report stage and Third Reading were taken on Friday, 20 March 1970, these debates again taking up almost all of the time available; the proceedings on the measure began at 11 a.m. and ended at 3.50 p.m., when the Third Reading was agreed to. The way was now open for consideration by the House of Lords.

The Earl of Longford had agreed to sponsor the Bill in the Lords and at 3.15 p.m. on 19 April he moved the Second Reading in the upper House. During his opening speech he spelled out the essential purpose of the legislation proposed. He said:

'My Lords, we are determined that henceforward, so far as lies in human power, the disabled shall no longer feel themselves to be second-class citizens in their own country. We are determined that they shall no longer suffer, as so many do, from a dread sense of isolation. We are determined that through this Bill not only shall they acquire a new sense of independence but at the same time shall obtain an integration within the community, a feeling of belonging fully to it, just like everybody else. Moreover, we are determined that they shall not be just passive beneficiaries of these welcome changes but shall be as actively concerned in administering the results as they have been in promoting the Bill. For the first time we are insisting that the problems of the disabled shall be looked at and treated as a whole, instead of allowing the provision . . . to emerge from the efforts of nine different departments as a sort of un-thought-out residual legacy.'

This debate and those of the remaining stages in the Lords were impressive because of the high standard of the debate and because a significant number of the participants spoke from personal experience of severe disablement. Two peeresses, Lady Darcy de Knayth and Lady Masham of Ilton, and two peers, Lord Crawshaw and Lord Ingleby, addressed the House from wheel-chairs positioned in front of the cross benches – the first three named were making their maiden speeches. Baroness Serota, Minister of State in the Department of Health and Social Security, welcomed the Bill on behalf of the Government and, shortly after 7 p.m. on this day, the Second Reading was formally approved and the Bill was committed to a Committee of the Whole House.

The Committee stage in the Lords was held on 30 April and 15 May, and the Report and remaining stages on 15 May 1970. The Lords amendments were considered in the Commons on 27 May. Moving the acceptance of the Lords Amendment to Clause 1, Mr Morris spoke appreciatively of the way in which Lord Longford and his colleagues had strengthened the Bill and paid tribute to Mr Giles Eccleston of the Public Bill Office and the late Mr Julian Elliston, Parliamentary Counsel, for their assistance in drafting the Bill. The concluding words were spoken by Dr John Dunwoody who said: 'I think this Parliament has done its best and we have in this legislation a base on which we can build in the future.' In the Second Reading debate on 20 March 1970, Mr John Page, M.P. had said of Mr Alfred Morris, the originator of the Bill: 'We all wish to congratulate him on this milestone in his Parliamentary career. I suspect that whatever heights he may go to in the long time he may be in this House he will enjoy no greater satisfaction than that which comes from having piloted this Bill.'

The Chronically Sick and Disabled Persons Bill was given precedence by the Government in the dying days of Parliament and the necessary Money Resolutions were approved: it received the Royal Assent on 29 May 1970, the day on which Parliament was prorogued. The main provisions of the statute are outlined below and the summary shows that whereas the original Bill contained 32 Clauses, the Act has 29 Sections. This, of course, arises from the alterations, additions and deletions which were effected in the course of its journey through the two Houses.

The Chronically Sick and Disabled Persons Act, 1970, has occasioned much international interest and its implementation will be watched closely by interested observers both at home and abroad. Only 600 000 cases of severe disablement were known to the public authorities at the time the Bill was prepared but the actual number is probably nearer to 2 millions. This is why Section 1 of the Act, which requires local authorities to compile a register of such persons and to make known to them the facilities which are available is so important.

The speed at which the Act is implemented is dependent to a large extent upon the sympathy and vigour with which its provisions are acted upon by the local authorities and administrative bodies concerned. Some councils are responding to the challenges presented with energy and determination but others are approaching their responsibilities more slowly. This variation in response illustrates one aspect of the difficulties which hold up the full implementation of important social legislation.

Main Provisions of the Chronically Sick and Disabled Persons Act, 1970

Section 1. Requires local authorities to ascertain details of all handicapped persons living in their area and to inform them of the kind of help which is available to them.

Section 2. Enables local authorities to make provision for the following forms of assistance:

(a) practical assistance in the home;

(b) supplying or helping to obtain radio, television, library and other recreational facilities;

(c) leisure pursuits and educational facilities;

(d) travel facilities to and from the home to take advantage of services available;

(e) adaptation of the home to secure greater safety, comfort and convenience (including, e.g. ramps, door widening, hand-rails, hoists, etc.);

(f) arranging suitable holidays;

(g) provision of meals;

(h) supplying or giving help in obtaining a telephone and, if necessary, the special equipment needed to make use of it.

Section 3. Requires local authorities to consider the provision of housing: keeping in mind the special needs of the chronically sick and disabled.

Sections 4–7. Deal with the provision of facilities for access to sanitary conveniences and require these to be provided in certain premises open to the public. In each case the special needs of handicapped persons are to be taken into account and appropriate signs are to be provided.

Section 8. Provides that universities, colleges and schools must make suitable provision to enable disabled persons to attend.

Sections 9–16. Require that sick and disabled persons shall be represented on committees and advisory bodies, etc. which are concerned with the aspects of welfare services and other matters which affect them.

Section 17. Instructs hospital authorities that as far as possible young patients who are in hospital or other institutions for a long period should be accommodated separately from older patients.

Sections 20–1. Extend facilities for the use of invalid carriages.

Section 22. Requires the Secretary of State, Department of Health and Social Security to present an annual report to Parliament on 'research and development work carried out by or on behalf of any Minister of the Crown in relation to equipment that might increase the range of activities and independence or well-being of disabled persons, and in particular such equipment that might improve the indoor and outdoor mobility of such persons'.

Section 23. Gives additional rights in matters relating to appeals on war pensions.

Section 24. Requires the Secretary of State to collate and present evidence to the Medical Research Council on the need for an institute of hearing research.

Sections 25–7. Direct attention to the need to improve the provision for the special educational treatment of deaf–blind, autistic and dyslexic children.

Sections 28–9. Empower the Secretary of State to make necessary regulations, and lay down the dates on which the various sections of the Act will come into force.

V Extracts from the Third Report of the Committee of Public Accounts for the Session 1969–70

Note: These extracts deal with matters appertaining to the Committee's investigation into delay by the Post Office in recovering sums due from Standard Telephone and Cable, an American firm of contractors.

A. *Report.* (This section outlines the issue under consideration and notes the assurances given by the Post Office on steps taken to improve the system which gave rise to cause for concern.)

'174. The Report of the Comptroller and Auditor-General drew attention to cases of substantial delay in recovering amounts shown to be due to the Post Office after final contract prices had been determined. The cases included a delay of 17 months in recovering £285,000 due to the Post Office on final settlement of a contract for submarine cable, and of four years in recovering £159,583 in respect of five contracts for submerged repeaters.

175. The submarine cable was delivered by 1963 but there was delay in completing the cost investigation and the final price was not agreed until December 1967. This fell short of the amount paid on account by £285,000, but the Post Office did not obtain the refund until May, 1969. Your Committee were informed that the delay occurred partly because the Contracts Division had, on grounds that were now thought to be unsound, associated the settlement with other matters which were being negotiated with the firm and partly because that Division failed to notify the Branch responsible for making the recovery that the refund was due.

176. The prices for the five contracts for submarine repeaters, all delivered by 1961, were finally agreed in May 1965. After minor adjustments made early in 1966, the final prices fell short of those paid provisionally by the Post Office by a total sum of £159,583, but recovery of this sum was delayed from early 1966 until May and June, 1969. Your Committee were informed that the delay was caused by the failure, on three separate occasions, of the officers responsible to carry out the recognised procedure. As a result of these administrative errors, the failure to recover remained undiscovered for three years.

177. The Post Office assured Your Committee that they had since developed a system which should prevent such delays in future. A senior officer in the Contracts Division had been made responsible for following up all contracts placed at prices to be negotiated. He received independently from purchasing, accountancy and technical cost branches, reports which enabled him to ensure that prompt action was taken to secure any recoveries due. The procedure would also be subject to internal audit.

178. Your Committee welcome this assurance that steps have now been taken to improve the system. They trust that these improvements will ensure that all amounts due to the Post Office on final settlement of prices are properly recorded by those responsible and that energetic action is taken to secure refunds promptly. They also trust that every effort will be made to restrict advances to contractors to a level which will avoid the need for refunds.'

B. *Minutes of Evidence.* (This section gives details of members present and witnesses called by the Committee and presents a verbatim report of part of the proceedings.)

'WEDNESDAY, 3rd December, 1969.

Members Present:

Mr. J. Boyd-Carpenter in the Chair

Mr. Joel Barnett   Mr. Robert Sheldon
Sir Douglas Glover   Sir John Vaughan-Morgan

Sir Bruce Fraser, K.C.B. and Mr. A. J. Phelps, called in and examined

POST OFFICE ACCOUNTS, 1968–69

TREASURY MINUTE RELATING TO PARAGRAPHS 110–150 OF COMMITTEE'S THIRD REPORT, 1968–69

Mr. A. W. C. RYLAND, C.B., Deputy Chairman and Chief Executive, Mr. E. W. SHEPHERD, C.B., Senior Director (Finance and Personnel) and Mr. K. H. CADBURY, M.C., Senior Director (Planning and Purchasing) Post Office, called in and further examined.

178. You had £285,000 outstanding for 17 months and £159,583 for four years? — Yes.

179. Can you compute what the rate of interest over that period would have been? — For the two, about £70,000.

180. Can you tell me as a general proposition, before we get into detail, why you make payments on account which turn out to be substantially larger than the amounts finally discovered to be due? — As a general proposition we do not now do this. The first of these cases was governed by an agreement that we had with the American Telephone and Telegraph Company and it is their practice to pay the full amount and to recover subsequently. We operated on that basis because of this particular association.

. . .

182. You pay on account the maximum price you conceivably could be called upon to pay? — No, Sir, I said in this particular case, because this is an American practice, we paid for this particular cable the maximum price. Normally we pay 90 per cent. The situation in case 2(b) was in fact different in the sense that we only paid the 90 per cent but the ascertained price turned out to be lower than 90 per cent. of the maximum price.

183. Taking first the general principle, I shall come in a moment to the two particular cases, you are telling the Committee that you entered into an agreement

312

with an American firm to pay them the maximum amount possible and called it a payment on account? — The agreement that we had was a joint agreement not with the manufacturer but with the American Telephone and Telegraph Company, who were to be the joint owners of the cable. There were two cables, one a transatlantic cable and one the Florida/Jamaica Cable, and we were acting as partners with the American Telephone and Telegraph Company. The firm that manufactured, also in American ownership, was Standard Telephones and Cables. It is the practice of the American Telephone and Telegraph Company in these cases to pay the maximum price and this was part of our agreement with them. We were following their procedure in this particular instance. It was not an agreement with an American firm of manufacturers, but an agreement with the American firm who were going to be our partners in the project.

184. Have you done this in any other case? — Certainly not in recent years. Our practice, as reported to the Committee earlier, is that we pay not more than 90 per cent. of the maximum price in cases where there is a maximum price, subject to cost investigation.

185. Do you ever intend to do it again? — No, Sir.

186. It was a mistake, was it not? — We did not particularly want to do it on that occasion, but this was part of the procedures with which we had to fall in because of the practice and the accounting arrangements of the American Telephone and Telegraph Company.

. . .

190. Would you agree with me it is a very undesirable practice? — It is not our practice and it is not a practice we adopt.

191. Because it gives the other party the reverse of an incentive to come to a final settlement? — Exactly.

192. And it involves making him almost certainly some interest free loan? — Yes.

193. Which adds to the real cost to you of whatever you are buying? — Certainly in those cases where the maximum price exceeds the actual price.

. . .

197. Taking paragraph 2(a), the submarine cable, do you think the firm were withholding their confirmation of the agreed price in order to put pressure on you for a more favourable arrangement to them on the associated work? Or were they simply using this as a red herring to defer payment of your interest free loan? — Looking back at this, may I just explain a little of the background to the handling of this case? It was handled personally by one of our senior officers in the Contracts Division. He himself felt it right to associate it with other matters which he was negotiating with the firm concerned. I think this was ill-advised, but it was his decision.

198. You think it was ill-advised? — Yes, Sir. This in fact was in part the reason why he did not take action to confirm the agreed price until the following April, some three or four months later, and why in the subsequent discussions with the firm he himself proposed to them at the time of getting confirmation of the agreed refund a basis for settling ships' loading; the initiative came from him. I would not wish to put this on the firm; I think it was clearly a red herring. I think the fault lay mainly with the Post Office.

199. The settlement was finally agreed in December 1967, was it not? — Yes, that is right.

200. Why at that point did you not simply deduct the refund from the payment due to Standard Telephones for other supplies? — For general accounting reasons we must first have a voucher, a credit note, from the firm concerned. This is not an

automatic deduction that we make. We get a credit note from the firm concerned as a voucher supporting our general accounting mechanism.

201. I think I understand that as a procedure, but my question goes to the substance. They were found to owe you a substantial sum of money which they had indeed owed to you for some time. You at the same time were making payments to them. Why did you not offset them? — Because we do not offset them until we get the credit note.

202. Why not? — I am advised this is a necessary and prudent accounting principle.

203. You say it is prudent, but it has the effect of leaving what is your money as an interest free loan with the other party. I see the prudence from their point of view, its prudence from your point of view I find a little difficult to follow? — May I ask Mr. Shepherd to elaborate on this point? — (Mr. Shepherd). The point is that normally in a case of this kind, when once the final price has been agreed, the conclusion following immediately upon that is for us to write to the firm and say, "Please send us a credit note to the agreed amount", and they do this. That passes through the normal accounting machine and results in an adjustment being made along with other payments to the firm and any other credits that there may be. The importance of this credit note is that it is a simple voucher which a paying clerk can handle without any special knowledge of the case and it provides a permanent record of what has happened. What went wrong in this case was that that simple and normally straightforward procedure was not followed because other things were in play with the firm as well, and we failed to write to the firm in the way that would normally have been done.

. . .

207. Mr. Ryland, have you issued any instructions as to the handling of this kind of situation in future? — (Mr. Ryland). Yes, we have; we have revised the system. Could I just comment on this last point? As is brought out in the C. and A.G's. report, one of the reasons why it was not considered, even had it been appropriate under the system to do so at that time, was the fact that the person handling the case in the Contracts Division did not in fact send a voucher or a note about this particular case to the paying branch where the deduction from outstanding accounts would have had to be made anyway. So they were not advised of it. This was one of the failures of the system.

208. What have you done to repair that part of the system? — What we have done to repair this and other parts of the system is firstly to make a senior officer in the Contracts Division responsible for watching all these cases. He now gets independently a report from purchasing branches, accountancy branches, technical cost branches, dealing with both the new and the cleared cases, in a way which enables him to check in each case whether there is delay, whether there is a hold-up, whether in fact a particular credit which is due has been notified from the purchasing branch to the accounts branch so they can follow up. So we have got a complete check, and this applies to all payments as well as credits, but the credits are drawn specifically to his attention. So he has now a complete register and personal responsibility to check and follow at all levels the particular cases being handled, whether senior to him or junior to him.

209. So in future a named officer will know if a firm owes you money? — Yes.

215. Are you satisfied none of your officers will leave £150,000 outstanding for four years and do nothing about it again? — (Mr. Ryland). I am satisfied that the system is such that it should not happen. I am satisfied, after a careful check, there are no cases of this kind in the system at the moment, and while I would not wish to say nothing will ever go wrong, because I think it would be unwise of me to say so, I am satisfied we have a very tight system which should prevent this kind of case occurring on this scale or with this kind of regularity in future.'

314

Glossary

Note: *The purpose of the glossary is to provide definitions of words and phrases used in the text or to expand the explanations already provided. Brief explanations of other words and phrases frequently used in political literature but not included in the text are also given.*

Ad hoc. For this purpose.

Adjournment (Parliament). The process of ending each day's sitting of the House of Commons. The House 'stands adjourned' until the time appointed for the next sitting.

A priori. The literal meaning of this phrase is 'from what is before' and its use implies an unprejudiced assumption that something has happened, the relevance or seriousness of which should be determined by further inquiry.

Audi alternam partem. This phrase, meaning 'hear the other side' expresses the principle that both sides in a dispute should be heard before a decision is given.

Autonomy. The right to act independently.

Back-bencher. Member of Parliament who is not a member of the Government or an official spokesman of the Opposition.

'Backwoodsmen'. Hereditary peers who are members of the House of Lords but do not normally attend meetings of the House. Standing orders were introduced in 1958 which ended the possibility of large numbers of this category coming to the House without notice and voting on a matter of concern to them.

Balance of migration. The rate of immigration measured against the rate of emigration in a given year.

Bar of the House. The delineated boundary in the House of Lords and the House of Commons which may not be passed by non-members.

Bicameral legislature. Law-making body consisting of two chambers.

Birth rate. The ratio of total live births to total population in a given year.

Black Rod (Chief Gentleman Usher of). An official of the Lord Chamberlain's department of the Royal Household who is Usher of the House of Lords. He summons Members of the House of Commons to hear the Queen's Speech.

Block Vote. Feature of voting system at Labour Party Annual Conference where a trade union casts all its votes (based on affiliated numerical strength) for or against a proposal under consideration.

Bona fide. In good faith, genuine.

By-election. An election specially held to fill a vacancy for an M.P. or a Councillor which has arisen because of the death or resignation of the previous member.

Canvass. A door to door inquiry by political party workers designed to produce a record of electors' voting intentions. Frequently associated with the idea of an organised attempt to persuade electors to accept the merits of one of the parties but this aspect is normally secondary to that described above.

Caucus. A meeting of a group of people at which a course of political action is determined. In British politics frequently used with connotation of a secret group meeting where actions may adversely affect political system. In U.S.A. political system 'caucus' meetings are routine party matters, e.g. in Congress and in nominating Conventions. The word derives from an Algonquin Indian word meaning to urge or to advise.

Central Office. The national headquarters of the Conservative and Unionist Association.

Civil List. The sum of money allocated to meet the expenses of the Queen and the Royal Family.

Civil Rights. The actual or alleged rights and privileges of individuals and groups (e.g. the right to vote or to have an equitable basis of representation). Used especially in connection with protest movements in U.S.A. and Northern Ireland.

Closure. The ending of a debate in the House of Commons. Used to expedite the rate at which the various measures are dealt with.

Congress. The name given collectively to the two Houses of the legislature in the United States, viz. the Senate and the House of Representatives.

Conservatism. Political doctrine involving disposition to maintain existing institutions or to reform them, in the light of experience. This doctrine places high value on individual freedom and expresses belief that politics is secondary in life; personal or spiritual concerns being of greater importance.

Conurbation. A term coined to indicate an extensive area which is heavily urbanised and densely populated, e.g. Greater London, Merseyside.

Co-opt. The process whereby an individual is invited to join a committee or other public body following a formally agreed decision of its existing members. Usually members are co-opted because of their special knowledge or experience and they have lesser rights than the original members, e.g. they cannot vote.

Count. The counting of votes cast in a parliamentary or local government election to decide which candidate or candidates has been elected.

Crown. The source of supreme executive power. The Crown symbolizes *both* the Sovereign and the Government.

Crown Office. The Office of the Clerk to the Crown in Chancery which issues election writs to returning officers and writs of summons to peers.

Culture. Used in the sociological sense, implies the total way of life of a society. 'Culture is that complex whole which includes knowledge, belief, art, morals, law, custom, and any other capabilities and habits acquired by man as a member of society.' (E. B. Tylor, *Primitive Culture,* 1871.) In indicating, e.g. age, regional or class variations within the total culture, it is usual to speak of *sub*-cultures, hence the terms teen-age sub-culture, working-class sub-culture, etc.

Death rate. The ratio of total deaths to total population in a given year.

Decentralisation. The arrangements made whereby powers of a central body are exercised in locations or by bodies away from the centre of government organisation.

De facto. This simply means 'in fact', and indicates e.g. that a government or body actually holds power whether this in 'in law' (*de jure*) or not.

Demography. The scientific study of human populations, especially their size, structure and development.

316

Devolution. Delegation of work or power from one body to another, e.g. from Parliament to the Board of nationalised industry. This may be functional or geographical.

Dissolution. The termination of a Parliament prior to a general election. The timing of this is announced by the Queen on the advice of the Prime Minister.

Election writ. See Writ of Election.

Established Church. The church established by law and which thereby has a number of rights and privileges.

Exempted business (Parliament). This includes matters which are exempted from the usual restrictions imposed by Standing Orders and which may, even though opposed, be taken after 10 a.m.

Ex officio. By virtue of office held.

Fabian Society. An association of intellectual socialists which concentrates on policies and background studies of political issues. Prominent Fabians have included George Bernard Shaw, Sydney and Beatrice Webb, H. G. Wells, G. D. H. and Margaret Cole. The viewpoint of the Society emphasises 'inevitability of gradualism' and importance of acting on basis of reliable information and data.

Father of the House. The M.P. who has the longest *continuous* service in the House.

Filibuster. Prolonged discussion and debate of a proposal before a legislature designed to delay or prevent the passage of the measure. In British Parliament this procedure is prevented by one or other of the methods of Closure.

Franchise. The right to vote. A suffrage.

Gavel. A chairman's hammer, which is banged to draw a meeting to order.

Gerrymander(ing). The practice of arranging constituency boundaries in such a way as to give electoral advantage to one party as against its rivals. (For an excellent account of the possible origin of the term see *Dictionary of American Politics* (Penguin, 1968), pp. 68–9.

Habeas Corpus (Writ of). A writ obtained from a High Court judge to order a gaoler to 'produce the body' of a person held by bringing him to court at a specified time.

Hansard. The verbatim Official Report of proceedings in Parliament. Named after Mr T. C. Hansard, who undertook the publication of reports on debates in 1811 and whose family carried on the business for nearly eighty years.

Horizontal mobility. This phrase indicates an individual's occupational movement to jobs of similar status (e.g. from teacher to social worker) as against vertical mobility (e.g. from teacher to headteacher).

Ideology. A set of ideas or beliefs concerning the nature of society or a political system.

In camera. Sittings, e.g. of court, held in private without the public being admitted.

Injunction. A writ issued by the High Court ordering a person not to do or to cease from doing an act not amounting to a crime.

Inter alia. Among others.

Isolationist. A policy urging non-involvement in the affairs of other countries. Applies particularly to groups in U.S.A. which opposed involvement of U.S.A. in European affairs before the Second World War.

'Knocking-up'. Visits made to the home of electors on election day by party workers in an effort to persuade them to go and vote.

Liberalism. Political doctrine which emphasises individual rights and freedoms. The Liberal Party in Britain advocates electoral reform, co-ownership in industry and supports the setting up of Scottish and Welsh parliaments.

317

Mace. The symbol of authority in the House of Commons which rests on the Table.

Mandate. The authorisation, actual or assumed, given by the electorate to the party winning a general election. (Derived from Latin, *mandatum*, meaning charge, order or message.)

Manifesto. The short statement of principle and policy issued by political parties at the time of a general election.

Marginal seat. A seat held by one party with a relatively small majority which is liable to be gained by the other party if it gains a higher percentage of the vote than at the previous election.

Norms (social or cultural). General ideas about the behaviour or attitudes of a given group to which members of the group are expected more or less to conform. Behaviour which does so accord is, therefore, normative.

Order in Council. An order made in the name of the Queen by the Privy Council under authority deriving from the royal prerogative or legislation.

Palace of Westminster. The buildings and surrounding area in which the Houses of Parliament are situated. The Houses of Parliament still form part of the Royal Palace and are controlled by the Lord Great Chamberlain, a hereditary 'Great Officer of State'.

Patronage. The power (e.g. of the Sovereign or Prime Minister) to bestow office, honours or other awards.

Political culture. That part of the total culture which is concerned with the political system involving people's perception of and attitudes towards political institutions and issues.

Prayer (Parliament). The act of moving an address to the Queen, e.g. for the annulment of an Order in Council or statutory instrument.

Precepting Authority. A local authority which is legally entitled to make a precept or demand on another (the Rating Authority) for the levying of a rate, e.g. under the existing pattern County Councils and Parish Councils submit precepts to Rural District Councils.

Prima facie. At first sight.

Primus inter pares. First among equals.

Prorogation. The formal procedure by which a Session of Parliament is ended. When the House is prorogued this automatically 'kills' bills which have not completed all the necessary stages.

Quorum. The minimum number of members in either House of Parliament or in any committee required for the legitimate conduct of business.

Rating Authority. A local authority which has power to fix and levy rates.

Recess. Technically this is the period between the prorogation of Parliament and the State opening of a new Session. The word is also used colloquially to describe the shorter breaks at Christmas and other times during the Session.

Returning Officer. The official appointed to supervise the conduct of elections.

Royal Prerogative. The right of the Sovereign to act without consulting Parliament.

Safe Seat. A constituency which one or other of the parties is virtually certain to win in an election because of the high proportion of supporters concentrated in the area.

Seebohm Committee. This committee was appointed to consider and make recommendations upon certain aspects of social welfare administration. It recommended that each local authority should have a single Social Service department to ensure a

318

co-ordinated approach for deprived families and groups. All of the Committee's major recommendations were accepted by the Government and implemented by the Local Authority Social Services Act, 1970.

Shadow Cabinet. The name given to the group of Opposition leaders who provide the Front Bench spokesmen.

Socialisation. The social process by means of which an individual's attitudes, assumptions and aspirations are largely determined. *Political* socialisation is that part of the process which affects political beliefs and attitudes.

Socialism. A political doctrine which advocates the public ownership and control of the means of production, distribution and exchange and which seeks to achieve equality of opportunity.

Sovereign. The reigning King or Queen. The person on whom the Crown is constitutionally conferred. (Term is interchangeable with King, Queen, Monarch but *not* the Crown.)

Sponsored candidate. A Labour parliamentary candidate whose candidature receives substantial financial aid from a trade union or other affiliated organisation. The amount which can be contributed in this way, or by the candidate himself, is limited by the party constitution.

Stormont. Area near Belfast in which the Northern Ireland legislature is situated. Frequently used to refer to this assembly.

Suffrage. The right to vote. A franchise.

Supply (Committee of; Supply Days). Technically the consideration of finance requested by the Government; in practice the policy of the Government is more generally discussed. The former Committee of Supply which considered the estimates was a Committee of the Whole House. Supply Days equal Opposition Days (see text).

Supreme Court (U.S.A.). The highest court in the United States' judiciary. Its major importance is a final court of appeal. It decides constitutional cases. Described by Woodrow Wilson as 'a kind of continuous constitutional convention'.

Tort. A civil wrong which gives rise to an action in the courts.

Transport House. The national headquarters of the Labour Party.

Ultra vires. An act declared to be 'beyond the powers' of, e.g. a local authority, and therefore unlawful.

Unicameral legislature. Law-making body consisting of a single chamber.

Unitary government. A state whose central government exercises full and undivided sovereign power over the whole of a country as in the United Kingdom. (cf. a federal state where power is divided between central government and state government.)

Veto. The power to reject legislation exercised by e.g. the House of Lords in Britain and the President of the U.S.A.

Ward. Smaller electoral areas into which a local government area other than a County or Rural District may be divided. Each ward elects a number of councillors and party organisation is frequently arranged on this basis.

Ways and Means. When the House of Commons discusses proposals for taxation and payments from the Consolidated Fund, it is concerned with 'Ways and Means' which were formerly considered in the Committee of that name.

Whips. (1) M.P. who is responsible to leader for discipline and voting of members of parliamentary party. (2) The written instructions on voting issued by party whip.

Whitehall. Part of London in which bulk of important government offices are situated. Sometimes used to refer to idea of civil servants generally and their supposed modes of procedure.

Woolsack. The red leather-covered sack of wool which forms the cushion on the Lord Chancellor's chair in the House of Lords.

Writ of Election. The legal document issued to authorise the holding of a parliamentary election.

Writ of Summons. The summons to the House of Lords which is sent to peers by the Crown Office.

Further Reading

GENERAL WORKS
S. H. Beer, *Modern British Politics* (Faber, 1965).
A. H. Birch, *The British System of Government* (Allen and Unwin, 1967).
I. Gilmour, *The Body Politic* (Hutchinson, 1969).
A. H. Hanson and M. Walles, *Governing Britain* (Fontana, 1970).
J. P. Mackintosh, *The Government and Politics of Britain* (Hutchinson, 1970).
R. M. Punnett, *British Government and Politics* (Heinemann, 1970).
R. Rose, *Politics in England* (Faber, 1965).
E. C. S. Wade and G. C. Philips, *Constitutional Law* (Longmans, 1967).

MORE SPECIALISED WORKS. These are listed by the chapter heading of the present book.

1 THE BASIS OF POLITICS
B. Crick, *In Defence of Politics* (Penguin, 1964).
J. D. B. Miller, *The Nature of Politics* (Penguin, 1965).
D. Pickles, *Introduction to Politics* (Methuen, 1964).
R. R. Raphael, *Problems of Political Philosophy* (Macmillan, 1970).
H. V. Wiseman, *Politics in Everyday Life* (Blackwell, 1966).

2 THE NATURE OF DEMOCRACY
R. Basset, *Essentials of Parliamentary Democracy* (Cassell, 1964).
S. I. Benn and R. S. Peters, *Social Principles and the Democratic State* (Allen and Unwin, 1959).
D. Pickles, *Democracy* (Batsford, 1970).
J. A. Schumpeter, *Capitalism, Socialism and Democracy* (Allen and Unwin, 1963).

3 THE ELECTORAL SYSTEM
D. E. Butler, *The Electoral System in Britain Since 1918* (Oxford University Press, 1963).
R. L. Leonard, *Elections in Britain* (Van Nostrand, 1968).
W. J. M. Mackenzie, *Free Elections* (Allen and Unwin, 1958).
P. G. J. Pulzer, *Political Representation and Elections in Britain* (Allen and Unwin, 1968).
J. F. S. Ross, *Elections and Electors* (Eyre and Spottiswoode, 1955).

4 POLITICAL PARTIES
S. D. Bailey, *The British Party System* (Hansard Society, 1953).
S. H. Beer, *Modern British Politics* (Faber, 1965).
I. Bulmer Thomas, *The Party System in Great Britain* (John Baker, 1966).
R. Fulford, *The Liberal Case* (Penguin, 1959).
Q. Hogg, *The Conservative Case* (Penguin, 1959).

R. Jenkins, *The Labour Case* (Penguin, 1959).
Sir I. Jennings, *Party Politics* vols I–III (Cambridge University Press, 1960–2).
R. T. McKenzie, *British Political Parties* (Heinemann, 1963).
P. Paterson, *The Selectorate* (MacGibbon and Kee, 1967).
A. Ranney, *Pathways to Parliament* (Macmillan, 1965).
M. Rush, *The Selection of Parliamentary Candidates* (Nelson, 1969).

5 PRESSURE GROUPS
V. L. Allen, *Trade Unions and the Government* (Longmans, 1960).
S. H. Beer, *Modern British Politics* (Faber, 1965).
H. Eckstein, *Pressure Group Politics* (Allen and Unwin, 1960).
S. E. Finer, *Anonymous Empire* (Pall Mall, 1966).
A. M. Potter, *Organised Groups in British National Politics* (Faber, 1961).
P. Self and H. Storing, *The State and the Farmer* (Allen and Unwin, 1962).
J. D. Stewart, *British Pressure Groups* (Oxford University Press, 1958).
H. H. Wilson, *Pressure Groups* (Secker and Warburg, 1961).

6 THE SOCIAL STRUCTURE
E. Butterworth and D. Weir, *The Sociology of Modern Britain* (Fontana, 1970).
Central Office of Information, *Britain; An Official Handbook* (H.M.S.O., annually).
D. V. Glass (ed.), *Social Mobility in Britain* (Routledge, 1953).
E. A. Johns, *The Social Structure of Modern Britain* (Pergamon, 1965).
R. K. Kelsall, *Population* (Longmans, 1967).
D. C. Marsh, *The Changing Social Structure of England and Wales* (Routledge, 1965).
R. Rose, *Politics in England* (Faber, 1965).
J. Ryder and H. Silver, *Modern English Society : History and Structure, 1850–1970* (Methuen, 1970).

7 THE PATTERN OF PARTICIPATION
D. Berry, *The Sociology of Grass Roots Politics* (Macmillan, 1970).
J. Blondel, *Voters, Parties and Leaders* (Penguin, 1965).
W. L. Guttsman, *The British Political Elite* (MacGibbon and Kee, 1968).
R. K. Kelsall, *Higher Civil Servants in Britain* (Routledge, 1955).
R. Rose, *Politics in England* (Faber, 1965).

8 VOTING BEHAVIOUR
A. J. Allen, *The English Voter* (English Universities Press, 1964).
M. Benney, A. P. Gray and R. H. Pear, *How People Vote* (Routledge, 1950).
J. Bonham, *The Middle-Class Voter* (Faber, 1954).
D. Butler and M. Pinto-Duschinsky, *The General Election of 1970* (Macmillan, 1971). See also studies of elections 1945–66 in this series.
D. Butler and D. Stokes, *Political Change in Britain* (Macmillan, 1969).
J. H. Goldthorpe and D. Lockwood *et al.*, *The Affluent Worker : Political Attitudes and Behaviour* (Cambridge University Press, 1968).
R. T. McKenzie and A. Silver, *Angels in Marble : Working-Class Conservatives in Urban England* (Heinemann, 1968).

9 PRIME MINISTER, GOVERNMENT AND MONARCHY
F. W. G. Benemy, *The Queen Reigns : She Does Not Rule* (Harrap, 1963).
H. Berkeley, *The Power of the Prime Minister* (Allen and Unwin, 1968).
Sir I. Jennings, *The Law and the Constitution* (London University Press, 1933).
  Cabinet Government (Cambridge University Press, 1959).
A. King (ed.), *The British Prime Minister* (Macmillan, 1969).
J. P. Mackintosh, *The British Cabinet* (Stevens, 1962).
G. Marshall and G. C. Moodie, *Some Problems of the Constitution* (Hutchinson, 1961).
Lord Morrison, *Government and Parliament* (Oxford University Press, 1964).

Sir H. Nicholson, *King George V; His Life and Reign* (Constable, 1952).
Sir C. Petrie, *The Modern British Monarchy* (Eyre and Spottiswoode, 1961).
E. C. S. Wade and G. C. Philips, *Constitutional Law* (Longmans, 1967).
P. Gordon Walker, *The Cabinet* (Cape, 1970).
H. V. Wiseman, *Parliament and the Executive* (Routledge, 1966).

10 THE HOUSE OF COMMONS
H. M. Barclay and S. C. Hawtrey, *Abraham and Hawtrey's Parliamentary Dictionary*
    (Butterworth, 1971).
R. Butt, *The Power of Parliament* (Constable, 1967).
S. Gordon, *Our Parliament* (Cassell, 1964).
A. H. Hanson and B. Crick (eds), *The Commons in Transition* (Fontana, 1970).
A. H. Hanson and H. V. Wiseman, *Parliament at Work* (Stevens, 1962).
Sir I. Jennings, *Parliament* (Cambridge University Press, 1957).
K. R. Mackenzie, *The English Parliament* (Penguin, 1959).
Sir T. Erskine May, *The Law, Privileges, Proceedings and Usages of Parliament*
    (Butterworth, 1971).
P. G. Richards, *Honourable Members* (Faber, 1964).
E. Taylor, *The House of Commons at Work* (Penguin, 1970).
S. A. Walkland, *The Legislative Process in Britain* (Allen and Unwin, 1968).

11 THE HOUSE OF LORDS
B. Crick, *The Reform of Parliament* (Weidenfeld and Nicholson, 1968).
P. A. Bromhead, *The House of Lords and Contemporary Politics* (Routledge, 1958).
S. D. Bailey (ed.), *The Future of the House of Lords* (Hansard Society, 1954).
Lord Chorley, B. Crick and D. Chapman, *Reform of the Lords* (Fabian Society, 1954).
A. Wedgwood Benn, *The Privy Council as a Second Chamber* (Fabian Society, 1957).

12 GOVERNMENT AND FINANCE
Lord Bridges, *The Treasury* (Allen and Unwin, 1964).
B. Chubb, *The Control of Public Expenditure* (Oxford University Press, 1952).
A. R. Prest, *Public Finance in Theory and Practice* (Oliver and Boyd, 1960).
A. Williams, *Public Finance and Budgetary Policy* (Allen and Unwin, 1963).

13 GOVERNMENT DEPARTMENTS
Central Office of Information, *Britain: An Official Handbook* (H.M.S.O., Annually).
B. Chapman, *The Profession of Government* (Allen and Unwin, 1959).
E. H. Gladden, *An Introduction to Public Administration* (Staples Press, 1966).
W. J. M. Mackenzie and J. W. Grove, *Central Administration in Great Britain*
    (Longmans, 1957).
F.M.G. Willson, *Administrators in Action: British Case Studies* (Allen and Unwin,
    1961).
    (ed.), *The Organisation of British Central Government* (Allen and Unwin, 1968).

See also volumes on individual Departments in the New Whitehall series published
by Allen and Unwin for the Royal Institute of Public Administration.

14 THE CIVIL SERVICE
B. Chapman, *British Government Observed* (Allen and Unwin, 1959).
T. A. Critchley, *The Civil Service Today* (Gollancz, 1951).
R. K. Kelsall, *Higher Civil Servants in Britain* (Routledge, 1955).
W. A. Robson, *The Civil Service in Britain and France* (Hogarth, 1956).
Cmd. 3638: *Report of the Committee on the Civil Service* (The Fulton Report)
    (H.M.S.O., 1968).
    The British Civil Service (Central Office of Information, 1971).

A *Northern Ireland*
R. J. Lawrence, *The Government of Northern Ireland* (Oxford University Press, 1965).

G. S. Pryde, *Scotland* (Benn, 1956).

E. Rhodes, *Public Administration in Northern Ireland* (Magee University College, Londonderry, 1967).

J. N. Wolfe, *Government and Nationalism in Scotland* (Edinburgh University Press, 1969).

B *Delegated Legislation*

Sir C. K. Allen, *Law and Orders* (Stevens, 1965).

J. A. G. Griffith and H. Street, *Principles of Administrative Law* (Pitman, 1967).

H. W. R. Wade, *Administrative Law* (Oxford University Press, 1961).

C *Public Corporations*

R. Kelf Cohen, *Twenty Years of Nationalisation* (Macmillan, 1969).

J. W. Grove, *Government and Industry in Britain* (Longmans, 1962).

A. H. Hanson, *Nationalisation : A Book of Readings* (Allen and Unwin, 1963).

W. A. Robson, *Nationalised Industry and Public Ownership* (Allen and Unwin, 1962).

D *Regionalism*

J. P. Mackintosh, *The Devolution of Power* (Penguin, 1968).

B. C. Smith, *Regionalism in England*, volumes I–III (Acton Society Trust, 1966).

D. Steel, *More Power to the Regions* (Fabian Society, 1964).

16 THE STRUCTURE OF LOCAL GOVERNMENT

J. M. Drummond, *The Finance of Local Government* (Allen and Unwin, 1962).

H. Finer, *English Local Government* (Methuen, 1950).

W. O. Hart, *Introduction to the Law of Local Government Administration* (Butterworth, 1962).

R. M. Jackson, *The Machinery of Local Government* (Macmillan, 1958).

W. E. Jackson, *Local Government in England and Wales* (Penguin, 1969).

W. A. Robson, *Local Government in Crisis* (Allen and Unwin, 1968).

K. B. Smellie, *A History of Local Government* (Allen and Unwin, 1957).

Cmd. 4040–1: *Report of the Royal Commission on Local Government*, vols. I–II (H.M.S.O., 1969).

17 LOCAL GOVERNMENT AT WORK

F. Bealey, J. Blondel and W. P. McCann, *Constituency Politics* (Faber, 1965).

A. H. Birch, *Small Town Politics* (Oxford University Press, 1959).

J. G. Bulpitt, *Party Politics in English Local Government* (Longmans, 1967).

R. J. Buxton, *Local Government* (Penguin, 1970).

W. Hampton, *Democracy and Community; A Study of Politics in Sheffield* (Oxford University Press, 1970).

G. W. Jones, *Borough Politics – 1888–1964* (Macmillan, 1969).

L. J. Sharpe, *Voting in Cities* (Macmillan, 1967).

Why Local Democracy?, Fabian Tract no. 361 (Fabian Society, 1965).

J. Stanyer, *County Government in England and Wales* (Routledge, 1967).

H. V. Wiseman, *Local Government at Work* (Routledge, 1967).

Cmd. 4040–II: *Report of the Royal Commission on Local Government in England*, vol. III (H.M.S.O., 1969).

18 THE ENGLISH LEGAL SYSTEM

P. Archer, *The Queen's Courts* (Penguin, 1963).

H. K. Black and D. K. Latham-Brown, *An Outline of English Law* (Methuen, 1966).

F. T. Giles, *The Criminal Law* (Penguin, 1954).

The Magistrates' Courts (Penguin, 1966).

H. G. Hanbury, *English Courts of Law* (Oxford University Press, 1967).

R. M. Jackson, *The Machinery of Justice in England* (Cambridge University Press, 1967).

E. Jenks, *The Book of English Law* (Murray, 1967).

P. Vingradoff, *Common Sense in Law* (Oxford University Press, 1959).

19 ADMINISTRATIVE JUSTICE

Sir C. K. Allen, *Administrative Jurisdiction* (Stevens, 1956).

'Justice', *The Citizen and the Administration: The Redress of Grievances* (Stevens, 1961).

W. A. Robson, *Justice and Administrative Law* (Stevens, 1971).

Cmd. 4060: *Report of the Committee on Ministers' Powers* (H.M.S.O., 1932).

Cmd. 218: *Report of the Committee on Administrative Tribunals and Inquiries* (H.M.S.O., 1957).

20 THE CONSTITUTION

L. S. Amery, *Thoughts on the Constitution* (Oxford University Press, 1964).

W. Bagehot, *The English Constitution* (Fontana, 1963).

A. V. Dicey, *Introduction to the Law of the Constitution* (Macmillan, 1961).

J. A. G. Griffith and H. Street, *Principles of Administrative Law* (Pitman, 1967).

Sir I. Jennings, *The Law and the Constitution* (London University Press, 1933).

The British Constitution (Cambridge University Press, 1961).

F. W. Maitland, *Constitutional History of England* (Cambridge University Press, 1961).

G. Marshall and G. C. Moodie, *Some Problems of the Constitution* (Hutchinson, 1961).

W. A. Robson, *Justice and Administrative Law* (Stevens, 1971).

E. C. S. Wade and G. C. Philips, *Constitutional Law* (Longmans, 1967).

K. C. Wheare, *Modern Constitutions* (Oxford University Press, 1951).

L. Wolff-Philips, *Constitutions of Modern States* (Pall Mall, 1968).

Index

329

331